"Jonathan Moore's acute analysis of the theology of grace espoused, taught, and argued by John Preston is more than a reliable account of one of the most influential early-seventeenth-century divines. It is an important corrective to an understanding of the theological differences of the time in terms of a simple 'Calvinist consensus' versus a contrary Arminianism. Moore demonstrates that Preston advocated hypothetical universalism, 'a new and much softer brand of Calvinism.' This accounts for Preston's puzzling conduct at the critically important York House Conference of 1626, which can only be understood in the light of his posthumously published works, on which Moore is now the leading authority."

— Patrick Collinson
Trinity College,
University of Cambridge

"Drawing on an impressive knowledge of primary sources and archival material, this study illustrates the breadth of opinion in Puritan and Reformed scholastic thought. By conclusively demonstrating that Preston presented an independent English version of hypothetical universalism that was distinct from French Amyraldianism, Moore corrects various recent interpretations of Preston's Reformed theology, calls into question simplistic categories and time-worn prejudices about Reformed scholasticism in general and Puritanism in particular, and invites us to adopt a more sophisticated methodology for the study of both phenomena in their historical context."

— Willem J. van Asselt
University of Utrecht

"It is a pleasure to commend Jonathan Moore's superb book. Moore has provided a fascinating and compelling study that is accessible not only to the academy but also to pastors who are concerned to understand more deeply the Reformed doctrine of the atonement. I hope it will be widely read."

— Rev. Ian Hamilton
Cambridge Presbyterian
Church, England

ENGLISH HYPOTHETICAL UNIVERSALISM

*John Preston and the Softening
of Reformed Theology*

Jonathan D. Moore

WILLIAM B. EERDMANS PUBLISHING COMPANY
GRAND RAPIDS, MICHIGAN / CAMBRIDGE, U.K.

Published 2007 by
Wm. B. Eerdmans Publishing Co.
2140 Oak Industrial Drive N.E., Grand Rapids, Michigan 49505 /
P.O. Box 163, Cambridge CB3 9PU U.K.

Printed in the United States of America

12 11 10 09 08 07   7 6 5 4 3 2 1

Library of Congress Cataloging-in-Publication Data

Moore, Jonathan, 1970-
English hypothetical universalism: John Preston and the softening
of reformed theology / Jonathan D. Moore.
p.   cm.
Includes bibliographical references.
ISBN 978-0-8028-2057-0 (pbk.: alk. paper)
1. Preston, John, 1587-1628. 2. Puritans — England — Doctrines —
History — 16th century. 3. Puritans — England — Doctrines —
History — 17th century. 4. Perkins, William, 1558-1602.   I. Title.

BX9339.P7M66   2007
230′.59092 — dc22

2007019883

www.eerdmans.com

For beloved Caragh

Contents

Bibliography

Foreword

The last two decades have seen nothing short of a renaissance of interest in the theological world of the late sixteenth and seventeenth centuries. Prior to that time, this territory was the preserve of an unholy mix of religious antiquarians on the one hand whose interest was driven by a desire to return the church to 'the old paths'; and, on the other, those modern systematicians, many under the influence of Swiss theologian Karl Barth, who wished to plunder the sources for evidence of the great apostasy from Calvin epitomized in the hackneyed phrase, 'Calvin against the Calvinists.'

In recent years, however, there has been a growing interest in the theology of this period from the perspective of a more nuanced, interdisciplinary intellectual history. Without doubt, the major influence in this field has been that of Richard Muller, who has brought to bear on the writings of this era the insights into medieval theology and the history of exegesis pioneered by Heiko Oberman and David Steinmetz. The result has been the development of a picture of the theology of this period that has highlighted not only the important connections between Reformed Orthodoxy and the prior Western intellectual tradition as a whole, but also the need for nuance and care with reference to the analytical categories that scholarship has traditionally used to describe the thought of the period. Terms such as 'Calvinism,' 'Arminianism,' 'supralapsarianism,' 'infralapsarianism,' and the like have been shown to be broad labels that can often hide important differences and nuances within the theological world of the time. Reformed theology was no more or less monolithic an entity; and even the great church confessions of the period embraced a spectrum of opinion. In addition, in the cognate field of church history proper, the work of figures such as Anthony Milton has called into question the use of such labels as adequate to describe the political parties within the various ecclesiastical conflicts of the time. Our understanding of the theological world of the late sixteenth and seventeenth centuries is today one that is both complex and diverse on all levels — theological, political, and social.

It is against this background of nuanced studies of the period that Jonathan Moore's outstanding monograph is to be understood. Where Muller and Milton have laid out their detailed arguments on a broad canvas, Dr Moore has focused in detail on the particular individual John Preston as a means of exploring issues surrounding the development of English Reformed Orthodoxy during the Elizabethan and Jacobean periods. The results are significant contributions to a number of debates in the current historiography. In addition to the now well-established positions on scholasticism as a method and the priority of original sources set within flexible historical-oriented models of interpretation rather than dogmatically driven, Procrustean frameworks, the following points are worthy of note:

First, Dr Moore dispatches to the ash can of history two of the central theses of the 'Calvin against the Calvinists' argument, as found in the influential work of R. T. Kendall. By demonstrating that Preston's hypothetical universalism could happily co-exist with his commitment to experimental predestinarianism, he cuts the tight connection between limited atonement and the latter upon which Kendall and his followers place so much weight. Further, by careful study of the decretal order in Reformed Orthodoxy, he also puts to death the simplistic connection drawn by Kendall, Clifford, and others between hypothetical universalism and Amyraldianism. The two are not different sides of the same coin, and are not connected in any significant organic or structural way; rather, hypothetical universalism was developed within an orthodox ordering of the decrees and, as one option within a heterogeneous English Calvinism, was not subject to the same public suspicion as Amyraldianism, though evidently was still a novelty in the evolving Jacobean church.

Second, Dr Moore takes care to place Preston and his thought in context. Not only is it unacceptable to judge later Reformed theology by some arbitrary criteria drawn from the writings of one man, typically John Calvin; it is no less illegitimate to compare the theology of men working in parishes in the context of an established, national Reformed church with that of a man attempting to bring about the Reform of a single city, populated by exiles, in the context of the politics of French emigration and the intricacies of Swiss politics.

Third, and here the task of the historian comes to an end and serves up raw material for the theologian and the pastor, he raises acute questions concerning predestinarian theology, Christology, the will of God to save, and the dogmatic underpinning of the message preached. It is, of course, almost heretical as a historian committed to the canons of scholarly historiography to say this, but Dr Moore's study leads the reader inevitably into those questions of pastoral practice that were so pressing for a man like Preston and remain so for those who self-consciously seek to preach in a confessionally orthodox, Reformed manner today. So, this book should be required reading not just for the scholar, but for any who have an active interest in the Reformed tradition, not as a blueprint for restoring 'the old paths,' but as an example of how one great Puritan pastor wrestled with the interface of theology and practice.

Dr Carl R. Trueman
Professor of Historical Theology
and Church History
Westminster Theological Seminary
Philadelphia

Acknowledgements

John Preston's predecessor at Lincoln's Inn, John Donne, rightly said that, "No man is an island." It is therefore fitting that I should begin by endeavouring to pay some recognition to those who make up in a more immediate fashion my part of the "continent." At the outset I would like to thank those who made the doctoral research that lies behind this book possible for me in the first place. Firstly, I would like to offer special thanks to Rev. Brian Norton, without whom I would never have undertaken postgraduate research, let alone become engrossed in the intricacies of seventeenth-century theological debate. I would also like to thank Rev. Iain Murray for kindly lending me his early editions of Preston and other rare seventeenth-century volumes at the outset of my theological studies. It was primarily these two pastors who introduced me to the world of Puritan divinity. Secondly, I would also like to thank the British Academy for awarding me a three-year Research Studentship, and Emmanuel College for a three-year External Research Studentship and repeatedly generous help from the Thorp Theological Studies Fund. Thirdly, hearty thanks are due to Professor Iain Torrance for so kindly taking it upon himself to champion my thesis for publication with Eerdmans, and to Bill Eerdmans Jr. and his team for being such a pleasure to work with in the process of preparing the final manuscript for publication.

Thanks are also due to numerous scholars who aided me in my research in some way or other, sometimes through highly stimulating conversation, but often also through pointers to new references and sources. These scholars include Dr Bill Black, Dr John Brouwer, Dr Alan Clifford, Dr John Coffey, Dr David Como, Dr Mark Dever, Dr Tom Freeman, Dr Randall Gleason, Dr Aza Goudriaan, Dr Polly Ha, Professor Brian Harrison, Professor Paul Helm, Mr Seán Hughes, Dr Arnold Hunt, Dr R. T. Kendall, Dr Peter Lake, Dr Vivienne Larminie and the editorial team of the *ODNB*, Dr Michael Lawrence, Dr

Acknowledgements

Samuel Logan Jr., Dr Jessica Martin, Dr Mary Morrissey, Professor Jim Packer, Dr Jason Peacey, Mr John Perkins, Dr Sebastian Rehnman, Dr Michael Thomas, Dr Carl Trueman, Dr Elliot Vernon, Dr Bruce Winter, and Dr Jason Yiannikkou.

I must also acknowledge the valuable help of the staff of the following libraries and archives: the University Library, Cambridge; the Divinity School Library, Cambridge; Tyndale House Library, Cambridge; the Seeley History Library, Cambridge; the Wren Library, Trinity College, Cambridge; Westminster College Library, Cambridge; the Forbes Mellon Library, Clare College, Cambridge; Wesley House Library, Cambridge; the Bodleian Library, Oxford; Queen's College Library, Oxford; the British Library, London; Dr Williams's Library, London; the Public Record Office, London; Lincoln's Inn, London; St John's College Library, Durham; the University Library, Durham; New College Library, Edinburgh; Buckinghamshire County Record Office, Aylesbury; Buckinghamshire County Local Studies Library, Aylesbury; the Church Office, St Mary's Church, Amersham; the Palace Library, Armagh; the Northamptonshire Record Office; the Essex Record Office; and the University Library, Sheffield. I would offer special thanks to Dr Peter Spreadbury and Dr Helen Carron for their work at Emmanuel College Library, Cambridge, and to Professor Barry Windeatt, also of Emmanuel College Library, for help in procuring the digital image of an oil portrait of Preston used on the cover of this book. I would also like to acknowledge the expert help of the late Dr Frank Stubbings, also of Emmanuel College Library. It was a happy providence indeed that it was as a privileged member of Emmanuel College that I was able to study the world of John Preston.

Special thanks are due to my Cambridge doctoral supervisor Professor Eamon Duffy, whose astute guidance and encouraging affirmation of my work and ideas were much appreciated. For further encouragement and helpful comments on my work in progress I would also like to thank Professor Patrick Collinson, Dr John Craig, Professor Alan Ford, Dr Anthony Milton, Dr Nicholas Tyacke, and Dr Paul Lim. I owe a great intellectual debt to the work of Nicholas Tyacke, as well as that of Professor Richard Muller. To Alan Ford I am particularly indebted for his moral support, and practical help with manuscript sources. I would also like to thank my doctoral examiners Professor John Morrill and Dr Brian Cummings for helpful feedback. But of course, despite the beady eyes of these esteemed scholars, any remaining mistakes and flaws in this book are fully mine.

But still it must be said, where would we be if our help only came from fellow scholars? My greatest earthly help in all this was undoubtedly my great 'help meet,' Caragh, whose price is far above rubies. For far too long, Caragh had to compete with John Preston for attention, but coped admirably. For Caragh's love, patience, and inspiration I am ever grateful, and to Caragh I dedicate this book. But of course, ultimately my help came from the LORD, the maker of heaven and earth. To him alone be glory.

With regard to quotations from primary sources, and particularly Preston's posthumously published sermons, I have not usually reproduced the liberal and often arbitrary use by seventeenth-century printers of italic fonts, unless the italics are unambiguously emphatic. Only when the original italics indicate direct speech or quotation have they been preserved by means of modern quotation marks. The precision of quotations from primary sources has been fully retained as to wording, but on those very rare occasions when certain peculiarities of spelling or printing were deemed unnecessarily and distractingly conspicuous (*e.g.*, 'vvhen' instead of 'when'), liberty has been taken to amend these, but only where no possible implications occur for the interpretation of the writer's meaning. Scripture abbreviations have been standardised throughout, including in quotations from primary sources. Unless otherwise stated, all Scripture quotations are from the Authorised Version.

This book is for the most part the substance of my doctoral dissertation. However, now no longer under the strict 80,000-word limit of the Cambridge Divinity School, I have taken the opportunity to make some minor corrections, expand the text and footnotes in some significant places, and incorporate into my argument a number of publications that appeared after my thesis was submitted, as well as a number of other lines of evidence from the primary sources, including more manuscripts. As such this book completely replaces my doctoral dissertation.

According to Patrick Collinson this study is a radical piece of revisionism.[1] I myself never tried to be radical, but merely to resolve certain conflicts I saw in the secondary literature concerning John Preston and the English Church. The success, usefulness, and radicalness of what I have achieved others will have to judge.

DR JONATHAN D. MOORE
Cambridge

---

1. Patrick Collinson, Sarah Bendall, & Christopher N. L. Brooke, *A History of Emmanuel College, Cambridge* (Woodbridge, UK: Boydell Press, 1999), pp. 216, 219.

Abbreviations

Abbreviations Used for Preston's Works

For full bibliographical details of the following references see the Bibliography.

The Breast-plate / STC 20213

The Breast-plate of Faith and Love. A Treatise wherein the Ground and Exercise of Faith and Love, as they are set upon Christ their Object, and as they are expressed in good Works, is explained. Delivered in 18 Sermons upon three severall Texts. Edited by Richard Sibbes & John Davenport. [1630] 5th ed., London: Robert Young for Nicholas Bourne, 1634 (1637).

The deformed Forme / STC 20216

The deformed Forme of a formall Profession. Or the Description of a true and false Christian, either excusing, or accusing him, for his pious, or pretended Conversation. Shewing that there is a powerfull Godlynes necessary to Salvation and that many have the Forme, but not the Power thereof. in handling whereof these three Things are plainely and powerfully explained and applied. What Godlines is. What the Power of it. What the Reasons why some have but the Forme thereof. Together with the Meanes, and Marks, both how to attaine, and to try ourselves whether we have the Power thereof or not. [1632] Another ed., Edinburgh: John Wreittoun, 1634.

Foure Treatises / STC 20223

Foure godly and learned Treatises, intituled, I. A Remedy against Covetousnesse. II. An elegant Description of spirituall Death and Life. III. The Doctrine of Selfe-Deniall. IV. Upon the Sacrament of the Lords Supper. Delivered in sundry Sermons. [1632] 4th ed., London: A. Griffin for Michael Sparke, 1636.

The Fulnesse of Christ / STC 20225

The Fulnesse of Christ for us. A Sermon preached at the Court before King James of blessed Memory. [1639] Another ed., London: J. Okes for John Stafford, 1640.

The golden Scepter / STC 20227

The golden Scepter held forth to the Humble. With the Churches Dignitie by her Marriage and the Churches Dutie in her Carriage. In three Treatises. The former delivered in sundry Sermons in Cambridge, for the weekely Fasts, 1625. The two latter in Lincolnes Inne. Edited by Thomas Goodwin & Thomas Ball. [1638] Another ed., London: R. Badger for Nicholas Bourne, and Rapha Harford and Francis Eglesfield, 1639 (1638).

Irresistibilitate Gratiæ convertentis / [Rotterdam]

De Irresistibilitate Gratiæ convertentis. Thesis. Habita in Scholis Publicis Academiæ Cantabrigiensis . . . Ex ipsius Manuscripto. 1st ed., Rotterdam: Jacobus Moxon, 1639.

Irresistiblenesse of converting Grace / Wing STC P3305

The Position of John Preston, Doctor in Divinity, sometimes Mr. of Emanuel Colledge in Cambridge, and Preacher at Lincolnes-Inn; concerning the Irresistiblenesse of converting Grace. 1st English ed., London: J. G. for Nathanial Webb & William Grantham, 1654.

The Law / STC 20230

The Law out lawed. Or, the Charter of the Gospell, shewing the Priviledge and Prerogative of the Saints by Vertue of the Covenant. Wherein these foure Points of Doctrine are properly observed, plainly proved, both by Scripture, and Reason: and pithily applied. Viz. 1. That he that is in the State of Grace lyeth in no knowne Sinne, no Sinne hath Dominion over him. 2. That Sinne though it doth not raigne in the Saints, yet it doth remaine and dwell in them. 3. That the Way to overcome Sinne, is to get Assurance of the Love, and Grace, and Favour of God, whereby it is forgiven them. 4. That whosoever is under the Law, Sinne hath Dominion over him. [1631] Another ed., Edinburgh: John Wreittoun, 1633.

Life and Death / STC 20278.5

A Sermon of spirituall Life and Death. Preached before the King, at White-Hall, November, 1626. [1630] Another ed., London: Thomas Cotes for Michael Sparke, 1630.

Life eternall / STC 20232

> *Life eternall or, a Treatise of the Knowledge of the divine Essence and Attributes. Delivered in 18 Sermons.* Edited by Thomas Goodwin & Thomas Ball. [1631] 2nd corrected ed., London: R. Badger for Nicholas Bourne & Rapha Harford, 1631.

A liveles Life / STC 20237

> *A liveles Life: Or Man's spirituall death in Sinne. Wherein is both learnedly and profitably handled these foure doctrines, The Spirituall Death in Sinne. The Doctrine of Humiliation. Mercy to be found in Christ. Continuance in sinne, dangerous. Being the substance of severall Sermons upon Ephesians 2:1-3. 'And you hath he quickened, who were dead in trespasses and sins.' Whereunto is annexed a profitable Sermon at Lincolnes-Inne, on Genesis 22:14.* [1633] 3rd ed., London: J. Beale for Andrew Crooke and Daniel Frere, 1635.

Lords Supper / STC 20281

> *Three Sermons upon the Sacrament of the Lords Supper.* [1631] Another ed., London: Thomas Cotes for Michael Sparke, 1631.

Love of Christ / STC 20240.3

> *A heavenly Treatise of the Divine Love of Christ. Shewing the Motives, the Meanes, the Markes, the Kindes thereof. Delivered in five Sermons.* [1638] 3rd ed., London: Thomas Paine for John Stafford, 1640.

The mysticall Match / Wing STC P3303

> *The mysticall Match between Christ and his Church . . . The leading Sermon to that Treatise of his called The Churches Marriage.* Edited by T. S. 1st ed., London: For Francis Eglesfield, 1648.

The New Covenant / STC 20247

> *The New Covenant or the Saints Portion: A Treatise unfolding the All-sufficiencie of God, Mans Uprightnes and the Covenant of Grace, delivered in fourteen Sermons upon Genesis 17:1, 2. Whereunto are adjoyned foure Sermons upon Ecclesiastes 9:1, 2, 11, 12.* Edited by Richard Sibbes & John Davenport. [1629] 9th corrected ed., London: J. Dawson for Nicholas Bourne, 1639.

Plenitudo Fontis / Wing STC P3304A

> *Plenitudo Fontis, or Christ's Fulnesse and Man's Emptinesse. A Sermon preached by John Preston.* [1639] New ed., London: For John Stafford, 1645.

Remaines / STC 20250

Remaines of that reverend and learned Divine, John Preston, Dr. in Divinity, Chaplaine in Ordinary to his Majesty, Master of Emanuel Colledge in Cambridge, sometimes Preacher of Lincolnes-Inne. Containing three excellent Treatises, namely Judas's Repentance. The Saints Spirituall Strength. Pauls Conversion. [1634] 2nd ed., London: R. Badger and J. Legate for Andrew Crooke, 1637.

Riches of Mercy / Wing STC P3306A

Riches of Mercy to Men in Misery. Or, certain excellent Treatises concerning the Dignity and Duty of Gods Children. [1658] Another ed., London: J. T. for Francis Eglesfield, 1658.

Saints daily Exercise / STC 20251

The Saints daily Exercise. A Treatise concerning the whole Dutie of Prayer. Delivered in five Sermons, upon I Thessalonians 5:17. Edited by Richard Sibbes & John Davenport. 1st ed., London: W. Jones for Nicholas Bourne, 1629.

Saints Infirmities / STC 20221

The Doctrine of the Saints Infirmities. Delivered in severall Sermons. Edited by Thomas Goodwin & Thomas Ball. [1636] Another ed., London: John Okes for Henry Taunton, 1638.

Saints Qualification / STC 20262

The Saints Qualification: Or a Treatise I. of Humiliation, in tenne Sermons. II. of Sanctification, in nine Sermons: Whereunto is added a Treatise of Communion with Christ in the Sacrament, in three Sermons. Edited by Richard Sibbes & John Davenport. 1st ed., London: R. Badger for Nicholas Bourne, 1633.

Saints Submission / STC 20266

The Saints Submission, and Sathan's Overthrow. Or, Sermons on James 4:7. 1st ed., London: J. Dawson for Peter Cole, 1638.

Sermons preached before His Majestie / STC 20274

Sermons preached before His Majestie, and upon other speciall Occasions: Viz. 1. The Pillar and Ground of Truth in I Timothy 3:15. 2. The New Life, I John 5:12. 3. A sensible Demonstration of the Deity, Isaiah 64:4. 4. Exact Walking, Ephesians 5:15. 5. Samuels Support of sorrowful Sinners, in I Samuel 12:20, 21,

22. Edited by Thomas Goodwin & Thomas Ball. [1630] 5th Corrected and amended ed., London: John Norton for Anne Boler, 1637.

Sinnes Overthrow / STC 20277

Sinnes Overthrow: or, a godly and learned Treatise of Mortification: wherein is excellently handled; first the generall Doctrine of Mortification: and then particularly, how to mortifie Fornication, Uncleanesse, evill Concupiscence, inordinate Affection, and Covetousnesse. All being the Substance of severall Sermons upon Colossians 3:5, 'Mortifie therefore your members'. [1633] 3rd Corrected and enlarged ed., London: Felix Kingston for Andrew Crooke and Daniell Frere, 1635.

Summe / [Manuscript]

ECL MS. 181.

Sun-beams / Wing STC P3307A

Sun-beams of Gospel-light, shining clearly from severall Texts of Scripture, opened and applyed. 1. A heavenly Treatise of the Divine Love of Christ. 2. The Christian Freedome. 3. The deformed Forme of a formall Profession. 4. Christs Fulnesse, and Mans Emptinesse. [1631, 1632, 1638, 1639] Reissue ed., London: For John Stafford, 1644.

Other Abbreviations

For full bibliographical details see the Bibliography.

AHR	*American Historical Review*
ATR	*Anglican Theological Review*
BDE	Larsen, Bebbington & Noll, eds. *Biographical Dictionary of Evangelicals,* 2003.
BHR	*Bulletin of (Institute of) Historical Research*
BL	British Library, London
Bod	Bodleian Library, Oxford
CCRB	Keeble & Nuttall, eds., *Calendar of the Correspondence of Richard Baxter,* 1991.
CH	*Church History*
CTJ	*Calvin Theological Journal*
CUL	The University Library, Cambridge
DNB	Stephen & Lee, eds., *Dictionary of National Biography,* 1921-22.

ECL   Emmanuel College Library, Cambridge

ERO   Essex Record Office, Chelmsford

EHR   *English Historical Review*

EP   Gisel, ed., *Encyclopédie du Protestantisme*, 1995.

EQ   *Evangelical Quarterly*

HJ   *Historical Journal*

HLB   *Harvard Library Bulletin*

HT   *History Today*

HTR   *Harvard Theological Review*

JBS   *Journal of British Studies*

JEH   *Journal of Ecclesiastical History*

JMH   *Journal of Modern History*

JTS   *Journal of Theological Studies*

NIDCC Douglas, ed., *The New International Dictionary of the Christian Church*, 1978.

NRO   Northamptonshire Record Office, Northampton

ODCC Cross & Livingstone, eds., *The Oxford Dictionary of the Christian Church*, 1997.

ODNB Harrison & Matthew, eds., *Oxford Dictionary of National Biography*, 2004.

OER   Hillerbrand, ed., *The Oxford Encyclopedia of the Reformation*, 1996.

P&P   *Past and Present*

PRO   Public Record Office, London

RRR   *Reformation & Renaissance Review*

SBET   *Scottish Bulletin of Evangelical Theology*

SCJ   *Sixteenth Century Journal*

SP   State Papers

SUL   The University Library, Sheffield

STC   Pollard, Redgrave, et al., eds., *Short-Title Catalogue*, 1986.

TCSM *Transactions of the Colonial Society of Massachusetts*

TRHS   *Transactions of the Royal Historical Society*

Wing STC Donald Wing et al., eds., *Short-Title Catalogue*, 1994.

WTJ   *Westminster Theological Journal*

SECTION I

Preston's Life

CHAPTER 1

A Biographical Introduction

". . . one who is beyond all exception for piety, Orthodoxnesse, and Learning, even Dr. Preston."[1]

Preston's Life[2]

Born in 1587 of a Northamptonshire farmer, Thomas, of Upper Heyford, who was to die before John Preston was thirteen years old, and baptised on 27th Oc-

1. Richard Baxter, *Aphorismes of Justification* (The Hague: Abraham Brown, 1655), p. 284.

2. The most important source of detail on Preston's life is Thomas Ball's (1590-1659) biography: Thomas Ball, *The Life of the Renowned Doctor Preston,* ed. Edward W. Harcourt (Oxford: Parker and Co., 1885). Unless otherwise stated, this is the edition I cite. Ball was Preston's pupil at Queens' College, and later a Fellow alongside Preston at Emmanuel College, not least due to Preston being deeply impressed with his theological acumen and godliness. According to Howes, Preston esteemed Ball, "not onely as his beloved Pupil, but as his bosome friend, and most intimately private familiar" (John Howes, *Real Comforts, extracted from moral and spiritual Principles* [London: S. Griffin for R. Royston, 1660], p. 39). Ball's biography was probably completed by the late 1630s, but possibly written as late as 1650. It cannot have been completed before 1636, still less written or published in 1628 as Schaefer claims (doubtless following Harcourt's 1885 title-page), because Ball cites Preston's *Saints Infirmities* which was not published until 1636 (Paul R. Schaefer Jr., "The Spiritual Brotherhood on the Habits of the Heart: Cambridge Protestants and the Doctrine of Sanctification from William Perkins to Thomas Shepard" [D.Phil. Dissertation, University of Oxford, 1994], p. 15; Ball, *Life of Preston,* p. 148). If it is argued that Ball refers only to a manuscript version of *Saints Infirmities,* then it still must have been completed after 5th July, 1635, because Ball mentions Sibbes's decease (Ball, *Life of Preston,* p. 149). Morgan gives no evidence for his assertion that it was "first circulated in manuscript form after [his] death" (Irvonwy Morgan, *Puritan Spirituality: Illustrated from the life and times of the Rev. Dr. John Preston* [London: Epworth Press, 1973], p. 124). It could have been written directly for the famous biographer Samuel Clarke. Ball's manuscript was published by

tober at Bugbrooke parish church, few would have predicted Preston's future greatness.[3] However, the Prestons were of a good stock. His mother, Alice, daughter of Lawrence Marsh of Northampton, had a rich uncle, Cresswell, who was childless and took a liking to Preston, and sent him to the free-school in Northampton.[4] Eventually, after further tuition in Bedfordshire, Preston matriculated as a sizar at King's College, Cambridge, on 5th July, 1604. He began by studying music, showing particular devotion to the lute. Unhappy in this he moved in 1606 to Queens' College and studied natural philosophy, proceeding B.A. in 1608, and then M.A. in 1611.[5] At this stage Preston's ambition

Clarke in 1651, replacing the brief life of Preston he had prepared himself (BL Harleian MS. 6037, f. 15v). Contrary to Kendall this was not an abridgement but a full reproduction of Ball's biography (R. T. Kendall, *Calvin and English Calvinism to 1649*, 2nd ed. [Carlisle, UK: Paternoster Press, 1997], p. 117). It was reprinted in 1660 and 1677, and new editions appeared in 1751, 1780, 1819, and 1885. These were mainly abridgements of Clarke's edition, but Harcourt's 1885 edition was a careful edition of an original manuscript from the Harcourt family library (Ball, *Life of Preston*, pp. iv, x, xv. I am grateful to Steven Tomlinson of the Bodleian Library for clarification of this point). There are a number of minor inaccuracies in Ball's biography, but his work remains a mine of useful facts and insight (Erasmus Middleton, *Biographia Evangelica* [London: J. W. Pasham for Alex. Hogg, 1779-86], II:467; Mark E. Dever, *Richard Sibbes: Puritanism and Calvinism in Late Elizabethan and Early Stuart England* [Macon, GA: Mercer University Press, 2000], p. 47; see also below, p. 9). Unless otherwise stated, biographical details concerning Preston are taken from the 1885 edition and my own entry in the *ODNB*. Emerson has described Ball's *Life* as a "brief masterpiece," following in the eulogistic tradition of Thomas Fuller who claimed that it was "so largely and learnedly written . . . that nothing can be added unto it" (Everett H. Emerson, *English Puritanism from John Hooper to John Milton* [Durham, NC: Duke University Press, 1968], p. 236; Thomas Fuller, *The Church-History of Britain* [London: For John William, 1655], XI:131; cf. Thomas Fuller, *The History of the Worthies of England* [London: J. G. W. L. and W. G., 1662], II:291. See also Richard Baxter's praise of this biography in his preface to Samuel Clarke, *The Lives of sundry eminent Persons in this later Age* [London: For Thomas Simmons, 1683]). Irvonwy Morgan has written the only modern biography of Preston, 'adding' in fact much to Ball's work from other manuscripts and printed sources (Irvonwy Morgan, *Prince Charles's Puritan Chaplain* [London: George Allen & Unwin Ltd, 1957]). Other recent accounts of Preston's life are by Patrick Collinson (Patrick Collinson, Sarah Bendall, & Christopher N. L. Brooke, *A History of Emmanuel College, Cambridge* [Woodbridge, UK: Boydell Press, 1999], pp. 215-21) and my own entry in the *ODNB*.

3. NRO MS. 53p/1/18r; Morgan, *Prince Charles's Puritan Chaplain*, p. 12; cf. Fuller, *Worthies of England*, II:291.

4. It would appear from SUL Hartlib MS. 48/3/1a that Preston had at least one sibling, namely, James.

5. Cf. John Venn & J. A. Venn, eds., *Alumni Cantabrigienses* (Cambridge: Cambridge University Press, 1922-27), III:393; Anthony A. Wood, *Fasti Oxonienses, Or the Annals of the University of Oxford*, ed. Philip Bliss, 3rd ed. (London: For F. C., and J. Rivington et al., 1815), col. 333. Upon the advice of Professor Brian Harrison I take Wood's date of 1610 for the M.A. to be incorrect.

was to pursue a career in the world of business or at Court. However, his first business venture, for which he had sold land inherited from Cresswell, came to nothing and so he returned to his books. His first pursuit was philosophy, and Aristotle quickly became "his tutelary saint."[6] In 1609 at the age of twenty-two he was elected a Fellow of Queens', where he soon became "the greatest Pupil-monger in England in mans memory."[7]

In 1610 Preston was made a lay Prebendary of Lincoln Cathedral, an office he held until his death.[8] However, Preston was at this time far from seeking ecclesiastical preferment, and, according to Ball, he "thought it below him to be a minister, & held the study of Divinity to be a kind of honest silliness." He rather turned his studies to medicine and astrology. However, it was "as he was in the Cælestial contemplations" that he was rudely awakened by "the hotter sort of Protestant."[9] John Cotton's plain, evangelical University sermon in Great St Mary's met widespread disapproval from an audience seeking more ostentatious rhetoric, and Cotton returned dejected to his Fellow's accommodation in Emmanuel College. Suddenly, however, Preston "knocks at his door, and coming in, acquaints him with his spiritual condition, and how it had pleased God to speak effectually unto his heart by that Sermon."[10] Not only did Preston and Cotton become lifelong comrades,[11] but Preston's view of the Christian ministry and the study of divinity was transformed, and soon he was immersing himself in the works of the schoolmen, delighted to find there so frequently quoted his old friend Aristotle. He was soon ordained

6. Ball, *Life of Preston*, p. 9; cf. BL Harleian MS. 6037, f. 15v.

7. BL Harleian MS. 7038, f. 137r; Fuller, *Worthies of England*, II:291 (Fuller means this in a complimentary way. Cf. Morris Fuller, *The Life, Letters and Writings of John Davenant* [London: Methuen, 1897], p. 60; cf. pp. 121-22).

8. Venn, ed., *Alumni Cantabrigienses*, III:393; Morgan, *Prince Charles's Puritan Chaplain*, p. 14.

9. Ball, *Life of Preston*, pp. 7, 16.

10. John Norton, *Abel being dead yet speaketh. Or, the Life & Death of that deservedly famous Man of God, Mr John Cotton* (London: Thomas Newcomb for Lodowick Lloyd, 1658), p. 14; cf. Samuel Clarke, *A Collection of the Lives of ten eminent Divines* (London: For William Miller, 1662), pp. 59-60; Cotton Mather, *Magnalia Christi Americana*, 3rd ed. (Hartford: Silas Andrus and Son, 1853), I:256; Evelyn S. Shuckburgh, *Emmanuel College*, University of Cambridge College Histories (London: F. E. Robinson & Co., 1904), p. 45. The exact date of Cotton's sermon is unknown. The old *DNB* and Haller give around 1611 while Morgan suggests 1612 (William Haller, *The Rise of Puritanism, or the Way to the New Jerusalem as set forth in Pulpit and Press from Thomas Cartwright to John Lilburne and John Milton, 1570-1643* [New York: Harper & Brothers, 1957], p. 71; Morgan, *Prince Charles's Puritan Chaplain*, p. 40).

11. Preston would advise "his near fledged pupils" to finish their training by spending time at Boston with Cotton, and he himself paid Cotton an annual visit for the rest of his life (Mather, *Magnalia Christi Americana*, I:260, 261).

Deacon in the Diocese of Peterborough on 19th June, 1614, and Priest on 20th June.[12]

Preston was also already beginning his rise to political fame. Samuel Harsnett, Master of Pembroke College and Vice-Chancellor of the University, prevailed upon Preston to engage in a public philosophical disputation before King James in March 1615. Preston excelled and gained the king's favour, debating the question as to "whether Dogs could make syllogismes." This "opened a way for Mr Preston at the Court if he were willing" but he was not, and his seeming indifference to the allurements of the Court offended many, some of whom suspected that "some inclination to puritanisme" lay behind his reserve.[13] But this did not stop Sir Fulke Greville and others from becoming his patrons, and Preston's reputation among 'the godly' was consequently advanced, resulting in an increasing influx of pupils for him at Queens' College. Strategic contacts at Court continued, and his reputation as a theologian grew. He received the B.D. in 1620 and soon became Dean and Catechist at Queens'. On 9th May, 1621, he was chosen by James Ussher, then Vice-Chancellor of Trinity College, to be Professor of Theological Controversies with him at Dublin, but Preston deliberated until 20th July before declining.[14] Preston's delay in replying was because he was also being considered, along with Samuel Ward, as a possible successor to John Davenant as the Lady Margaret Professor of Divinity in Cambridge, Davenant having been elected Bishop of Salisbury in June 1621. Yet it seems that now Preston quietly had his sights on being chosen to serve as Chaplain in Ordinary to Prince Charles, "that he might feel the Pulse of the Court."[15] This honour finally came to him

12. Venn, ed., *Alumni Cantabrigienses*, III:393.

13. Ball, *Life of Preston*, pp. 23, 27, 29; cf. p. 41; Frank L. Huntley, *Bishop Joseph Hall 1574-1656: A Biographical and Critical Study* (Cambridge: D. S. Brewer Ltd, 1979), p. 6 (an unreliable account). This is the same Harsnett whose anti-Calvinist sermon will be discussed in Ch. 2.

14. Preston did *not* accept, contrary to Venn, ed., *Alumni Cantabrigienses*, III:393.

15. John P. Mahaffy, *The Particular Book of Trinity College, Dublin. A Facsimile from the Original, with Introduction and Appendices* (London: T. Fisher Unwin, 1904), f. 187r; James Ussher, *The whole Works of the most Rev. James Ussher*, ed. Charles R. Erlington (Dublin: Hodges and Smith, 1847-64), XVI:370-72; John Hacket, *Scrinia Reserata: A Memorial offer'd to the great Deservings of John Williams* (London: Edward Jones for Samuel Lowndes, 1693), I:204. Ball reports that Preston was informed concerning the chair that "the election would be easily carryed for him" if he wanted it. Preston sought John Dod's advice in this decision, who dissuaded him from taking the chair in favour of preaching in plain English (Ball, *Life of Preston*, pp. 71-72). Preston's visit to the continent was not really to learn Latin in preparation for this post, as Ball suggests, but was a covert political mission. Schaefer is therefore wrong to conclude that Preston rejected Dod's advice (Schaefer, "The Spiritual Brotherhood," pp. 187-88). The evidence is that he was of one mind with Dod in this matter (cf. below, pp. 9, 21). Preston's letter to Ussher just cited shows that Erlington is also incorrect in stating that Preston declined Ussher's offer in or-

later that year, thanks to his close relationship with George Villiers the Duke of Buckingham, who was considered at that time "the most popular man in England."[16] Had Preston not been made chaplain to Prince Charles, he could well have been made chaplain to the queen of Bohemia at The Hague.[17]

On 21st May, 1622, Preston was elected to succeed John Donne as the Preacher to the Honourable Society of Lincoln's Inn, an extremely influential London pulpit with many Parliament men in attendance. Although still based in Cambridge, Preston preached twice here on Sabbaths during term time, as well as on numerous other occasions for the rest of his life.[18] On 3rd October, 1622, Preston was admitted as Master of Emmanuel College, to succeed Dr Laurence Chaderton who had occupied this position for thirty-eight years, but who was still to outlive Preston.[19] It was done lawfully, but secretly, suddenly, and behind locked gates in order to avoid a perceived downgrade as had happened at Christ's College after Valentine Cary was imposed as Master

der to become Master of Emmanuel (Ussher, *Works*, I:56). We will meet Ussher and Davenant again in Ch. 7.

16. Ussher, *Works*, I:55; XVI:370-72 (Overtures had also been made to Preston "by the fellows and some in the court" to replace Davenant as Master of Queens'); Morgan, *Prince Charles's Puritan Chaplain*, pp. 74, 124. For an account of how Buckingham finally became most unpopular, see Thomas Cogswell, "The People's Love: The Duke of Buckingham and Popularity" in *Politics, Religion and Popularity in Early Stuart Britain: Essays in Honour of Conrad Russell*, ed. Thomas Cogswell, Richard Cust, & Peter G. Lake (Cambridge: Cambridge University Press, 2002), pp. 211-34. Ball suggests that a motive for Preston's promotion by King James might actually have been to "divide him from [the Puritans]" (Ball, *Life of Preston*, p. 68; cf. p. 100; Collinson, *History of Emmanuel College*, p. 217). But Peter Heylyn saw it as an attempt by Buckingham to "gain a party by him," a view that has been commonly adopted (Peter Heylyn, *Cyprianus Anglicus: Or the History of the Life and Death, of the most reverend and renowned Prelate William* [London: For A. Seile, 1668], p. 156; James Granger, *A biographical History of England* [London: For T. Davies, J. Robson, G. Robinson, T. Becket, T. Cadell, and T. Evans, 1775], II:175; Daniel Neal, *The History of the Puritans* [London: For William Baynes and Son, 1822], II:138, 175; Haller, *Rise of Puritanism*, p. 72; Emerson, *English Puritanism*, p. 238). Whatever the case, according to Hacket, Preston visited the Duke's "Bedchamber at least thrice a Week with a fly Audacity" (Hacket, *Scrinia Reserata*, I:204). We will meet the Duke again in Ch. 6.

17. PRO SP 84/105/38 (a letter from Preston to Sir Dudley Carleton); cf. Morgan, *Prince Charles's Puritan Chaplain*, p. 84.

18. *Records of the Hon. Society of Lincoln's Inn: The Black Books* (London: Lincoln's Inn, 1898), II:234-35; Morgan, *Prince Charles's Puritan Chaplain*, p. 111; cf. Ussher, *Works*, XVI:395. Much of Preston's printed legacy is comprised of sermons from this pulpit. Baxter saw this as a time when Preston was a 'blessed Light' to the city of London (Richard Baxter, *A Sermon of Judgement, preached at Pauls before the Honorable Lord Maior and Aldermen of the City of London, Dec. 17 1654. And now enlarged* [London: R. W. for Nevil Simmons, 1655], p. 3Av).

19. ECL Archive Col. 14.1 f. 27. According to Joseph Mede, the election itself took place on 2nd October (BL Harleian MS. 389, f. 235r). Chaderton finally died in 1640.

in 1609.[20] In this particular case one of the rivals was Dr Elias Travers, and again the Duke of Buckingham loaned his influential powers. Once made known, Preston's new position "created a national sensation."[21] His court connections gave to Emmanuel the prestige it needed to offset its increasing reputation as a subversive 'Puritan' institution. Yet Preston finally fell out of favour with the Fellows who had elected him, because he was so absorbed with Court affairs that he had little time to bring in the reforms to the College statutes that the Fellows were expecting.[22]

Meanwhile, Preston had caught the eye of Arthur Chichester, who in 1623 requested the king for the company of Preston on his proposed visit to Cologne concerning peace negotiations for the war in the Palatinate. Chichester, with Sir Edward Conway and Buckingham, then obtained a D.D. for Preston, through a personal mandate of the king dated 15th July, and conferred on 17th July. It was thought improper for a Master of a College in the University to be seen abroad without one.[23] Thus Preston had become Chaplain to Prince Charles, Preacher at Lincoln's Inn, Master of Emmanuel College, and Doctor of Divinity all in the space of two years.[24] In addition, Preston turned down a variety of other lucrative positions, including an offer of

20. James Heywood & Thomas Wright, *Cambridge University Transactions during the Puritan Controversies of the 16th and 17th Centuries* (London: Henry G. Bohn, 1854), II:312-13. Chidester has no grounds for saying this was done dishonestly (Evelyn A. Chidester, "John Preston: Puritan Divine and Writer of the early Seventeenth Century" [M.A. Dissertation, Texas College of Arts and Industries, 1956], p. 25). For an outline of the transformation of Christ's College under Cary see Samuel T. Logan Jr., "Theological Decline in Christian Institutions and the Value of Van Til's Epistemology" *WTJ* 57 (1995): 145-63.

21. Christopher Hill, *Puritanism and Revolution: Studies in Interpretation of the English Revolution of the Seventeenth Century* (London: Secker & Warburg, 1958), p. 241.

22. Morgan, *Prince Charles's Puritan Chaplain*, p. 115. Walter Foster "was once a Fellow of Emmanuel in Cambridge but could never cotten with Dr Preston who therfore sought to gaine him by all meanes but in vaine" (SUL Hartlib MS. 28/1/36b). See also Anthony Tuckney's recollection in 1635 of these "broyles" in BL Harleian MS. 3785, f. 58 and CUL MS. Mm.1.45, ff. 129-30. Preston himself, however, believed that by 1624 even his adversaries acknowledged that he had greatly reformed the college (PRO SP 14/171/15). Even before he took his oath as Master, Preston had negotiated terms such that his involvement in the London political scene would not be hindered by the traditional requirements of Cambridge residency (ECL Archive Col. 14.1 f. 27). Possibly he knew that Chaderton would continue to watch over the college in his absence. Chaderton continued to live across the street from the college throughout Preston's mastership *(ODNB)*. For Preston's early involvement in litigation at Emmanuel College, even when he was still a Fellow of Queens' College, see CUL MS. UA.V.C.Ct.III.23 ff. 190-212(vii).

23. PRO SP 14/148/69, 14/148/84, 14/148/110, 14/148/111; CUL MS. Mm.1.43 f. 365. Kendall and Schaefer incorrectly give the date as 1624 (Kendall, *Calvin and English Calvinism*, p. 117; Schaefer, "The Spiritual Brotherhood," p. 180).

24. Morgan, *Prince Charles's Puritan Chaplain*, p. 117.

the Deanery of Westminster, seeing them as less strategic for the cause of 'the godly.'[25]

This desire to place a higher priority on 'godly' preaching than on financial gain came to the fore in 1624 over the vacancy of the Trinity Lecturer.[26] This town lectureship had been established in 1610 for the popular Richard Sibbes and would be worth £80 a year to Preston. But when this position became vacant, in order to keep the suspect Court chaplain out of such a position, the king and bishops not only promised the unpopular Paul Micklethwayte, a Fellow of Sydney Sussex, a reward if he would campaign for it, but also offered Preston any bishopric or other preferment he desired. Yet Preston's heart was set on preaching, and he was finally confirmed lecturer at Trinity Church by Nicholas Felton, the Bishop of Ely, amidst much controversy and opposition from the Vice-Chancellor.[27] Preston seems to have practised what he preached:

> [P]referment, which should make a man more usefull and profitable both to God and his Church, to how many is it made a snare, who make it the end of their desires? Thus when a man is in favour with the Prince or some great man whereas he should make the use of it which Nehemiah did, yet he useth it for his own turne, for sinister endes.[28]

It seems fair to say, with Morgan, that theological concerns overrode Preston's more natural inclinations to prolong his period of political favour.[29] Nevertheless Preston "still continued, and increased in the favor of the King, and Duke." Fuller tells us that it was "much observed, that on the day of King James his death, he rode with Prince, and Duke, in a Coach shut down from Theobolds to London, applying comfort now to one now to the other, on so sad an occasion."[30] This was officially "against the rules of the Court," but "it

25. Hacket, *Scrinia Reserata*, I:205.

26. Cf. Ball, *Life of Preston*, p. 96.

27. Dever, *Richard Sibbes*, pp. 38-40; PRO SP 14/164/39, 14/164/41, 14/165/71, 14/170/58, 14/171/15. Preston "did not appeal to the town, though Micklethwait had only 18 voices out of 100" (PRO SP 14/164/41). Cf. Fuller, "The History of the University of Cambridge," appended to Fuller, *Church-History of Britain*, pp. 163-64; Heylyn, *Cyprianus Anglicus*, p. 156. Ball's claim that this lectureship became vacant in 1615 due to Sibbes being deprived has been disproved by Mark Dever (Ball, *Life of Preston*, p. 149; Dever, *Richard Sibbes*, pp. 43-48, 212-14; Mark E. Dever, "Moderation and Deprivation: A Reappraisal of Richard Sibbes" *JEH* 43 [1992]: 396-413).

28. John Preston, *Saints Submission*, pp. 142-43; cf. John Preston, *Riches of Mercy*, pp. 5, 228.

29. Morgan, *Prince Charles's Puritan Chaplain*, p. 208.

30. Fuller, *Church-History of Britain*, XI:119.

was said, the King was so over charged with grief, that he wanted the comfort of so wise and great a man."[31] In April 1625 Mede could still describe Preston as "a man in speciall favour with the king," and for a while Buckingham continued to seek Preston's preferment.[32] That same year he nominated Preston for the newly vacant position of Lord Keeper, although Thomas Coventry, formerly of Emmanuel College, finally received the post.[33] However, Buckingham was quietly undergoing a change of allegiance in an anti-Calvinist direction, following the new king, Charles. In February 1626 at the York House Conference, Richard Montagu escaped the clutches of his would-be oppressors, and Buckingham's new agenda became clear to Preston.[34] Preston committed to writing his new assessment of the Duke and court politics in general, but the satirical, sealed letter, "being unluckily dropp'd out of his Pocket," was "found in Smithfield broken open," and then taken up by Sir Henry Spiller who spilled his findings to the Duke. A wedge was driven between him and Preston, and Preston's influence at Court began to wane, so much so that he even considered escaping to Basel.[35]

Having "made much noise in the World," Preston was now past his peak. Peter Heylyn bitingly remarks that Preston, having been "gazed on for a time, like a new Court-Meteor; and having flashed and blazed a little, went out again, and was forgotten."[36] It is certainly true that Preston's career was cut short. Within two years his health had begun to fail, and, "flying from pulpit to pulpit in London and Cambridge and taking his due turns preaching at court, Preston burned out the last two or three years of his life."[37] Again

31. Gilbert Burnet, *Bishop Burnet's History of his own Time* (London: For Thomas Ward, 1724-34), I:19.

32. BL Harleian MS. 389, f. 428; quoted in Collinson, *History of Emmanuel College*, p. 219.

33. Heylyn disputes that Preston was ever offered this post (Peter Heylyn, *Examen Historicum: Or, a Discovery and Examination of the Mistakes, Falsities, and Defects of some modern Histories* [London: For Henry Seile and Richard Royston, 1659], I:198; cf. Fuller, *Church-History of Britain*, XI:131; Burnet, *History of his own Time*, I:19).

34. For more on the York House Conference see Ch. 6.

35. Heylyn, *Cyprianus Anglicus*, p. 157; William Sanderson, *A compleat History of the Life and Raigne of King Charles from his Cradle to his Grave* (London: For Humphrey Moseley, Richard Tomlins, and George Sawbridge, 1658), pp. 119-20; cf. Fuller, *Church-History of Britain*, XI:126; Fuller, *Worthies of England*, II:291. Sanderson tells how Preston's supporters allegedly bribed the Duke's barber "to finger the Letter out of the Dukes pocket" and return it to Preston. Sanderson and Heylyn emphasise that Buckingham never had any liking for Preston in the first place, but had merely used him up to this point in an attempt to gain control of Preston's "party" (Sanderson, *A compleat History of the Life and Raigne of King Charles*, pp. 119-20; Heylyn, *Examen Historicum*, I:198).

36. Heylyn, *Cyprianus Anglicus*, p. 156; cf. Heylyn, *Examen Historicum*, I:198.

37. Haller, *Rise of Puritanism*, p. 74.

we find Preston practising what he preached: "spend your fat and sweetnesse for God and man; weare out, not rust out; flame out, not smoke out; burne out, bee not blowne out."[38] On 27th May, 1628, Sibbes wrote to Ussher, informing him that Preston was "inclining to a consumption" and that his state was "thought doubtful to the physicians."[39] Preston spent his last months travelling to see friends and hoping that the country air would do him good. He finally returned to his home county of Northamptonshire and to his friend Sir Richard Knightley at "the puritan shrine of Fawsley," enabling him to renew fellowship with his old friend Dod, who "prayed by him when he lay a dying." He was also visited by Chaderton and Lord Saye and Sele.[40] Then at five o'clock in the morning, on the Sabbath of 20th July,[41] Preston died just short of his forty-first birthday. He was buried on 28th July in Fawsley parish church, intentionally without elaborate ceremony. Dod preached the funeral sermon, "and a world of Godly people came together."[42] Not long afterwards Preston was being heralded as "one of the greatest men in his age."[43] As Christopher Hill notes, "[t]here is scarcely an eminent Puritan divine of the fifty years after Preston's death who does not refer to him as one of the greatest au-

38. John Preston, *Foure Treatises,* p. 100.

39. Ussher, *Works,* XVI:522; Richard Sibbes, *The Complete Works of Richard Sibbes,* ed. Alexander B. Grosart (Edinburgh: James Nichol, 1862-64), I:xciv. Preston's own physician, Dr Ashworth, mistakenly deemed his condition to be "the scorbate" or scurvy (Ball, *Life of Preston,* pp. 168, 170). It is generally understood to have been tuberculosis (Hill, *Puritanism and Revolution,* p. 244; Collinson, *History of Emmanuel College,* p. 220).

40. Collinson, *History of Emmanuel College,* p. 220; John Preston, *The golden Scepter,* p. A5r; Samuel Clarke, *A general Martyrologie, containing a Collection of all the greatest Persecutions which have befallen the Church of Christ, from the Creation, to our present Times* (London: For William Birch, 1677), II:172; John Preston, *The New Covenant,* p. A4r; Sibbes, *Works,* I:xcvi; Ball, *Life of Preston,* p. 176.

41. Ball makes much of the fact that it was on "the Lord's Day" that Preston died (Ball, *Life of Preston,* pp. 174-76). Ball incorrectly states that the 20th July was Preston's funeral date, and Morgan that 28th July was a Sunday (Morgan, *Prince Charles's Puritan Chaplain,* p. 203).

42. Ball, *Life of Preston,* p. 175. In Preston's will, made on 30th July, 1618, and proved on 30th July, 1628, Preston's beneficiaries included Lord Chichester, Lord Saye his executor, Dod, Sibbes, Cotton, Thomas Hooker, and other "godly preachers" (PRO PROB. 11/154, f. 102v). In a codicil to his will he left £200 to Emmanuel College to support two poor scholars (Shuckburgh, *Emmanuel College,* pp. 67-68; Collinson, *History of Emmanuel College,* pp. 111, 221). Ball claims that Preston waived his 1618 will and replaced it with this "deed of guift" to Lord Saye, "with such restrictions & limitations as he thought good" (Ball, *Life of Preston,* pp. 171-72). Certainly Preston would not have been entirely happy with his 1618 will, leaving as it did £50 to Queens' College, but nothing to Emmanuel.

43. Mather, *Magnalia Christi Americana,* I:256. The way Heylyn saw things was that Preston's "party . . . look'd upon [him] with such a reverence as came near Idolatry" (Heylyn, *Examen Historicum,* I:198).

thorities."[44] With the extensive publication of his sermons Preston's influence was to stretch far and wide, not least to the New World. Meanwhile at home, his printed sermons in the 1630s "helped to maintain the Puritan ethos at the time when Laud was suppressing the Puritan preachers."[45] Had Preston not died so early, his influence would doubtless have been even greater, being, as he was, "perhaps the most influential of godly divines in the 1620s."[46]

A Puritan?

At the outset of a consideration of Preston's place in the early Stuart Church, and given the extensive literature that has accumulated in recent years over the vexed term 'Puritan,'[47] the question arises as to whether or not Preston is suitably styled 'a Puritan,' and if so, in what sense. Hitherto Preston has almost universally been known as a Puritan. Preston's contemporary biographer and devoted pupil continually portrays Preston as the leader of "the Puritans," and the only modern biography of Preston (written by Irvonwy Morgan) is entitled *Prince Charles's Puritan Chaplain*.[48] Almost all recent treatments of Preston have followed in this vein, not only describing him as 'a Puritan,' but also usually seeing him as *a* or *the* leader of a 'Jacobean Puritan movement,'[49] if not "the puritan pope of all En-

44. Hill, *Puritanism and Revolution*, p. 244. Hill also gives a list of some who were influenced by Preston's published sermons (p. 245). See also Morgan, *Prince Charles's Puritan Chaplain*, pp. 204-6.

45. Morgan, *Prince Charles's Puritan Chaplain*, p. 204.

46. Heylyn, *Cyprianus Anglicus*, pp. 156-57; Emerson, *English Puritanism*, p. 236; Derek Hirst, *Authority and Conflict: England 1603-1658* (London: Edward Arnold, 1986), p. 70 (whose is the quotation); cf. Mark R. Shaw, "William Perkins and the new Pelagians: Another Look at the Cambridge Predestination Controversy of the 1590's" *WTJ* 58 (1996): 267-301, p. 283.

47. It is too extensive to list here, but useful introductions to this discussion are Peter G. Lake, "Defining Puritanism — Again?" in *Puritanism: Transatlantic Perspectives on a Seventeenth-Century Anglo-American Faith*, ed. Francis J. Bremer (Boston: Massachusetts Historical Society, 1993), pp. 3-29, and Collinson in *OER*, III:364-70.

48. Ball, *Life of Preston*, pp. 30, 45, 55, 66, 68, 100; cf. p. 41. Echard calls him the "Head of the Puritan Party" as does Burnet (Lawrence Echard, *The History of England. From the Beginning of the Reign of King Charles the First, to the Restoration of King Charles the Second* [London: For Jacob Tonson, 1718], II:72; Burnet, *History of his own Time*, I:19; cf. Emerson, *English Puritanism*, p. 33; J. Sears McGee, *The Godly Man in Stuart England: Anglicans, Puritans, and the Two Tables, 1620-1670* [New Haven: Yale University Press, 1976], p. 6).

49. E.g., Norman Pettit, "The Heart renewed: Assurance of Salvation in Puritan spiritual Life" in *Transatlantic Encounters: Studies in European-American Relations. Presented to Winfried Herget*, ed. Udo J. Hebel & Karl Ortseifen (Trier, Germany: Wissenshaftlicher Verlag Trier, 1995),

gland."[50] But Schaefer, still labouring, it seems, under a perception that Puritanism is almost synonymous with nonconformity, is rather bemused by this "rather complex fellow" and finds it hard to imagine how one who knew "such a life of preferment and honours" could ever have been a Puritan.[51] Nicholas Tyacke in a similar vein has sent out a warning signal against an uncritical use of what was often a pejorative label when referring to Preston.[52]

But although to define Puritanism exclusively in terms of a zealous desire for further ecclesiastical reform is now somewhat problematical and dated, it is still an important area to consider in any assessment of Preston's puritan credentials. We have already seen how Preston was early on in his career suspected of "some inclination to puritanisme."[53] However, no tangible evidence seems to have been given in support of this charge, other than his opposition to one of his pupils appearing in a stage play as a woman. Yet in the historiography of dissent Preston was soon to become enshrined, without evidence, as a 'sufferer for nonconformity.'[54] According to Fuller, the term 'Puritan' originally "was only taken to denote such, as dissented from the

---

14-28, p. 26; Daniel W. Doerksen, *Conforming to the Word: Herbert, Donne, and the English Church before Laud* (Cranbury, NJ: Associated University Presses, 1997), p. 45; Yong Jae Timothy Song, *Theology and Piety in the Reformed Federal Thought of William Perkins and John Preston* (Lewiston, NY: Edwin Mellen Press, 1998), p. 13; Geoffrey Treasure, ed., *Who's Who in British History: Beginnings to 1901* (London: Fitzroy Dearborn Publishers, 1998), II:1004; cf. Haller, *Rise of Puritanism*, p. 61.

50. Collinson, *History of Emmanuel College*, p. 220; cf. p. 15.

51. Schaefer, "The Spiritual Brotherhood," p. 187. Schaefer affirms that Preston nevertheless was a Puritan, due to his "associations and his preaching itself" (p. 181).

52. Nicholas R. N. Tyacke, *Anti-Calvinists: The Rise of English Arminianism c. 1590-1640*, 2nd ed. (Oxford: Clarendon Press, 1990), p. 171; cf. Tom Webster, *Godly Clergy in Early Stuart England: The Caroline Puritan Movement, c.1620-1643* (Cambridge: Cambridge University Press, 1997), p. 85; Collinson, *History of Emmanuel College*, p. 216.

53. See p. 6.

54. Neal, *History of the Puritans*, II:128. Another example of Preston being 'claimed' in later, popular dissenting literature is Helen Campbell, *Anne Bradstreet and her Time* (Boston, MA: D. Lothrop Company, 1891), pp. 26-27, where Preston is described as "a noted Nonconformist." Cf. *CCRB*, II:159. Similarly, Preston's life is also included in the following works: Benjamin Brook, *The Lives of the Puritans: Containing a biographical Account of those Divines who distinguished themselves in the Cause of Religious Liberty, from the Reformation under Queen Elizabeth, to the Act of Uniformity, in 1662* (London: For James Black, 1813), II:352-61; Thomas Smith, *Select Memoirs of the Lives, Labours, and Sufferings, of those pious and learned English and Scottish Divines, who greatly distinguished themselves in promoting the Reformation from Popery; in translating the Bible; and in promulgating its salutary Doctrines by their numerous evangelical Writings; and who ultimately crowned the venerable Edifice with the celebrated Westminster Confession of Faith* (Glasgow: D. Mackenzie, 1828), pp. 342-48.

Hierarchie in Discipline, and Church-Government."[55] Two objective standards, therefore, for measuring a man's inclination to Puritanism in a narrow
ecclesiastical sense are the stance taken towards episcopacy and to the established forms of worship.[56] On the first score, Preston proves elusive. Fuller
gives no grounds for styling Preston as the "Patriarch of the Presbyterian
Party," and neither does William Sanderson for his belief that Preston "was
esteemed indeed a proper Patron for the Puritan Presbyter." Preston seems to
be on record nowhere as having spoken against episcopacy, although some
did see him as a threat to the episcopal system.[57] Preston did turn down bish-
oprics, as we have already seen, but never on the stated grounds of an unease
with the office itself, but always because he saw the cause of 'the godly' as
better served in some other sphere of service. He also maintained close and
enduring friendships with numerous bishops, particularly Ussher and
Davenant, who both published defences of episcopacy, albeit Ussher's being
too weak for many.[58] If Preston did indeed think that the episcopal system

55. Fuller, *Church-History of Britain*, IX:66; cf. Henry Parker, *A Discourse concerning Puritans: A Vindication of those, who unjustly suffer by the Mistake, Abuse, and Misapplication of that
Name. A Tract necessary and usefull for these Times*, 2nd ed. (London: For Robert Bostock, 1641),
p. 10.

56. Cf. Roland G. Usher, *The Reconstruction of the English Church* (London: D. Appleton
and Co., 1910), II:355-57.

57. Fuller, *Church-History of Britain*, XI:131; cf. Wood, *Fasti Oxonienses*, col. 333. Charles
Erlington also gave Preston this dubious title, following Samuel Ward of Ipswich (Ussher,
Works, I:55-56). Sanderson, *A compleat History of the Life and Raigne of King Charles*, p. 119. Cf.
Morgan, *Prince Charles's Puritan Chaplain*, pp. 130, 195. Haller presents Preston as basically a
strict Presbyterian, yet cites no evidence (Haller, *Rise of Puritanism*, p. 70). Although Collinson
cites a preface to a book by Clarke to this effect, only "the later" in the list were actually "zeal-
ously affected towards *Presbyterial* Government," and Preston is one of 'the former' (Samuel
Clarke, *The Marrow of Ecclesiastical Historie, contained in the Lives of the Fathers, and other
learned Men, and famous Divines, which have flourished in the Church since Christ's Time to this
present Age* [London: William Du-gard, 1650], p. b2v; Patrick Collinson, *Godly People: Essays on
English Protestantism and Puritanism* [London: Hambledon Press, 1983], p. 516). Lancelot
Andrewes was one bishop who saw his own office as under threat from Preston (Ball, *Life of
Preston*, pp. 53-54).

58. James Ussher, *The Reduction of Episcopacie unto the Form of synodical Government received in the ancient Church* (London: E. C. for R. Royston, 1656); John Davenant, "The
Determinationes, Or Resolutions of certain theological Questions, publicly discussed in the
University of Cambridge" in *A Treatise on Justification*, trans. Josiah Allport (London: Hamil-
ton, Adams, & Co., 1846) II:199-539, II:437-48. However, Ussher himself was accused by some to
King James of being a "Puritane" (Nicholas Bernard, *The Life & Death of the most reverend and
learned Father of our Church Dr. James Ussher* [London: E. Tyler for John Crook, 1656], p. 50;
Clarke, *A general Martyrologie*, II:287; cf. Peter Heylyn, *Respondet Petrus: Or, the Answer of Peter
Heylyn D.D. to so much of Dr Bernard's Book entituled, The Judgement of the late Primate of Ire-*

had no biblical sanction, then, unlike Chaderton, his predecessor at Emmanuel, he did a good, and we must say strategic, job of concealing it. As Hacket noted, "he had more Skill, than boisterously to propound to [Buckingham] the Extirpation of the Bishops, remembring [*sic*] what King James had said in the Conference at Hampton-Court . . . 'No Bishop, No King.'"[59]

On the second score, however, there is a small amount of evidence that Preston was indeed chafing under the collar of his mother church. Early on in his career, Preston nearly lost his place at Queens' when accused of being "a Non-Conformist" and "an enemy to formes of Prayer." On 23rd January, 1620, Preston clashed with Dr Robert Newcome, commissary of the Archdeacon of the diocese of Ely, and with Lancelot Andrewes, recently departed Bishop of Ely, over his failure to use the Book of Common Prayer at a lecture in St Botolph's church, Cambridge, and his preaching a sermon when explicitly forbidden to do so by Newcome. Yet the incident is clouded by personal enmity against Preston on the part of Newcome for matters wholly unrelated to ecclesiastical affairs, and may well have been a trap. At any rate, Preston reaffirmed his full allegiance to the Prayer Book at St Botolph's, in what was made to be seen as an enforced recantation sermon, and he signed a written apology to Newcome. Preston thereby evaded the moves by Andrewes to have him expelled from the University. As if to play to *both* galleries, Preston in this sermon endorsed set forms of prayer *and* extempore prayer as each being useful in its own place.[60]

---

land [London: For R. Royston and R. Marriot, 1658], *passim*). This accusation was to increase in frequency under King Charles (Ussher, *Works*, XIII:348). This is another example of how this word was a term of abuse. We will meet Ussher and Davenant again in Ch. 7.

59. Hacket, *Scrinia Reserata*, I:204; cf. Parker, *Discourse concerning Puritans*, p. 13. In his *Summe*, which is a concise overview of all the *locii* of systematic theology that Preston taught at Emmanuel College, Preston is tantalisingly brief in his *locus* on ecclesiology. He simply states that in order that "the church be rightly constituted" and "be so kepte," it is necessary to appoint "good officers[,] & here the doctrine of church governores is to be handled" (Preston, *Summe*, f. 5). How Preston exactly "handled" it behind the closed doors of Emmanuel College is not clear. The presence of this *locus* within the *Summe* does not in and of itself suggest anti-episcopalian sympathies, since church government is there set alongside the equally brief *locii* of family and civil government as part of a comprehensive whole. On the other hand, in a college known for its Puritan sympathisers, Preston evidently did not want to make church government a taboo subject, despite its potentially subversive tendencies. Preston's *Summe* is an unpaginated manuscript (ECL MS. 181), so here I give my own pagination. For an introduction to Preston's *Summe* see Ball, *Life of Preston*, pp. 39-42 and Morgan, *Prince Charles's Puritan Chaplain*, pp. 34-40.

60. CUL MS. UA.V.C.Ct.III.24 ff. 87-88; CUL MS. UA.Comm.Ct.I.13 ff. 14r-15r; CUL MS. UA.V.C.Ct.I.9 ff. 173v-74r; Ball, *Life of Preston*, pp. 42-59; Morgan, *Prince Charles's Puritan Chaplain*, pp. 29, 46-50; cf. Kenneth Fincham & Peter G. Lake, "The Ecclesiastical Policy of King James I," *JBS* 24 (1985): 169-207, p. 193. The sermon is not extant, but was on 2 Peter 3:17, 18 —

We can be certain that in principle Preston had no fundamental problem with the established liturgy of the Church of England, and was happy to
defend his liturgical heritage before the highest in the land. On another occasion he was urged to preach on set forms of prayer, this time before James at
Hinchingbrooke. The bulk of the sermon turned out to be an anti-Arminian
polemic, but towards the end Preston obliged with a defence of set forms of
prayer, and an exhortation to obey the commands of the Church. Ball tells us
that "the King sate all ye while very quiet, & never stirred or spake to anybody,
but by his lookes discovered he was pleased." The whole court greatly appreciated this sermon and it ultimately led to Preston being appointed Court
Chaplain in 1621.[61] There appears to be no surviving evidence of Preston's attitude to vestments or the signing of the cross in baptism. Perhaps this speaks
for itself. Any tendencies to nonconformity that Preston may have had were
clearly never so great as to cost him considerable preferments in church and
state.[62] In order to secure for himself the Trinity Lectureship, for example, it
would appear from Bishop Felton's letter to Conway that Preston was willing
to make "professions of all conformitie."[63]

However, it cannot be said with total certainty that Preston was completely free from a 'puritanical' instinct to purge the church of the remnants

---

verses sufficiently irrelevant to the point at issue. Harry Porter sees the enmity alluded to above
as relating to Preston's revenge on Newcome *after* the clash at St Botolph's, but this is contrary
to Ball's account (Porter's only cited source), which suggests it may well have been a cause
(Harry C. Porter, *Reformation and Reaction in Tudor Cambridge* [Cambridge: Cambridge University Press, 1958], p. 263; Ball, *Life of Preston*, p. 52).

61. Ball, *Life of Preston*, pp. 62-69; cf. Brook, *Lives of the Puritans*, II:357. The sermon was
finally published, and subsequently cited in defence of set forms of prayer (Richard Capel,
Capel's Remains. Being an useful Appendix to his excellent Treatise of Tentations [London: T. R.
for John Bartlet, 1658], p. A8r; James Ussher, *The Judgement of the late Arch-Bishop of Armagh*
[London: For John Crook, 1659], pp. 327-29). For the section on set forms, see John Preston, *The
Fulnesse of Christ*, pp. 22-26 and John Preston, *Plenitudo Fontis*, pp. 16-18. For the problematic
publication history of this sermon see below, pp. 238-39. For another defence of set forms of
prayer, this time preached at Lincoln's Inn towards the end of his life, see John Preston, *Saints
daily Exercise*, pp. 80-84.

62. In this Preston is similar to his friend Richard Sibbes. Sibbes was *not* "an open conformist. He was a hesitator, and a questioner, but not a dissenter," subscribing as he did to the
Three Articles in December 1616 (Ball, *Life of Preston*, p. 149; Dever, *Richard Sibbes*, Chs. 2-4, especially pp. 45-48; Dever, "Moderation and Deprivation," p. 406; cf. Capel, *Remains*, p. A8r). According to Grosart, Preston and Sibbes "loved one another with a love that was something wonderful. They were as David and Jonathan in earlier, and as Luther and Melanchthon in later,
days. They were never found apart when anything was to be done for their Master. To the last it
was so" (Sibbes, *Works*, I:l-li).

63. PRO SP 14/170/58. See above, p. 9.

of corrupt religion. James for one continued to be suspicious of Preston and tried to curb his influence.[64] John Hacket, later Bishop of Coventry and Lichfield, describes how Preston was "not well affected to the Church," and was "zealous for a new Discipline, and given to Change." Preston did not want the Duke of Buckingham to be "among those that are Protestants at large, and never look inward to the Center of Religion," but rather to be "a warm and zealous Christian." He wanted the Duke, in this spirit, to help him "strenuously to lop off from this half-reformed Church, the superfluous Branches of Romish Superstition, that much disfigured it." By this he meant "the Quire-Service of Cathedral and Collegiate Churches, with the Appennages [*sic*], which were maintained with vast Wealth, and Lands of excessive Commodity, to feed fat, lazy, and unprofitable Drones." He lamented that "all that Chanting and Pomp hindred the Heavenly Power, and Simplicity of Prayer: And furthered not the Preaching of the Gospel." However, Hacket writes with clear polemical intent to style Preston's proposal of the dissolution of Cathedral Chapter lands, to finance the armies in the Palatinate, as sacrilegious and pernicious, and to number him among that carnal "Generation of malecontents." In this connection he also claims that Preston was working for the Scottish followers of John Knox, and sees in Preston's proposal an anti-episcopal agenda, since the Deans and Chapters were "the Seminary from whence the ablest Scholars were removed to Bishopricks."[65] Hacket, writing in the 1650s, cites no sources for this narrative, however, and it is impossible to know how accurate these claims are. They could be mere mud slinging, or it could be that they indicate that Preston's public outward conformity was a conscious strategic decision.

That some mud should have stuck should not surprise us, however. Preston enjoyed close and enduring friendships with those renowned for a more defiant stance towards their mother church, and was master of Emmanuel, a college notorious for its nonconformity.[66] He may or may not have

64. Ball, *Life of Preston*, pp. 99-101; cf. Schaefer, "The Spiritual Brotherhood," p. 192. James is reported to have joked about having in Preston a chaplain "who could not say Prayers, for he scrupled the use of our Liturgy" (Rapin de Thoyras, *The History of England*, trans. N. Tindal [London: For James, John and Paul Knapton, 1732-33], II:199).

65. Hacket, *Scrinia Reserata*, I:203-5; cf. II:231. McCullough also recognises that Hacket was "not above some partisan resentment" (Peter E. McCullough, *Sermons at Court: Politics and Religion in Elizabethan and Jacobean Preaching* [Cambridge: Cambridge University Press, 1998], p. 201). Hacket left his library to the University of Cambridge, including ten books by Preston (CUL Syn.7.63.309; Syn.7.63.409; cf. Brian North Lee, *British Bookplates: A pictorial History* [Newton Abbot, UK: David & Charles, 1979], pp. 32-33).

66. Ball, *Life of Preston*, p. 79; Shuckburgh, *Emmanuel College*, pp. 35-37; Peter G. Lake, *Moderate Puritans and the Elizabethan Church* (Cambridge: Cambridge University Press, 1982),

shared the nonconformist leanings of Cotton or Arthur Hildersham, but he was sufficiently behind them to negotiate their liberty to preach again after they had been silenced.[67]

Although when addressing the Lincoln's Inn congregation in February 1624 Preston had publicly taken an ambivalent attitude towards "Impropriations," stating that some but not most opposition to them was legitimate,[68] it is still likely that Preston gave crucial support and guidance to the Feoffees for Impropriations, a potentially subversive scheme whereby funds were raised to buy patronage rights for strategic or simply neglected pulpits, and thereby secure 'godly' and even openly nonconformist preaching, even when the local bishop would have normally been able to prevent it.[69] In keeping with his characteristic shrewdness, there appears to be no direct evidence for Preston's involvement, but Heylyn, Laud's key informant during the ensuing crackdown in the Court of the Exchequer, perceptively makes a connection between the formalisation of this long-running project in February 1626 and Preston's influence upon "the Affairs of the Puritan Faction" at that time.[70] It is perhaps also not without significance that the Trust for the pur-

pp. 45-46; Collinson, *History of Emmanuel College*, pp. 178-86; cf. Joan S. Ibish, "Emmanuel College: the Founding Generation, with a biographical Register of Members of the College, 1584-1604" (Ph.D. Dissertation, Harvard University, 1985), pp. 301-17, 322.

67. Ussher, *Works*, XVI:371; Morgan, *Puritan Spirituality*, p. 74; Fincham & Lake, "Ecclesiastical Policy," pp. 178-79; Webster, *Godly Clergy*, p. 86; cf. Francis J. Bremer, *Congregational Communion: Clerical Friendship in the Anglo-American Puritan Community, 1610-1692* (Boston: Northeastern University Press, 1994), p. 84; *CCRB*, II:74, 88, 93, 117-18, 159. Interestingly, it was Davenant who tried, unsuccessfully, to persuade Cotton to conform (Fincham & Lake, "Ecclesiastical Policy," p. 178). For more on Hildersham, see below, p. 139.

68. Preston, *Foure Treatises*, p. 203.

69. Cf. Heylyn, *Examen Historicum*, I:210.

70. Heylyn, *Cyprianus Anglicus*, p. 209. The project began informally around 1613. For early accounts of the investigation of the legality of the Feoffees for Impropriations and seventeenth-century assessments of their significance see William Laud, *The Works of the most reverend Father in God, William Laud*, ed. William Scott & James Bliss, Library of Anglo-Catholic Theology (Oxford: John Henry Parker, 1847-60), III:216-17, 253, IV:100-101, 175-76, 303-4; William Prynne, *Canterburies Doome. Or the first Part of a compleat History of the Committment, Charge, Tryall, Condemnation, Execution of William Laud* (London: John Macock for Michael Spark Sr, 1646), pp. 385-89, 537-39; Fuller, *Church-History of Britain*, XI:136-37, 143; William Gouge, *A learned and very useful Commentary on the Whole Epistle to the Hebrews* (London: A. M. T. W. and S. G. for Joshua Kirton, 1655), pp. b2v-c1r; Heylyn, *Examen Historicum*, I:208-11; Heylyn, *Cyprianus Anglicus*, pp. 209-10; John Rushworth, *Historical Collections* (London: J. A. for Robert Boulter; J. D. for John Wright and Richard Chiswell; for Richard Chiswell & Thomas Cockerill, 1680-1701), II:8, 150-52; John Barnard, *Theologo-historicus, or the true Life of the most reverend Divine, and excellent Historian Peter Heylyn* (London: J. S. for Ed. Eckelston, 1683), pp. 147-50; Mather, *Magnalia Christi Americana*, I:322-23.

chase of Impropriations was formally set up on 15th February, just four days after Preston had been hit by the realisation at the York House Conference that the Duke of Buckingham had turned against him.[71] It should also not go unnoticed that Preston was later to assign the posthumous publication of his sermons to two Feoffees, namely, Richard Sibbes and John Davenport.[72]

It might be concluded therefore that Preston was styled a 'Puritan' often as a term of abuse, and more because he was associated with certain 'undesirable' people and institutions, than because of any public stance with regard to worship or polity.[73] Outwardly, or at least publicly, Preston fully conformed, and Schaefer's dilemma is partly solved by the fact that James tended to view Puritanism as only a matter of refusing to conform outwardly and not of private doctrinal opinion.[74] Thus the path to promotion remained relatively clear for Preston, and he successfully "trod the line between conformity and nonconformity."[75]

71. For a detailed study of the York House Conference, see Ch. 6. For treatments of the Feoffees for Impropriations which, following Heylyn, mention Preston as a background influence, see Charles Webb Le Bas, *The Life of Archbishop Laud* (London: For J. G. & F. Rivington, 1836), pp. 149-52; Ethyn W. Kirby, "The Lay Feoffees: A Study in militant Puritanism," *JMH* 14 (1942): 1-25, p. 4; Morgan, *Prince Charles's Puritan Chaplain*, pp. 178-83; Hill, *Puritanism and Revolution*, p. 244; McGee, *The Godly Man*, p. 12; Webster, *Godly Clergy*, pp. 17, 81-86. For other modern treatments see Henry A. Parker, "The Feoffees of Impropriations," *TCSM* 11 (1907): 263-77; Isabel M. Calder, "A seventeenth-century Attempt to purify the Anglican Church," *AHR* 53 (1948): 760-75; Isabel M. Calder, ed., *Activities of the Puritan Faction in the Church of England, 1625-33* (London: SPCK for the Church Historical Society, 1957); Haller, *Rise of Puritanism*, pp. 80-82; Christopher Hill, *Economic Problems of the Church from Archbishop Whitgift to the Long Parliament* (Oxford: Clarendon Press, 1956), pp. 245-74.

72. See below, p. 230.

73. The Arminian Heylyn saw Preston as one who tirelessly pursued "the Puritan Interest" and who "gained a strong Party in the City" of London, even to the point where his bishop-like influence would have rivalled that of Laud had Preston lived a little longer (Heylyn, *Cyprianus Anglicus*, pp. 156-57).

74. See p. 13; Parker, *Discourse concerning Puritans*, p. 14; cf. Fincham & Lake, "Ecclesiastical Policy," p. 205. Samuel Harsnett, "a zealous asserter of ceremonies" whom we will meet in Ch. 2, loathed such "conformable puritans, who practiced it out of policy, yet dissented from it in their judgments" (Fuller, *Church-History of Britain*, XI:144). Baxter looked up to Preston as one of the exemplary "old Conformists" (Richard Baxter, *A Defence of the Principles of Love, which are necessary to the Unity and Concord of Christians; and are delivered in a Book called The Cure of Church-divisions* [London: For Nevil Simmons, 1671], p. 12; cf. *CCRB*, II:118, 139).

75. Norman Pettit, *The Heart Prepared: Grace and Conversion in Puritan Spiritual Life*, 2nd ed. (Middletown, CT: Wesleyan University Press, 1989), p. 76; Pettit, "The Heart Renewed," p. 26. The recent description of Preston as being "a nonconforming Anglican" must be rejected (Kenneth Hylson-Smith, *The Churches in England from Elizabeth I to Elizabeth II* [London: SCM Press, 1996-98], I:198).

Yet as the work of Collinson and Lake has made abundantly clear, it is unsatisfactory to define Puritanism solely, if at all, in terms of church polity and nonconformity. Puritanism was primarily a style of piety and divinity.[76] It is in this more subjective realm of piety, divinity, and preaching that Preston shows himself to have been definitely the 'hotter sort of Protestant.' In terms of strictness of life, Preston was a born disciplinarian. Long before he turned to divinity, he had to be reprimanded by his tutor for excessive studying to the neglect of the body, and, once a preacher, this zeal seems only to have been reinforced. Heylyn singled him out as a renowned Sabbatarian.[77] But to those who found him too strict, Preston had this to say: "All the carnall men in the world finde fault with strictnesse &c; but another mans chief trouble is, that hee cannot bee strict enough."[78] Although his preaching was on occasions militantly anti-Papist and anti-Arminian, and his court sermons frequently addressed the contemporary political scene,[79] Preston's works are almost entirely consumed with

76. For an insightful introduction to the literature behind this statement see Lake, "Defining Puritanism — Again?"

77. Heylyn, *Respondet Petrus*, p. 94. William Perkins is also mentioned in this connection.

78. Ball, *Life of Preston*, p. 10; cf. p. 19; Preston, *The golden Scepter*, I:217.

79. Preston would exhort his congregation to "shew your zeal by hating and abhorring Poperie" (Preston, *Riches of Mercy*, p. 91; cf. John Preston, *Breast-plate*, II:87). Henry Burton, in his Epistle Dedicatory to the Duke of Buckingham in his attack on the Papal Bull of 1626, leans on Preston's court preaching for support (Henry Burton, *The Baiting of the Popes Bull. Or, an Unmasking of the Mystery of Iniquity, folded up in a most pernitious Breeve or Bull, sent from the Pope lately into England* [London: W. Jones for M. Sparke, 1627], pp. **3v-**4r; cf. Morgan, *Prince Charles's Puritan Chaplain*, p. 193). According to Ball, Preston's anti-papal activities extended to writing, if only in a joint-authorship capacity, a tract against the Spanish Match (Ball, *Life of Preston*, pp. 59-60). Morgan argues that Preston's letter was known as "Mr Alured's" letter against the Spanish Match, numerous copies of which survive (Morgan, *Prince Charles's Puritan Chaplain*, pp. 54-59; BL Add. MS. 18201, ff. 20v-28r; 40629, ff. 117r-22r; 4149, ff. 158r-162v; Bod Tanner MS. 290, ff. 55r-57v; Tanner MS. 299, 44r-45v; PRO SP 14/115/67). Lake, Fincham, and Charles Hill assume Preston was the author, but others still assume that Alured was the author (Fincham & Lake, "Ecclesiastical Policy," p. 199; Charles P. Hill, *Who's Who in Stuart Britain: Being the Fifth Volume in the Who's Who in British History Series* [London: Shepheard-Walwyn, 1988], p. 64; Thomas Cogswell, *The Blessed Revolution: English Politics and the Coming of War, 1621-1624* [Cambridge: Cambridge University Press, 1989], p. 45). The *ODNB*'s entry for Thomas Alured is non-committal on this point, but Collinson finds Morgan's arguments plausible (Collinson, *History of Emmanuel College*, p. 219). According to Hunt, Preston was also probably behind the presentation to King James of what he called a "stinging" petition, calling for the stricter enforcement of recusancy laws (William A. Hunt Jr., *The Puritan Moment: The Coming of Revolution in an English County* [Cambridge, MA: Harvard University Press, 1983], p. 179). William Prynne in his own anti-Arminian publication gives an extensive list of places in Preston's works where Arminianism is refuted (William Prynne, *Anti-Arminianisme. Or, the Church of Englands old Antithesis to new Arminianisme* [London: Eliz. Allde for M. Sparke, 1630], p. 212). Some deemed

matters of spiritual experience and practical piety. Particularly prominent are the themes of preparation for salvation, the quest for full assurance of faith, and the need for self-examination when partaking of the Lord's Supper. In that sense, Preston was an exemplary 'experimental predestinarian' and well qualifies for the term 'Puritan.'[80] For one reason or another, Preston's brand of Puritanism was more concerned about promoting a generic unity within 'the spiritual brotherhood' than pressing home potentially divisive distinctives.[81]

In terms of preaching, we have already seen how Preston gave it a very high priority, and his pulpit style was "as plain as any Puritan style to be met with anywhere."[82] It also appears to have been to some degree innovative in so far as many began to emulate the way he made "Practical Uses upon maine fundamental Theoretical points" as found, for example, in his *Life eternall*.[83] Although Preston was a highly successful politician of the utmost cunning,[84] his primary passion still seems to have been preaching, including to the ordi-

---

Preston's powerful court sermons to have been prophetic (Morgan, *Prince Charles's Puritan Chaplain*, pp. 187-91).

80. It was Kendall who coined this label to be used in distinction to mere "credal predestinarianism" (Kendall, *Calvin and English Calvinism*, pp. 8, 80). Lake and Hughes endorse this distinction. However, Tyacke, Schaefer, and Anthony Milton reject it as too rigid (Peter G. Lake, "Calvinism and the English Church 1570-1635," *P&P* 114 [1987]: 32-76, pp. 39, 58; Seán F. Hughes, "The Problem of 'Calvinism': English Theologies of Predestination c.1580-1630" in *Belief and Practice in Reformation England: A Tribute to Patrick Collinson from his Students*, ed. Susan Wabuda & Caroline Litzenberger [Aldershot, UK: Ashgate Publishing Company, 1998], 229-49, pp. 235, 247; Tyacke, *Anti-Calvinists*, p. ix; Schaefer, "The Spiritual Brotherhood," p. 247; Milton, personal communication). Both Kendall and Lake label Preston an experimental predestinarian (Kendall, *Calvin and English Calvinism*, p. 118; Lake, "Calvinism and the English Church," p. 41). Preston preached a series of sermons on 2 Peter 1:10, "the biblical banner for the experimental predestinarian tradition" (R. T. Kendall, "John Cotton: First English Calvinist?" in *The Puritan Experiment in the New World* [London: The Westminster Conference, 1976], 38-50, p. 46). These sermons were about to be published but are now lost (Prynne, *Anti-Arminianisme*, p. 212). However, we know that Preston believed that "the maine errand for which wee came into the world" was "to make our calling and election sure" (Preston, *The golden Scepter*, I:200).

81. Cf. the testimony of Miles Corbett in John Barkstead, *The Speeches, Discourses, and Prayers, of Col. John Barkstead, Col. John Okey, and Mr. Miles Corbet; upon the 19th of April, being the Day of their Suffering at Tyburn* (London: n.p., 1662), pp. 41-42.

82. See p. 9; cf. John Preston, *Sinnes Overthrow*, p. 102 cited in Capel, *Remains*, p. A6r; John Preston, *Saints Qualification*, I:298. Emerson, *English Puritanism*, p. 238.

83. SUL Hartlib MS. 29/2/51b-52a.

84. Cf. Fuller, *Church-History of Britain*, XI:131; Fuller, *Worthies of England*, II:291; Heylyn, *Cyprianus Anglicus*, p. 156; Echard, *The History of England*, II:72; Granger, *History of England*, II:175; Hill, *Puritanism and Revolution*, p. 260; John Chandos, ed., *In God's Name: Examples of Preaching in England from the Act of Supremacy to the Act of Uniformity, 1534-1662* (London: Hutchinson & Co., 1971), p. 287.

nary people. Desiring to see many 'conversions,' he was willing to "bow his more sublime and raised parts to lowest apprehensions."[85] Edward Leigh told the following story about Preston to illustrate this point:

> Doctor Preston being asked, Why he preached so plainly, and dilated so much in his Sermons: answered, He was a Fisherman: Now Fishermen, said he, if they should winde up the Net, and so cast it into the Sea, they should catch nothing but when they spread the Net then they catch the Fish; I spread my Net (said he) because I would catch the Fish, that is, I preach so plainly and dilate so much in my Sermons, that I may win souls to Christ.[86]

Many attributed their spiritual awakening to Preston's preaching, including some eminent 'Puritans' such as Thomas Shepard of New England fame.[87]

85. Editorial preface to John Preston, *Sermons preached before His Majestie*, p. A3r; cf. Preston, *The New Covenant*, p. A4r; John Preston, *Sun-beams*, pp. B1r-B1v. See also above, p. 6. Preston's popular preaching style transformed Thomas Goodwin's approach to preaching, and continued to be praised right into the nineteenth century (Thomas Goodwin, *The Works of Thomas Goodwin*, ed. John C. Miller [Edinburgh: James Nichol, 1861-67], II:lxv-lxvii; John Wilkins, *Ecclesiastes: Or, a Discourse concerning the Gift of Preaching, as it falls under the Rules of Art*, 9th ed. [London: For W. Churchill and M. Lawrence, 1718], pp. 91, 237; Edward Williams, *The Christian Preacher: Or, Discourses on Preaching, by several eminent Divines, English and Foreign*, 5th ed. [London: For Thomas Tegg, 1843], p. 305). In some ways, Goodwin saw his own ministry as building on the foundation Preston had laid (SUL Hartlib MS. 29/2/60a).

86. Edward Leigh, *A Systeme or Body of Divinity consisting of ten Books* (London: By A. M. for William Lee, 1654), pp. 464-65.

87. Thomas Shepard, *God's Plot: The Paradoxes of Puritan Piety: Being the Autobiography & Journal of Thomas Shephard*, ed. Michael McGiffert (Amherst, MA: University of Massachusetts Press, 1972), pp. 41-42, 45, 47, 73; Mather, *Magnalia Christi Americana*, I:381. It may be that Shepard is referring to the same sermon on Romans 12:2 that deeply affected Thomas Goodwin, preached in October 1622 in Emmanuel College Chapel upon Preston's election to the mastership. However, the evidence is not conclusive (Goodwin, *Works*, II:xvii, lxv-lxvii). Shepard, on hearing Preston at Emmanuel deemed him to be "the most searching preacher in the world" (Shepard, *God's Plot*, p. 42). Others Preston greatly influenced included Samuel Fairclough (Morgan, *Prince Charles's Puritan Chaplain*, p. 45), Prynne (Heylyn, *Cyprianus Anglicus*, p. 156; Anthony A. Wood, *Athenæ Oxonienses*, ed. Philip Bliss, 3rd ed. [London: For F. C., and J. Rivington et al., 1817], III:845; see below, p. 237), Martin Holbeach *(ODNB)*, Henry Burton (Morgan, *Prince Charles's Puritan Chaplain*, p. 193), Sir William Roberts *(ODNB)*, John Bastwick (Morgan, *Prince Charles's Puritan Chaplain*, pp. 194-95), Miles Corbett (Barkstead, *Speeches, Discourses, and Prayers*, pp. 28, 38, 42), and probably Henry Lawrence *(ODNB)*. As preacher to Lincoln's Inn, Preston would probably also have influenced John Milton, Oliver St. John, William Lenthall, and William Sheppard (Emerson, *English Puritanism*, p. 279; Bremer, *Congregational Communion*, p. 52). Preston's dying prayers were for the raising up of "able preaching ministers" to take his place in the various pulpits he was to leave behind (Ball, *Life of Preston*, p. 173).

Furthermore, although Preston never was given a cure of souls, he was highly sought after as a spiritual counsellor concerning the inward motions of the human heart. His most demanding service in this area would have been the infamous case of Joan Drake.[88] If 'Puritan' is to be defined in terms of the spiritual brotherhood who pursued this approach to piety, whether it was merely an *ecclesiola in ecclesia* or in fact 'the religion of Protestants,' then Preston was indeed a Puritan.[89] If regard to outward conformity, or rather lack of it, is also to be included in the term 'Puritan,'[90] then Preston was a 'moderate Puritan' in the sense outlined by Lake, or as Doerksen calls Preston, a "fully conforming" Puritan.[91] Yet Doerksen's description is in danger of implying that Preston, preoccupied with the motions of the heart, was happily complacent about the ecclesiastical *status quo,* which he seems quietly not to have been. It was not for nothing that he "had made a science of skirting the edges of conformity."[92] Better still then, although the term 'Puritan' drops away altogether, Preston was also "a conforming reformer."[93]

---

88. Joan Drake was understood to be in the grip of Satan and suicidal until she was finally delivered through the prolonged counselling of Preston and others. For the main sources on this much-publicised affair see *The Firebrand taken out of the Fire. Or, The Wonderful History, Case, and Cure of Mrs Drake, sometimes the wife of Francis Drake of Esher in the County of Surrey Esq. Who was under the Power and severe Discipline of Satan for the Space of ten Yeares; and was redeemed from his Tyranny in a wonderfull Manner a little before her Death, by the great mercy of God; and (instrumentally) by the extraordinary Paines, Prayers and Fasting, of foure Reverend Divines, whose Names are here subscribed, viz. B. Usher, M. Hooker, D. Preston, M. Dod* (London: For Thomas Mathewes, 1654); George H. Williams, "Called by Thy Name, Leave Us Not: The Case of Mrs. Joan Drake, a formative Episode in the pastoral Career of Thomas Hooker in England," *HLB* 16 (1968): 111-28, 278-303; Clarke, *A general Martyrologie,* II:170-71. Ever since George Thomason's seventeenth-century attribution, John Hart has been traditionally viewed as the author of the pseudonymously published *The Firebrand.* However, Williams in his article shows that it was in fact written by the London barrister Jasper Heartwell.

89. Cf. Patrick Collinson, *The Religion of Protestants: The Church in English Society, 1559-1625* (Oxford: Clarendon Press, 1982).

90. Collinson still insists on this although Lake does not (Collinson, *History of Emmanuel College,* p. 177; Lake, "Defining Puritanism — Again?" p. 6).

91. Lake, *Moderate Puritans, passim;* Doerksen, *Conforming to the Word,* p. 21; cf. p. 109; Fuller, "The History of the University of Cambridge," pp. 162-63; Ball, *Life of Preston,* p. 74; Morgan, *Prince Charles's Puritan Chaplain,* pp. 46-50, 130, 195. In terms of the taxonomy of Preston's contemporary Mede, writing in 1623, Preston was thus mainly a "morall Puritan" and to some extent a "Political Puritan," but not an "Ecclesiastical Puritan" (BL Harleian MS. 389, f. 314; quoted in Collinson, *History of Emmanuel College,* p. 216; cf. Parker, *Discourse concerning Puritans,* pp. 10-11).

92. Bremer, *Congregational Communion,* p. 83.

93. Dever, "Moderation and Deprivation," p. 410 (speaking of Sibbes). Tyacke preferred to see Preston as "a Calvinist conformist" (Nicholas R. N. Tyacke, "Puritanism, Arminianism &

It is with some justification, then, that Patrick Collinson describes Preston as "one of the more enigmatic figures in the history of religion, and of politics."[94] Not only has the term 'Puritan' been used in connection with Preston in order to imply a nonconforming Genevan bent, but it is also true that in terms of his theology proper he "has received little direct attention from modern scholars," and "his thought has, for whatever reason, not undergone the intense scrutiny that scholars have given to the thinking of Perkins, Sibbes, Cotton, and Shepard."[95] Supplementing the recent work of Schaefer and Song, this book is an attempt to continue to rectify this situation, whilst also relocating Preston in his historical context. In particular its purpose is to ascertain Preston's position on the controverted points of predestination, the extent of the satisfaction of Christ, and the nature of the gospel call, and to unfold some of the implications of this for our understanding of the wider historical developments of the period. This is no easy task, however, due to the nature of the sources[96] and the complexity of the theological issues at stake. A very close and exhaustive reading of Preston's works has therefore proved necessary in order to achieve progress on this front. Interaction with a considerable amount of modern literature, by both professional historians and historical theologians — including some in the Reformed tradition for whom the writings of Preston remain living theological texts — serves to enrich our understanding of Preston's contribution. Collinson has stated that "to comprehend the motivation and strategy of Preston's career will be to have some small understanding of the nature of both religion and politics in seventeenth-century England."[97] To achieve this comprehension, we must first turn to Preston's theological heritage.

Counter-Revolution" in *The Origins of the English Civil War,* ed. Conrad Russell [London: Macmillan, 1973], 119-43, p. 129). For those who persist in associating Puritanism with a cantankerous and marginalised nonconformity, then Preston will certainly continue to be "an unusual puritan" (Schaefer, "The Spiritual Brotherhood," p. 179).

94. Collinson, *History of Emmanuel College,* p. 215.

95. Schaefer, "The Spiritual Brotherhood," p. 182. Stearns lamented in 1941 that "there are no good studies of" Preston (Raymond P. Stearns, "Assessing the New England Mind," *CH* 10 [1941]: 246-62, p. 262; cf. Song, *Theology and Piety,* p. iii).

96. See below, pp. 230-40.

97. Collinson, *History of Emmanuel College,* p. 215.

SECTION II

Preston's Heritage

CHAPTER 2

William Perkins and Elizabethan Particularism

"[I]f wee looke backe upon that Generation of Queene Elizabeth; how are we changed! they were zealous, but here is another generation come in their roome, that is dead, and cold, and yet we have their light."[1]

Introduction

Before we carefully assess the position taken by John Preston with regard to the divine decree, the death of Christ, and the gospel call, we must seek to appreciate Preston's heritage in late Elizabethan Reformed divinity. For reasons that will become clear, we begin with an examination of the theology of William Perkins. Perkins was born in 1558 and in 1577 entered Christ's College, Cambridge, where he was tutored by his lifelong friend Laurence Chaderton. Having been made Fellow in 1584, he took up the only other position of his career in 1595, namely, Lecturer at Great St Andrew's, Cambridge, a post he held until his death in 1602. Although his life only just spanned the years of Elizabeth's reign, Perkins' output as a preacher and theological writer was astounding. Between 1590 and 1618 approximately 210 books were printed by the primary publishing house in Cambridge. Of these Perkins wrote no fewer than fifty,[2] a fact consistent with the contemporary opinion that Perkins was a pillar of Protestant orthodoxy.[3] Nevertheless,

---

1. John Preston, *The golden Scepter*, I:12; cf. Preston, *Saints Qualification*, I:168; Preston, *Riches of Mercy*, p. 91.
2. Harry C. Porter, *Reformation and Reaction in Tudor Cambridge* (Cambridge: Cambridge University Press, 1958), p. 264; cf. p. 267.
3. Helena Hajzyk, "The Church in Lincolnshire, c.1595-c.1640" (Ph.D. Dissertation, Uni-

Perkins was viewed by some in his day as "an obscure fellow,"[4] whose works were "a lump of extreame follies."[5]

However, in generations immediately after his death, Perkins was held up by many as an archetype of the perfect combination of rigorous doctrine and fervent piety.[6] William Ames stated that Perkins "for many yeares held forth a burning and shining light, the sparks whereof did flie abroad into all corners of the land."[7] Perkins was certainly "a formidable patristic scholar,"[8] and rose to be "perhaps the most eminent English Reformed theologian of the late sixteenth century."[9] He was not only "the most widely known theologian of the Elizabethan church," but was also "the first English Calvinist to win a major European reputation."[10] While one recent scholar is prepared only to say that Perkins "may well have been the most important figure in the emergence of Reformed scholasticism in England," another can go so far as to say that "Perkins was doubtless the most influential English theologian of his time. Any account of the development of Reformed theology in either England or the Netherlands must place him at the centre of the intellectual narrative."[11]

---

versity of Cambridge, 1980), p. 232. See also the central place given to Perkins' defence of orthodoxy against Romanism and Arminianism in the plate between John Russell, *The Spy, discovering the Danger of Arminian Heresie and Spanish Trecherie* (Amsterdam: n.p., 1628), pp. A2v-A3r. Perkins is portrayed as being the capstone of the castle of Reformation orthodoxy. This pamphlet was not actually published at Strasbourg as the title-page states, but at Amsterdam.

4. William Barrett in John Strype, *The Life and Acts of John Whitgift* (Oxford: Clarendon Press, 1822), II:236.

5. William Williams in Hajzyk, "The Church in Lincolnshire," p. 234.

6. Cf. Samuel Clarke, *The Marrow of Ecclesiastical Historie, contained in the Lives of the Fathers, and other learned Men, and famous Divines, which have flourished in the Church since Christ's Time to this present Age* (London: William Du-gard, 1650), pp. 414-18.

7. Ames writing in the preface to Paul Baynes, *The Diocesans Tryall. Wherein all the Sinnewes of Doctor Downhams Defence are brought into three Heads, and orderly dissolved* (London: n.p., 1621 [*i.e.* 1644]), p. A2v.

8. Ian Breward in *NIDCC*, p. 765; cf. Ian Breward, ed., *The Work of William Perkins* (Abingdon, UK: Sutton Courtenay Press, 1970), p. 102.

9. Richard A. Muller, *Christ and the Decree: Christology and Predestination in Reformed Theology from Calvin to Perkins*, Revised ed. (Grand Rapids, MI: Baker Book House, 1988), p. 131; cf. Richard A. Muller, "Perkins' *A golden Chaine*: Predestinarian System or Schematized *Ordo Salutis?*," *SCJ* 9 (1978): 69-81, p. 69. Munson sees Perkins as "the unsurpassed Puritan theologian of Tudor times" (Charles R. Munson, "William Perkins: Theologian of Transition" [Ph.D. Dissertation, Case Western Reserve University, 1971], p. 181).

10. Breward, ed., *The Work of William Perkins*, p. xi; Patrick Collinson, *The Elizabethan Puritan Movement* (London: Jonathan Cape, 1967), p. 434.

11. Dewey D. Wallace Jr., *Puritans and Predestination: Grace in English Protestant Theology, 1525-1695* (Chapel Hill, NC: University of North Carolina Press, 1982), p. 55; Carl R. Trueman in *BDE*, p. 520. For more on Perkins' reputation see Mark R. Shaw, "The Marrow of

But it is not only Perkins' greatness in his own right that makes him a necessary subject for this study. Perkins bore much resemblance in his own generation to Preston in his. Not only did both these Cambridge men exercise a wide influence through published works, but both are commonly seen as renowned national leaders of 'the Puritan movement,' both having climbed the hierarchy of 'Puritan' colleges.[12] Certainly, both held to the worldview that was later to be so perturbed by the challenge of Laud. Even if it is denied that previous usage of the term 'Puritan' is a sure guide to any analysis today, a comparison of the specific churchmanship of the two men also brings out, theology proper apart, the close bonds of inheritance between them. Both men were sometimes accused of nonconformist tendencies, but pursued a moderate course, devoted to their mother the established Church.[13] In terms

---

Practical Divinity: A Study in the Theology of William Perkins" (Th.D. Dissertation, Westminster Theological Seminary, 1981), pp. 3-6.

12. Collinson, for example, sees Perkins, in his capacity as "virtually the first puritan theologian in the systematic sense," as "the prince of the puritan theologians and the most eagerly read." Christopher Hill sees Perkins as "the high priest of the Puritans," and "the key figure in the systematization of English Puritanism." McGiffert sees Perkins in his own day as "the mastermind of puritanism" (Collinson, *Elizabethan Puritan Movement*, pp. 434, 125; Christopher Hill, *Society and Puritanism in Pre-Revolutionary England* [London: Secker & Warburg, 1964], p. 140; cf. pp. 25, 29, 342, 502; Christopher Hill, *Puritanism and Revolution: Studies in Interpretation of the English Revolution of the Seventeenth Century* [London: Secker & Warburg, 1958], p. 236; Michael McGiffert, "Grace and Works: The Rise and Division of Covenant Divinity in Elizabethan Puritanism," *HTR* 75 [1982]: 463-502, p. 496; cf. Hill, *Puritanism and Revolution*, pp. 64, 215, 216; Christopher Hill, *God's Englishman: Oliver Cromwell and the English Revolution* [London: Weidenfeld & Nicolson, 1970], p. 40; Jan Rohls, *Reformed Confessions: Theology from Zurich to Barmen* [Louisville, KY: Westminster John Knox Press, 1998], p. 25; Alister E. McGrath, *Historical Theology: An Introduction to the History of Christian Thought* [Oxford: Blackwell, 1998], p. 174). For Preston's puritanism, see above, pp. 12-13.

13. Heylyn accused Perkins of being "a professed Presbyterian" (Peter Heylyn, *Aerius Redivivus: Or, the History of the Presbyterians* [Oxford: John Crosley for Thomas Baffet, 1670], p. 342), but for Perkins' conformity see Thomas Fuller, *The Church-History of Britain* (London: For John William, 1655), IX:211; Hill, *Puritanism and Revolution*, p. 216; Breward, ed., *The Work of William Perkins*, p. 22; Paul R. Schaefer Jr., "The Spiritual Brotherhood on the Habits of the Heart: Cambridge Protestants and the Doctrine of Sanctification from William Perkins to Thomas Shepard" (D.Phil. Dissertation, University of Oxford, 1994), pp. 23-29, 35. Baxter saw Perkins as a stricter nonconformist than himself, claiming that Perkins reluctantly conformed "rather than cease Preaching" (Richard Baxter, *An Apology for the Nonconformists Ministry* [London: Thomas Parkhurst and D. Newman, 1681], p. 70; Richard Baxter, *A second true Defence of the meer Nonconformists, against the untrue Accusations, Reasonings and History of Dr Edward Stillingfleet* [London: For Nevil Simons, 1681], p. 39). Cf. Breward, ed., *The Work of William Perkins*, p. 113; Arnold G. Matthews, ed., *The Savoy Declaration of Faith and Order, 1658* (London: Independent Press, 1959), p. 72. For the nature of Preston's conformity see above, pp. 14-17.

of a tradition of piety, both men were exemplary 'experimental predestinarians.'[14] Both subsequently became revered role models in Puritan New England and were highly influential in establishing a new spiritual genre of devotional publications, including through foreign language editions.[15] As Breward puts it, Perkins and Preston together "dominated ministerial training in early New England and profoundly shaped what godly students discerned in the word of God and the workings of their own hearts."[16] It is only fitting, therefore, that a consideration of Preston's intellectual and spiritual heritage should begin by dealing with Perkins' thought.[17]

Perkins and the Divine Decree

When we turn to consider Perkins' theological system we are in a considerably easier position than in the case of Preston. Preston's printed legacy is largely sermonic material, whereas Perkins' theological works consist mainly of theological treatises. In terms of Perkins' predestinarian theology we are particularly well provided for. Amidst the furore of the Barrett-Baro controversy,[18] Perkins wrote two detailed treatises devoted specifically to this topic. The first, *A golden Chaine,* reached its third Latin edition by 1592 and its eighth English edition by 1600.[19] Here we find "the fullest exposition of his

14. Cf. above, p. 21.

15. Miller ranked Perkins and Preston in the top three teachers who were most influential in the development of the "New England creed" (Perry Miller, *The New England Mind: The Seventeenth Century* [Cambridge, MA: Harvard University Press, 1954], p. x; cf. pp. 12, 209, 374, 432, 476, 520; Perry Miller, *The New England Mind: From Colony to Province* [Cambridge, MA: Harvard University Press, 1953], pp. 221, 233). See Breward, ed., *The Work of William Perkins,* p. 130 for an extensive list of Perkins' foreign language publications, and below, p. 241 for Preston's.

16. Breward, ed., *The Work of William Perkins,* p. 111.

17. Despite the fact that their careers never overlapped, Preston has also been styled as Perkins' 'disciple' (Munson, "William Perkins: Theologian of Transition," p. 177; Hill, *Puritanism and Revolution,* pp. 216-17; cf. Everett H. Emerson, *English Puritanism from John Hooper to John Milton* [Durham, NC: Duke University Press, 1968], p. 46).

18. Thorough accounts of this controversy are found in Porter, *Reformation and Reaction,* pp. 314-90 and Peter G. Lake, *Moderate Puritans and the Elizabethan Church* (Cambridge: Cambridge University Press, 1982), pp. 201-42. See also Mark R. Shaw, "William Perkins and the new Pelagians: Another Look at the Cambridge Predestination Controversy of the 1590's," *WTJ* 58 (1996): 267-301.

19. The English translation was produced by Robert Hill at Perkins' request. For a study of Hill's zealous yet pastorally sensitive promotion of Perkins' theology, see Julia F. Merritt, "The pastoral Tightrope: A Puritan Pedagogue in Jacobean London" in *Politics, Religion and Popular-*

systematic theology."[20] The second treatise, *A Christian and plaine Treatise of the Manner and Order of Predestination,* did not prove as immediately popular, but found a place, together with *A golden Chaine,* in Perkins' collected works which were reprinted periodically up until, significantly, 1631.[21] Its importance is clear when it is realised that "the basic document of Arminianism," namely Jacobus Arminius' *Examen Modestum Libelli,* was in fact a response to this very treatise.[22] In addition to these two works, Perkins also gives predestination a most detailed treatment in his exposition of the Apostles' Creed. This work was first published in English in 1595 and had reached its sixth edition by 1631 as well as also featuring in Perkins' collected works. These books were the first English discussions of predestination to be published overseas and they contributed significantly to international debate.[23] It is upon these three works that we will mostly rely in this consideration of Perkins' theology of the divine decree, although confirmative recourse will also be made to other treatises.

Perkins taught an eternal, immutable, and all-embracing decree of God.[24] Perkins accommodates this predestinarian theology to the problem of sin by asserting, in classic Anselmian fashion, that sin as such does not exist. There is simply no metaphysical reality of evil. Sin is "privative" and not "positive," being "the absence of that good which ought to be in the creature." It is not a substance that needed to be created.[25] This definition of sin facilitates Perkins in his positioning of the Fall of man within the absolute decree of God. This, coupled with a distinction between God's permissive or

---

ity in Early Stuart Britain: Essays in Honour of Conrad Russell, ed. Thomas Cogswell, Richard Cust, & Peter G. Lake (Cambridge: Cambridge University Press, 2002), pp. 143-61.

20. Munson, "William Perkins: Theologian of Transition," p. 63. For a chronology of Perkins' works, see Donald K. McKim, *Ramism in William Perkins' Theology* (New York: Peter Lang, 1987), pp. 149-50.

21. Cf. below, p. 229.

22. Carl Bangs, *Arminius: A Study in the Dutch Reformation* (Nashville, TN: Abingdon Press, 1971), p. 209; James Arminius, *Iacobi Arminii veteraquinatis Batavi, S. Theologiæ Doctoris eximii, Examen modestum Libelli* (Leiden: Godefridi Basson, 1612).

23. Breward, ed., *The Work of William Perkins,* pp. 88-89. Perkins' "formal analysis of predestination [is] one of the most exegetically oriented analyses of the early orthodox period" (Muller, *Christ and the Decree,* p. 163).

24. William Perkins, *The Workes of that famous and worthy Minister of Christ in the Universitie of Cambridge, Mr. William Perkins* (London: John Legatt & Cantrell Legge, 1616-18), III:(i)131.

25. Perkins, *Workes,* I:18. This contradicts Boughton's claim that Perkins "equated evil with the nature of a being rather than . . . as privation or displacement of that good that was due to a particular nature" (Lynne C. Boughton, "Supralapsarianism and the Role of Metaphysics in Sixteenth-Century Reformed Theology," *WTJ* 48 (1986): 63-96, p. 87).

general will and his positive or special will, enables Perkins to reconcile God's sovereignty and holiness with the presence of sin in the world he created. According to Perkins, "the voluntary fall of Adam" was "permitted," yet not "by [God's] bare permission, or against his will: but rather miraculously, not without the will of God, and yet without all approbation of it."[26] Although Perkins taught that "God decreed Adams fall," he was at pains to point out that "thence it followeth not, that hee is the author of mans sinne," because

> God's will is twofold, generall, and speciall. God's generall will is, to permit that which is evill, not simply, but because with God evill hath some respect of good, and in this respect we say God decreed Adams fall. God's speciall will, is his approving will; whereby he taketh pleasure and delight in that which is good: and in this regard God nilled Adams fall, and mans sinnes: and yet in some respect he may bee said to wil them. A magistrate, though he take no comfort or delight in the death and execution of a malefactor, yet, he decreeth and appointeth it, and so may be said to will it.[27]

God stands in the same relation to all evil actions throughout history as he did to the Fall. It is vital to "make distinction betweene sinne itselfe and the permission thereof." This means that "sinne itselfe is no effect, but onely the consequent of the decree."[28] This means "God permitteth evil by a certain voluntary permission, in that hee forsakes the second cause in working evill. And he forsaketh his creature either by detracting the grace it had, or not bestowing that which it wanteth." Similarly to the Fall, there is also a sense in which God also positively wills evil actions. We must realise that "God is not onely a bare permissive agent in an evill worke, but a powerfull effectour of the same." Of course, God wills evil in a different way to willing good,[29] but Perkins still declares that God "voluntarily doth permit evill; because it is good that there should bee evill." According to Perkins, God

> hath most justly decreed the wicked workes of the wicked. For if hee had nilled them, they should never have been at all. . . . in respect of Gods decree they are some ways good: for there is not anything absolutely evill. . . . The thing which in its owne nature is evil, in God's eternal

26. Perkins, *Workes*, I:287; I:19; cf. II:606.
27. Perkins, *Workes*, III:(ii)298; cf. II:299.
28. Perkins, *Workes*, I:287.
29. Perkins, *Workes*, I:16; II:624.

counsell is respectively good, in that it is some occasion & way to manifest the glorie of God in his justice, and his mercie.[30]

As regards predestination, or "Gods decree, in as much as it concerneth man,"[31] Perkins distinguishes his own position from three other rival views. He repudiates firstly the Pelagian view in which "the causes of God's predestination" are "in man," in so far as "God did ordaine men either to life or death, according to as he did fore-see, that they would by their naturall Free-will, either reject or receive grace offered." He also repudiates the Lutheran view which, although teaching unconditional election, states that reprobation is "because he did eternally fore-see that they would reject his grace offered them in the Gospell." Perkins' third group of enemies are "Semi-Pelagian Papists" who "ascribe God's predestination, partly to mercie, and partly to mens fore-seene preparations and meritorious workes." This leaves the fourth and Reformed orthodox view held by Perkins. In contradistinction to all the above, this schema teaches that

> the cause and execution of God's predestination, is his mercy in Christ, in them which are saved; and in them which perish, the fall and corruption of man: yet so, as that the decree and eternall counsell of God concerning them both hath not any cause beside his will and pleasure.[32]

By this latter proviso, Perkins means that God "did upon his meere pleasure elect some, & reject others eternally, not mooved or urged thereunto by any thing whatsoever out[side] of himselfe."[33]

Perkins' doctrine of double predestination is nowhere more strikingly portrayed than in his famous, and some would say notorious, diagram that was published as part of *A golden Chaine*.[34] The visual impression given is

---

30. Perkins, *Workes,* I:12, 15; cf. III:(i)199; (ii)298.

31. Perkins, *Workes,* I:16.

32. Perkins, *Workes,* I:9.

33. Perkins, *Workes,* I:109.

34. Perkins, *Workes,* I:10 (opposite). This chart was reprinted in Breward, ed., *The Work of William Perkins,* p. 168; Harry C. Porter, ed., *Puritanism in Tudor England* (London: Macmillan and Co., 1970), pp. 296-97; Muller, "Perkins' *A golden Chaine,*" pp. 774-75; Edward Hindson, ed., *Introduction to Puritan Theology: A Reader* (Grand Rapids, MI: Baker Book House, 1980), p. 139; Alasdair I. C. Heron, ed., *The Westminster Confession in the Church Today* (Edinburgh: Saint Andrew Press, 1982), p. 54 (opposite); and James B. Torrance, "The Concept of Federal Theology: Was Calvin a Federal Theologian?" in *Calvinus Sacrae Scripturae Professor: Calvin as Confessor of Holy Scripture,* ed. Wilhelm H. Neuser (Grand Rapids, MI: Eerdmans, 1994), 15-40, p. 40. For a consideration of the influence of Ramism on this schematisation, and on Perkins' theology in general, see McKim, *Ramism in William Perkins' Theology.*

that there is complete symmetry between election and reprobation. The extent to which Perkins really held to a symmetrical double predestination becomes clearer when he engages in elaborate explanation of his diagram. Perkins defines election as "God's decree, whereby of his owne free wil, he hath ordained certaine men to salvation, to the praise of the glorie of his grace."[35] This election "is unchangeable; so as they which are indeede chosen to salvation cannot perish, but shall without faile ataine to life everlasting."[36] Reprobation on the other hand, "is that part of predestination, whereby God, according to the most free and just purpose of his will, hath determined to reject certain men unto eternall destruction, and misery, and that to the praise of his justice."[37] Elsewhere, Perkins states that it is "a worke of God's providence, whereby he hath decreed to passe by certaine men, in regard of supernaturall grace, for the manifestation of his justice and wrath in their due destruction."

From the historical perspective, reprobation can also be said to be "his will, whereby he suffereth some men to falle into sinne, and inflicteth the punishment of condemnation for sinne." In order to avoid any miscommunication, Perkins divides the decree of reprobation into "two acts." The first of these parts is "the purpose to forsake some men, and to make knowne his justice in them. This act hath a finall cause, but no impulsive cause out[side] of God," arising as it does out of "God's meere good pleasure."[38] The first act of reprobation is therefore not for sin, for "sinne is not the cause of reprobation." However, the second act "is the ordaining of them to punishment or due destruction. . . . For as men are actually damned for sinne: so God hath decreed to damne them for the same sinne."[39]

Perkins understandably anticipated numerous objections to this doctrine. However, none of these objections left him without an equally rigorous refutation. The first objection is that it is "very hard to ascribe unto God who is full of bountie and mercie, such a decree" of reprobation. To this Perkins defended God's unimpeachable prerogative to predestinate. Perkins asserted that

35. Perkins, *Workes*, I:24.

36. Perkins, *Workes*, I:281.

37. Perkins, *Workes*, I:105. Perkins' teaching that reprobation is a subset of predestination escapes Peter White's assertion that "in sixteenth-century scholarly usage ['predestination'] was usually a synonymn for election, and excluded reprobation" (Peter White, *Predestination, Policy and Polemic: Conflict and Consensus in the English Church from the Reformation to the Civil War* [Cambridge: Cambridge University Press, 1992], p. 5).

38. Perkins, *Workes*, II:610.

39. Perkins, *Workes*, II:611; cf. I:105, 109, 287.

it stands more with equitie a thousand fold, that all the creatures in heaven and earth should jointly serve to set forth the glorie and majestie of God the Creator in their eternall destruction, than the striking of a flie or the killing of a flea should serve for the dignitie of all men in the world.

Elsewhere Perkins argues that "God doth none wrong, although he chuse not all; because he is tied to none: and because he hath absolute soveraigntie and authoritie over all creatures."[40] Thus, even if there were not also a decree of election, man could in no way rightly complain at the decree of reprobation.

To another objection that "it is a point of cruelty with God to purpose to create a great part of the world to damnation in hell fire," Perkins replies that "by the virtue of this decree God cannot be said to create any to damnation, but to the manifestation of his justice & glory in his due and deserved damnation: & the doing of this is absolute justice." Perkins also denies that his doctrine results in God hating "his owne creature, and that before it is," for "God's purpose to hate" must be distinguished from his "actuall hating." By this Perkins means that

God before all worlds did purpose to hate some creatures: and that justly so farre forth as his hating of them will serve for the manifestation of his justice: but hee neither hates them indeede . . . before they are: and therefore actuall hatred comes not in till after the creation. Whom God hath decreed . . . to hate, them being once created, he hates in Adam with actuall hatred.

Perkins also denied the charge that his doctrine of reprobation made God the author of sin. Those who allege that it does, argue that "he which ordaines to the end, ordaines to the meanes of the end," and therefore seeing as "God ordaines men to . . . damnation: therefore he ordaines them to . . . sin." Firstly, Perkins evaded this charge by denying the premise. A man

may be ordained to the end simply, the end being simply good; & yet not be simply ordained to the meanes, because they may be evill in themselves, and onely good in part, namely, so far forth as they have respecct of goodnesse in the minde of the ordainer.

Secondly, Perkins denied the assumption lying behind the charge. He claimed that

40. Perkins, *Workes*, I:287; II:608.

35

> the supreame end of God's counsel is not damnation, but the declaration of his justice in the just destruction of the creature: neither doth God decree mans damnation as it is damnation, that is, the ruine of man and the putting of him forth to punishment, but as it is a reall execution of justice.

In the third place, Perkins called for his by now familiar "distinction betweene sinne itselfe and the permission thereof," adding to this the other important distinction "betweene the decree of rejection, and actuall damnation." Perkins' readers had to realise that "the permission of sinne, and not sinne it selfe properly is the subordinate meanes of the decree of rejection," which means that "sinne itselfe is no effect, but onely the consequent of the decree: yet so, as it is not onely the antecedent, but also the efficient and meritorious cause of actuall damnation."[41]

Given the nature of the elaborate and subtle qualifications that Perkins attaches to his doctrine of absolute and unconditional reprobation, Richard Muller seems justified in his assessment that Perkins "does not establish reprobation as the exact coordinate of election."[42] To this extent, Perkins' perfectly symmetrical chart in *A golden Chaine* has misled some. However, this must not be overemphasised, as the only possible conclusion to be drawn from the above is that Perkins was a very strict double predestinarian.

This strictness of formulation also extends into the realm of the *ordo rerum decretarum*. Very early on in *A golden Chaine* the reader is confronted with Perkins' supralapsarianism. Perkins styles the creation and fall as mere "meanes of accomplishing Gods Predestination."[43] In terms of election,

> the first act is a purpose, or rather a part & beginning of the divine purpose, whereby God doth take certaine men which are to be created,[44] unto his everlasting love and favour, passing by the rest, and by taking maketh them vessels of mercie and honour: and this act is of the sole will of God, without any respect either of good or evill in the creature.

---

41. Perkins, *Workes*, I:287-88; cf. I:109.

42. Muller, *Christ and the Decree*, p. 164; cf. p. 170.

43. Perkins, *Workes*, I:16. Munson writes that "Perkins could not accept any view which made the divine decree of election subsequent to the fall, for then the fall becomes a purpose rather than a means" (Munson, "William Perkins: Theologian of Transition," p. 76).

44. It is clear from what follows and from elsewhere in his *opera* that, by the phrase "which are to be created," Perkins was referring to conceptual priority within the decree and did not merely mean "which are to be created in time." For example, Perkins states that "when God with himselfe had decreed to manifest his glory in saving some men by his mercy, hee ordained further the creation of man in his own image, yet so as by his owne fal he should infold himself & all his posterity under damnation" (Perkins, *Workes*, I:282).

Having decreed concerning men considered as yet uncreated, God is to be seen conceptually as proceeding to a "second act" within the decree of election, which consists in "the purpose of saving or conferring glory, whereby hee doth ordaine or set apart the very same men, which were to fall in Adam, unto salvation and celestiall glory." This second act of election "is not of men to be created as was the former, but of men falne away. Therefore in this act God respecteth the corrupted masse of man kind." Perhaps fearing the charge of being over-precise in such lofty matters, Perkins is quick to add that this second act "is in no wise to be severed from the former, but to bee distinguished in the minde (for orders sake, and for the better unfolding of it)."[45]

Contrary to the frequent claim that theologians such as Perkins were guilty of falling into a rigid predestinarian metaphysic, the christocentricity of Perkins' supralapsarian formulations is clear.[46] Perkins avoids the common charge against supralapsarianism, namely of subordinating Christ to the decree, by seeing the decree as trinitarian. In this way, Christ himself is both the subject and the object of predestination. Firstly, Christ is the author of predestination, for "as he is God, we are predestinate *of him,* even as we are predestinate of the Father and the holy Ghost." Secondly, and conceptually subsequent to the decree of the creation and the fall, God "also decreed that the Word should be incarnate actually, to redeeme these out of the former misery, whom hee had ordained to salvation. Christ therefore him selfe was first of all predestinate as hee was to be our head." The elect are therefore "predestinate *in him,*" because "God ordained that the execution of mans election should be in him."[47]

Although the emphasis in the exposition of *A golden Chaine* is on election, Perkins does not shy away elsewhere from delineating the supralapsarian nature of the decree of reprobation also. Perkins is adamant that "sinne is not the cause of reprobation." His followers must realise that "when God had decreed to passe by some men, he withall decreed to the permission of sinne, to which permission men were ordained." As a result it is true to say that everyone

> is unto God, as a lumpe of clay in the potters hand: and therefore God according to his supreme authoritie doth make vessels of wrath, he doth not find them made. But he should not make them, but find them made, if we say that God willed in his eternall counsell, to passe by men only as they

45. Perkins, *Workes,* II:607-8.
46. Cf. Muller, "Perkins' *A golden Chaine,*" *passim.*
47. Perkins, *Workes,* I:282.

are sinners, and not as they are men for causes most just, though unknowne to us.[48]

Perkins' fully articulated supralapsarianism should now be evident.[49]

Perkins and the Death of Christ

The first point to note about Perkins' particularist doctrine of the death of Christ is that he is convinced he is giving full recognition to the universal language in Scripture concerning the work of Christ. Perkins is not only completely uninhibited about employing Scripture's own universal language, but he seems to relish an opportunity for doing so. He seems determined not to be open to the charge of so forcing his own system upon the text of Scripture that he can no longer use the very language of Scripture itself to explain his position. For example, we are told that at Calvary "God powred upon [Christ] . . . such a sea of his wrath, as was equivalent to the sinnes of the whole world."[50] As a result, Christ "hath perfectly alone by himselfe accomplished all things that are needful for the salvation of mankinde," in that he made "satisfaction to his Father for the sinne of man."[51]

More specifically, Perkins saw the necessity for retaining Scripture's universal language in regard to Christ's satisfaction being of infinite intrinsic value. In Thomist fashion, he believed that "[t]he vertue and efficacie of this price beeing paid, in respect of merit and operation is infinite."[52] Thus it follows that "if we regard the value and sufficiencie of the death of Christ," then it is "as general as the sin of Adam."[53] Thus, "the sacrifice of Christ offered upon the crosse . . . doth infinitely exceede all the sinne of the whole world."[54] Indeed, regarding its "potentiall efficacie" the price Christ paid "is in it selfe

---

48. Muller, "Perkins' *A golden Chaine*," p. 80; Perkins, *Workes*, II:611, I:288, II:610.

49. Muller cites a number of places where he sees Perkins indulging in infralapsarian notions (Muller, *Christ and the Decree*, pp. 162, 164-65). Yet all these places are not strictly to the point, and are mainly extrapolations from Perkins' frequent employment of the concept of 'divine permission.' They in no way stand in conflict with Perkins' unmistakably clear supralapsarian formulations noted above. In the last analysis, Muller too is happy to style Perkins, without qualification, as a supralapsarian (Muller, *Christ and the Decree*, p. 172; Muller in *OER*, III:336).

50. Perkins, *Workes*, I:28; cf. I:5

51. Perkins, *Workes*, I:1, 4; cf. I:25, 27, 70, 186.

52. Perkins, *Workes*, II:609; cf. I:296.

53. Perkins, *Workes*, II:248.

54. Perkins, *Workes*, II:606.

sufficient to redeeme every one without exception from his sins, albeit there were a thousand worlds of men."[55] Perkins' rationale for such statements is the divine nature of Christ corresponding to the infinitely evil nature of sin, due to its violating "the infinite justice of God."[56] Perkins' concern in such statements is therefore christological and not decretal.

Perkins can even go so far as to write, "I doe willingly acknowledge and teach universall redemption and grace, so farre as it is possible by the word," and he admits that "Universall redemption of all men, we grant: the Scripture saith so."[57] However, when Perkins states that "Christ offered himselfe a sacrifice to the Father for the sinnes of the world," he is simultaneously maintaining that Christ died "only for those which are elected and predestinated." This is because Perkins sees that "there is an universalitie among the Elect and beleevers." Similarly, Perkins can concede that "Christ died for all men in the sense of Scripture," but simultaneously denies that "Christ died for every man without exception."[58]

Muller notes that in Perkins' chart for his *A golden Chaine,* there are no lines between the ineffectually called reprobate and Christ's work.[59] It is already clear that Malone is exaggerating when he says that "Perkins was addicted to adding the qualifying phrase 'for the elect' to universalist Biblical statements."[60] However, that this feature of the chart is no accident is clear from the numerous references in Perkins' treatises to the particular nature of Christ's redemptive work. It is clear that Perkins' doctrine of particular redemption was intimately linked with three main areas of his thought: predestinarianism, federalism, and the doctrine of the unity of Christ's priestly work.

55. Perkins, *Workes,* II:609; cf. I:296.

56. Perkins, *Workes,* I:159; cf. I:87, 173.

57. Perkins, *Workes,* II:605; I:297. If for no other reason, Perkins was constrained to admit as much due to the second of the Thirty-Nine Articles (cf. Thomas Rogers, *The English Creede, consenting with the true ancient catholique, and apostolique Church in all the points and articles of Religion which everie Christian is to knowe and beleeve that would be saved* [London: John Windet for Andrew Maunsel, 1585], pBi). Ever undeterred, Baxter even argued that in his ordinary preaching Perkins denied practically the particular redemptionism which in debate he claimed to hold (Richard Baxter, *Universal Redemption of Mankind, by the Lord Jesus Christ* [London: For John Salusbury, 1694], pp. 176-84, citing Perkins, *Workes,* I:625-34). Yet Baxter is conveniently ignoring Perkins' consistent use of judicial categories, as outlined below, p. 46 (cf. Perkins, *Workes,* II:625).

58. Perkins, *Workes,* II:609; I:297; III:(i)251; cf. II:621.

59. Muller, "Perkins' *A golden Chaine,*" p. 77; cf. Munson, "William Perkins: Theologian of Transition," p. 92; McKim, *Ramism in William Perkins' Theology,* p. 189.

60. Michael T. Malone, "Doctrine of Predestination in the Thought of William Perkins and Richard Hooker," *ATR* 52 (1970): 103-17, p. 113.

We have already seen how Perkins conceded that the "potentiall efficacie" of the atonement is infinite. He was quick to add, however, that more important is the "actuall efficacie." From this latter perspective,

> the price is payd in the counsell of God, and as touching the event, only for those which are elected and predestinated. For the Sonne doth not sacrifice for those, for whom he doth not pray: because to make intercession and to sacrifice are conjoyned: but hee prayeth onely for the elect and for beleevers.

In case his readers are still in any doubt as to his doctrine, Perkins adds: "wee utterly denie, that [Christ] died for *all and every one alike in respect of God*, or as well for the damned as elect, and that effectually on God's part."[61]

But Perkins does not rest in an equivocal distinction between the sufficiency and efficiency of the atonement. The sufficiency is really only a hypothetical consideration from the christological perspective, and not an ordained reality from the decretal perspective.[62] He does not shy away from stating bluntly of the reprobate that God "giveth them no Saviour. For Christ is onely the Redeemer of the Elect, and of no more."[63] He exhorts his readers to "looke for whome Christ is an advocate." Then it is that they shall see that

> to them onely is he a redeemer; for redemption and intercession, which are parts of Christ's priesthood, the one is as generall and large as the other, and so surely united and fastened together, as one cannot be without the other. But Christ is onely an advocate of the faithfull.[64]

The conclusion, for Perkins, is inescapable: "the price is appointed and *limited to the elect alone* by the Fathers decree, and the Sonnes intercession and

---

61. Perkins, *Workes*, II:609, 621.

62. Yet it must be admitted that Perkins, despite his supralapsarianism and vigorous polemical agenda against universal redemptionists, at least once slipped into a brief admission that there might be some validity in the sufficiency-efficiency distinction that supralapsarian Beza had largely spurned (Theodore Beza, *Ad Acta Colloquii Montisbelgardensis Tubingœ edita Theodori Bezœ Responsionis* [Geneva: Joannes le Preux, 1589], II:217, 221). Admitting that "Christ died for all (for so the Scripture saith)," Perkins asserts that "hee died not alike effectually for all" (Perkins, *Workes*, III:(i)118). However, this vague and cursory comment is overwhelmingly outweighed by the preponderant emphasis of his explicit and detailed teaching in the numerous places to be quoted below.

63. Perkins, *Workes*, I:415. Perkins cannot accept a universal donation of Christ since "this donation is not single but mutuall. As Christ is given to us, so wee [*i.e.* the elect church] againe are given to Christ" (Perkins, *Workes*, I:299; cf. I:298).

64. Perkins, *Workes*, I:108.

oblation."[65] In this Perkins does not see himself as advocating novel doctrine. When he reasons that "Christ doth sanctifie onely the elect and such as beleeve, therefore hee was a sacrifice only for them," he adds immediately that "this was the judgement of the ancient Church in this point," and there follow copious patristic and Medieval quotations.[66]

It is not only Perkins' predestinarianism that drives him to this particularism, but, as has already been emerging in the above quotations, a developed federal theology. Perkins insists that regarding his passion, "Christ must not be considered as a private person: for then it could not stand with equitie that hee should bee plagued and punished for our offences, but as one in the eternall counsell of God set apart to be a publike surety or pledge for us."[67] That is to say, Christ was set apart to "be a publike person to represent all the Elect in his obedience and sufferings."[68] Thus, Christ, as "the head of the faithful, is to bee considered as a publike man sustaining the person of all the elect," and "consequently, whatsoever Christ did as a Redeemer, the same did all those in him, and with him which are redeemed."[69] For example, in his resurrection

> Christ rose againe not as every private man doth, but as a publike person representing all men that are to come to life eternall. For as in his passion, so also in his resurrection, he stood in our roome and place: and therefore when he rose from death, we all, yea the whole Church rose in him, & together with him.[70]

This is true because

> the raising up of Christ is . . . his actuall absolution from their sins, for whom he died; for even as the Father by delivering Christ to death, did in very deede condemne their sinnes imputed unto Christ, for whome he died; so by raising him up from death, even *ipso facto* hee did absolve Christ from their sins, and did withall absolve them in Christ.[71]

---

65. Perkins, *Workes*, II:609 (emphasis added). Kendall suggests that "[t]his may be the first time in English theology the word 'limited' is used concerning Christ's death for the elect" (R. T. Kendall, *Calvin and English Calvinism to 1649*, 2nd ed. [Carlisle, UK: Paternoster Press, 1997], p. 58).

66. Perkins, *Workes*, II:609-10.

67. Perkins, *Workes*, I:186-87.

68. Perkins, *Workes*, I:282.

69. Perkins, *Workes*, I:78; II:609.

70. Perkins, *Workes*, I:235. Muller's statement that this strictly federal passage is evidence that Perkins held that "Christ's resurrection represents victory over death for the sake of *all men*" is misleading (Muller, *Christ and the Decree*, p. 149; emphasis added).

71. Perkins, *Workes*, II:609; cf. Schaefer, "The Spiritual Brotherhood," p. 59.

That Perkins does not see himself as teaching a clever embellishment of the gospel is clear when he states that if this federal construction of Christ's resurrection is "not considered, wee do not conceive aright of Christ's resurrection, neither can we reape sound comfort by it."[72] Perkins also reveals how this federal theology leads him to his strict statements against the reprobate having any part at all in Christ's death. He argues that a "wicked man which perisheth for his sin, cannot be said to have risen again with Christ; and therefore Christ did not beare his person upon the crosse." Thus, for a federalist like Perkins, Christ's redemption cannot be as general as Adam's fall for "Christ is . . . a roote . . . of the elect onely. . . . Hee cannot be said to be the root of all, and every singular man." Perkins must conclude that "it was not Christ's purpose to give himselfe for a ransome for all & every one alike."[73]

Sufficient evidence has now been given to demonstrate beyond doubt that Perkins was a rigorous particular redemptionist. However, it will be seen later how John Preston uses the standard twofold division of Christ's work as priest in order to hold to a hypothetical universalist position. In order that Preston's strong difference with Perkins on this issue might be clear, it is rewarding to examine more closely Perkins' doctrine of the particularity of Christ's priestly work which he saw as having two parts: satisfaction followed by intercession.[74]

In his *A golden Chaine*, Perkins states that God "punished the sinnes of the Elect, in his Sonnes own person." Thus, Christ's satisfaction is "that, whereby Christ is a ful propitiation to his Father for the elect." He divides Christ's satisfaction itself into two parts: his Passion and his fulfilling of the whole law. He says of his passion that Christ "satisfied God's justice, and appeased his anger for the sinnes of the faithfull." "Christ's marvelous passion" is therefore "a perfect ransome for the sinnes of all and every one of the elect."[75] Perkins defines Christ's priestly ministry of intercession as that "whereby Christ is an advocate & intreater of God the father for the faithfull." This means that "Christ maketh intercession . . . by desiring the salvation of the elect," and "for them onely which are elected and shall beleeve in him, he makes intercession."[76] More specifically, we are to appreciate the fact that Christ "alone doth continually appeare before his father in heaven, making the faithfull, and all their prayers acceptable unto him, by applying of the merits of this owne perfect satisfaction to them." Perkins, on the basis of John

---

72. Perkins, *Workes*, I:235.
73. Perkins, *Workes*, II:609; I:108; II:621.
74. Perkins, *Workes*, I:27, 169, 235.
75. Perkins, *Workes*, I:95, 27, 29; cf. I:28.
76. Perkins, *Workes*, I:29; I:415; cf. I:169.

17:9, notes that "Christ makes no intercession for the world." By 'the world' we are to understand "all such as are not the Fathers, & were never given to Christ" by the Father.[77] Limited satisfaction and limited intercession go hand in hand for Perkins. As we have already seen above, "to make intercession and to sacrifice are conjoyned," the intercession being "the meanes of applying the satisfaction." Thus redemption and intercession are "so surely united and fastened together, as one cannot be without the other."[78]

So far, we have examined Perkins' doctrine of particular redemption in its positive sense, that is to say, defined positively in terms of his predestinarianism, federalism, and doctrine of the unity of Christ's priestly work. But more can be learned of Perkins' precise position in these matters from his negative writings against the opposing position of 'universal redemption.' Perkins was not sparing in his open denunciation of this position, attacking it at length in numerous places in his collected works. Nor was he afraid of using colourful language in his crusade against it. Perkins styles universal redemption as "a meere devise," "very absurd," and "flat against Gods word."[79] Perkins saw it as a "forgerie of mans brain," and "the conceit of popish writers."[80] By making "God's will hang on the will of man,"[81] this doctrine renders Christ only a "halfe redeemer."[82] Indeed, it "may fitly be tearmed the Schoole of universall Atheisme. For it puls downe the pale of the Church, and laies it waste as every common field: it breeds a carelessnes in the use of the meanes of grace, the word and Sacraments."[83] It is not altogether surprising, therefore, that Baxter thought that no one had written "more confidently against Universal Redemption" than Perkins.[84]

But more than rhetoric was needed if Perkins' was to be believed. He needed a carefully argued rebuttal of the whole position, beginning first with a careful defining of the enemy doctrine. It must be recognised that the position Perkins was now at pains to refute was not the later development of Amyraldianism, still less of English hypothetical universalism. Rather, it was the less subtle universal redemptionist formulations of semi-Pelagianism or of Perkins' archenemy Jacobus Arminius, the father of Arminianism. This larger system was known to Perkins as 'universal grace'

77. Perkins, *Workes*, I:5, 296.
78. Perkins, *Workes*, II:609; I:296, 108; cf. Muller, *Christ and the Decree*, p. 142.
79. Perkins, *Workes*, III:(i)187; II:628; III:344; cf. I:293; III:(i)230.
80. Perkins, *Workes*, III:(i)118, 242; cf. I:296.
81. Perkins, *Workes*, III:494.
82. Perkins, *Workes*, II:622.
83. Perkins, *Workes*, I:296.
84. Baxter, *Universal Redemption*, p. 176.

and had three parts: universal election, universal redemption, and universal vocation.[85] Universal redemption taught that God "decreed the universall Redemption of all and every man actually by Christ, so be it they will beleeve in him." It taught that "God giveth . . . unto all men such measure of grace, whereby (if they will themselves) they may beleeve, repent, and be saved," and "that God giveth grace sufficient unto all, whereby they might be saved, if they by their malice and sinne did not abolish the same."[86] A fundamental tenet of this semi-Pelagian or Arminian position is a universal satisfaction. It is on Perkins' refutation of a universal satisfaction that attention will now be focused.

A popular argument for a universal satisfaction is the incarnation itself, in which Christ is understood to have taken upon himself human nature in general. Perkins was willing to grant that in one sense Christ is Mediator "[b]etwixt God and al men: for being both God and man, he doth participate with both extreames."[87] However, this is no ground for a general redemption on two accounts. Firstly, such reasoning would mean that "Christ redeemed his owne humanitie, which cannot be any waies possible." Secondly,

> [e]very woman doth partake the humane nature of every man, yet is not every man each womans husband, but hers alone, with whome by the covenant in matrimonie, hee is made one flesh: and in like sort Christ did by his incarnation . . . take also upon him mans nature, and that common to all Adams progenie, yet is he the husband of his Church alone, by another more peculiar conjunction, namely the bond of the spirit and of faith. And by it the Church is become flesh of his flesh, and bone of his bone. . . . therefore shee alone may justly claime title to the death of Christ, and all his merits.

That Christ took upon himself the same human nature as have the reprobate is therefore almost incidental. It certainly does not lead logically to a propitiation being made for them.[88]

Far more common objections to particular satisfaction come from the texts of Scripture that stand in seemingly plain opposition to this doctrine. Yet these held no weight with Perkins. Firstly, Scripture's use of the word 'all' in connection with the scope of Christ's work came under particular scrutiny.

85. Perkins, *Workes*, I:295.
86. Perkins, *Workes*, I:293; III:(ii)280; cf. III:(i)242.
87. Perkins, *Workes*, I:27.
88. Perkins, *Workes*, I:108.

According to Perkins "we must understand, that 'All' is not alwaies taken generally, but sometimes indefinitely for many."[89] Just as when "Christ is said to have healed 'every disease'" we have no choice but to read "every kinde of disease," so we are to "understand by 'all' of all sorts some, not every singular person of all sorts."

Such an approach enables Perkins, for example, to remove the ground for a universal redemption in Romans 11:32, "that he might have mercy upon all." Perkins claims that the word 'all' "must be understood of all that are to be saved, both of Jewes and Gentiles." To Perkins this is the only possible interpretation, for

> if we should expound the word 'all' for every particular man, as some would have it, Paul must contradict himselfe, who said before that God would have mercy on whom he will have mercy, & whom he wil he hardeneth, & in this very chapter his drift is to proove the rejection of the Jewes, & the calling of the Gentiles.[90]

Perkins also goes to great length to refute a universal redemption based on Scripture passages that speak of 'the world' as being the scope of Christ's work. He writes,

> this word 'world' . . . doth not signifie both all and every man that descended from Adam, but all nations in this last age of the world. . . . [A]ll the like places in scripture . . . are to bee understood of some men to bee called out of every nation and countrie after the death of Christ.[91]

Regarding the famous text of John 3:16 therefore, Perkins is quick to remind his readers that by the word 'world' "wee must not understand every particular man in the world, but the elect among the Jewes and Gentiles."[92] This Perkins demonstrates from Romans 11:12, 15 and 2 Corinthians 5:19. In the latter text "by 'the world,' we are to understand all beleevers through the whole world."[93] Perhaps 1 John 2:2 is a universal redemptionist's favourite proof text with its statement that Christ "is the propitiation for our sins: and not for ours only, but also for the sins of the whole world." But even here, according to Perkins, 'world' in this context can only mean "[t]he congregation of the

---

89. Perkins, *Workes*, III:(ii)108; cf. I:109; III:125, 494, 516.

90. Perkins, *Workes*, I:296; cf. II:248.

91. Perkins, *Workes*, II:622.

92. Perkins, *Workes*, I:296; cf. I:187 where Perkins states that the donation of Christ, as well as the love, in this text is also particular.

93. Perkins, *Workes*, I:297; II:248.

elect, dispersed over the face of the whole earth, & to be gathered out of the same."[94]

There is a third class of texts brought out to support universal redemption which Perkins sought to defuse of their potential threat to his system. Romans 14:15 reads, "Destroy not him with thy meat, for whom Christ died," and 2 Peter 2:1 speaks of false teachers "denying the Lord that bought them." In the several places in which Perkins deals with these texts, they are taken in a strictly judicial manner. He first points out that "we must not understand such places meant of al reprobates, but of such as are for a time in the Church." In the second place such false prophets or weak brethren "are said to be redeemed, justified, & sanctified, both in their own judgements, & the churches also, in as much as they make an external profession of the faith. But this is a judgment of charity, not of certainty." But they were never redeemed "in God's decree . . . for then had they been saved."[95] It seems that no 'problem text' could pose any problems for Perkins.

However, Perkins' attack on a universal satisfaction consisted of more than mere negative reactions to various problem texts. His main objection to a universal atonement was its inevitable dilution of the very concept of propitiation. In short, universal satisfaction was in conflict with his doctrine of penal substitution. Perkins reasoned as follows:

> If Christ became once before God a reconciliation for all mens sinnes, yea and also satisfied for them all, it must needs follow that before God all those sins must bee quite blotted out of his remembrance. . . . [S]atisfaction with God, doth necessarily imply the very reall and generall abolishment of the guilt and punishment of sinne.[96]

For this very same reason that "satisfaction doth necessarily abolish fault," it cannot be maintained "that Christ was crucified and died no lesse to make satisfaction for the sinnes of the damned, than for the sinnes of Peter and Paul & the rest of the Saints." Universal redemption implies that "all and every one are reconciled unto God," and if this is to have any real meaning, then universal redemptionists should iron out these inconsistencies and become full-blown universalists.[97]

94. Perkins, *Workes*, I:109. However, Perkins did occasionally slip from this high ground to a citation of this text with regard to the universal sufficiency of the "meanes of salvation" (Perkins, *Workes*, I:5; cf. I:1).

95. Perkins, *Workes*, I:109; III:521; cf. I:296.

96. Perkins, *Workes*, I:108.

97. Perkins, *Workes*, I:296; II:621.

Neither did Perkins feel that this was a rather harsh and austere system that he was propounding, and could not possibly prove attractive to ordinary Christians. When Perkins teaches that "God would have some particular men deprived of grace and redemption by Christ," indeed, "the greatest part of mankinde," he refuses to have sympathy with the claim that this is "hard speech." Rather, "it is a wonder, that all without exception are not damned," "for God in his justice without all crueltie might have condemned every man." Therefore it is "his endlesse mercie, that he hath given Christ to be a Saviour unto some, and that any are made partakers of this salvation by Jesus Christ." The problem is one of perspective:

> Wee must not esteeme of the mercie of Christ by the number of men which receive mercie . . . but we must rather measure it by the efficacy and dignitie thereof . . . For it was a more easie thing to destroy all by sinne, than by grace to save but one.[98]

Thus, for the truly humbled saint, there is no offence here but only cause for thanksgiving. Conversely, the apparently friendlier face of universal redemptionism is but a deceitful mask. Says Perkins,

> I appeale to the judgements of all men, whether in this manner of consolation, be any great comfort to the conscience afflicted.
> Christ died for all men.
> Thou art a man:
> Therefore Christ died for thee.[99]

Perkins' meaning is that given that some men are indeed damned, we would have to conclude that Christ died for them nevertheless. Thus the death of Christ *per se* is no real source of assurance for the believer. It guarantees nothing. The face of Perkins may initially appear more austere, therefore, but, in the long run and to the believer, it is proven to be genuinely friendly.

Perkins and the Gospel Call

The defence of Perkins' particularist system was not yet complete, for in the light of his strictures on the absolute and supralapsarian decree of reprobation and the limited extent of Christ's satisfaction, Perkins had to justify the

---

98. Perkins, *Workes*, III:(i)251; II:621; III:(i)251; I:108.
99. Perkins, *Workes*, I:109.

Church's commission to preach the gospel to 'every creature.' This commission might appear inconsistent with Perkins' high particularism, and God might seem hypocritical in the offering of a non-existent salvation to the reprobate. Perkins did not appeal to paradox, but offered a clear solution.

As we have seen, Perkins is militantly opposed to any attempt to deduce a universal grace from the universal command to "preach the gospel to every creature." To illustrate the futility of any such extrapolations, Perkins repeatedly points out that despite this New Testament command, in actuality the gospel has never been preached to all men, either under the Old or New Covenants. Perkins knew that "the meanes to receive grace, is the hearing of the word." However, given that "all men in all ages never had [this] vouchsafed unto them," we must conclude that in actuality God has never called all men without exception to faith.[100] Perkins uses the fact that the church was "for so long a time" only "a small remnant, among the people of the Jewes only," with "not one of tenne thousand" Gentiles having faith, in order to deny a "universall calling of all and every man to the estate of grace and salvation."[101] There is therefore no universal grace or universal, conditional covenant here, since "a benefit to be apprehended by faith, if it be unknowne, is no benefit."[102]

Perkins defends this teaching from the text "many are called, but few chosen." He concludes that "God would not have all men called unto Christ," which is evident from Christ's own restriction of his own and his disciples' preaching ministry. This is why there "be many millions of men, which have not so much as heard of Christ," and why the "greatest part of the world hath ever bin out of the covenant of grace." To the objection to this teaching that Perkins is focusing too much on the preaching of the Word and overlooking the fact that the written Scriptures are available to all, Perkins replies that "the Scriptures were commited to the custodie of the Church of God, & every one was not credited with them." Perkins' particularism is everywhere.[103]

Perkins therefore rejects as a "very unreasonable position" an actual universal call of the gospel, holding that there is no revelation of the gospel in the created order, and that just as the Scriptures are not read by all, so preachers, in practice, never get to preach to all men without exception. However, this does not mean that Perkins does not uphold a hypothetical universal call

---

100. Mark 16:15; Perkins, *Workes,* III:(ii)333.

101. Perkins, *Workes,* III:(ii)165.

102. Perkins, *Workes,* II:250; cf. II:641. Andrew Woolsey also finds in Perkins a strict particularity of the covenant of grace (Andrew A. Woolsey, "Unity and Continuity in Covenantal Thought: A Study in the Reformed Tradition to the Westminster Assembly" [Ph.D. Dissertation, University of Glasgow, 1988], II:207).

103. Matthew 20:16; Perkins, *Workes,* I:111; cf. I:5.

in that all without exception who come under the sound of the preaching of the gospel are to be called in God's name to repentance: "the Ministers of the Gospell ought indifferently to exhort all and every one to repent."[104] So what does in fact occur when the gospel, in the sovereign purposes of God, *is* preached to some of the reprobate?

We have already seen how Perkins taught that "Christ maketh intercession . . . by desiring the salvation of the elect," and that "God would not have all men called unto Christ." But does Christ desire the salvation of the reprobate in any way at all? While Perkins is willing to concede that "God doth love all his creatures," and while he saw Christ's tears over the children of Jerusalem as a manifestation of "a tender compassion over their miserie to come," he adamantly denied any will or desire in God to save the reprobate.[105] Due to his polemical context this denial is a dominant strain in Perkins' theology. Perkins was concerned to defend the unity of God's will. "God's will is onely one, considered in it selfe, as God is one." Perkins conceded that from our point of view the will of God needed to be "distinguished" in terms of "either absolute, or revealed" will. However, when God commands the sinner to be saved, this is not to be taken as revelation that the ever blessed God desires that he be saved, but he is rather "revealing unto him . . . what he will have man to doe . . . if he desire to come to life, and would not be condemned." God wills the conversion of the reprobate "onely in respect of approbation, exhortation, and meanes" from the human point of view, but not in his being in which there is no conflict. Thus, God, by his commandments, "sheweth what hee liketh, & what he willeth that we should do to him, not what he will do to us or in us." Perkins' theology revolves entirely around God's purposes for the elect. God "doth in part only so farre forth propound his will, as he knoweth it expedient for the salvation of the elect."[106]

Perkins had to maintain this doctrine in the face of the traditional Pelagian defence of a universal saving will in God, which cites for support Ezekiel 33:11 and 1 Timothy 2:4. Perkins argues that Ezekiel 33:11, with its statement that God has "no pleasure in the death of the wicked," "is to be understood not simply but in respect." That is to say, firstly, "of the twaine God rather wills the repentance of the sinner than his death." Secondly, God "wils not the death as it is the destruction of his creature," but rather "he wils the

104. Perkins, *Workes*, I:111; II:608.

105. Perkins, *Workes*, I:108; III:(i)131 (referring to Luke 19:41). Indeed, Perkins was even prepared to say, in connection with Christ's earthly ministry, that the will of Christ as man is no sure guide in this connection, for "there is one will in Christ as God; another, as man" (Perkins, *Workes*, I:26).

106. Perkins, *Workes*, III:(i)131; II:608-9.

same as it is a meanes of the manifestation of his justice." Therefore God *does* "will the death of a sinner," but only "as it is a punishment, that is, as it is a meanes to declare & set out his divine justice." Perkins concludes that

> therefore it is an untruth for a man to say, that God would have none condemned. For whereas men are once condemned, it must be either with Gods will, or without it: if without it, then the will of God must needs suffer violence, the which to affirme is great impietie; if with his will, God must needes change his sentence before set downe, but we must not presume to say so.[107]

God is not a sadist, but neither is he a spectator.

First Timothy 2:4 states that God "will have all men to be saved, and to come to the knowledge of the truth." For his own interpretation of this text, Perkins assembles an extensive list of reasons amounting to three double-column folio pages. Firstly, "the place is not to be understood, of all the posteritie of Adam, but properly of those which live in the last age of the world." Secondly, Perkins sees a universality amongst the elect: "God wils that all men bee saved, that is to say, of those that are saved." Thirdly, Perkins consciously follows the Augustinian interpretation of this passage, and sees the text as meaning "God will not have every one of every kinde, but the kinds of every one to bee saved; that is to say, of every estate and condition some." Fourthly, we are to understand the verse judicially in terms of the visible church. The apostle "speaketh in this place according to the charitable judgement of Christians: and not according to the judgement of secret and infallible certaintie." At this point, Perkins challenged the use of the distinction between God's "precedent and consequent will." Rather than delighting at this point in such scholastic subtleties as "a wishing will," Perkins simply reasoned that "whatsoever any one desireth and earnestly willeth, that will he bring to passe, unlesse he bee hindred." Yet the divine will never "stands doubtfull" and is always accomplished even when not all are saved. Fifthly, it is clear that God does not will the blessednes of all angels without exception, so why should it be so concerning men? Sixthly, "if God wil that al men, as they are men, be saved: in like manner he wil, that all sinners, as they are sinners, bee damned." Seventhly, Perkins argues for the absoluteness of God's antecedent will on the basis of Romans 9:19, and argues in an Augustinian manner that God's antecedent will, and not any consequent will, is known "by the event." Eighthly, Perkins argues that because the text added "and to come to the

---

107. Perkins, *Workes,* I:296, 109; cf. III:(ii)494.

knowledge of the truth," then faith cannot be a "condition" upon which the divine will in this text hangs. Lastly, Perkins quoted Augustine's exegesis of this text to the effect that the text "is to be understood of them which are actually saved: because all men which are saved, are saved by the will of God."[108] The great length to which Perkins goes to defend his interpretation of 1 Timothy 2:4 is indicative of how dangerous to his system Perkins considered the notion of a universal saving will in God to be. He was convinced it led to Arminianism, for if God would have all men to be saved, then why are not all saved? The answer would have to be that "Men will not keep the condition and beleeve." But this "is flat to hang God's will upon mans wil, to make every man an Emperour, and God his underling, and to change the order of nature by subordinating God's will, which is the first cause, to the will of man, which is the second cause."[109] It is clearly erroneous, therefore, for Timothy Song — without offering any evidence — to ascribe to Perkins the doctrine of "the well-meant gospel call" in the sense advocated by the modern Reformed theologian Anthony Hoekema.[110]

Perkins refused to concede that his position rendered the gospel call to the reprobate insincere if not downright deceitful. He felt able to prove that "there is no delusion" in this regard.

> God must not bee said to mocke men, if by the word preached he do outwardly call those, whome he will not have to be saved: for by this meanes he shewes unto them the riches of his grace, and declares that they perish by their owne fault, because they will not receive salvation offered. . . . [T]hat inability whereby they cannot, is voluntarie, and borne together with us, not infused into us by God: and therefore it cannot bee excused.[111]

The main reason why the gospel is preached to the reprobate wicked is because the ministers of the gospel do not know who the "mingled" elect are, and "therefore" must adopt the policy of preaching "indifferently" or indiscriminately. The salvation of the elect is always of paramount concern in Perkins' thought. The preaching of the gospel is not to announce God's general love to all, but is "an ordinance of God appointed for the gathering to-

---

108. Perkins, *Workes,* II:623-25; cf. I:109, 296; II:625; III:(i)118.

109. Perkins, *Workes,* I:295; cf. III:494.

110. Yong Jae Timothy Song, *Theology and Piety in the Reformed Federal Thought of William Perkins and John Preston* (Lewiston, NY: Edwin Mellen Press, 1998), pp. 144, 212; Anthony A. Hoekema, *Saved by Grace* (Grand Rapids, MI: Eerdmans, 1994), pp. 68-79. Hoekema does not mention Perkins, but condemns his views, taking an opposite position to Perkins on Ezekiel 33:11, Matthew 23:37, 2 Corinthians 5:20, and 2 Peter 3:9.

111. Perkins, *Workes,* I:297; II:625.

gether and the accomplishment of the number of the Elect." The whole of human history exists that the elect might be saved. Thus, "grace & salvation is offered principally and directly to the elect, and onely by consequent to them which are ordained to just damnation." However, the second and subordinate, but nevertheless very real, reason why the gospel is preached to at least some reprobate is that they might be hardened and left inexcusable. "For the offering of grace doth not onely serve for the conversion of a sinner, but also to be an occasion by mens fault, of blinding the minde, and hardning the heart, and taking away excuse in the day of judgement."[112] Perkins held that "God sometimes giveth a commandement not that it should bee actually done, but that men may bee tried, and that they may be convicted of their naturall infidelity before God in the last judgement."[113]

In Perkins the gospel call may be said to be the universal proclamation of a particular promise. Perkins explicitly and frequently denies that the gospel promise is something that belongs to all or is made to all. This doctrine is one of the "waightie points to bee knowne and beleeved" concerning God's "speciall mercy." To affirm "that the promises of the Gospel . . . belong to all and every man whatsoever, unlesse he will reject them, is a device of mans braine." Rather, the biblical teaching is that "the promise of remission of sinnes, and life everlasting in the Messias, is not universall to all, but indefinite to many of all sorts, kinds, and estates."[114] "[T]he promise is not made to the worke, but to the worker, and to the worker, not for the merit of his worke, but for the merit of Christ."[115] The promises of the gospel are universal in the sense that they are "universall indeede to all that overcome." But we are ever to remember that "that is a propertie which restraines them wholly to true beleevers." Perkins held to the particularity of the promise because "life eternall is not promised to every man as he is a man comming of Adam; but to a man as he is in Christ by faith, and a new creature."[116] This did not mean that Perkins could not consistently preach the gospel to 'every creature,' since "[w]ith the promise there is joyned an exhortation, or commandment to beleeve: which is more generall than the promise."[117] God, therefore, never once promises to save the reprobate, and therefore he never once breaks his promise by instead casting them into hell. They hear this annunciation of the gospel promise made by God in Christ to the universality of the elect, but

112. Perkins, *Workes*, I:297; II:608; cf. II:625.
113. Perkins, *Workes*, II:625.
114. Perkins, *Workes*, III:(i)117; III:(ii)281; cf. III:(i)187.
115. Perkins, *Workes*, II:392-93.
116. Perkins, *Workes*, III:(ii)281; cf. II:248, 608.
117. Perkins, *Workes*, II:608.

they do not obey the accompanying command to repent and believe in Christ. But to the elect, the universal proclamation of this particular promise draws them to Christ, believing that "he is faithful that promised."[118]

We have already seen how Perkins asserts that the reprobate have no "title to the death of Christ" whatsoever.[119] However, it is necessary to appreciate an important qualification Perkins makes to this by way of his judicial ecclesiology and high sacramentology. The reprobate do not have any title to the death of Christ *qua* reprobate, but as those whom God has made outward members of church they do have such a title. Similarly, the universal gospel call does *not* consist in being called upon to believe that one "is effectually redeemed by Christ." However, "Every one in the Church, by God's commandment 'Believe the Gospell' is bound to beleeve that he is redeemed by Christ; yea even the reprobate as well as the elect."[120] This is Perkins' way of discouraging morbid introspection as to the vexed question of whether one is elect or not, and one for whom Christ did in fact die. Just as "the ministers of God, not knowing his secret counsel, in charitie think al to be elect," so all church members are to work out their own salvation in fear and trembling *as Christians* and not in order that they might *become Christians*. They work out their salvation from *within* the covenant, not in order to enter it, and do so on the basis of their very real judicial standing and sacramental privileges.[121] Although, as we have seen, the covenant of grace and the gospel promise for Perkins are strictly particular, he is prepared to say that "God the Father hath made an Evangelicall covenant with his church."[122] This results in a relaxing of his particularist provisos within the visible church, since this is, after all, to be considered as the company of God's elect. Thus, within this 'Evangelicall

---

118. Chalker therefore entirely misrepresents Perkins in this respect when he asserts that for Perkins "Christ does not so much reveal God as Savior as he reveals a way of salvation offered by God" (William H. Chalker, "Calvin and some Seventeenth-Century English Calvinists: A Comparison of their Thought through an Examination of their Doctrines of the Knowledge of God, Faith and Assurance" [Ph.D. Dissertation, Duke University, 1961], p. 96). On the contrary Christ promises absolutely and unconditionally to save his elect people. This promise is not a mere offer, and never once fails. Cf. Victor L. Priebe, "The Covenant Theology of William Perkins" (Ph.D. Dissertation, Drew University, 1967), pp. 87-88; Munson, "William Perkins: Theologian of Transition," pp. 92-93; Woolsey, "Unity and Continuity in Covenantal Thought," II:207.

119. See p. 44.

120. Perkins, *Workes*, II:625.

121. Perkins, *Workes*, I:297.

122. Perkins, *Workes*, I:299. Thus Christ as "a grant" is also to the church only (Perkins, *Workes*, I:299). As we shall see in Ch. 7, this is to be contrasted with John Davenant's formulation of an 'Evangelical covenant' with the whole world, head for head.

covenant with the church' Perkins can say that "the Evangelical promises are indefinite and doe exclude no man, unlesse peradventure any man do exclude himselfe." The two sacraments then "do to everyone severally apply indefinite promises, and therefore are very effectuall to enforce particular assurance or pleropherie of forgiveness of sinnes." In baptism, the water "signifieth, that the partie baptized doth receive the internall washing, which is by the blood of Christ, or at the least that it is offered unto him." The distribution of the elements at the Lord's Supper "sealeth the action of God offering Christ unto all, yea, to the hypocrites: but giving him indeede unto the faithfull, for the daily increase of their faith, and repentance."[123] On one level at least, the polarity between the elect and the reprobate in Perkins' thought thus knows a short respite in the realms of ecclesiology and sacramentology. In distinction from the world of the heathen, the church in history is the company of the redeemed. The eternal division between elect and reprobate does not so control his ecclesiology that he has a doctrine of dual church membership, as found in post-Restoration Puritanism under the leadership of Baxter.[124] Perkins wants a particularism that magnifies the sovereignty of God and glorifies the free grace of God, but not one that chokes the life and diminishes the privileges of the church militant. It is to the church that Perkins acknowledges Christ makes 'offers.' To the world of the lost, Christ makes no offers. To them the gospel is presented as a divine command, and the particular promise is generally proclaimed. There is therefore in Perkins still no conditional gospel promise.[125] In Perkins the Christian works at all times within the sphere of the covenant.

It pays at this point to recall the eminence and sustained influence of Perkins as a popular preacher and trainer of ministers in Cambridge.[126] It was while propounding and emphasising such a system of doctrine that he won notable admirers across the spectrum of the English Church. The books from which the above quotations have been taken were reprinted remarkably frequently, and while the English presses heaved with Perkins' heavy tomes, no

123. Perkins, *Workes*, I:87, 74, 75.

124. E.g., Richard Baxter, *A Petition for Peace: With the Reformation of the Liturgy. As it was presented to the right reverend Bishops, by the Divines appointed by his Majesties Commission to treat with them about the Alteration of it* (London: n.p., 1661), p. 67. For a recent study of Baxter's ecclesiology, including church membership, see Paul Chang-Ha Lim, *In Pursuit of Purity, Unity, and Liberty: Richard Baxter's Puritan Ecclesiology in Its Seventeenth-Century Context* (Leiden: Brill, 2004).

125. This is not, of course, to deny that Perkins frequently styles faith as a 'condition' in terms of a *sina qua non* of the gospel (e.g., Perkins, *Workes*, I:32; II:299, 625).

126. See above, pp. 27-28.

publications against Perkins' theology accompanied them, at least not in his lifetime. It might appear then that Perkins was advocating a 'received' position that, in English Reformed circles at least, was largely accepted. But was this really the case? It transpires that the system of doctrine that we have seen Perkins espousing was neither original to English theology, nor went unchallenged in Elizabethan England. However, we will also see now that the context and very nature of the challenges actually serve to support the contention that Perkins' system is largely the form that Tyacke's 'Calvinistic consensus' took in late Elizabethan England.

Perkins as Representative Elizabethan Churchman

London's outdoor pulpit at Paul's Cross, dating from 1241, was "a national pulpit and barometer of doctrinal change."[127] In 1571, John Bridges, prebendary of Winchester, and Fellow of Pembroke Hall, Cambridge, since 1556, preached at Paul's Cross on John 3:16, a text found in the gospel reading for that day. In his preface to the published version, and in tones typical of the period, Bridges pleads that the sermon was so widely admired and appreciated, that he could finally no longer withstand the pleas of friends to have it published. But lest the clamour to have it published be taken in the wrong way, he was quick to add how now "al the world may see, there was nothing in [this sermon] but that was even 'Commune Sanctorum' (as they say) such matter as every one of [the congregation] did knowe alreadie, as well and better than I could tell them."[128] He considerably expanded the sermon for the press, to form what amounts to a small treatise advocating particular grace from the famous 'universalist' passage of John 3:16. Bridges dedicated the sermon to Lord Burghley.

In this sermon, Bridges reveals certain supralapsarian tendencies, and

---

127. Peter E. McCullough, *Sermons at Court: Politics and Religion in Elizabethan and Jacobean Preaching* (Cambridge: Cambridge University Press, 1998), pp. 46, 1. During Paul's Cross sermons "the hourglass was turned twice" (McCullough, *Sermons at Court*, p. 129). Throughout this section I am particularly indebted to Nicholas Tyacke's excellent work on the English Calvinist consensus, and in particular on Paul's Cross sermons. For more on Paul's Cross sermons, albeit of a later date than those considered here, see Mary E. Morrissey, "Rhetoric, Religion & Politics in the St Paul's Cross Sermons, 1603-1625" (Ph.D. Dissertation, University of Cambridge, 1998).

128. John Bridges, *A Sermon, preached at Paules Crosse on the Monday in Whitson Weeke Anno Domini. 1571* (London: Henry Binneman for Humfrey Toy, 1571), Epistle Dedicatorie p. A2v.

holds that God "created the wycked to an evyll daye, that is, even unto damnation."[129] But his main concern is to limit the desire in God to save the elect alone. His first task was to define the word 'world' in John 3:16, a task made all the more urgent because "by mistakyng thereof, great errours have growne." It does not mean "universally all Creatures," nor "all the world in generall and every man," nor "the wicked worldelyngs," for "[t]hose whome hee loved, even unto the ende hee loved them." Thus 'world' here means "the elect of God." One reason he gives for this interpretation is that the elect are "dispersed through out the world and are of al sorts and kynds of the world. . . . the worlde is all Nations, kyndredes, conditions, states, orders, personages, sexes, ages, and all degrees of persones: soo the Electe are of all sortes. . . . There is . . . [no] respecte of difference in Gods election: and therefore the electe may well bee called the Worlde."[130] Bridges is convinced that it is due to the failure to interpret 'world' as "the elect of God out of this worlde" that "divers have staggered at this and suche other sentences, and fallen into grevous errours."[131]

A second related emphasis in this sermon is that God only desires to save the elect. Bridges relies on Augustine for guidance at this point, following him in his contention that "all men" in 1 Timothy 2:4 means "not every man, but men of every sort, without respect of person, place, tyme, dignitie, or any other regarde than of hys owne choyce and wyll."[132] In accordance with the irresistibility of God's will, Bridges concludes that "as he wolde not that every one should be damned, so he wolde not that every one sholde be saved."[133] Bridges attacks the papist notion of a *voluntas antecedens* opposing a *voluntas consequens,* holding it to be blasphemous thus to create "division" in God. The only acceptable distinction in the will of God is that made by "the ancient and godly learned Fathers" namely "of *Voluntas signi,* and *Voluntas beneplaciti.*" But the response of the reprobate to God's revealed will is exactly according to God's secret will.[134]

While implying that the Father's donation of Christ in John 3:16 is to the elect alone, Bridges does not explicitly touch on the subject of the extent of Christ's satisfaction. Perhaps what he has already said makes it unnecessary

---

129. Bridges, *Sermon,* p. 23. He is of course quick to add that this does not mean that God "delyghteth in theyr destruction whome hee hardeneth, or is the author or partaker of their wyckednesse . . . for Gods workes to the wicked are just and righteouse." But cf. pp. 17, 91.

130. Bridges, *Sermon,* pp. 13, 15, 16, 19; cf. p. 46.

131. Bridges, *Sermon,* p. 21. Bridges suggests Origen and Pelagius.

132. Bridges, *Sermon,* p. 23; cf. pp. 31-32.

133. Bridges, *Sermon,* p. 24; cf. pp. 27, 32.

134. Bridges, *Sermon,* pp. 28, 32, 33.

to labour this point further.[135] Bridges' main concern was now to uphold the universal call of the gospel. He held that "this gift is offered by the preaching of the woorde unto all, to all nations, tongs, and people, to all sortes, ages, sexes, degrees, and all kynde of persons what so ever." The gospel is "thus generally proclaymed to all," and "some receive this gifte so freely by the worde offered unto them."[136] Considerations of God's secret will are not to impede this important duty

> bycause wee are not devisers of Gods privie counsel, but voyces of criers and proclaimers of Gods open offer: therfore so farre as our commission stretcheth, we travel to all, we cal all, we preache to all, we teach all, we exhort all, we reprove all, we labour to win all, we exempt none, we drive away none, we debarre it from none, nor none from it, we bid none despaire, but all to truste and beleve in God, and to take this gift thus freely offered to them, whereof wee be appointed the bringers and the offerers.[137]

The universal gospel call in no way implies an ability in the hearers to respond.[138]

With theology such as this, Bridges was made D.D. in 1575, and was installed dean of Salisbury in 1578. From this vantage point, he was extensively involved in defending the established form of ecclesiastical government against a rising proto-Presbyterianism, refuting the arguments of Beza and Calvin in a book of over one thousand pages.[139] He took part in the Hampton Court conference in 1604, and a month later was consecrated bishop of Oxford by Whitgift.[140] His high Calvinism was clearly not the product of a radical Genevan bent, nor did it marginalise him ecclesiastically. It should be noted that when Bridges preached this sermon, Perkins was only about thirteen years old.

135. Bridges, *Sermon*, pp. 141, 142. Certainly, concerning John 3:16, Bridges' unusual rendering of the more usual 'that whosoever believeth' as "that al that beleve on him," suggests that he was committed to the view that Christ's death was particularly designed for the elect. Because "al that beleve on him" are the elect alone, "so many even at the fyrste choppe, are quite dashte out," and so "this worde *All*, is restrayned to a marvelous small numbre, in comparison of *All* those that are none of all these, which receyve this benefite" (Bridges, *Sermon*, title-page, p. 145).

136. Bridges, *Sermon*, p. 145; cf. pp. 176-77.

137. Bridges, *Sermon*, p. 146.

138. Bridges, *Sermon*, p. 179.

139. John Bridges, *A Defence of the Government established in the Church of Englande for ecclesiasticall Matters* (London: John Windet for Thomas Chard, 1587). Salisbury was where John Davenant was later to be made bishop in 1621.

140. *ODNB*.

On 27th October, 1594, Samuel Harsnett (1561-1631), then Fellow of Pembroke Hall, Cambridge, preached a sermon at Paul's Cross, London, on Ezekiel 33:11.[141] Harsnett's intention was to refute the belief that "God should designe many thousands of soules to Hell before they were, not in eye to their faults, but to his own absolute will and power, and to get him glory in their damnation." This "monstrous" opinion of a "fancied decree, of eternall designement to Hel without sin" states "that not one or two, but millions of men should fry in Hell; and that [God] made them for no other purpose, than to be the children of death and Hell, and that for no other cause, but his meer pleasure's sake." It not only makes "God the Author of sin," but "takes away from Adam in his state of innocency all freedome of will, and liberty not to sin," and "maketh in God two Wills, the one flat opposite to the other."[142]

As the sermon begins it might seem that Harsnett is attacking only a grossly exaggerated form of supralapsarianism, from the standpoint of a mild infralapsarian system. However, that something far more adventurous is afoot soon becomes apparent. Harsnett saw in his text the following six tenets:

---

141. Tyacke dates this sermon 1584, the year Perkins became a Fellow of Christ's College (Nicholas R. N. Tyacke, *Anti-Calvinists: The Rise of English Arminianism c. 1590-1640,* 2nd ed. [Oxford: Clarendon Press, 1990], p. 164). Tyacke is doubtless following Harsnett's publisher in 1656 who stated that it was preached in "Anno Reginæ Elizabethæ 26" (Samuel Harsnett, "A Sermon preached at S. Pauls Cross in London, the 27. Day of October, Anno Reginæ Elizabethæ 26" in *Three Sermons preached by the reverend, and learned, Dr. Richard Stuart, Dean of St. Pauls, afterwards Dean of Westminster, and Clerk of the Closset to the late King Charles. To which is added, a fourth Sermon, preached by the right reverend Father in God, Samuel Harsnett, Lord Arch-Bishop of Yorke,* ed. Richard Steward [London: For Gabriel Bedel and Thomas Heath, 1656], pp. 121-65, title-page; cf. Henry Hickman, *Historia Quinq-Articularis Exarticulata; Or, Animadversions on Doctor Heylin's Quinquarticular History* [London: For Robert Boulter, 1674], p. 202). Porter, Hargrave, and Breward also date the sermon as 1584, and Peter White 1585 (Porter, *Reformation and Reaction,* p. 382; O. T. Hargrave, "The Doctrine of Predestination in the English Reformation" [Ph.D. Dissertation, Vanderbilt University, 1966], p. 226; Breward, ed., *The Work of William Perkins,* p. 84; White, *Predestination, Policy and Polemic,* p. 99). However, both dates are probably wrong. Tyacke seems right to suggest that John Dove's Paul's Cross sermon of 1597 on Ezekiel 33:11 (see below, p. 63) was a conscious refutation of Harsnett's sermon on the same text (Tyacke, *Anti-Calvinists,* p. 252). This leads us to accept as more reliable the testimony of a manuscript copy of Harsnett's sermon, unreferred to by the scholars above, which gives the date as 1594 (Rawlinson MS. 1349 ff. 156r-69r. Slight variations in wording occur from the 1656 edition). The significance of this for our purposes is that it now allows for the possibility that Harsnett was consciously opposing the teaching of Perkins, whose first publications did not see the press until 1590. Certainly Perkins' cherished doctrines are violently assailed.

142. Harsnett, "Sermon," pp. 133-34, 164, 135, 137.

1. God's absolute will is not the cause of Reprobation; but sin.
2. No man is of absolute necessity the childe of Hell, so as by God's Grace, he may not avoid it.
3. God simply willeth and wisheth every living Soul to be saved, and to come to the Kingdome of Heaven.
4. God sent his Sonne to save every Soule, and to bring it to the Kingdome of Heaven.
5. God's Son offereth Grace effectually to save every one, and to direct him to the Kingdome of Heaven.
6. The neglect and contempt of his Grace, is the cause why every one doth not come to Heaven; and not any privative Decree, Counsel, or determination of God.[143]

In this scheme the Fall need not have happened,[144] and now that it has happened, God desires to save all men without exception. The reason why he does not finally save as many as he desires to save is to be found in man and not in God. Not even the mildest infralapsarian Reformed divine would have said this.

Of particular interest to us here is Harsnett's handling of certain key texts. Firstly, he uses 1 Timothy 2:4 to prove that God desires to save all men without exception.[145] Harsnett resolved the difficulty arising from the fact that some souls finally *are* damned, by appealing to the distinction between God's irresistible "absolute Will" and "his Will with condition." Men are only saved if they meet certain conditions:

> The first condition was in Paradise . . . 'Eat not, and thou shalt live': and that we would not keep. The second was under the Law . . . 'Do this, and thou shalt live': and that wee could not keep. The third is under the Gospel . . . 'Believe, and thou shalt live': and that we may all keep.[146]

If anyone does not meet this condition, he only has himself to blame. Harsnett explicitly repudiates "the Genevian conceit" which "hath dealt with this gracious bounty of God, and this blessed saying," and "hath curtail'd the grace of God at the stumps" by claiming that it

> must not bee meant, that God would have every living soule to come to Heaven; but one or two out of every Order and Occupation to come unto

---

143. Harsnett, "Sermon," pp. 148-49.
144. Harsnett, "Sermon," p. 151.
145. Harsnett, "Sermon," p. 153.
146. Harsnett, "Sermon," pp. 154-55.

heaven. As if our gracious God were fallen out of liking with Christian souls, and suddenly fallen in love with Orders and Occupations.[147]

Such exegesis "would teach us thus to say: God would have all to be saved, that is, God would have a few to be saved: God would not have any to perish, that is, God would that almost all should perish." Harsnett is leaning on 2 Peter 3:9, and "the spirit of Peter" is "a great deal wiser than that of Geneva." God speaks so "plainly" in that text, and Harsnett trusted that "wee shall have grace to believe him; since himselfe can better tell what himselfe would have, than the men of Geneva can."[148]

Another Genevan doctrine for which Harsnett had nothing but scorn, was that of particular redemption. We are to understand that "Almighty God (in his infinite love and mercy towards man) sent his Son to dye and suffer hellish Torments, not for Peter, James and John, and a few of the Elect only; but for the sins of every sinfull Soul in the world." He maintained, citing John 1:29 and 1 John 2:2, that "this Doctrine is so clear in the Book of God, as that the Sun at mid-day shines not more bright." Thus he lamented that

> the new Synechdoche chops of [sic] at a blow from the death of Christ all the sensible parts in the world, and leaves him onely the center to carry his wares in. For it would teach us thus to say . . . so God loved the world, that is, so God loved a smal number in the world: this is the Saviour of the world, that is, a Saviour of a handfull of the World.

This is nothing but a "silly shift." Furthermore, Harsnett also attacks even the scholastic distinction between the sufficiency and efficiency of Christ's death, seeing it as yet another "silly shift" and "gay interpretation." The problem with this "device" is that it implies that Christ "meant not the good of his death to all," and thus "shaddowes the wisedome of our Saviour Christ."[149]

According to Harsnett, the doctrine of particular redemption also results in "delusion" taking place when the gospel is preached. Only a universal satisfaction and desire to save can secure a sincere universal gospel call. Otherwise, according to "this new devise," "Christ calls and invites all to repentance and amendment of life," but "meaneth not as he saith; for he would not

147. Harsnett, "Sermon," p. 153.
148. Harsnett, "Sermon," pp. 156, 153, 154; cf. p. 147.
149. Harsnett, "Sermon," pp. 155-58. Positively, Harsnett himself taught that "Christ by his death and passion made a full satisfaction, for the sins of all the sinfull souls in the whole world. Which since he did, it stood as much with his ease and more with his goodnesse, to communicate his goodnesse, and the benefits of his precious death unto us all, than to appropriate them to a few" (Harsnett, "Sermon," p. 157).

have every one to repent and amend. Is God as a man that he should dissemble?"[150] Under this "Genevian supposition" Israel might have said, "O God of our Fathers, what meanest thou to say unto us, why will ye die, when thou hast from all eternity decreed, that we cannot but die?" Similarly,

> the tenour of our Saviours deploration must then needs have been this: Oh Jerusalem, Jerusalem; thou that killest the Prophets, and stonest them that are sent unto thee; how often would I have gathered thee together, as an hen gathereth her chickens under her wings! but ye could not, for I and my Father have sate in councell in Heaven, and from all eternity have made a decree, that ye should never come to heaven, though I my selfe a thousand times should be crucified for you.

Matthew 23:37 proves a key text in Harsnett's argument, and he derided those who "devised . . . that our Saviour should weep over these Jewes, as man, and laugh at them as God (himselfe having decreed their destruction from all eternity)." This is nothing but "a very bad and profane device. For it would make our Saviour Christ to shed Crocodiles teares, to laugh and lament both at once."[151]

In opposition to this, Harsnett held that "Christ offers saving Grace effectually to all, to direct them to the Kingdome of Heaven; and all and every one may be saved, that doth not despise nor abuse the Grace of God."[152] He even rejected "Bellarmines dreaming" that "Christ offers Grace to all sufficiently; but it is not effectuall or saving Grace." He argued that since "there is nothing sufficient for any thing, which is not efficient to that use too," this was "verily as drowsy a dreame, as ever dropped from that Phlegmatique head." Thus "Christ offers saving Grace effectually to all," a grace "which hath power, strength, and vertue to save all." Sadly, many "despise and abuse" this grace, but we must maintain that "the very same saving Grace, that is a savour of Life unto one, is the savour of Death unto another." Just like the ten virgins, we have "Lamps and Light alike to light us to the Kingdome of Heaven: yet, but five of us with wise usage, shall keepe our Lamps, and Light, and enter in; and five of us, by foolishnesse, shall let our Lamps out, and stand without."[153] In order totally to clear God from any causation in the damnation of a sinner by means of any "privative decree, councell, or determination," Harsnett is willing to go so far as to say that

150. Harsnett, "Sermon," pp. 157, 160, 158.
151. Harsnett, "Sermon," pp. 163-65.
152. Harsnett, "Sermon," p. 158.
153. Harsnett, "Sermon," pp. 160, 161.

there was never man so desperately wicked, but at some time or other, he felt this sparke of Gods Spirit, glowing in his heart. He that blowes that spark, may have a flame to light him to the Kingdome of Heaven; and he that spits upon it, makes himselfe a brand fit to increase the fire of Hel.

Thus the sinner's damnation rests entirely in the "contempt and neglect" of saving grace.[154]

In his sermon, Harsnett, ironically perhaps, warns as much against the Papist error of relying "upon our freewill," and the Pelagian error of relying "upon our Nature," as against the "Puritan" error of "laying the burthen of our sins upon [God's] shoulders, and the guilt of them at his everlasting doores." At first glance, it might appear that Harsnett's repudiation of all these extremes places him in Peter White's happy *via media,* and that there cannot have been many divines with "Genevian" opinions in sixteenth-century England.[155]

Not so. Tyacke has shown that this was the only clearly anti-Calvinist Paul's Cross sermon in Elizabethan England.[156] For this sermon Harsnett "was checked by the Lord Archbishop Whitguifte, and commanded to preach no more of it, and he never did."[157] It is important to notice that even as he preached, Harsnett knew he was up against an overwhelmingly powerful consensus of opinion. Of the system he seeks to refute in this sermon, Harsnett says: "This opinion is growne huge and monstrous (like Goliath) and men doe shake and tremble at it; yet never a man reacheth to Davids sling to cast it down."[158] This goes to explain why his sermon was not published until more tolerant days in 1656 and 1658. His university disputations on this theme, probably from this same period, must also therefore be seen as the objections of a tiny minority.[159] This is also borne out by the way Baro was opposed for expressing similar views to Harsnett in the 1590s.[160] As Breward notes, the disputes of the 1590s "made it clear that Perkins was much nearer the midstream of the Elizabethan church than Baro and Hooker, and that his account of predestination and grace seemed eminently sound and scriptural to many of his peers."[161]

154. Harsnett, "Sermon," pp. 162, 163.
155. Harsnett, "Sermon," pp. 165, 154.
156. Tyacke, *Anti-Calvinists,* p. 253.
157. *Journals of the House of Lords,* 19th May, 1624, III:389.
158. Harsnett, "Sermon," 1656, p. 134.
159. Tyacke, *Anti-Calvinists,* p. 164; BL Harleian MS. 3142, ff. 54-61v.
160. Porter, *Reformation and Reaction,* pp. 376-90.
161. Breward, ed., *The Work of William Perkins,* pp. 87-88.

On 6th February, 1597, John Dove (1561-1618) had the opportunity to preach at Paul's Cross a sermon from Ezekiel 33:11 very different from that of Harsnett's. Tyacke actually suggests that this choice of text was possibly a conscious response to Samuel Harsnett's anti-Calvinist Paul's Cross sermon of 1594.[162] The evidence certainly lends support to this claim. Both sermons focus on three key texts: Ezekiel 33:11, 1 Timothy 2:4, and Matthew 23:37. Both are at odds on absolute reprobation, particular redemption, and the gospel call. Whatever the case, Dove was determined to defend a rigorous particularism.

In his sermon, and in direct opposition to Harsnett, Dove clearly articulates the doctrine of absolute and unconditional election and reprobation. He states that "the onely rule of predestination, and reprobation, whereby God is directed, and the only law which he tieth himself to observe therin, is his will: so that no part of our election is ascribed to our selves, or any thing which may be in us."[163] This means, for example, that "the cause why he decreed that men shoulde bee damned is only in himself, because his owne wil is the cause of that decree."[164] In fact, Dove goes even 'higher' than Perkins in his predestinarian formulations, returning, incidentally, to a view held by Calvin. In the realm of the problem of evil, Dove rejected any attempts to hide behind a divine 'permission,' affirming that God

> doth not onely suffer the wicked to do evill, but himselfe is a doer, and principall agent therein. I knowe there bee some of greater modestie than judgement in divinity, which for reverance to the person of God, do affirme, that all the actions of sathan, and the wicked, are not done by the will, but onely by the permission & sufferance of God: by which opinion of theirs they fall into two absurdities: the one is, they deny his providence which doth so moderat & dispose of al things, that nothing can come to passe otherwise than he hath appointed and decreed before. The other is, they derogate much & detract from his omnipotencie, as if he should suffer any thing to be done against his wil.[165]

---

162. Tyacke, *Anti-Calvinists*, p. 252. Tyacke is even prepared to suggest this while dating Harsnett's sermon 1584 instead of 1594 (see above, p. 58).

163. John Dove, *A Sermon preached at Paules Crosse, the Sixt of February, 1596. In which are discussed these three Conclusions. 1. It is not the Will of God that all Men should be saved. 2. The absolute Will of God, and his secret Decree from all Eternitie, is the Cause why some are predestinated to Salvation, others to Destruction, and not any Foresight of Faith, or good Workes in the one, or Infidelitie, Neglect, or Contempt in the other. 3. Christ died not effectually for all* (London: T. Creede for R. Dexter, 1597), p. 34.

164. Dove, *Sermon*, p. 40.

165. Dove, *Sermon*, p. 55; cf. John Calvin, *Institutes of the Christian Religion*, ed. John T. McNeill, trans. Ford Lewis Battles (Philadelphia, PA: Westminster Press, 1960), III.xxiii.8. Yet, if

Instead, Dove held it necessary "to distinguish of evils: one is a sinne, the other a punishment, God is the cause wee do evill, but as wee doo it, it is sinne, as hee doth cause it, it is no sin, but a punishment for our sinnes. And so as it is a punishment or revenge, God is the authour, Sathan is the executor of the same."[166]

It is from such a standpoint that Dove defends the heading of his sermon, namely, "It is not the will of God that all men should be saved."[167] Dove's interpretation of 1 Timothy 2:4 is an Augustinian treatment, almost identical to that of Perkins and the kind which Harsnett had ridiculed, namely that which takes "all men" to be "all kinds of men."[168] The words of Jesus in Matthew 23:37 similarly presented no problem to Dove's system, though used so powerfully by Harsnett. Citing Augustine as his authority, he states that the will of God is not "made frustrate" here. "Nay, rather Jerusalem in deed, forasmuch as lay in her, would not have her children gathered together, but his will was not frustrate for as much as hee against her will gathered together as many of them as seemed good to his owne will and pleasure."[169] Thus, "in as much as they did contrary to the will of God, in them so doing was fulfilled the will of God."[170] Dove's strict particularism continues to control his handling of the apparently universal text of John 1:9, where Christ "lighteth every man that cometh into the world." Dove warned that this "is not so to be understoode, as if all men were lightened of him, but so, that no man is lightened but by him."[171]

Yet if Harsnett was in fact under fire, the stated purpose of Dove's ser-

---

Dove is stricter that Perkins on the will of God in relation to evil, he is arguably happier with infralapsarian formulations. Dove taught "that the whole lumpe of which the vessels of wrath are framed, had beene damned before in Adam" (Dove, *Sermon*, p. 38; cf. p. 35). Furthermore, Dove might arguably be construed as teaching from John 3:16 a general love of God to "all sinners" without exception. However, elsewhere Dove in certain contexts takes "all" to mean "all sortes" along the lines of the concept of the 'world of the elect' (Dove, *Sermon*, pp. 11-12; cf. pp. 20, 65). This passage remains inconclusive.

166. Dove, *Sermon*, 1597, p. 59.

167. Dove, *Sermon*, title-page.

168. Dove, *Sermon*, p. 20; cf. pp. 17, 19. Nearly ten years previously, a treatise by Thomas Wilcox, published in London along with a treatise by Beza, had also denied that God willed to save all men (Theodore Beza & Thomas Wilcox, *Two very learned Sermons of M. Beza, togither with a short Sum of the Sacrament of the Lordes Supper,* trans. Thomas Wilcox [London: Robert Waldegrave for T. Man and T. Gubbins, 1588], pp. 215-16).

169. Dove, *Sermon*, p. 16.

170. Dove, *Sermon*, p. 17. Perkins is somewhat 'lower' than Dove at this point, explaining this text as referring only to God's revealed will through preaching (Perkins, *Workes*, II:638; III:[ii]345).

171. Dove, *Sermon*, p. 18.

mon was to contend that "Christ died not effectually for all" against that Lutheran "brocher of new and strange opinions," Samuel Huberus.[172] This Dove does in a manner very similar to Perkins, namely a close conceptual linking of Christ's satisfaction with his intercession. Thus, "to those for whom Christ doth not pray, to them the death of Christ dooth nothing availe, to those his death is of no effect."[173] Although "the death of Christ were sufficient for the redemption of all mankind, yet hee dyed not effectually for all, for as much as all men are not saved, therefore to manie, that is, to them which are not saved, the deathe of Christ is of no effect."[174] Dove denies that Christ's "death appertained to all, or that he died effectually for all, but onely for the beleevers." The death of Christ does not 'seal salvation' "to any more than to the faithfull." Like Perkins, he interprets texts that appear to teach that some for whom Christ died finally perish, in terms of judicial church membership, as opposed to "in truth and in veritie."[175] Dove deems Huberus to have come to "absurde conclusions" in teaching that to "hold with Calvin, that Christ dyed not to save all, but onely those which in his will hee had predestinated, were plaine Mahometisme, Paganisme, Sarasinisme." Rather, this doctrine that "Christ died onely for them whom hee hath predestinated before" is a great comfort to the justified man.[176]

Yet none of this undermines a universal call of the gospel as Harsnett claimed. While expounding 1 Timothy 2:4 as outlined above, Dove does add a qualification not mentioned by Augustine. In terms of the distinction not between God's absolute and conditional will but between his secret and revealed will, it *is* God's revealed will in terms of the universal proclamation of the gospel that all be saved. No one can exclude himself from the invitation to come to Christ, for in "his revealed will he commandeth that the Gospel should be preached to all."[177] Thus, although "salvation is offered unto all,"

> God is not contrarie to himselfe, albeit his revealed will, and his secrete will, are not one: for the will of God in it selfe is one, but it is saide to bee diverse, as it appeareth unto us, whose dulnesse is such, that we cannot conceive how in diverse respects he he [*sic*] will, and he will not.[178]

---

172. Dove, *Sermon*, p. 64; cf. title-page, pp. 43-54.

173. Dove, *Sermon*, p. 64.

174. Dove, *Sermon*, p. 63. Dove quotes John 17:9.

175. Dove, *Sermon*, pp. 65, 66, 71.

176. Dove, *Sermon*, pp. 74, 76.

177. Dove, *Sermon*, pp. 21, 77.

178. Dove, *Sermon*, pp. 66, 24. Dove quotes Calvin as an authority.

Shunning all prying into the divine decree we are therefore not to "despaire of any mans conversion unto the fayth."[179] Yet it is to be noticed that undergirding this universal call is no more than a divine command.

In his preface, Dove speaks of

> the soundnesse of the doctrine therin conteined, which is warranted by the authoritie of the scriptures, . . . the consent of both the Fathers of the primitive Church, and the now writers of our times, which do concurre in judgement, and agree upon the same interpretation.[180]

Yet Dove seems to have sensed an influential antipathy to "such deepe poynts of divinitie."[181] In this same preface he writes to the Lord Chancellor, Sir Thomas Egerton, that he had despaired of "any Ecclesiastical preferment in this corrupt and simoniacall age, (had I not bene by your Honor preferred)."[182] However, it would be quite wrong to take Dove for a radical, hardline Genevan on the 'puritan' fringe of the English Church, despite his self-pity. He was a "Preacher of Note in the University," and had the Lord Chancellor as a protégé. Just three months before this sermon, Archbishop Whitgift had secured him the rectory of St Mary, Aldermary in London, and Tyacke argues that it was most probably Whitgift who licensed the publication of this sermon.[183] Dove later was to dedicate the published sermon to Egerton, who had formerly secured him a living at the rectory of Tidworth, Wiltshire.[184] Dove was also able to preach once more at Paul's Cross a few years later.[185] Nor was Dove's position typically 'puritanical.' While he opposed Romanism, and published against the Jesuits, he also, like John Bridges above, opposed Presbyterianism and a puritanical approach to ecclesiastical ceremonies. This is clear from his published defences of the established form of church government and the use of the sign of the cross in baptism.[186] In

179. Dove, *Sermon*, p. 77.
180. Dove, *Sermon*, p. A3v.
181. Dove, *Sermon*, p. 78.
182. Dove, *Sermon*, Epistle dedicatorie, p. A3v.
183. Richard Newcourt, *Repertorium Ecclesiasticum Parochiale Londinense: An ecclesiastical Parochial History of the Diocese of London* (London: Benjamin Motte for Christopher Bateman, Benjamin Tooke, Richard Parker, Jon. Bowyer and Henry Clements, 1708-10), I:435-36; Tyacke, *Anti-Calvinists*, p. 34.
184. Dove, *Sermon*, pA3r; *ODNB*.
185. John Dove, *Of Divorcement. A Sermon preached at Pauls Crosse the 10. of May 1601* (London: T. Creede, 1610).
186. John Dove, *An Advertisement to the English Seminaries, amd* [sic] *Jesuites: Shewing their loose kind of Writing* (London: N. Okes for S. Waterson, 1610); John Dove, *A Defence of*

July 1596, just six months before this rigorously particularist sermon, Dove had been made D.D. at Christ Church, Oxford.[187] Dove was preaching doctrine acceptable to the establishment.

Another source of indications of the theological climate of late Elizabethan England is the popularity of a number of important continental volumes published in England in translation. Naturally, the popularity of the numerous English editions of Beza are of special significance at this point. But Beza's particularism has already been treated at length by numerous scholars, and space does not permit another account here.[188] But Harsnett's association of a rigorous particularism with "Geneva" should not be taken so as to exclude the Heidelberg school. In this connection two outstanding but now less well-known divines should be mentioned, namely Jeremias Bastingius and Jacobus Kimedoncius. These divines, in works that were repeatedly published in England in the 1580s and 1590s, offered 'Perkinsian' interpretations of such texts as John 3:16, 1 Timothy 2:4, 2 Peter 3:9, and 1 John 2:2.[189] Kimedoncius explicitly taught what Ussher and Davenant were later to condemn as the doctrine of 'bare sufficiency.'[190] He also taught that Christ's priestly satisfaction and intercession were only for the elect;[191] that under the preaching of the gospel, sinners are not required to believe that Christ died for them personally;[192] that a universal gospel call does not necessitate a de-

---

Church Government. Dedicated to the high Court of Parliament. Wherein is proved that subjects ought to conforme themselves to the state ecclesiasticall. Together with a Defence of the Crosse in Baptisme (London: T. Creede for H. Rockit and by J. Hodgets, 1606).

187. Tyacke, *Anti-Calvinists*, p. 33.

188. A useful entry point into this literature on Beza is G. Michael Thomas, *The Extent of the Atonement: A Dilemma for Reformed Theology from Calvin to the Consensus* (Carlisle, UK: Paternoster Press, 1997), pp. 41-65.

189. Jeremias Bastingius, *An Exposition or Commentarie upon the Catechisme of Christian Religion, which is taught in the Schools and Churches both of the Low Countries, and of the Dominions of the Countie Palatine* (Cambridge: John Legat, 1595), p. 31v; cf. pp. 53r, 70r-70v, 72r, 161v; Jacobus Kimedoncius, *Of the Redemption of Mankind. Three Bookes: Wherein the Controversie of the Universalitie of Redemption and Grace by Christ, and of his Death for all Men, is largely handled. Hereunto is annexed a Treatise of Gods Predestination in one Booke*, trans. Hugh Ince (London: Felix Kingston, 1598), pp. 32, 39-42, 45, 46, 54, 58-59, 61, 69, 70, 72, 74-75, 78, 79, 80, 91-92, 104, 107-29, 169, 182, 187, 192, 198, 202, 210, 233, 261, 264, 331-32, 367, 389-90, 405-6.

190. See Ch. 7. Kimedoncius, *Of the Redemption of Mankind*, pp. 36, 38, 39, 80, 95, 177, 205, 213.

191. Kimedoncius, *Of the Redemption of Mankind*, pp. 33, 173, 188, 210-11, 329-30.

192. Kimedoncius, *Of the Redemption of Mankind*, p. 151; cf. pp. 94-99. Additionally, in this connection, he refuted the charge that particular redemption hinders assurance, asserting, like Perkins, that it is rather an unlimited satisfaction that provides no ground for comfort (Kimedoncius, *Of the Redemption of Mankind*, pp. 146-51, especially p. 148).

sire in God to save the reprobate;[193] and that the gospel promise is strictly particular.[194] Kimedoncius' work was personally licensed by Bishops Richard Bancroft of London and Richard Vaughan of Chester.[195] Kimedoncius' work therefore serves as an example of how strict Elizabethan particularism, with the blessing of the establishment, was also nourished by continental sources.

In conclusion, it is to be noted that in late Elizabethan England it was fashionable to draw up very clear battle lines. Either Christ came to save the elect only or he did not; either God desires to save all or he does not. There was no great rush to answer "yes, according to one scholastic category" but "no, not according to another scholastic category." A reconciliatory *via media* seems to have been as unnecessary as undesirable; no appeasing grey areas; no paradoxical mysteries. It was not to last. The Harsnetts of the age were not to be silenced or ignored forever.

193. Kimedoncius, *Of the Redemption of Mankind*, p. 171; cf. pp. 156-58, 320, 359, 360, 391, 395. This belief was not something proceeding only from Heidelberg. In London in 1563 a treatise of Beza had been published in which the purpose of God in sending preaching to the reprobate is described solely in terms of bringing about their hardening (Theodore Beza, *A briefe and pithie Summe of the Christian Faith made in forme of a Confession, with a Confutation of all suche superstitious Errours, as are contrary thereunto*, trans. R. Filles [London: Rouland Hall, 1563], p. 52v). Even when the writings of an infralapsarian Reformer such as Peter Martyr Vermigli reached the English press, this view was also supported. In an English translation of Vermigli's *Loci Communes* with appended additional material which was "Seene and allowed according to the Queenes Majesties Injunctions" and published in London in 1583, Vermigli categorically denies that the gospel call to the reprobate involves God 'dallying' with them, despite him not desiring to save them. The only purpose he mentions in God sometimes sending the gospel call to the reprobate *qua* reprobate (as opposed to their simply being intermixed with the elect, whose salvation in distinction God does will through the preaching of the gospel) is in judgment to render them without excuse, and to make the elect more thankful for sovereign and particular grace. Quoting Isaiah 6:10, Vermigli states that therefore "this kind of calling is of force, to the blinding and hardening of men for their ill deserts" (Peter Martyr Vermigli, *The Common Places of the most famous and renowmed* [sic] *Divine Doctor Peter Martyr, divided into foure principall Parts: With a large Addition of manie theologicall and necessarie Discourses, some never extant before*, trans. Anthony Marten [London: Henry Denham and Henry Middleton, 1583], IV:Air; II:30 [III.i.42]; IV:122).

194. Kimedoncius, *Of the Redemption of Mankind*, pp. 101, 142, 148, 150, 153, 154, 183, 263-64.

195. Edward Arber, ed., *A Transcript of the Registers of the Company of Stationers of London, 1554-1640* (London: Private publication, 1875-94), III:43v.

SECTION III

Preston's Theology

CHAPTER 3

The Divine Decree

"[W]hatsoever he doth, though thou seest no reason for it, yet justifie thou him in all; when thou seest him . . . denying his grace to many thousands, and the like, yet doe thou justifie him in all his wayes."[1]

Introduction

Hitherto Preston has usually been seen as a 'thorough Calvinist,' who had "an orthodox belief in Calvinism."[2] It is therefore commonly understood that he continued in the tradition of William Perkins, who had explicitly taught the attainment of personal assurance within a framework of double predestination and particular redemption. However, a careful reading of Preston indicates that with regard to predestination and the death of Christ, this background consensus contained significant variation in practical application and emphasis. In the first place, with regard to predestination, Preston's works[3] show a somewhat different presentation of the divine decree from Perkins. It would seem that this is at least partly because Preston has become particularly sensitive to the charge of encouraging passivity under the preaching of

---

1. John Preston, *Life eternall*, II:79-80.

2. James Reid, *Memoirs of the Lives and Writings of those eminent Divines, who convened in the famous Assembly at Westminster, in the Seventeenth Century* (Paisley, UK: Stephen and Andrew Young, 1811-15), I:131; Evelyn S. Shuckburgh, *Emmanuel College*, University of Cambridge College Histories (London: F. E. Robinson & Co., 1904), p. 53.

3. By 'Preston's works' is meant all his published works, listed on pp. xv-xix, together with Preston's *Summe*, which was introduced above on p. 15. Surviving material concerning the York House Conference is not included by this term and will be treated separately in Ch. 6 in light of this examination of his works.

God's sovereignty. He desires to vindicate Reformed orthodoxy from growing anti-Calvinist aspersions that the whole system was detrimental to responsible, holy living, and earnest endeavours in the Christian life.[4] Exactly how Preston went about this task is the subject of this chapter. While Lynne Boughton finds Preston presenting "a vision of God that was bleak and forbidding," it will be seen that this was far from Preston's intention.[5]

Fundamental Axioms

The existence of significant variation from Perkins in Preston's presentation of the divine decree does not mean that Preston did not stand in a most rigorous tradition of predestinarian theology. Preston was in no way reticent to speak of the "absolute and peremptory Decree of God." He understood God's decree to be "the purpose of his will whereby whatsoever he hath judged to be done he determines to doe in due season," and through which "god is knowne." In keeping with his Reformed heritage, Preston held that the "onely reason of the Decree" is "Gods meer good pleasure."[6] This pleasure operates in conjunction with God's purpose to glorify himself and to reveal himself that he might be glorious.[7] God "is desirous of glory" and so he "made the world . . . for his glories sake."[8] Just as "the Lord will not lose his glory" and is "exceeding tender of his glory," so "all things worke for his glory."[9] In Preston's theology it is therefore the glory of God which is the controlling principle and the ultimate end of all things.

God's glory is achieved by means of decrees that are eternal, immutable, and all-embracing. Firstly, they are eternal. Preston taught that

> all the decrees, all the counsells, and all the acts of his will, that ever were in him, they were in him from all eternity: that is, there is not a vicissitude of counsells, thoughts and desires upon the passages of things in the world, as there is in men; for then hee should be subject to change. . . . Therefore looke backe to all times, in your imaginations and thoughts, as

4. For a witty exploration of the issues involved in this charge against Reformed orthodoxy see Richard A. Muller, "The Myth of 'Decretal Theology,'" *CTJ* 30 (1995): 159-67.

5. Lynne C. Boughton, "Supralapsarianism and the Role of Metaphysics in Sixteenth-Century Reformed Theology," *WTJ* 48 (1986): 63-96, p. 89.

6. John Preston, *Irresistiblenesse of converting Grace*, p. 17; Preston, *Summe*, f. 2.

7. John Preston, *Riches of Mercy*, p. 30.

8. John Preston, *Lords Supper*, p. 71; Preston, *Riches of Mercy*, p. 29.

9. John Preston, *The New Covenant*, p. 522; John Preston, *Remaines*, p. 262.

to the making of the world; all those acts, those counsels that have bin executed upon all men, they were in him from everlasting.[10]

Secondly, it follows that the decrees are also unchangeable: "whatsoever purpose or decree, or counsell hee takes to him, hee is immutable in it."[11] Therefore "all the wisdome, and strength, that a man hath, is not able to turne God from his purpose, it is not able to evacuate and to frustrate his decrees, but they shall come to passe."[12] Thirdly, nothing escapes the embrace of this eternal and immutable decree, there being "nothing that comes to passe in the World, but it was in Heaven before all eternity."[13] As "all things come from God whether they be good things or bad," so not even a grain of dust escapes the sovereign decree.[14] In Preston's theology therefore the divine decree concerns the whole of life and at every point the believer has recourse to the decree for ultimate explanation.

The Origin of Evil and the Cause of the Fall

Naturally such teaching raises important concerns regarding human responsibility and the origin of evil. Although Preston saw that "there is a *secret* will of God," whereby he performs things "for reasons best known to himself,"[15] Preston was not one to shirk these questions where he believed Scripture was not silent. In the context of the divine decree he was thus led into a treatment of the Fall and "the Mystery of Election and Reprobation."[16] Preston taught that "so farre as Sinne it Selfe is a Being, God is the cause of it."[17] The heritage of Preston in the high Calvinism of Perkins is reflected when he goes on to assert that "God onely is the Author of good and evill," and in one sense can be said to be the cause even of sinful actions.[18] Preston could say of his God that "good and evill are done by him alone," and that "no creature can . . . doe good or evill without God."[19] The "sinnes of Reprobates," Preston claims, "in-

10. Preston, *Life eternall*, II:80; cf. I:159; II:79.

11. Preston, *Life eternall*, II:72; cf. II:92.

12. Preston, *The New Covenant*, p. 549; cf. p. 557.

13. John Preston, *Sinnes Overthrow*, p. 94; cf. p. 95.

14. Preston, *Sinnes Overthrow*, p. 94; Preston, *The New Covenant*, pp. 163-64.

15. Preston, *Riches of Mercy*, p. 422.

16. John Preston, *The Breast-plate*, I:8.

17. Preston, *Irresistiblenesse of converting Grace*, p. 16; cf. p. 17.

18. John Preston, *Saints Qualification*, I:261; Preston, *The New Covenant*, p. 562.

19. John Preston, *Sermons preached before His Majestie*, p. 26; Preston, *Sinnes Overthrow*, p. 71; cf. Preston, *Saints Qualification*, I:253.

fallibly follow from the determinate counsell of God, who hath decreed their event." Of evil men it can be said that God "is present with their mindes, and knowes their counsells, and moves their hearts, and disposeth of all their counsells." Consequently, there "is no man that speakes for us or against us, that doth us either hurt or good, but God is present with him, and stirres him up to it, whatsoever it be." Preston was not ashamed of this but saw in it a call to worship: "therefore let us give to the Lord, this great Prerogative of his; That he onely doth good and evill, and let no man question it."[20]

However, by citing medieval schoolmen, Preston could considerably empty this teaching of its problematical implications. He taught that although "God is the cause of the whole Being," he is "not the efficient cause of sinne" because sin, as Perkins had taught, is actually "not a being, but rather a defect of what should be in a faculty or act." Rather, the efficient cause of sin is "a deficient will."[21] God being the cause of sin is to be understood in terms of permission only. It was Amos who asked the question, "Shall there be evil in a city, and the LORD hath not done it?" Preston sees Amos as asking, "What evill is committed and is not first permitted by God to be done?"[22] Thus God causes sin by leaving men to their own sinfulness,[23] but this abandonment, as has been noted, does not mean that God is not still actively ruling and moving the individual when he sins.

While God permitted the Fall, he was not its efficient cause. The first fall was that of the angels, and Preston locates the efficient cause of this in two areas, "self-dependence" and negligence. The angels were self-dependent when they "would stand of themselves" and so "they fell downe to the lowest pitt."[24] Concerning their negligence, Preston points out that it is here "worth observing" what "some Divines hold concerning the fall of the Angels, that it was onely through the want of stirring up those excellent things, and lights of knowlege which were in them, that brought them to their fall."[25] The second fall was that of man, and so Adam too, and not God, must bear responsibility for the sin in this world. According to Preston the "phylosophers were all deceived at this poynt, from whence corruption should come," for "it came from

---

20. Preston, *Irresistiblenesse of converting Grace,* p. 17; Preston, *Life eternall,* II:153, 156; Preston, *Saints Qualification,* I:254.

21. Preston, *Irresistiblenesse of converting Grace,* p. 15; William Perkins, *The Workes of that famous and worthy Minister of Christ in the Universitie of Cambridge, Mr. William Perkins* (London: John Legatt & Cantrell Legge, 1616-18), I:18.

22. Amos 3:6; Preston, *Sinnes Overthrow,* p. 95.

23. Preston, *Life eternall,* I:36.

24. Preston, *Riches of Mercy,* p. 240; John Preston, *The deformed Forme,* p. 7.

25. John Preston, *Saints Submission,* pp. 219-20.

Adam."[26] Like the angels, Adam fell through self-dependence or pride and through negligence.[27] Preston also claimed that the inward cause of the Fall can be said to be Adam's "owne free will or mutabilitie of his owne minde, in that he considered not all that was to be considered & so he fell into infidelitie in not believing Gods worde." This whole process and intermingling of factors constituted "Rebellion" and the whole human race fell into misery.[28] Thus it can be seen that Aristotelian fourfold causality is foundational to Preston's formulation of his theology of the decrees of God.

Predestination

Having considered Preston's theology of the divine decree in general, we now come to consider the decree specifically as it regards the purpose of God for his moral creatures. Although Boughton believes that "Preston considered theology to be a fit subject for speculation," Preston's treatment of predestination is accompanied with warnings against going beyond that which is revealed. Rather than "searching and prying into the counsel of God," in order to ask "why so many are damned, and so few saved . . . how the infallibilitie of Gods will and the libertie of mans will can stand together . . . why he suffered the Gentiles to walke in the vanitie of their own mindes so long a time," we should realise that "Gods decree concerning salvation and damnation must be admired at, not pryed into."[29]

However, without 'prying,' Preston still felt he could make certain matters quite plain. First of all, anticipating the likely reaction of his hearers, Preston is at pains to discharge God from any semblance of injustice or cruelty in predestination by upholding God's freedom to do as he pleases. In this respect this Jacobean divine freely admits that salvation *is* about free will — God's free will![30] So free does Preston deem God to be that he goes so far as to place God above the law, reasoning that if "the Lord be without all cause, this we may gather then, that he doth not will any thing, because it is just, or desire it, because it is good, or love any thing, because it is pleasant; for there is no cause without him, all perfection is in him originally." Thus

---

26. John Preston, *Foure Treatises*, p. 140.

27. Preston, *Saints Submission*, pp. 219-20; Preston, *Riches of Mercy*, p. 240; Preston, *Summe*, f. 3.

28. Preston, *Summe*, f. 3.

29. Boughton, "Supralapsarianism and the Role of Metaphysics," p. 90; Preston, *Life eternall*, I:100; Preston, *Sinnes Overthrow*, p. 142.

30. Preston, *The Breast-plate*, II:4.

"every thing is just because he wils it; it is not that God wils it, because it is good or just."[31]

Thus even to question the rightness of God, "the governor of the world," in a discriminating predestination of all men is nothing more than bold presumption on the creature's part. "If God will take a few out of a Nation, and destroy all the rest, who can say any thing to him? They are his owne; as he is without all cause, so he is without all end." Echoing Paul in Romans 9, Preston reminds us that

> all the creatures are made, as pots are made by the potters; and therefore, as they have an author of their being, so they doe serve for another end; so that the potter he may appoint what end hee will and no man can say, why doest thou it? So God, because hee is the first cause, hee may have what end he will, and no man can say, why doest thou so? Hee may make some vessels of honour, and some of dishonour, and all for himselfe, and his owne glory; therefore, when you see that he did not spare the Angels, but cast them downe into hell, there to be reserved in chaines of darkness till the last day; when you see him not sparing the old world, when you see him suffering the Gentiles to walke in their owne wayes; when you see him to suffer a great part of the world to be damned, and to perish; when you see him let the Churches to be made havocke of, you should be ready to say thus, 'To him be glory for ever': that is, you should not murmure against him, but glorifie him, and reverence him for ever.[32]

It should also be noted that Preston frequently employed the concept of double predestination. In the sermon that won him his chaplaincy, he urged King James to see God as "putting difference betwixt man and man in the matter of Salvation and Damnation."[33] He could speak in terms of "predestination to death or life" and, like Perkins, asserted that this "doctrine of predestination . . . consistes of 2 Partes. Election or Reprobation."[34] Put simply this means that "some hath hee chosen, and some not; some he loves, and some hee hates; some hee hath mercy upon, and some he hardens."[35] Neither does anyone escape this double decree, for

---

31. Preston, *Life eternall*, I:143.

32. Preston, *Riches of Mercy*, p. 234; Preston, *Life eternall*, I:145-46.

33. John Preston, *Plenitudo Fontis*, p. 9. The anti-Arminian passage from which this comes was "deleted" from the editions of 1639 and 1640 (see below, pp. 238-39).

34. Preston, *Foure Treatises*, pp. 64-65; Preston, *Summe*, f. 4; cf. Perkins, *Workes*, I:24.

35. Preston, *Life eternall*, II:96.

all are either elect or reprobates: God hath divided all the world into these two, either they are the Lords portion, or the Divels portion . . . God hath made all men to be vessels of honour, or of dishonour, there is no vessell of an indifferent or middle use.[36]

In Pauline fashion, Preston used the case of Esau and Jacob to illustrate the decree of election and reprobation. God "might have chosen Esau and not Jacob; or if hee would have chosen the younger; then hee might have brought him first out of the wombe, but he will not, because he is most free in his choice, he will save Jacob and cast off Esau." God "might have chosen Simon Magus, as well as Simon Peter, but he will not."

> [T]here cannot a reason be given, wherefore he should chuse the one and not the other; he will choose the wife and not the husband, hee will choose the husband and not the wife, he will choose the childe and not the father, and he will chuse the father and not the childe. . . . surely there can be no reason given of it, but because the Spirit is free to choose, and choose not.[37]

Preston defines election as "a decree of god whereby he hath chosen some to life & leadeth them to it by infallible meanes to the practice [*sic; lege* praise] of the glorie of his grace."[38] It is a decree whereby "God determined with Himselfe to save some persons selected from the common Masse." Thus election "is nothing else but this, God hath taken some to life, and makes them holy." The objects of election are thus "set apart to good." Preston gives at least two characteristics of "the prosecution of [God's] decree . . . of Election."[39] Firstly, it is unchangeable, and secondly it is unconditional or absolute. God "useth a libertie . . . in election, he chooseth one and refuseth another, and that for no other reason, because it pleaseth him."[40] Because "Gods meer good pleasure" is "the onely reason of the Decree . . . [i]t necessarily followes, that God hath absolutely decreed to save some." Preston loathed the Arminian doctrine of "a conditionall Decree grounded on the praescience of Faith."[41]

---

36. Preston, *The New Covenant*, p. 486.

37. Preston, *Remaines*, pp. 169-70; cf. Preston, *Riches of Mercy*, pp. 113-14.

38. Preston, *Summe*, f. 4. In Morgan's transcript, "*the* decree" is inaccurate (Morgan, *Prince Charles's Puritan Chaplain*, p. 38).

39. Preston, *Irresistiblenesse of converting Grace*, p. 16; Preston, *Saints Qualification*, II:150; John Preston, *Love of Christ*, p. 82; Preston, *Riches of Mercy*, p. 114.

40. Preston, *The New Covenant*, p. 512; cf. Preston, *Life eternall*, II:95; Preston, *Remaines*, pp. 168-70; Preston, *Riches of Mercy*, pp. 113-14.

41. Preston, *Irresistiblenesse of converting Grace*, pp. 4, 17; cf. p. 16.

Consequently, in Preston's theology, election is inextricably linked to irresistible grace. In his treatise *Irresistiblenesse of converting Grace,* Preston grounds his case in the doctrine of election. We must remember that "the Decree of Election . . . is absolute, and therefore doth necessarily and infallibly attaine its effect." As a result, "Conversion and Faith doe follow the absolute Decree of God" in an irresistible manner. And it could not be otherwise, for "if converting grace move the will after a manner, that may be resisted by it, God cannot infallibly foreknow, who shall believe, and who not; and consequently, all election should be utterly taken away."[42] Preston could describe the same in a less abstract manner by resorting to his favourite imagery: "Now his Father from eternity had ordained this Wife for his Sonne, and therefore hee must have her, and he could have no other."[43] Thus, for this first branch of predestination Preston took the characteristics of predestination as a whole, and, without qualification, applied them to his doctrine of election.

With reprobation, however, Preston treads more carefully. According to Preston, God in the decree of reprobation "passed by so many thousands," and these he has "appointed unto damnation" and "ordained to death."[44] Preston affirms that the decree of reprobation, like election, is immutable. Just as "tares will never be wheate, so they that are reprobated, will never convert."[45] The reprobate "are men set apart to evill, appointed to destruction; as some men are set apart to good, so are these to evill. They are shut up in prison, such as God hath set himselfe against. His eyes are continually upon them for evill."[46] Reprobation is also eternal. God loved Jacob and hated Esau, and in the theology of Preston, God most surely hates the reprobate, and does so from all eternity.[47] We must know that "all the . . . hatred, that [God] hath now since the world was made . . . hee had it from all eternity."[48]

However, this most free and eternal hatred is firmly set in the context of a response to sin. Preston never affirms absolute reprobation without making

---

42. Preston, *Irresistiblenesse of converting Grace,* pp. 16, 17, 19. This is a translation of John Preston, *Irresistibilitate Gratiæ convertentis.* Miller saw this treatise as "the best study of regeneration in psychological terms" he had encountered (Perry Miller, *The New England Mind: The Seventeenth Century* [Cambridge, MA: Harvard University Press, 1954], p. 517).

43. John Preston, *The golden Scepter,* II:2-3.

44. Preston, *The Breast-plate,* II:77 (cf. Preston, *The golden Scepter,* I:63); Preston, *Sinnes Overthrow,* p. 87; John Preston, *A liveles Life,* I:70.

45. Preston, *Remaines,* p. 267.

46. Preston, *Love of Christ,* p. 82; cf. John Preston, *Saints daily Exercise,* p. 100.

47. Preston, *Foure Treatises,* p. 193; Preston, *Love of Christ,* pp. 13-14; Preston, *The New Covenant,* p. 465; Preston, *Saints Qualification,* I:114, 126-27.

48. Preston, *Life eternall,* II:79; but cf. Preston, *Sinnes Overthrow,* pp. 59-60, 170.

precondemnation a part of preterition. For this second branch of predestination Preston took the characteristics of predestination as a whole, but only with qualification did he apply them to his doctrine of reprobation.[49] As we shall see, Preston was sensitive to the fact that the doctrine of absolute reprobation was becoming increasingly unpopular with many in Jacobean England. However, his first response to any objections to his doctrine of reprobation was to show that the very spirit of objection is a matter of sinful arrogance. God is above reproach in this whole matter of reprobation. It is his prerogative to do as he pleases, and we are wrong even to question his actions. We are to know our place and humbly remember

> that if thousands perish, it is nothing to him; hee cares no more for the destruction of the whole world, than thou doest for the throwing away of a little dust; he is full of excellencie and perfection; you see how often hee sweepes away whole kingdomes with the bosome of destruction, nay, he swept away the world by the Floud, as you doe sweepe a little dust out of your houses. Therefore do not thou dispute with God, and aske why are so many damned? Why are so many swept away? Thinke with thy selfe, that hee, that was before all things were, will be when they are gone: therefore learne with Paul, to reverence his judgements, to feare and tremble before him. He is full of being, and though thou perish, what is that to him? Wilt thou dispute with God? Thou art but a particle of dust. What art thou that contendest with him? Let the potsherd strive with potsherds of the earth, but not with God. Shall the clay say to him that fashions it, what makest thou?[50]

Preston acknowledged, however, that some questions could be legitimately posed at this point, and he was not short in providing answers. To the question, "Why do so many perish while it is in his power to save them?" Preston's attempted answer is twofold. Firstly, "though God indeed be exceeding rich in mercy, yet that doth not contradict his other Attributes . . . though he be rich

---

49. Of course, Perkins and Preston both insisted that "God cannot be said to create any to damnation," and that "none were made for damnation" (Perkins, *Workes,* I:287; Preston, *Saints Qualification,* III:21). Perhaps both men were consciously alluding to the Lutheran Saxon Visitation Articles of 1592. Article IV(ii) states that "God created no man for condemnation; but wills that all men should be saved and arrive at the knowledge of the truth." However, the Lutherans then used this to undergird the universal call of the gospel, and this immediately follows the assertion of Article IV(i) that "Christ died for all men, and, as the Lamb of God, took away the sins of the whole world" (Philip Schaff, ed., *The Creeds of Christendom, with a History and Critical Notes* [Grand Rapids, MI: Baker Books, 1993], III:185).

50. Preston, *Life eternall,* I:127; cf. I:101, 145.

in mercy yet that contradicts not his justice, therefore he must deal with the wicked according to their sins." Secondly,

> though he be rich in mercy, yet his mercy contradicteth not his libertie, he hath a libertie to do what he pleaseth, having a soveraigntie over all creatures, he is free to chuse more or fewer to his kingdom, as he pleaseth, and to exercise his severitie as he will.[51]

Thus problems with reprobation flow from an overemphasis on one attribute of God to the detriment of others, such as justice or liberty. Once again, as for his general doctrine of predestination, and now even more so for its severe subdivision of reprobation, Preston sees the revelation of the glory of God as the only way we can begin to understand this doctrine.

> Will he cast men to hell? Will hee damne them for his owne glory? Yes . . . all his actions even that also is for his own sake . . . This is enough, he hath no end, no cause above himselfe; and therefore it is reason enough, he doth it because he will doe it.

It is therefore God's prerogative to do as he pleases, and we must acquiesce with Preston's formulation of "the prosecution of [the Spirit's] decree . . . of . . . Reprobation."[52]

But having acquiesced with it, we are not to overemphasise it. Preston considered himself a minister of the gospel, and, as such, could say "wee doe not preach damnation, our end is Salvation."[53] Although elsewhere in other contexts Preston says more than once that he *does* preach damnation and will continue to do so,[54] this demonstrates that Preston was concerned with a matter of emphasis and motivation, and was perhaps seeking to stem the excesses of some of the Elizabethan divines. His concern may also have been reinforced by the pastoral problems he experienced with Joan Drake.[55] Preston was also aware that the doctrine of reprobation was open to abuse and misapplication, and he warned his hearers against this. The right use of the doctrine of God's immutable rejection of sinners is "that wee might tremble at his judgements, and that we might rejoyce in his favour with joy unspeakable and glorious." Therefore, this "being the end why it is revealed,

---

51. Preston, *Riches of Mercy*, pp. 32, 33.
52. Preston, *Remaines*, p. 170; cf. Preston, *Riches of Mercy*, pp. 113-14.
53. Preston, *Saints Qualification*, I:83.
54. Preston, *The Breast-plate*, II:32; Preston, *Love of Christ*, p. 32.
55. See above, p. 23.

it ought to be applied onely to these uses," and not in any way to curious speculations.[56]

Preston's desire to avoid a harmful emphasis on the doctrine of reprobation and its misapplication is reflected in his consistently asymmetric portrayal of the double decree. Unlike the famous diagrammatical schemes of Beza and Perkins, Preston shunned portraying the decree of double predestination as symmetrical. God's "primarie intent" was not to display his wrath in damnation but "was to shew mercy to all creatures, to men and angels both." Similarly Preston expressed the "unchangeable Decree concerning the salvation of men" as either "giving grace" or "denying grace."[57] Preston formulated the decree in this way to avoid the objection that "those whom God hath rejected, do sinne irresistibly." He was quick to "deny that there is the same reason of both":

> for although Faith be the effect of predestination, yet infidelity is not the proper effect of Reprobation. Whereas Faith requires a cause of it selfe efficient, which hath a true and proper influence into its effect. But there is no efficient cause required to unbeliefe; but deficient (because it followes upon the meere defect and absence of that cause by which Faith should be wrought). As to the illumination of the aire; there is required the Sun or some other efficient cause, having influence into that effect; but the absence of the Sunne is enough to cause darknesse. In like manner, although the sinnes of Reprobates do infallibly follow from the determinate counsell of God, who hath decreed their event; yet Conversion and Faith doe follow the absolute Decree of God after a much different manner; sinnes do follow infallibly indeed, but onely by a necessity of consequence; that is, God not at all causing or effecting, but onely permitting: but Faith and good Workes follow by a necessity of the consequent, as of which God must most properly be called the Author, according to all Divines.[58]

Although the above quotations on the asymmetry of the decree of predestination might already suggest that Preston was of the infralapsarian school, it is still not immediately clear whether Preston had a supralapsarian or infralapsarian understanding of the decree. Unlike Perkins, he never consciously and explicitly defended one viewpoint to the exclusion of the other.

---

56. Preston, *Life eternall*, II:97; cf. II:148. Goodwin and Ball in their "Dedicatorie" to *Life eternall* state that Preston there presents us with "those lofty speculations of the schools . . . digested into usefull applications" (Preston, *Life eternall*, pp. A6v-A7r).

57. Preston, *Riches of Mercy*, p. 33; Preston, *Life eternall*, II:92.

58. Preston, *Irresistiblenesse of converting Grace*, p. 17.

This should hardly surprise us since in the year following Preston's promotion to chaplain to Prince Charles, the King issued his famous directions concerning preachers. Amongst other restrictions, James declared that "noe preacher, of what title soever, under ye degree of a Bishop, or Deane at the least, doe from henceforth presume to teach in any popular auditory the deepe points of Predestination, Election, Reprobation."[59] Charles's royal proclamation of 1626 "for the establishing of the Peace and Quiet of the Church of England" had a similar effect.[60] Perhaps Preston was still feeling the pressure of such edicts while in Cambridge in 1628, when he carefully wrote that

> the Lord looking down from heaven . . . made of one heape of clay severall creatures, and appointed to every one his several end, which end they must observe and aime at; and if they doe not, they wrong him that made them; and therefore it is hee destroyes them.[61]

Although Preston is speaking in the context of God's sovereignty, by 'end' he is merely referring to the calling every human being has in this world. If a man does not fulfil his occupational vocation to the glory of God, he will be justly destroyed. Despite the strong allusions to Romans 9:21, Preston is only speaking here about social callings or 'ends' and not the secretly predetermined destiny of the individual. Yet Preston did teach that "God determined with himselfe to save some persons selected from the common Masse." But was this "heape" or "common Masse" of humanity conceptually fallen or unfallen?[62]

Boughton, on a reading of *The New Covenant* and *Life eternall* alone, is persuaded that Preston was a supralapsarian. Boughton reasons that a theologian must have been a supralapsarian if he held, as Preston did, that God designed all things "for his own pleasure even if this meant the destruction of most intelligent creatures," and that this "could not be judged by men to be an unfair condemnation of being prior to its existence." However, the distinctive tenet of supralapsarianism is not that the decree results in a "condemnation of being prior to its existence," for this is common to the infralapsarian position which teaches that men are irrevocably condemned in Adam before they exist.

59. Bod Tanner MS. 299, ff. 47-50, #3; cf. John P. Kenyon, ed., *The Stuart Constitution, 1603-1688: Documents and Commentary,* 2nd ed. (Cambridge: Cambridge University Press, 1986), p. 129.

60. James F. Larkin & Paul L. Hughes, eds., *Stuart Royal Proclamations* (Oxford: Clarendon Press, 1973-83), II:90-93.

61. Preston, *Life eternall,* I:146. Emerson incorrectly locates these sermons in 1626 (Everett H. Emerson, *English Puritanism from John Hooper to John Milton* [Durham, NC: Duke University Press, 1968], p. 241).

62. Preston, *Irresistiblenesse of converting Grace,* p. 16.

Rather it is that the conceptual object of the decree of predestination is unfallen humanity,[63] and nothing in *The New Covenant* and *Life eternall* or the rest of Preston's works would suggest that he held to this position. Boughton also asserts that Preston reasoned that since "God had being without succession his acts and judgments were all done at once." Were this standard tenet the sum of Preston's thoughts on the matter then it would be impossible for him to be either a supralapsarian or an infralapsarian. But this whole debate never pretended to be concerned with any temporal sequence in the divine mind (a total impossibility in the scholastic doctrine of God), but rather a conceptual one, and it is clear that Preston envisaged a conceptual sequence in the divine decree. We have already seen how Preston taught that God does not will things because they are just, but that they are just because he wills them.[64] Boughton concludes from this that Preston was actually teaching that "God was devoid of qualities such as justice."[65] Yet before this is allowed in any way to bolster an alleged supralapsarianism, it must not be forgotten that God being above the law might be just as necessary to defend the infralapsarian position, since God could have determined to save every fallen human being, and had the power to accomplish this, yet chose not to do so.

Furthermore, coupled with Boughton's lack of positive evidence that Preston was a supralapsarian, there is positive evidence that he was in fact an infralapsarian. Preston defines reprobation as "a decree of God whereby he passeth by some men before they had done either good or evill & beinge vessells of wrath by sin are destinated [*sic*] to destruction that his anger & power may be knowne."[66] Here it is clear that although the decree is in eternity ("before they had done either good or evill") the object of predestination is a fallen and not an unfallen humanity ("beinge vessells of wrath by sin"). Thus, in response to the question "What is this Gospell?" Preston the infralapsarian can say that it "is nothing but this, when God looked on mankinde, as fallen in Adam, he tooke a resolution in himselfe to recover them againe, by giving his Sonne to them."[67]

---

63. *The Oxford Dictionary of the Christian Church* is totally unsatisfactory at this point, as are the definitions provided by Kenyon, Sharpe, and Secor (*ODCC*, pp. 1320, 1552, 1560; Kenyon, ed., *The Stuart Constitution*, p. 132; Kevin Sharpe, *The Personal Rule of Charles I* [New Haven, CT: Yale University Press, 1992], pp. 296-97; Philip B. Secor, *Richard Hooker: Prophet of Anglicanism* [Tunbridge Wells, UK: Burns & Oates, 1999], p. 117).

64. See above, p. 75.

65. Boughton, "Supralapsarianism and the Role of Metaphysics," p. 89; cf. p. 65.

66. Preston, *Summe*, f. 4.

67. Preston, *Saints Qualification*, III:16. Although Muller claims that supralapsarianism alone constitutes "a fully double predestination," and that infralapsarianism is "frequently

Reprobation in Time?

According to Preston, the eternal decree of election and reprobation is realised in history under the preaching of the gospel. The elect are saved by the preaching and the reprobate come under God's judgment for resisting the very same preaching. It is concerning this divine rejection of the stubborn hearers of the gospel that Preston's theology has been misrepresented, especially concerning his doctrine of reprobation. The responsible act of the rejecting of the gospel was to Preston the most grievous sin possible to fallen man. He claimed that "of all the sins that can be committed . . . all our personal rebellions provoke not God so much to anger, as the rejection of his Son." The most grievous sin receives therefore the most grievous punishment. Because "the Law makes way for the Gospell," the gospel is "the uttermost" and "therefore the sentence, and condemnation of the Gospell is peremptory, and terrible, and nothing beyond it."[68] Furthermore,

> in this New Testament, in these days of grace, the Lord is much more quick and peremptory in rejecting men and casting them off, the time is shorter; he will not wait so long as he was wont to do in those times, he will sooner swear in his wrath now, that you shall not enter into his rest.[69]

Developing this theme of Psalm 95, which is picked up by the writer to the Hebrews, Preston elaborated a doctrine of God's rejection in history of those who 'hardened their heart' under the preaching of Christ.[70] According to Preston, Psalm 95:11 concerns the time when, as in Genesis 6:3, "God suffers his Spirit to strive no longer."[71] He also sees a "resemblance" of rejecting

---

called single predestination" (Richard A. Muller, *The Dictionary of Latin and Greek Theological Terms Drawn Principally from Protestant Scholastic Theology* [Grand Rapids, MI: Baker Book House Co., 1985], pp. 235, 292), this study finds this dichotomy misleading, and seeks to reserve the concept of single predestination for the Lutheran schema involving conditional reprobation. Preston's system was infralapsarian in formulation, seeing the objects of reprobation as fallen, but still has reprobation as a positive decree, and to some extent coordinate with the decree of election. Preston can therefore still be described as a double predestinarian, just as Song has done (Yong Jae Timothy Song, *Theology and Piety in the Reformed Federal Thought of William Perkins and John Preston* [Lewiston, NY: Edwin Mellen Press, 1998], pp. 189-90).

68. Preston, *Riches of Mercy*, p. 427; Preston, *Saints Qualification*, I:77; cf. Preston, *Love of Christ*, pp. 85-86.

69. Preston, *The New Covenant*, p. 421; Preston, *The golden Scepter*, II:50.

70. Cf. Psalm 95:8-11; Hebrews 3:15–4:11.

71. Preston, *Plenitudo Fontis*, p. 15; cf. Preston, *The golden Scepter*, II:68; Preston, *Saints Qualification*, II:100-101.

Christ, when the Jews, before entering Canaan, "refused the offer that God made to them." God therefore swore "in his wrath that they should not enter into his rest," and in so doing "cut them off." However, God's final rejection of the Jews had not yet come, for

> God was angry afterwards with them many times, yet his wrath came not upon them to the uttermost till they had refused Christ, because the Gospel was preached so freely, and Christ offered unto them, and they refused it, therefore the wrath of God came upon them, as it is to be seen at this day.[72]

Psalm 95 is therefore a forerunner of the divorcement of the Jews for rejecting their Messiah, and has its application today to all those who reject the offer of Christ in the gospel: "By this therefore we may see the danger of refusing the Gospel, God had endured their provocations, yet now for their refusing of Christ he cut them off, and so he will do to every particular person, for there is no Law that can be preached that is so dangerously refused as the Gospel."[73]

Preston could therefore entreat his hearers with the following words:

> defer not the taking of his offer, take heed lest God swear in his wrath you shall not enter into his rest, if you refuse this excellent gift, Remember that though it be true, that the whole time of this life be a time of grace, yet there is an opportunity in which God offereth grace, and after that offer, it is no more. And therefore he would offer Jerusalem no more peace, because she knew not the time of her visitation, and afterwards God either offered her none at all, or gave her not an heart to take it.

Elsewhere Preston addresses his hearers in the following words:

> Beloved, there is double time: a time of the comming forth of this decree, and a time of preparing and trying, while the doore stands open. Therefore take heed that that acceptable time doe not passe away.[74]

While it seems clear that Preston had in mind here a divine judicial abandonment, he frequently was ambiguous in his terminology in this connection. This led James Veninga mistakenly to construe Preston as teaching that the divine decree of reprobation is to be viewed as occurring in time and contin-

---

72. Preston, *Riches of Mercy*, p. 427.

73. Preston, *Riches of Mercy*, p. 429; cf. Preston, *The Breast-plate*, II:209; Preston, *Plenitudo Fontis*, pp. 14-15.

74. Preston, *Riches of Mercy*, p. 432; Preston, *Life eternall*, II:98.

gent upon man's sinful actions. The importance of a correct understanding of Preston on this point is clear when it is realised that Preston considered the doctrine of divine judicial abandonment as central to his whole understanding of the role of preaching the gospel. It was vital to understand this danger: "Doe not thinke this is a case that seldome comes, it is done every day, continually upon some."[75] Preston's doctrine of divine judicial abandonment needs therefore to be examined more closely and the claims of Veninga evaluated.

Veninga, relying especially on *Life eternall,* understands Preston to have taught that "there is a time span in the life of the Christian . . . a time of preparation, in which he attempts to live up to the covenantal requirements. Upon failure, a moment arrives when God, unbeknown to the Christian, rejects the individual." Because, as has been noted, Preston sometimes used the word 'decree' in this connection, Veninga equates this rejection with the decree of reprobation.[76] Veninga therefore interprets *Life eternall* as teaching that "there is a period of time granted to the individual in which he is to prepare for the experience of grace. Preston seeks to exhort his listeners to pray and to be obedient. Should they fail in this task, God is likely to send forth his decree of reprobation" or "a decree that they are outside the covenant."[77] Therefore the nominally eternal decree of reprobation is "finalized" "during the lifetime of the individual." Thus "the decree of reprobation only becomes actualized after the individual turns away from his conditional covenant obligations."[78] Furthermore, "should the individual still be able to seek God, the decree most likely has not yet been made."[79] All this is seen as part of Preston's "softening the implications of the doctrine of election," with a view to being able to "continue to affirm the doctrine of election, while prodding his listeners to live a life of obedience."[80] So great was Preston's "desire to soften the doctrine of election," that he formulated his theology so that "the doctrine of election is relaxed to the point of granting to the individual the power to permit God to respond to the individual in a gracious manner." Indeed, concerning Preston's system as a whole, Veninga claims that "the type of compromise that takes place in Preston, certainly allows for an incorporation of some of the attitudes of the Arminians, without becoming an exponent of free will."[81]

---

75. Preston, *Life eternall,* II:83.

76. James F. Veninga, "Covenant Theology and Ethics in the Thought of John Calvin and John Preston" (Ph.D. Dissertation, Rice University, 1974), pp. 210, 211.

77. Veninga, "Covenant Theology and Ethics," pp. 233, 214.

78. Veninga, "Covenant Theology and Ethics," pp. 335, 345.

79. Veninga, "Covenant Theology and Ethics," p. 213; cf. pp. 214, 216.

80. Veninga, "Covenant Theology and Ethics," pp. 213, 215.

81. Veninga, "Covenant Theology and Ethics," pp. 334, 233; cf. pp. 332, 345.

According to Veninga, therefore, Preston saw reprobation as a response to provocation and not as unconditional or absolute. Passivity under predestinarian teaching is eliminated for so "long as one can still prepare, through prayer and holy living, the decree has not been made." But even then, the small group who can no longer prepare, should not be discouraged, for "a change of heart will make God respond."[82] Thus, according to Veninga, Preston

> wishes to argue that while God decrees the reprobation of some individuals from eternity, this decree is not actualized until a certain moment arrives in the lives of those individuals. Until that moment occurs, these individuals are allowed a time of 'preparing and trying.' Should their prayer and holy endeavors result in the gracious response of God, they will become members of the particular elect. In this case, Preston wishes to say, the decree itself has not changed: for that decree is based on the sinfulness of the individual. Rather, the individuals have changed, making possible the gracious attitude of God.

Strangely, Veninga thinks that Preston, with his logic "pressed to the point of breaking," and at a time of a rising anti-Calvinism, was able to lead 'the godly' unchallenged in his maintaining that "that the decree of reprobation is carried out only after the individual fails to prepare for God's mercy." Veninga admits that Preston's "departure from Calvin's doctrine of election is significant, and leads to the conclusion that Preston is compromising with the Arminian challenge."[83] But could Preston really have taught this?

Despite our having already demonstrated that Preston was a double predestinarian, a closer look at Preston's doctrine of reprobation and abandonment in connection with gospel preaching is evidently necessary. It is clear that Preston taught that when Christ is presented to sinners with the command to repent and believe in him, and they refuse to comply, three things are involved in God's rejection of them. The first is the termination of offers of grace. "There is a day . . . after which God will not offer grace: . . . The Jewes had their day; but because 'they accounted themselves unworthy of everlasting life, Paul did turne from them to the Gentiles.'"[84] Still today God's "Spirit shall not always strive with men" and after a time Christ may "never be a suter" to a sinner again.[85] Thus there are "certain acceptable times, after which God

---

82. Veninga, "Covenant Theology and Ethics," p. 216; cf. pp. 214, 335.

83. Veninga, "Covenant Theology and Ethics," pp. 335, 336, 216, 336; cf. p. 345.

84. Preston, *Foure Treatises*, p. 171.

85. Preston, *The golden Scepter*, II:68. For more on Christ as suitor, see below, pp. 134-35.

offereth grace no more."[86] This withdrawing of "the offer of grace" is akin to 'the removal of the candlestick.'[87] The "pardon" then becomes "out of date" to the sinner, and "it is too late" for him to be saved.[88] This termination of offers of grace is actually an expression of God's hatred. When a man rejects and forsakes God, "he is left to himselfe," which "is properly called the hatred of God, for then God with-drawes from a man his Spirit and speciall providence, because he loathes him."[89] Preston finds ground for this teaching in 2 Corinthians 6:2 where Paul's statement that "this is the accepted time, this is the day of salvation," implies "that all time is not the accepted time."[90]

This rejection is not, however, a merely passive abandonment. There is an active rejection of the sinner also. Upon persistent rejection of the offer of Christ, God sends out a curse or irreversible sentence of condemnation. We are to "know that there is a thunderbolt always following this lightening" of "offering you Christ." That is why "when John the Baptist came and preached the Gospel, he tels them presently of the curse that was to follow." It is even actually the Christ who is preached who does the cursing. Even "as Christ cursed the figtree . . . [s]o when Christ is offered, and this Gospell preached, and thou refusest this grace, thou mayest find Christ so curse thee, that thou be ever barren in the matter of grace." In this context "a curse is but a separation, when a man is cast aside and set apart for such a purpose," and the actual execution of the curse need not be for many years. This curse need not, however, have immediately noticeable effects.[91]

In the third place, Preston also speaks in terms of God's unnoticeable and irreversible swearing of an oath or sending forth of a decree against the offender. There is abundant evidence that these two concepts are synonymous in Preston's thought. He calls God's 'swearing in his wrath' in Psalm 95:11 "a decree," and elsewhere says that "when God takes an oath the decree is peremptory, and never to be reversed." The decree is unnoticeable, for when it is passed upon a man "no man sees it, no not he himselfe, but he comes to Church, and heares the word from day [*sic; lege* day to day]. But yet remember that God is unchangeable."[92] It is also irreversible both as an oath and decree.

---

86. Preston, *Plenitudo Fontis*, p. 13; cf. Preston, *The New Covenant*, pp. 420-22. In the corrupted 1640 edition (see below, pp. 238-39) these words are followed by "to them that wilfully refuse" (John Preston, *The Fulnesse of Christ*, p. 17).

87. Preston, *Remaines*, pp. 70-71.

88. Preston, *The golden Scepter*, II:47-48.

89. Preston, *Sinnes Overthrow*, p. 59.

90. Preston, *The golden Scepter*, II:48.

91. Preston, *The Breast-plate*, II:209; Preston, *Love of Christ*, p. 82.

92. Preston, *Life eternall*, II:82; Preston, *Saints Qualification*, I:138; cf. Preston, *Foure Trea-*

When God "comes to sweare, there is no retracting of it then, wheresoever you finde an oath in the Scripture, there is no reservation, when he sware, he never returned againe." Therefore it can be said that there is

> a double time: a time of preparing and trying before this unchangeable decree come forth. . . . [T]here is a time, when the decree is past; and when this is not past, there is a doore of hope opened: but when the decree is come forth, then you are past hope.[93]

Preston finds textual warrant for this usage of the term 'decree' in terms of the swearing of an oath in Zephaniah 2:1-2, which reads "Gather yourselves together, yea, assemble, O nation not desired; Before the decree bringeth forth, before the day passeth as the chaff, before the fierce anger of the LORD cometh upon you." He comments in this context that it is "a thing worthy of observation, that there is a double time . . . a time of preparing, and threatning, and no more but threatning, and a time of *executing* the decree." There

> is a time of whetting his glittering sword, and fitting the arrow to the bow, before the blow be given; there is a time of patience, triall and long-suffering, before he 'sweares in his wrath they shal not enter into his rest'; . . . Therefore . . . before the stroke be given, before the decree bee come forth, let us search our selves and meet him, to prevent it.[94]

Preston's doctrine of divine judicial abandonment can be better understood when his accounts of its occurrence to two biblical characters is considered, namely, that of Saul and Cain. Preston frequently used Saul as a notorious example of abusing the mercy of God and incurring a divine judicial abandonment as a result, which was nevertheless not fully worked out for many years. Saul, as king of Israel, had

> the will of God . . . revealed clearly to him, he was bid by a cleare command, 'Goe and kill all the Amalekites, and leave not any of them alive': Saul now had a heart contemning God in this commandment, therefore also God came to a resolution and decree, to cast him off.[95]

---

tises, p. 171; Preston, *The golden Scepter*, II:48-50; Preston, *Life eternall*, II:83, 91, 98; Preston, *Love of Christ*, pp. 85-86; Preston, *Sermons preached before His Majestie*, p. 87.

93. Preston, *Saints Qualification*, II:101; Preston, *Life eternall*, II:83.

94. Preston, *Sermons preached before His Majestie*, p. 87 (emphasis added); cf. Perkins, *Workes*, III:(ii)411.

95. Preston, *Life eternall*, II:81; cf. John Preston, *The mysticall Match*, p. 12.

So "when Saul had failed in one thing, God cast him off. . . . Saul had a naturall heart to doe evill, although his profession was good; yet when he was put to the triall, whether he would take the fat sheepe and the oxen, he did it; yet, you must know, it was not for that, that God cast him off, but because the frame of his heart was not good; for he would have done it againe and againe, an hundred times over." "Saule had his day, hee had common gifts and profited not, therefore God forsooke him," and "he was rejected."[96]

God also at this time "made a separation between God and him," for "a curse is but a separation, when a man is cast aside and set apart for such a purpose." However, "though Saul lived many yeares after, yet you could see no change in him, there was no alteration in his outward behaviour." Yet God's decree against Saul was irreversible, and Preston applied this with urgency to his own hearers:

> If God be unchangeable, take heede then, lest hee come to this, that hee cast thee off as hee did Saul: for if ever hee doe it, he will never repent, never alter, never retract his decree. . . . [I]t is most fearefull, 'God doth not repent': it is not with him as it is with man, for he may be intreated, and may repent; but 'the Lord is not as man that he should repent.'[97]

But it must never be thought that Saul's destiny was ever in the balance. He was reprobate from all eternity, and his rejection in time was but the outworking of this. God "shewed mercies to Saul [as well as to David], but they were another kind of mercies, Saul was not one he had chosen to himself, and therefore his mercies continued not, for indeed he never loved Saul with that unchangeable love." It was because God had reprobated Saul in eternity that "Saul was set apart for evill" in time.[98]

Another example of divine rejection used by Preston was the case of Cain. All his life Cain had had "but Gods common favour," and it did not become apparent that he was "a wicked man" until he murdered his brother Abel. For this he was cursed but still had "Cains priviledge," which was that none should kill him "presently." "Cains prosperity" was only that, although "the curse lay upon him," yet "he had his life continued." Likewise today, those who reject the offer of the gospel may have prosperity, but "the time of

---

96. Preston, *Saints Qualification*, II:68-69; Preston, *Foure Treatises*, p. 171; Preston, *The mysticall Match*, pp. 19-20.

97. Preston, *The Breast-plate*, II:209; Preston, *Life eternall*, II:80-81; cf. Preston, *Sermons preached before His Majestie*, p. 87.

98. Preston, *The Breast-plate*, II:36, 209.

execution is not yet come." To such Preston can say, "Thou mayest enjoy thy health and wealth, and no man lay hold on thee here to hurt thee. But thou art reserved to a more solemne day of punishment."[99]

Veninga's assessment of Preston's formulation of the doctrine of reprobation therefore will not stand. To Preston, just as the eternal and absolute decree of election is realized in time by the giving of repentance and faith, so the eternal and absolute decree of reprobation may be realized in time by way of the divine judicial abandonment of church members. Preston himself calls this the "executing" of the decree.[100] For both elect and reprobate it becomes manifest in time what is decreed in eternity. This no more renders reprobation conditional than election is rendered conditional by faith being a *sine qua non* of the salvation experience. Reformed orthodoxy always saw instrumental causes as subsumed in an absolute decree.

Veninga is well aware that part of Preston's formulation of this decree of rejection involves covenant theology.[101] Yet he fails to see the crucial significance of this. While Preston does not say so in so many words, the import of his judicial rejection or 'casting out' is little more than divine excommunication. The phraseology of 'casting out' is in keeping with the Old and New Testament terminology for excommunication. Yet the whole concept of excommunication is totally absent from Veninga's thought.[102] For Preston, Ishmael provides one such example of a member of the outward covenant who was finally excommunicated or judicially abandoned in time. Ishmael "lived in the family, as well as Isaac," but only "till the time that God would have him cast out." For an unregenerate church member today "it may bee, the time of casting out is not yet come, but in due time, when the right season shall come, then Ismael shall be cast out, and every one with whom the Covenant indeed is not established."[103] This divine excommunication might not be made manifest through the wielding of the keys in the visible church — and indeed very rarely ever would be in the English state church — yet it continually presented itself upon Preston's horizon. When Preston's temporal decree of rejection is properly examined, therefore, it is apparent that Veninga has no real grounds to doubt that Preston held to eternal reproba-

---

99. Preston, *Love of Christ*, pp. 82-83; Preston, *The Breast-plate*, II:209.

100. Preston, *Sermons preached before His Majestie*, p. 87.

101. E.g., Veninga, "Covenant Theology and Ethics," pp. 210, 214.

102. Cf. Veninga, "Covenant Theology and Ethics," p. 215. It is also absent from Song's thought when he wrestles with this same area of Preston's preaching. In contrast to Veninga, however, Song merely resorts to 'dialectical tension' and 'biblical paradox' in his defence of Preston's orthodoxy (Song, *Theology and Piety*, pp. 196-97).

103. Preston, *The New Covenant*, pp. 464-65.

tion, decreed while men were "not yet born, neither having done any good or evil."[104]

It can therefore be seen that Preston stood in a most rigorous tradition of predestinarian theology, and that his sermons are replete with predestinarian language and themes.[105] This is all the more striking when seen in the context of James's directions to preachers and Charles's declaration on the Thirty-Nine Articles.[106] Schaefer is certainly right to reject R. T. Kendall's exaggerated claim that Preston "makes the doctrine of predestination itself virtually pointless; it has become a mere theory."[107] However, it must also be said that Preston stands in a school of Jacobean predestinarianism that seeks 'lower' formulations than the 'high' predestinarianism we have seen in Elizabethan England. Yet while Veninga's analysis is somewhat crude and stretches Preston's statements in order to hold an interpretation that they simply will not bear, Veninga is nevertheless correct in detecting that Preston is struggling with his task of presenting the sovereignty of God in terms of his covenant theology and its call for mutual engagement with God. It is true to say that in this area a certain discontinuity exists between Preston and the Elizabethan Calvinism we have encountered. Double predestination has become far less symmetrical, and also overtly infralapsarian. The language of reprobation is stretched to the limits and given new meaning so as to maximise human responsibility. Not only has the decree of God been softened by Preston's infralapsarianism, but even the way in which reprobation is preached has been significantly modified. On the purely theological level, Veninga is inclined to explain Preston's approach as a simple tactic to avoid

104. Romans 9:11; Veninga, "Covenant Theology and Ethics," p. 209; cf. pp. 213, 233.

105. The case of Preston clearly contradicts Munson's exaggerated notion that "[p]redestination received so little attention among the seventeenth century [sic] covenant preachers that its lack can be considered one of the marks of covenant theology" (Charles R. Munson, "William Perkins: Theologian of Transition" [Ph.D. Dissertation, Case Western Reserve University, 1971], p. 180).

106. See above, p. 82.

107. R. T. Kendall, *Calvin and English Calvinism to 1649*, 2nd ed. (Carlisle, UK: Paternoster Press, 1997), p. 123; Paul R. Schaefer Jr., "The Spiritual Brotherhood on the Habits of the Heart: Cambridge Protestants and the Doctrine of Sanctification from William Perkins to Thomas Shepard" (D.Phil. Dissertation, University of Oxford, 1994), p. 208. Long before Kendall, Munson had presented Preston's theology similarly, with the claim that although Preston was "a disciple of Perkins," he "spoke of reprobation only in minimal terms." According to Munson, "Preston was not saying anything that Perkins would not say, but the essential difference was in the fact that the covenant had replaced predestination; no longer was predestination a prominent theme as it had been for Perkins. Under these circumstances, if a man is not in the covenant, the tendency is to consider that it is his own doing; election, and particularly reprobation, tend to be minimized" (Munson, "William Perkins: Theologian of Transition," pp. 177-78).

antinomianism amongst his hearers, and to preserve a need for obedience and holiness in the face of God's decree.[108] However, he also shows awareness of Preston's context and sees Preston's position very much as a "response to the Arminian challenge."[109] In subsequent chapters it will be seen how this response also affected other areas of Preston's theology.

108. Veninga, "Covenant Theology and Ethics," p. 215. McGiffert is of the opinion that reprobation is downplayed in Preston's theology due to his federalist doctrine of a prelapsarian covenant of works (Michael McGiffert, "The Perkinsian Moment of Federal Theology," *CTJ* 29 [1994]: 117-48, p. 124).

109. Veninga, "Covenant Theology and Ethics," p. 345; cf. pp. 233, 334, 336, 338, 342. Nearer to home, Preston would have been encouraged in this position by Cotton (see above, pp. 5, 11, 18) who himself, in the 1620s, promulgated a concept of "conditional reprobation" (McGiffert, "The Perkinsian Moment of Federal Theology," p. 142; David R. Como, "Puritans, Predestination and the Construction of Orthodoxy in Early Seventeenth-Century England" in *Conformity and Orthodoxy in the English Church, c.1560-1660*, ed. Peter G. Lake & Michael C. Questier [Woodbridge, UK: Boydell Press, 2000], 64-87, pp. 78-81; cf. Kendall, *Calvin and English Calvinism*, p. 112).

CHAPTER 4

The Death of Christr

*"My dissolution is at hand, let me go to my home, and Jesus Christ
who hath bought me with his precious blood."*[1]

Introduction

What exactly did Preston mean when he taught that Christ, as "the Saviour of
the world," came "to take away the sinnes of the world"? What did he mean
when he said that the gospel of Christ is "the way that the Lord hath appointed
mankinde to be saved by"? When Preston spoke of "Christ the surety of mankind" who "comes and undertakes for us," he could have meant that Christ was
mankind's only surety, or that he was the surety of all men without exception,
although he only came to 'undertake' effectually for the elect.[2] In the early seventeenth century clarifying such questions had become an extremely conten-
tious affair with tremendous political as well as theological ramifications. Papists, Calvinists, and Remonstrants clashed theological swords over these
ambiguous phrases, and within the Reformed fold even more subtle distinctions were being made between strict particular redemptionists and those who
desired a more nuanced and universal framework for the work of Christ.[3] We

1. John Preston from his deathbed (Thomas Ball, "The Life of Doctor Preston" in *A
generall Martyrologie, containing a Collection of all the greatest Persecutions which have befallen
the Church of Christ from the Creation to our present Times*, ed. Samuel Clarke [London: A. M.
for Thomas Underhill and John Rothwell, 1651], 473-520, p. 520).

2. John Preston, *The Breast-plate*, I:152; John Preston, *Sermons preached before His
Majestie*, p. 135; Preston, *The Breast-plate*, II:4; John Preston, *Riches of Mercy*, p. 151; cf. John Preston, *Saints Qualification*, I:187.

3. Peter White states that "[a]t perhaps no point were the tensions within international

have already seen how the writings of Boughton and Veninga display considerable confusion over Preston's predestinarian thought. With regard to these subtle distinctions concerning the death of Christ, other scholars have similarly tended to obscure the real Preston from view, as will now be shown.

It was Kendall who considerably popularised certain implications of the claim that John Calvin, as a dynamic theologian of the humanist school, was a universal redemptionist, whereas his scholastic successor at Geneva, Theodore Beza, and through him Perkins in England, were particular redemptionists.[4] That Beza and Perkins were proponents of particular redemption is beyond question. That Calvin was a universal redemptionist is highly controversial and has been debated on and off for centuries.[5] In light of this fact, and in view of Kendall's claim that the whole of Puritanism after 1600 was an

---

Calvinism more acute than on the extent of the Atonement" (Peter White, *Predestination, Policy and Polemic: Conflict and Consensus in the English Church from the Reformation to the Civil War* [Cambridge: Cambridge University Press, 1992], p. 187).

4. For a brief, classic statement of the 'Calvin versus the Calvinists' school, see Basil Hall, "Calvin against the Calvinists" in *John Calvin*, ed. Gervase E. Duffield (Abingdon, UK: Sutton Courtenay Press, 1966), pp. 19-37. One of the most influential books to promote this theory was Brian G. Armstrong, *Calvinism and the Amyraut Heresy: Protestant Scholasticism and Humanism in Seventeenth-Century France* (Madison, WI: University of Wisconsin Press, 1969).

5. For a selection of modern examples arguing that he was, see Armstrong, *Calvinism and the Amyraut Heresy;* James William Anderson, "The Grace of God and the Non-elect in Calvin's Commentaries and Sermons" (Th.D. Dissertation, New Orleans Baptist Theological Seminary, 1976); Stephen A. Strehle, "The Extent of the Atonement within the Theological Systems of the Sixteenth and Seventeenth Centuries" (Th.D. Dissertation, Dallas Theological Seminary, 1980); Curt D. Daniel, "Hyper-Calvinism and John Gill" (Ph.D. Dissertation, University of Edinburgh, 1983); M. Charles Bell, "Calvin and the Extent of the Atonement," *EQ* 55 (1983): 115-23; M. Charles Bell, *Calvin and Scottish Theology: The Doctrine of Assurance* (Edinburgh: Handsel Press, 1985), pp. 13-40; Kevin D. Kennedy, "Union with Christ as Key to John Calvin's Understanding of the Extent of the Atonement" (Ph.D. Dissertation, Southern Baptist Theological Seminary, 1999); and that he was not, see Roger Nicole, "Moyse Amyraut (1596-1664) and the Controversy on Universal Grace, First Phase (1634-1637)" (Ph.D. Dissertation, Harvard University, 1966); Roger Nicole, "John Calvin's View of the Extent of the Atonement," *WTJ* 47 (1985): 197-225; Richard A. Muller, *Christ and the Decree: Christology and Predestination in Reformed Theology from Calvin to Perkins*, Revised ed. (Grand Rapids, MI: Baker Book House, 1988); Jonathan H. Rainbow, *The Will of God and the Cross: An Historical and Theological Study of John Calvin's Doctrine of Limited Redemption* (Allison Park, PA: Pickwick Publications, 1990); Paul Helm, *Calvin and the Calvinists* (Edinburgh: Banner of Truth Trust, 1998). For studies that take a mediating position see Robert A. Peterson, *Calvin's Doctrine of the Atonement* (Phillipsburg, NJ: Presbyterian and Reformed Publishing Co., 1983); Hans Boersma, "Calvin and the Extent of the Atonement," *EQ* 64 (1992): 333-55; G. Michael Thomas, *The Extent of the Atonement: A Dilemma for Reformed Theology from Calvin to the Consensus* (Carlisle, UK: Paternoster Press, 1997); G. Michael Thomas, "Calvin and English Calvinism: A Review Article," *SBET* 16 (1998): 111-27.

essential extension of Perkins in distinction from Calvin, and its supposed source, the exact position of Preston on this issue comes to be of considerable interest.

It has usually been the case that the works of Preston have been quoted as coming from a typical Reformed Puritan or experimental predestinarian who of necessity held to a doctrine of particular redemption in the manner of his predecessors such as Perkins. However, modern treatments of Preston's theology have never attempted to demonstrate this assumption. Kendall goes so far as to claim that "Preston's works as a whole show him clearly to have embraced the thinking of that already seen in the more fully developed experimental predestinarian tradition."[6] By this Kendall is predominantly referring to the tradition of Perkins.[7] David Parnham has more recently contrasted the "Calvinism" of Perkins and Preston with that of Sir Henry Vane, who, among other aberrations from "the heavily fortified conventions of orthodox federal theology," actually "asserted the universality of the atonement."[8]

Yet Preston had an earlier reputation of being a hypothetical universalist. Baxter, a famous near contemporary of Preston's, repeatedly cited Preston in support of his own brand of universal redemptionism.[9] The only Baxter

6. R. T. Kendall, *Calvin and English Calvinism to 1649*, 2nd ed. (Carlisle, UK: Paternoster Press, 1997), p. 118; cf. White, *Predestination, Policy and Polemic*, p. 230.

7. Kendall insists that the "experimental predestinarian tradition may also be called the Beza-Perkins tradition" (R. T. Kendall, "The Nature of Saving Faith from William Perkins [d.1602] to the Westminster Assembly [1643-1649]" [D.Phil. Dissertation, University of Oxford, 1976], pi). I am grateful to Dr Kendall for especially waiving the thirty-year prohibition of access to this thesis in the Bodleian, so that I could consult the preface and introduction that are not found in the published editions.

8. David Parnham, *Sir Henry Vane, Theologian: A Study in Seventeenth-Century Religious and Political Discourse* (Cranbury, NJ: Associated University Presses, 1997), p. 264. Other recent treatments of Preston that suffer from a lack of awareness of Preston's hypothetical universalism include Paul R. Schaefer Jr., "The Spiritual Brotherhood on the Habits of the Heart: Cambridge Protestants and the Doctrine of Sanctification from William Perkins to Thomas Shepard" (D.Phil. Dissertation, University of Oxford, 1994), pp. 203-4; John von Rohr, *The Covenant of Grace in Puritan Thought* (Atlanta, GA: Scholars Press, 1986), p. 129; and Yong Jae Timothy Song, *Theology and Piety in the Reformed Federal Thought of William Perkins and John Preston* (Lewiston, NY: Edwin Mellen Press, 1998), *passim* but especially pp. 175-77, 198-212, 232, 234. Not only is Song comparing the theological systems of Preston and Perkins, but he is even comparing Preston with Perkins on the nature of the gospel call, and expunges the crucial phrase "Christ is dead for him" from his consideration of Preston's position (Song, *Theology and Piety*, p. 200). For why this phrase cannot be thus ignored, see below, pp. 116-24.

9. E.g., Richard Baxter, *Plain Scripture Proof of Infants Church-membership and Baptism* (London: For Robert White, 1651), p. 275; Richard Baxter, *Richard Baxter's Apology against the modest Exceptions of Mr T. Blake. And the Digression of Mr G. Kendall* (London: T. Underhill and Francis Tyton for Jos. Nevil and Jos. Barbar, 1654), II:71; Richard Baxter, *Certain Disputations of*

reference in Kendall's bibliography is Baxter's autobiography. Yet even this posthumously published book contains claims to the effect that Preston was a universal redemptionist.[10] By 1657 Baxter's authority for this claim was Ball's biography. It is unlikely that Baxter was referring to Ball's manuscript, as Reformed church historian David Lachman claims, but to the first printed edition of 1651.[11] It was possibly on the basis of Baxter's testimony that Peter Toon in 1967 cited Preston as a universal redemptionist. Norman Douty in a popular and polemical treatment of the extent of Christ's satisfaction had also claimed in 1972 that Preston was a universal redemptionist.[12] In view of

---

Right to Sacraments and the true Nature of Visible Christianity (London: William Du-Gard for Nevil Simmons, 1657), pp. B2v, C2r; Richard Baxter, *Richard Baxter's Catholick Theologie: Plain, pure, peaceable: For Pacification of the dogmatical Word-Warriors* (London: Robert White for Nevill Simmons, 1675), IV:50, 52; Richard Baxter, *Universal Redemption of Mankind, by the Lord Jesus Christ* (London: For John Salusbury, 1694), p. 480. Baxter was profoundly influenced by Preston's writings and thoroughly recommended them (Richard Baxter, *Aphorismes of Justification* [The Hague: Abraham Brown, 1655], pp. 283-88; Richard Baxter, *The Saints Everlasting Rest: Or, a Treatise of the blessed State of the Saints in their enjoyment of God in Glory* [London: Robert White for Thomas Underhil & Francis Tyton, 1650], p. A3v; Richard Baxter, *A Christian Directory: Or, a Summ of practical Theologie, and Cases of Conscience* [London: Robert White, for Nevill Simmons, 1673], I:60, 581, 922, 924; Richard Baxter, *A Treatise of justifying Righteousness, in two Books* [London: For Nevil Simons and Jonathan Robinson, 1676], II:47, 84; *CCRB*, I:405, II:57). For a recent study of Baxter's doctrine of universal redemption, see Hans Boersma, *A Hot Pepper Corn: Richard Baxter's Doctrine of Justification in Its Seventeenth-Century Context of Controversy* (Zoetermeer: Uitgeverij Boekencentrum, 1993), pp. 195-220.

10. Richard Baxter, *Reliquiae Baxterianae: Or, Mr Richard Baxter's Narrative of the most memorable Passages of his Life and Times*, ed. Matthew Sylvester (London: For T. Parkhurst, J. Robinson, J. Lawrence and J. Dunton, 1696), I:206. For more on this testimony see below, p. 174.

11. David C. Lachman, *The Marrow Controversy 1718-1723: An Historical and Theological Analysis* (Edinburgh: Rutherford House Books, 1988), p. 25; see above, p. 3. This would be consistent with the fact that Preston is missing from Baxter's list of universal redemptionists in 1650 (Baxter, *The Saints Everlasting Rest*, p. A4v). Lachman's idea is not impossible, however, for Baxter was Clarke's close friend, and wrote the preface to another compilation of *Lives* in the year of Clarke's death (*ODNB*; Samuel Clarke, *The Lives of sundry eminent Persons in this later Age* [London: For Thomas Simmons, 1683]).

12. Peter Toon, *The Emergence of Hyper-Calvinism in English Nonconformity 1689-1765* (London: The Olive Tree, 1967), p. 23; Norman F. Douty, *The Death of Christ: A Treatise which answers the Question: 'Did Christ die only for the Elect?'* (Swengal, PA: Reiner Publications, 1972), pp. 101-2; cf. Norman F. Douty, *Did Christ die only for the Elect? A Treatise on the Extent of Christ's Atonement*, 2nd ed. (Eugene, OR: Wipf & Stock Publishers, 1998), p. 145. Douty quotes Preston, *The Breast-plate*, I:8-9 as his proof — a passage examined at length below, pp. 116-24. Given that Toon wrote the preface to the first edition of Douty's work, having reviewed a first draft (Douty, *Did Christ Die Only for the Elect?*, p. 173), it could be that Toon was also thinking of *The Breast-plate* and supplied Douty with this reference. Postdating Kendall's work, Curt Daniel

this earlier perception that Preston was a universal redemptionist, Kendall's use of him as an example of how distorted a theologian's doctrine becomes when he departs from Calvin's (alleged) doctrine of universal redemption, is decidedly curious.[13]

On the other hand, Lachman, writing in the Reformed tradition, has sought to prevent Preston from being charged with being something less than Kendall's faithful follower of Perkins. Lachman acknowledges that "there is . . . some question as to the position of . . . Preston in regard to the extent of the atonement," but considers it "an open question for further research." He insists that although some manuscript evidence "would seem to indicate that Preston endorsed the position of Calvinistic universalists, in the absence of any positive evidence to the same effect in his published writings, the question must be left open." It is now time to produce such positive evidence and close this question. In the next two chapters Preston's works will be examined in order to see what exactly, according to Preston, is involved in "the punishment of Christ our Surety."[14]

The Particularity of the Atonement

In his *opera* Preston never explicitly states that Christ died 'for the elect.' Nowhere is there a 'Perkinsian' treatment of classic universalist texts involving 'all' or the 'world.' However, Preston does not hesitate to take up scriptural imagery of particular grace with regard to the death of Christ, and he does sometimes employ terminology associated with particular redemptionist formulations. Christ came "to take away the sinnes of his people; hee came to take away sinnes of all sorts."[15] Christ "hath purchased his Wife with his owne bloud," and "such a relation there is between Christ and us," as "between the

---

cited Preston as a universal redemptionist, but without documentation, despite his claim that Preston among others "made a specific point of emphasizing [his] rejection of limited atonement" (Daniel, "Hyper-Calvinism and John Gill," p. 735).

13. On 26th March, 1974, Kendall consulted Packer's thesis on Baxter and also overlooked Packer's quotation of Baxter's preface regarding Preston's universal redemptionism (James I. Packer, "The Redemption and Restoration of Man in the Thought of Richard Baxter: A Study in Puritan Theology" [D.Phil. Dissertation, University of Oxford, 1954], p. 225, flyleaf of the Bodleian copy).

14. Lachman, *The Marrow Controversy*, pp. 25, 27; Preston, *Saints Qualification*, I:118. More recently Michael Thomas has echoed Lachman's uncertainty, stating that Preston was "possibly" a universal redemptionist (Thomas, "Calvin and English Calvinism: A Review Article," p. 126).

15. Preston, *The Breast-plate*, I:248.

Shepherd and the Sheep; the Shepherd that gives his life for the sheep, and the sheep that are redeemed."[16] Preston also taught that

> as in the time of the Law, the Priest was to offer up sacrifices for the people in all humilitie, so Christ in the Gospell on the Crosse with a broken and a contrite spirit, offered a sacrifice for all his children, and makes them acceptable unto God.[17]

When Preston expounds 1 Corinthians 1:30 he curiously feels the need to include in the word 'redemption' deliverance from all and every trouble in this life. He says that "any evill, though it be but a small evill, a small disease, a little trouble" from which we are delivered is to be seen in terms of Christ's redemption, for "it is Christ that redeemes us from the least evill, as well as from hell it selfe." Immediately he is faced with a problem, since the wicked also experience deliverances and recoveries from sickness. Yet Preston will not withdraw his statement: "It is true indeed, there are some general workes of Gods providence that all men taste of; but there is no evill that the Saints are freed from, but it is purchased by the blood of Christ."[18] Here Preston clearly suggests that though the wicked know deliverances from tribulation and sickness in this life, this cannot be linked with Christ's death in the way that the saints' deliverances in this world can — if it can be linked at all.

As well as describing Christ's death in terms of its relation to the Church, Preston is also to be found relating it to the conditions of those individuals to whom his preaching comes. In a manner very characteristic of particular redemptionists, Preston sometimes linked Christ's satisfaction only with those who are convicted of their need of its benefits. Thus, Christ is styled as "a Saviour offered up for all that are wounded for sinne." Furthermore, in one sense at least, Christ died only for such. For "none are Christ's souldiers, or those whom he came to redeeme, but such as are described" in Isaiah 61:1-3. These verses of Isaiah speak specifically and only of "the meek," "the brokenhearted," "the captives," "them that are bound" and "all that mourn . . . in Zion." These are clear references to the elect under conviction of sin, and it is only these, according to Preston in this place, that Christ, in this sense, came to redeem.[19]

It is more characteristic of Preston, however, to emphasise that Christ died 'for believers.' He was thus able to escape the issue of the extent of the

---

16. Preston, *The Breast-plate*, II:142; John Preston, *The mysticall Match*, p. 14.

17. John Preston, *Remaines*, p. 237.

18. Preston, *The Breast-plate*, I:39; cf. Preston, *Riches of Mercy*, p. 210.

19. John Preston, *A liveles Life*, I:61; John Preston, *Saints Submission*, p. 276.

atonement and stress in a pastoral manner the necessity of faith on the part of his hearers. On the cross "the Lord Jesus out of his love and free favour, undertakes for the poor believer, and payes his debt."[20] His death, resurrection, and ascension were therefore "for the poor believing soul, and he had not done it but for him." Again, Preston paraphrased Christ's words to Paul on the road to Damascus as, "I am Jesus that was crucified for thee, I am Jesus that gave my body for thee, and as many as receive me." Similarly, in response to the affirmation of Hebrews 9:28 that "Christ was once offered to bear the sins of many," Preston merges this statement with the second part of the verse which reads, "and to them that look for him he shall appear the second time without sin to salvation." As a result he can ask, "For whom was hee offered? . . . To as many as looke for his comming againe."[21] Thus in Preston's systematic theology Christ died in a special manner for the elect. In Preston's surviving articulation of that theology, however, this is never stated explicitly but is always ambiguously expressed as Christ having died for believers.

The Efficacy of the Atonement

We have seen that Preston allowed for a special design of Christ's death. But on what grounds, if any, should Christ's satisfaction be for the reprobate in a broader sense? The bulwark of the Elizabethan particular redemptionist position was the effectual nature of Christ's satisfaction. That is to say, that the death of Christ actually achieves, rather than merely makes possible, the salvation of sinners. By this definition, satisfaction not only need not, but cannot have a reference to the reprobate who are in no way redeemed by the blood of Christ. Overtones of the Reformed language of efficacy are to be found in Preston's works, yet it will be seen that it is a relatively weak theme.

In broad terms Preston taught that Christ could never fail of his intent. For "whatsoever the Lords end is, he never failes of."[22] Because the Father "is not willing to have his Sonnes bloud spilt in vain,"[23] there must be an efficacy to Christ's satisfaction, at least on one level or for some people. This teaching occasionally filtered down into Preston's presentation of the death of Christ itself. Generally speaking, the "effect of the blood of Christ" is "grace."[24] This

20. Preston, *Riches of Mercy*, p. 148; cf. p. 147.
21. Preston, *Riches of Mercy*, p. 151; Preston, *Saints Qualification*, III:41; Preston, *The Breast-plate*, II:68.
22. Preston, *Saints Qualification*, II:20.
23. John Preston, *The golden Scepter*, I:275.
24. Preston, *Riches of Mercy*, p. 189.

includes the effectual procurement of the forgiveness of sins. Without sins actually being forgiven "the cross of Christ had beene of none effect, and his mediation of no use." Therefore just as "no man will doe any thing, especially so great a matter as to kill himselfe for no end," so Christ "dyed for the forgiveness of sins."[25] Thus Preston could tell his people that "the blood of Christ is more effectuall to rench thy conscience, and to purge it from dead workes, to take away, both the guilt of sinne, and likewise the power, and staine of it."[26] The forgiven sinner is then effectually made zealous in the cause of Christ. Because "Christ came to redeem them for this end that they might be zealous," and "Christ will not lose his end," then "they that Christ will save shall be zealous."[27]

Thus in Pauline fashion and with echoes of Perkins' *A golden Chaine*, Preston saw the fruits of an applied atonement forming an irresistible chain. Because "the vertue of his death is never disjoyned from the merit of his death," it follows, for example, that "where ever he forgives sin, he cures sinne." That is to say, that where God justifies he also always sanctifies.[28] It would appear, however, that a key question concerning Preston's theology is the cause of the application of Christ's satisfaction. Sanctification might well irresistibly follow justification, but what causes the initial justification? What exactly secures the "sprinkling of the bloud on the doore-posts of thy soule"?[29] Is it the fruit of the very death of Christ itself, covenantally understood, or does it stem from a propitiation whose application stems from another disconnected source?

The echoes of Perkins' *A golden Chaine* in Preston are soon muffled when it becomes clear that for Preston this irresistible chain is not to be grounded in the death of Christ itself but only in the intercession of Christ in the light of this general satisfaction. In an important but neglected collection of Preston's sermons entitled *Riches of Mercy,* Preston explicitly limited the intercession of Christ to the elect and grounded the efficacy of Christ's death in this intercession alone, and emphatically not in redemption itself. Preston insisted that "the intercession and prayer of Christ doth not fall upon his death, to make that belong to some and not to others." He implies therefore that the death of Christ belongs, at least in one sense, equally to all without exception. Furthermore he explicitly repudiates the notion that "the death of Christ belongeth to such only as he made intercession for." Christ's sacerdotal

25. John Preston, *The Law*, p. 14.
26. John Preston, *Saints daily Exercise*, p. 130.
27. Preston, *Riches of Mercy*, p. 90; cf. Preston, *Remaines*, II:138.
28. Preston, *Saints Qualification*, II:88; cf. II:93.
29. Preston, *Saints Qualification*, III:51.

prayer of John 17 is, however, a prayer for the elect only: "I pray for them, I pray not for the rest that belong not to my election." The prayer therefore "falleth upon the persons to whom his death is effectual." Indeed, wherever Christ's intercession is found in Scripture "it falleth not on the act of his redemption, but on such to whom his death is made effectual."[30] Preston denies that limited intercession should make the death of Christ "belong to some and not to others, for that is not mentioned in the intercession."[31] Preston therefore drives a significant wedge between the twofold high-priestly work of Christ as atonement-maker and intercessor. The effectual source of the 'golden chain' is not Christ's satisfaction itself, but an almost separate work of Christ, namely his intercession. The extent of the former can be totally different from that of the latter. Christ as High Priest makes satisfaction for all without exception, but Christ as High Priest makes intercession only for the elect. It would appear that the decree of election can be removed almost altogether from propitiation and lodged solely in the limited and discriminating intercession of Christ.

This might seem like an unnatural tension between the twofold ministry of Christ as priest, especially in the theology of a federalist. Although it enabled Preston to attain to a measure of consistency within a hypothetical universalist framework, it seems that on occasions he was unable to maintain such a sharp division between Christ's satisfaction and intercession. In Luke

30. It should be conceded that Perkins, on the basis of John 17:9, notes that "Christ makes no intercession for the world," and concludes that "therefore his redemption is not effectuall to al men, For the intercession is the meanes of applying the satisfaction" (William Perkins, *The Workes of that famous and worthy Minister of Christ in the Universitie of Cambridge, Mr. William Perkins* [London: John Legatt & Cantrell Legge, 1616-18], I:296). Taken in isolation it might appear that here Perkins too limits a universally sufficient satisfaction by a limited intercession that makes this satisfaction effectual. However, from Perkins' writings as a whole, it is indisputable that in Perkins' theology the intercession of Christ is limited because it follows on from a limited satisfaction. It is not limited only because it follows on from a decree to apply a universal satisfaction in a particular manner, as Preston teaches here.

31. Preston, *Riches of Mercy*, pp. 425-26. That Preston avoided portraying Christ's satisfaction as being also limited in extent like the intercession of Christ seems to be reflected in his systematic formulation of the threefold mediatorial office of Christ as found in the *Summe*. Christ is appointed "to be a mediatore betwixte God & us," and this general office of mediator consists of three parts: "a kinge a prophet a prieste." Christ is a king to "exalte his Church," a prophet "to teach his Church," and a priest "to make atonement" (Preston, *Summe*, f. 3). The words "for his Church" are conspicuous by their absence in the treatment of Christ's third office, where a literary parallelism would be expected. This literary parallelism is not lacking in Perkins' statement on the same theme: Christ is "a King, a Priest, and a Prophet: a King to gather & withall to governe his Church and people: a Priest, to make satisfaction & intercession for the sinnes of the elect: a Prophet to reveale & teach his people the will of God his father" (Perkins, *Workes*, I:169).

22:32 Christ says to Peter that he has prayed for him "that his faith fail not." Preston says that this intercessory ministry of Christ for Peter "is a privilege Christ hath purchased for every believing soul."[32] But if this is so then redemption purchases and causes the intercession of Christ. On Preston's own admission the intercession is limited to the elect and secures every believer's perseverance. The satisfaction as well as the intercession of Christ must therefore be, in some sense at least, limited.

Elsewhere Preston also closely links the propitiatory and intercessory ministries of Christ, even implying that atonement and intercession are a continuous process: "We fall into sinne from day to day; but, if we knew really what it is to have Christ an Intercessour, to have him our Priest, to make atonement for our sinnes every day, we should learne to prize him more." The concept of a continuing atonement is also found, surprisingly, in Preston's sacramental theology. In a manner almost resembling his Papist foes, Preston states that when "we come to the Sacrament, there is a reconciliation, an atonement to be made in a speciall manner."[33] It should be noted, however, that, according to Preston, Christ makes atonement "by satisfaction & intercession." His inclusion of intercession within the concept of atonement he understood in the following way. Christ's "satisfaction" was his "suffering" and "righteousnes & conformity to Gods will in his nature and actions," whereas his intercession consists in "offering up a sacrifice in offeringe up prayers & that presently when he died, continually to this daye."[34] Despite all this, when it came to the extent of this atonement, Preston was happy to divide the priestly work of Christ into two works with differing objects.

Thus it would appear that when Preston speaks of the death of Christ not failing in its purpose, he does not mean that the death of Christ in itself is effectual, but that together with the intercession of Christ it becomes effectual for those to whom it is destined to be applied. As an event in history, it facilitated a certain and definite outcome, which it did not necessitate. Clearly this distinction allowed Preston to hold to a universal extent of Christ's satisfaction while preserving something of the particularity of his Reformed heritage by strictly limiting the intercession of Christ to the elect.

It might seem surprising that with such an explicit treatment of the extent of Christ's satisfaction in relation to the limited extent of Christ's intercession it has remained doubtful for so long in modern scholarship as to whether Preston was in fact a hypothetical universalist. However, when in

---

32. Preston, *Riches of Mercy,* p. 158.

33. Preston, *Saints Qualification,* II:183-84; I:61.

34. Preston, *Summe,* f. 3.

1651, 1654, and 1657 Baxter went into print claiming Preston as support for his own universal redemptionism,[35] not all Preston's works had yet been published. If they had been, then perhaps Baxter would also have quoted as his authority the above section of Preston's *Riches of Mercy,* which went through two editions in 1658. But by 1675 Baxter was in the habit of citing Ball's *Life* as his published authority and perhaps was unaware of Preston's latest book.[36] The result of this seems to be that Preston's *Riches of Mercy* has been entirely overlooked by scholars as source material for Preston's theology.[37] Indeed, this last compilation of sermons by Preston to be published in the seventeenth century was not deemed worthy of treatment by Kendall, who asserted that this book did not "seem useful to list" as it contained "no theological variance."[38]

35. See above, pp. 96-97.

36. It does not appear listed in Baxter's library catalogue (Geoffrey F. Nuttall, "A Transcript of Richard Baxter's Library Catalogue: A bibliographical note," *JEH* 2 & 3 [1952]: 207-21 & 74-100). Alternatively, this may possibly have been one of many testimonies for universal redemption that Baxter claimed he threw away when Daillé's work was published (Baxter, *Universal Redemption,* p. 480). However, this is unlikely, since Daillé's *Apologia pro duabus Ecclesiarum in Gallia Protestantium Synodis Nationalibus,* to which Baxter is referring, appeared in 1655 (Amsterdam: Joannis Ravesteynii), and Baxter in all probability would therefore have seen it before 1658. There has been some confusion over which of Daillé's books is cited in this particular place, but Boersma has settled the matter in favour of Daillé's *Apologia* of 1655 (Boersma, *A Hot Pepper Corn,* pp. 336-37).

Initially, before coming to rest his case on Ball's account of Preston, Baxter cited Preston, *The Breast-plate,* I:8-10 for evidence of his universal redemption. See below, pp. 116-24, for a detailed treatment of this important passage. But Baxter does not appear to cite it again, possibly because he finds the account of Preston at York House more compelling. For more on this account, see Ch. 6.

37. I am aware of only four modern scholars who have quoted from this volume, but even then, they almost always quote from Preston's homiletical treatise *A Patterne of Wholesome Words* and not from the other sermons. See Perry Miller, *The New England Mind: The Seventeenth Century* (Cambridge, MA: Harvard University Press, 1954), pp. 202-3; Christopher Hill, *Puritanism and Revolution: Studies in Interpretation of the English Revolution of the Seventeenth Century* (London: Secker & Warburg, 1958), pp. 269, 270, 272; Christopher Hill, *Society and Puritanism in Pre-Revolutionary England* (London: Secker & Warburg, 1964), p. 46; Irvonwy Morgan, *Puritan Spirituality: Illustrated from the life and times of the Rev. Dr. John Preston* (London: Epworth Press, 1973), pp. 11-16; Everett H. Emerson, *English Puritanism from John Hooper to John Milton,* 1st ed. (Durham, NC: Duke University Press, 1968), p. 45. The Emerson quotation is unattributed but comes from Preston, *Riches of Mercy,* p. 320. One exception is Morgan, *Puritan Spirituality,* p. 93. For more on the background of Preston's *Riches of Mercy* see below, p. 239.

38. Kendall, *Calvin and English Calvinism,* p. 118. Perhaps Kendall was relying on the reported approbation of Sibbes, himself a particular redemptionist (Richard Sibbes, *The Complete Works of Richard Sibbes,* ed. Alexander B. Grosart [Edinburgh: James Nichol, 1862-64], II:179;

The Sufficiency of the Atonement

In the light of this it is not surprising to find Preston repeatedly stressing that in a very real sense Christ's atoning work was sufficient to redeem the whole world head for head. Christ *could* save the whole world, but if men do not receive him, he will not save them. Commenting on John 3:16 Preston asserted that "there is a sufficiencie in Christ to save all men, and he is that great Physician that heales the soules of men; there is righteousnesse enough in him to justifie all the world."[39] Such a sufficient atonement is made available to all in the gospel, and so Preston could proclaim to his congregation that "the sprinkling of the bloud of Christ thus offered is sufficient to cleanse your consciences."[40] Preston could speak in these terms of the universal sufficiency of Christ's atoning work against his background teaching that there is an infinite fullness in Christ ready to be tapped by those who believe in him. Christ is "full of love, full of patience, full of tender compassion which may invite us to come to him." Not only was Christ "ful as a Priest, full of favour with God," but still he is "alwais full of Compassion to man" and "full of merit." Because of this he is "ready to entertaine any suits or Suitors" and "sure to prevaile in all his receipts and Intercessions." Consequently sinners are to reason thus:

> though there be a fulnesse of sin and guilt in us, yet is there a fulnesse of Grace in him able to remove it, and take it away. A fulnes of mercy to receive our Supplications, a fulnes of merit to make an Attonement for our foulest sins: a fulnes of Favour to prevaile with his Father in any requests.[41]

While the infinite intrinsic sufficiency of Christ's satisfaction is quite consistent with a particular redemptionist schema, Preston argued for the sufficiency of the atonement in a distinct way. The superabundance Preston saw in the atonement stemmed from the following syllogism:

1. The price Christ paid for sin is of infinite value.
2. Even the most wicked of sins are still finite in scope.
3. Therefore no one can say they have committed sins greater than the price Christ paid for them.

V:345, 385-408, 516-17; cf. Mark E. Dever, *Richard Sibbes: Puritanism and Calvinism in Late Elizabethan and Early Stuart England* [Macon, GA: Mercer University Press, 2000], pp. 105-6). See below, p. 239.

39. Preston, *The Breast-plate*, I:43; cf. Preston, *Riches of Mercy*, p. 423.
40. Preston, *The golden Scepter*, I:261.
41. John Preston, *Plenitudo Fontis*, pp. 2, 7.

Preston could therefore reason thus with those in his congregation: "If thy sinnes be exceeding great and many, yet they are not Infinite, that is, they doe not exceed the price payed for them. But God is infinite in mercy, and therefore exceeds all thy sinnes."[42] To those who would object that God could not forgive us "exceeding great" sins, Preston asserted that there is no sin God cannot forgive due to

> the price which was payed and which no sin can goe beyond, indeed if Christ had payed but a finite pryce, we feare that our sins should not be forgiven, if a man were in debt two thousand pound and there were one payd, he might be discouraged, but when there is infinitely more payed than the debt is, this should make us believe our sins are forgiven us whatsoever they be, seeing they be all but finit.[43]

Clearly Preston did not consider Christ's payment of a debt in a strictly quantitative way. Perkins had taught that sin cannot be seen as finite in scope since a sin committed against an infinitely holy God is therefore infinitely wicked.[44] No sin can be little or less than infinite, since there is no little or less than infinite God to sin against. Within such a framework a quantitative approach to Christ's payment for sin is still possible. A satisfaction of infinite value is no more than infinite sins require and so Christ's satisfaction precisely meets the needs of sinners. However, we have seen how Preston saw sin as finite in scope and Christ's atoning work of infinite value. This meant that to tie the atonement-concept to the particular sins of particular people was an unnecessary and irrelevant consideration, failing to appreciate the infinite fullness of Christ's atoning work. There is no formal reciprocity between the debt incurred by sin and the price paid for sin. Thus Preston's congregation was told that

> the price that was paid answers for the greatest sinnes as well as the least; he is readie to forgive a thousand pound upon satisfaction as well as ten groats: and therefore if thou hast Christ for thy ransome, it is no matter what thy sinnes have beene, great or small, for the same price may as well stand for the one as for the other.[45]

---

42. Preston, *Remaines*, pp. 293-94; cf. p. 208. Perkins would have disagreed with Preston's second premise (Perkins, *Workes*, I:159, 173).

43. Preston, *The Law*, p. 15.

44. Perkins, *Workes*, I:159, 173.

45. Preston, *Sermons preached before His Majestie*, p. 135. However, once a universal satisfaction has been applied to a given believer, Preston does indeed betray a sympathy for a dis-

Consequently, in Preston's theology, Christ paid more than was necessary, and can be said to have over-redeemed the world. Preston can therefore speak of "the transcendency of that sufficiency in Christs bloud to cleanse us."[46] This "abondance of sanctification and redemption" consists in the fact that "he hath over-bought us." Preston explains what he means by the following illustration:

> If you should see a flocke of sheepe, and heare that such a man hath paid such a price for them, farre beyond their worth, you will bee ready to say, let him have them, he is well worthy of them. And shall Christ be denied that which he hath so dearely bought?[47]

To all believers Preston can therefore say, "you are his, hee hath bought you, yea he hath over-bought you, he hath paid a price more worth than we, he hath bought us with his bloud."[48] Given that not all men are saved, this super-abounding sufficiency in the atonement hangs as a general and unapplied reality in Preston's theology.

The Inefficacy of the Atonement

We have now seen how Preston's doctrine of the universal sufficiency of the atonement results in a shift in focus from the accomplishment of redemption to "the application of redemption."[49] Redemption is at first only made possible, although for all, and in the case of the reprobate it must therefore remain ineffectual. We would expect to find in Preston's sermons, therefore, the concept of the death of Christ being in vain for such people. Christ dying 'in vain' and the cross of Christ being made 'of none effect' are biblical concepts.[50] However, particular redemptionists such as Perkins did not see in these concepts the meaning that this was what had actually happened or

---

tinctly commercial understanding of Christ's death: "This is the ground of all our comfort . . . hath he not been satisfied and paid for our sinnes, by Christ? and his justice will not suffer him to require a second payment" (Preston, *The golden Scepter*, I:259). Similar commercial imagery is also present in *The Breast-Plate*, where Preston argues that "[i]f a man have an acquittance, although the debt remaine the same in the Booke, yet there can no more be required at the hands of him that hath taken the acquittance" (Preston, *The Breast-plate*, I:52).

46. Preston, *The golden Scepter*, I:261.
47. Preston, *Remaines*, p. 206; John Preston, *Love of Christ*, p. 48.
48. Preston, *The Breast-plate*, II:45.
49. Preston, *Summe*, f. 3; cf. Preston, *Saints Qualification*, I:13.
50. Cf. Galatians 2:21; 1 Corinthians 1:17.

genuinely might happen. Rather they took such texts as being rhetorical devices concerning a hypothetical proposition, employed in order to evoke a concerned response amongst professing believers and to make a point more powerfully.

Preston frequently used the concept of the death of Christ being in vain in this purely rhetorical manner. Christ would hypothetically have died in vain if at least three things did not happen. Firstly, Christ would have died in vain if there had been no universal gospel call. Preston's "first stated reason" for the gospel call is

> because God would not have the death of his Son to be of none effect, he would not have the blood of his Son spilt in vain, . . . so say I, if God did not send out his messengers to beseech and persuade and command men to believe, the death of Christ would be in vain.

Secondly, Preston frequently states how Christ would have died in vain were there to be no conversions. Paul "would not preach with eloquent words, because then he should convert none to Christ and if none be converted to Christ, 'the death of Christ should be in vain and of none effect.'"[51] Thirdly, Christ would have died in vain if the Sacrament did not give believers assurance. If this were to happen then also "the death of Christ should be of none effect."[52] However, seeing as quite evidently there *is* a gospel call, there *are* conversions, and believers *do* come to assurance through the Sacrament, then Christ did not die in vain at all in this respect, and Preston's usage of the concept is purely hypothetical and rhetorical.

However, Preston also took the biblical concept of Christ dying 'in vain' and the cross of Christ being made 'of none effect' and applied them to situations in such a way as to teach that in a very real sense Christ did actually and not merely hypothetically die in vain. In this he differed from the particular redemptionist position on the death of Christ. First of all it can be said that Christ died in vain when believers are not as godly as they ought to be. For example, if they do not pray as they ought Christ has died in vain. Prayer "is a privilege purchased by the blood of Jesus Christ," and "Christ dyed for this end, it cost him the shedding of his blood" that believers might be able to pray. Therefore if we neglect prayer then "so farre as is in you, you cause his

---

51. Preston, *Riches of Mercy,* p. 420; cf. Preston, *The Breast-plate,* I:94, 97; Preston, *The golden Scepter,* I:275; Preston, *The Law,* p. 14; Preston, *Remaines,* p. 297; Preston, *Saints Qualification,* II:162; III:20-21; Preston, *Riches of Mercy,* p. 274. For further treatment of Preston on the gospel call, see Ch. 5.

52. Preston, *Saints Qualification,* III:23.

blood to be shed in vaine: for if you neglect the priviledges gotten by that blood, so farre you neglect the blood, that procured them."[53] Few would deny that believers often neglect the privilege of prayer, and so, according to Preston, Christ in one sense has died in vain. Secondly, Christ died in vain when the call of the gospel is rejected. Preston taught that "when Christ is offered, it is not such an offer as when a man offereth a thing," for then "if it be not taken the party offering loseth nothing." Rather "it is such an offer" that "if it be not received and taken," it is "spilt and lost." Thus it is not like "when a man inviteth another to a feast and he cannot come," for then "the master is at no charge." Rather it is akin to "when the promise is made, and the dinner prepared, and then the guests not to come," for that "is loss." Similarly,

> so it is in this offer of Christ, all is ready Christ is slain, and his blood is poured out, if you do not come and take it, you put away from you the blood of Christ, and so in as much as in you lieth you make the death of Christ of none effect, and so by consequence you shall be guilty of the blood of Christ . . . if you had put God to the loss of silver and gold and precious stones it had been no great loss, but you have put him to the loss of Christ and his blood, so that whosoever refuseth Christ is guilty of the spilling of his most precious blood.[54]

Similarly, concerning "every man that neglects" or "hearkens not to" the "blood of Jesus Christ," Preston can say that this is "to cause the blood of Jesus Christ to be shed in vaine, to trample it underfoot, and to count it a common thing."[55] The important point to grasp is that Preston sees this trampling underfoot of the blood of Christ by reprobates as actually — and not merely hypothetically — making "the death of Christ to be of none effect." It constitutes an example of when the death of Christ "doth no good, when it is not improved for the purpose it was shed for."[56]

This same idea is again reinforced in Preston's teaching that those who reject the gospel call reject the blood that was shed for them. Evidently aware of the Remonstrant charge that the Reformed gospel call must be insincere and hollow, Preston chooses to ground the sincerity of the call in the fact that the blood of Christ was actually shed for some who reject it:

53. Preston, *Saints daily Exercise*, p. 19.
54. Preston, *Riches of Mercy*, pp. 427-28; cf. p. 420.
55. Preston, *Saints Qualification*, I:77.
56. Preston, *The Breast-plate*, I:94. This comment comes in the same series of sermons in which Preston said "Christ is dead for every man," a phrase that will be considered at greater length below, pp. 116-24.

> I say consider this, that if thou refuse [the free offer], it is the greatest sin that thou canst commit: . . . for . . . hee is not a bare suter, but a suter that hath paid deare for his wife; hee hath purchased thee at a deare price, with the shedding of his owne blood: so that if thou wilt not heare his sute, hee looseth not only his labour in suing, but the price that he paid for thee, for the very blood of Jesus Christ shall bee put upon thy score.[57]

Hence to Preston, Christ 'losing the price he paid,' or the shedding in vain of his blood, is not only a hypothetical concept used pastorally in order to evoke a passionate response, but is a present reality — and a very common one at that.

The efficacy of Christ's satisfaction therefore becomes conditional in Preston's theology. Borrowing an old illustration he declares that "the death of Christ is like a medicine, that hath efficacy enough to heal all mankind, if they will apply it, now if men will not take it, and receive it, it is not out of defect in the thing itself, but out of the contempt and stubborness of their own will."[58] Preston wittingly or unwittingly implies here that the death of Christ has done all it can, and now salvation hangs on the individual's response to the evangel. Yet the particular redemptionists taught that in the economy of redemption the propitiatory work of Christ itself (and not just election executed by the intercession of Christ) procures the willingness to believe the gospel, unbelief being one of the very sins covered by that atoning work.[59] But when the preaching of the gospel is constructed in terms of a hypothetical redemption belonging to the reprobate conditionally on terms of its reception, then the individual's response can become the focus of the preaching, and not what Christ has done. Preston could sum up his position by saying that "all the matter is, if we be willing to apply this pardon to our selves."[60]

Since many are unwilling to apply Christ's pardon to themselves, Preston's position ultimately led him to the position that Christ's death does not achieve all for which it was designed. Preston maintained that

> when we peach the Gospell, this is the great Jubile, every man may be free, the Son comes to that end, and it is the end of the Truth to make men free:

57. Preston, *The golden Scepter*, II:34-35.

58. Preston, *Riches of Mercy*, p. 423; cf. Preston, *The Breast-plate*, I:12-13, 43. Preston does not indicate his source for this illustration, but his likely twofold source, namely Prosper and Ussher, is revealed below, p. 177.

59. This concept was expressed in Preston's lifetime in Article 8 of the Second Head of the Canons of Dort (Philip Schaff, ed., *The Creeds of Christendom, with a History and Critical Notes* [Grand Rapids, MI: Baker Books, 1993], III:587).

60. John Preston, *Sinnes Overthrow*, p. 179.

The Son comes to deliver every man out of the Gaole, if he will, but men will not be at liberty, they will be servants still, because they were never humbled.

Therefore Preston saw it as a very real danger that his hearers might miss out on what Christ had actually prepared for them. He urged his congregation that "except . . . you taste how bountifull the Lord is, and what a Feast Christ hath prepared for you; all our labour is to no purpose." Since Preston acknowledges that there are "only a few whose hearts are sprinkled with the bloud of the Lambe,"[61] it would seem that much of Preston's labour was in fact to no purpose, just as Christ's preparation of a feast for many reprobate who never came to eat of it was to no purpose. We have seen therefore from a consideration of the particularity, efficacy, sufficiency, and inefficacy of the atonement that Preston's system gives strong evidence of his being a consistent hypothetical universalist. That Preston did indeed hold Christ's death to be, on one level at least, designed for the reprobate *qua* reprobate becomes even clearer in the context of the gospel call.

61. Preston, *Saints Qualification*, I:20; III:93; I:239.

CHAPTER 5

The Gospel Call

"*If thou doest open thy heart and let him in, he offers his Son to thee to believe in . . . the fair, free, large, and great offer of Grace made in the Gospel.*"[1]

Introduction

The doctrine of the gospel call is intimately connected with formulations of the extent of Christ's satisfaction. This is reflected by the fact that Preston's doctrine of the gospel call has already been touched upon in Chapter 4. Yet the whole doctrine of the universal gospel call in Preston's thought is worthy of deeper consideration, since it not only forms a dominant theme in Preston's theology, but also furnishes us with further evidence of Preston's hypothetical universalism. It will be seen that a universal redemption partly undergirds Preston's formulations of the gospel call, and that the two themes are intimately connected in his mind. Not only are Preston's sermons replete with appeals to the unconverted to come to Christ, but in a number of places Preston recorded his formal reflections on the doctrine of the gospel call, as well as its doctrinal implications for Reformed dogmatics. Nevertheless, he did this with a certain unwillingness, lamenting the fact that the doctrine that "God inviteth man to come" can be made "a point of controversy" rather than "a point of singular and great comfort," which he preferred to make it.[2]

---

1. John Preston, *Riches of Mercy*, p. 177.
2. Preston, *Riches of Mercy*, pp. 419-20.

The Donation of Christ

The call of the gospel in Preston's thought, as we might expect, goes out to all indiscriminately "without all exceptions of persons or sins," and "without having respect to election."[3] Thus "whosoever will, may goe free and be delivered," and it is quite wrong to "interline and restraine" this general pardon.[4] Preston saw this free offer in terms of the donation of Christ. The Great Commission itself could be described in the words, "goe and tell every man under heaven that Christ is offered to him, he is freely given to him by God the Father."[5] Here the donation of Christ is seen in terms of the Father's giving of Christ. This was the first aspect of the donation of Christ in Preston's thought, and he habitually cited Isaiah 9:6 in this connection, often seeing it in terms of giving in marriage, and sometimes in terms of being given in the Lord's Supper.[6] The second aspect of the donation of Christ is Christ's giving of himself.[7]

As for the donation of Christ made by the Father, it was performed to "mankinde, as fallen in Adam" in order to "save [the sonnes of men] from their sinnes."[8] As well as Isaiah 9:6, therefore, Preston also naturally based his concept of the donation of Christ on the famous 'universal' text of John 3:16.[9] This universal donation of Christ parallels a universal donation of the righteousness of God which is "given to every man, there is not a man excepted."[10] The donation of Christ is therefore merely an outward donation, for the reprobate do not in actuality receive Christ's righteousness. Christ is thus "freely given to all, yet God intends him onely to the Elect."[11] Preston explains: "*Giving* is but a Relative, it implies that there is a *receiving* or *taking* required: for when Christ is given, unless he be taken by us, he doth us no

---

3. Preston, *Riches of Mercy,* p. 420; John Preston, *The Breast-plate,* I:8; cf. I:11, 84, 150; II:144; John Preston, *Life eternall,* I:72; John Preston, *Love of Christ,* p. 6; John Preston, *Remaines,* pp. 187, 296; John Preston, *Saints Qualification,* I:19; John Preston, *Sinnes Overthrow,* p. 178; Preston, *Riches of Mercy,* pp. 419, 426. Of course, this does not mean the gospel call actually reaches everybody, or that many respond (Preston, *Love of Christ,* p. 86; Preston, *Saints Qualification,* II:186; Preston, *Riches of Mercy,* p. 423).

4. John Preston, *A liveles Life,* I:73-75; Preston, *The Breast-plate,* I:11.

5. Preston, *The Breast-plate,* I:75; cf. I:9, 13, 48, 74, 100; II:2; Preston, *Love of Christ,* p. 6; Preston, *Saints Qualification,* II:172.

6. Preston, *The Breast-plate,* I:73; II:142; Preston, *Love of Christ,* pp. 6, 65; Preston, *Saints Qualification,* III:24; John Preston, *The mysticall Match,* pp. 15-16.

7. Preston, *Saints Qualification,* II:171.

8. Preston, *Saints Qualification,* III:16.

9. Preston, *The Breast-plate,* I:7, 9, 10, 13, 43, 45.

10. Preston, *The Breast-plate,* I:7.

11. Preston, *The Breast-plate,* I:9.

good, he is not made ours. If a man be willing to give another any thing, unlesse he take it, it is not his."[12] Thus the universal donation does not profit anyone without "the gift of faith" which "is a fruit of election."[13] This is what Preston calls "a mutuall act of giving and receiving." This is not to say that there is no particular aspect to the donation of Christ in Preston's thought. He acknowledges that God "never gives his Son to any, but he gives them the Spirit of his Son too." However, Preston rarely ever speaks of the donation of Christ in particular terms. No sooner has he said that the Father "gives Christ, and freely," and that "to give him, is nothing else, but to make him ours," than he immediately adds, "But to give him is nothing, it is not enough except we take him likewise, for giving and taking are Relatives, remove one, and the other is taken away."[14] The donation of Christ is therefore general and outward and does not in itself guarantee anyone's salvation. This is in stark contrast to Perkins, who saw the donation of Christ in both Isaiah 9:6 and John 3:16 to be to the elect only.[15]

Despite its outward and conditional nature, the donation of Christ in Preston's thought is not to be seen as a cold and formal action, but as flowing forth from a general love of God to all mankind. God

> was willing out of his goodnesse to make Men and Angells, and to provide abundantly for them; and afterwards when all mankind were at one throw lost, and he might have left us, as he left the Angells that fell without any possibility of salvation, out of his φιλανθρωπία, his love to mankind, his love to the nation, he gave his Sonne to redeem us.[16]

Similarly Preston sees God's attitude to fallen humanity as opposed to the fallen angels in terms of "mercy." He urges his hearers to

> be thankful to God . . . for whereas all men might have perished as the Devils did, as the Angels that fell did, yet God hath shewed this mercy to

---

12. Preston, *The Breast-plate*, I:43; cf. Preston, *Saints Qualification*, II:172.

13. Preston, *The Breast-plate*, I:10; cf. Preston, *Love of Christ*, p. 6.

14. Preston, *Saints Qualification*, II:171; Preston, *The Breast-plate*, I:79; Preston, *Saints Qualification*, II:172.

15. William Perkins, *The Workes of that famous and worthy Minister of Christ in the Universitie of Cambridge, Mr. William Perkins* (London: John Legatt & Cantrell Legge, 1616-18), I:187, 296, 298.

16. John Preston, *The golden Scepter*, I:180. With "nation" Preston is playing on Luke 7:5. The Religious Tract Society editors of the 1836 edition truncated this passage, although they did retain in altered form the words "out of his love to mankind he gave his son to redeem us" (John Preston, *The golden Sceptre held forth to the Humble* [London: Religious Tract Society, 1836], p. 155).

mankinde, he hath given them *Secundam Tabulam post naufragium,* and that is this light, which is the thing you have cause to be thankfull for.[17]

A further noticeable feature of this preaching is that it implies that God gave his Son so that we, unlike the angels, would have "the advantage of the possibility of being saved."[18] Such theology echoes frequently throughout Preston's preaching, and this statement is in complete harmony with the schema of hypothetical universalism, although of course not exclusive to it. It might be no exaggeration to say that in Preston's theology, God's free grace is not so much magnified by the distinction between the elect and the reprobate, as in Perkins, but between mankind and the fallen angels. In response to the question "What is this Gospell?" Preston replies that God's "resolution in himselfe to recover mankinde" by "giving his Sonne to them"

> must be manifested to men, therefore he sends his messengers to declare to the sonnes of men, to let them know their estate by nature, and to tell them that he hath given them his Sonne to save them from their sinnes, and to reconcile them to himselfe, to give them title to the kingdome, from the hope of which they were fallen.[19]

Preston moves on to apply this definition of the gospel:

> Consider therefore the greatnesse of Christs love, that he should regard us so much, as to take our Nature, to cloath himselfe with our flesh and bloud, that he might be crucified, in that, I say, this is an extraordinary love: Compare but our condition with the Angels that were fallen, and we shall see the greatnesse of this love: The Angels that were fallen (and we were sunk in the same mire) when God looked downe from heaven, and saw the miserable condition of both, . . . he had compassion on us, but on the Angels he had not compassion: Which difference shewes his liberty, and magnifieth his mercy toward us, as you shall finde in Malachy, the Lord reasoning with Israel, 'Thus have I loved you, and yet you say, Wherein hast thou loved us?' Saith hee, 'Was not Esau Jacobs Brother, and yet Jacob have I loved, and Esau have I hated.' So, I say, the Lord hath loved us, in doing this for us, in giving this body of his to be broken, and his bloud to be shed, he hath loved us, and hated them.[20]

17. Preston, *Saints Qualification,* I:192; cf. Preston, *The Breast-plate,* I:32; Preston, *Riches of Mercy,* p. 430.

18. Preston, *The golden Scepter,* I:180.

19. Preston, *Saints Qualification,* III:16.

20. Preston, *Saints Qualification,* III:39-40; cf. III:21. The reference is to Malachi 1:2, 3.

It would appear from the context that Preston means that God loved fallen humanity and hated the fallen angels. Nevertheless it is seeing the love of God for him in particular that a sinner is first to be moved to come to Christ:

> he sees God exceeding kind and merciful, and willing to put away all his sins, and willing to accept the sincerity of his obedience, though there be not a perfection of obedience. Now he begins to change his opinion, both of God and of all his laws and precepts. When he sees God's kindness towards him, and his compassion and readiness, to forgive him, then his heart begins to relent towards the Lord again, he begins to magnify God's goodness and to condemn himself, he believes those promises, and thence he grows up in love towards God.[21]

Thus the call of the gospel to all without exception flows from "the love of [God's] own heart" and there is no "greater love" than that Christ should "set himselfe out for all to take him, and that freely too." The purpose of the gospel call, therefore, is "to show forth the riches of God's mercy and the abundance of his love to mankind."[22]

Grounded in a Universal Atonement

It follows logically that if what drove Christ to the cross was a love for mankind in general, then Christ was dying for mankind in general. Although it was not Preston's usual practice to ground the universal gospel call in a universal atonement,[23] yet one of the most explicit statements of hypothetical universalism in Preston's work — and certainly the most controversial in a later century[24] — comes in the context of the free offer of the gospel. Mark 16:15 reads, "Go ye into all the world, and preach the gospel to every creature." Preaching at Lincoln's Inn in 1625,[25] Preston calls this "the Charter of God himself," and to the question "What is that?" is able to reply that it means

> Goe and tell every man without exception, that there is good newes for him, Christ is dead for him, and if he will take him, and accept of his

21. John Preston, *The New Covenant*, pp. 339-40; cf. John Preston, *Foure Treatises*, p. 249.

22. Preston, *Riches of Mercy*, p. 177; Preston, *Sinnes Overthrow*, p. 149; Preston, *Riches of Mercy*, p. 420.

23. His preferred emphasis is that "the ground of this offer is the sure Word of God" (Preston, *The Breast-plate*, I:37; cf. Preston, *A liveles Life*, I:73-75).

24. Cf. the great Marrow Controversy in eighteenth-century Scotland.

25. That is to say, after the Synod of Dort, and before the York House Conference.

righteousnesse, he shall have it; restraine it not, but goe and tell every man under Heaven.[26]

It would appear that here is evidence that Preston, in common with all hypothetical universalists, explicitly grounded the universal call of the gospel, at least in part, in a universal aspect to Christ's satisfaction. In this place Preston is teaching that by way of the gospel call the very righteousness of Christ "is given to every man, there is not a man excepted." Christ's "righteousness and salvation" is therefore every man's without exception by virtue of "a conditionall Covenant of Grace, which is common to all."[27] This is the language of hypothetical universalism and was identified as an error by some in Preston's circles, including the particular redemptionist Thomas Goodwin, who had been deeply influenced by Preston and was later to edit some of Preston's sermons for publication.[28]

In 1726, during the great Marrow Controversy in Scotland that revolved partly around a quotation of Preston at this point, Thomas Boston defended "Preston's evangelistic mandate"[29] and argued that it came from a consistent particular redemptionist.[30] Lachman follows Boston's reasoning in this and seeks to prevent Preston from being charged conclusively with hypothetical universalism at this point. Concerning Preston's phrase "Christ is dead for him," Lachman, echoing Boston, has this to say:

> Preston is presenting the gospel offer and makes no reference to the extent of the atonement. In such a context the phrase 'Christ is dead for

---

26. Preston, *The Breast-plate*, I:7-8. This is to be compared with the similar phraseology later on in the same treatise and on the same text, which although not at all in the same way controversial, nevertheless does follow an offer from Preston of Christ's hand in marriage, which he makes to the unregenerate 'outside of the Covenant,' on the basis that "the Son gave himselfe to thee" (Preston, *The Breast-plate*, II:143). There, Preston merely paraphrases Mark 16:15 as "goe tell every man, without exception, whatsoever his sinnes bee, whatsoever his rebellions bee, goe tell him this glad tidings; that is, to preach the Gospell to him, that if hee will come in, I will accept him, he shall be saved" (Preston, *The Breast-plate*, II:144).

27. Preston, *The Breast-plate*, I:7, 32.

28. "There is an Error in Dr Prestons Treatise of faith [i.e., *The Breast-plate*] about the general Offer which Mr Goodin [*sic*] can refute best" (SUL Hartlib MS. 29/3/20a for the year 1635). For Preston's earlier influence on Goodwin, see above, p. 22. For Goodwin's role as editor, see below, p. 230.

29. Curt D. Daniel, "Hyper-Calvinism and John Gill" (Ph.D. Dissertation, University of Edinburgh, 1983), pp. 531-32.

30. Edward Fisher, *The Marrow of Modern Divinity: in two Parts. Part I. The Covenant of Works and the Covenant of Grace. Part II. An Exposition of the Ten Commandments*, ed. Thomas Boston (Philadelphia, PA: Presbyterian Board of Publication, 1910), pp. 127-30.

him' can only be understood as a paraphrase of the gospel offer, that Christ is available to all. There is no ground here for interpreting it as importing the doctrine of universal redemption.[31]

That is to say, Preston is "merely proclaiming a substitutionary atonement with no reference to the identity of those for whom the Saviour died."[32] More recently still, William Philip has followed Lachman in this, claiming that "'Christ is dead for him' is merely a paraphrase of the gospel offer."[33] It must be acknowledged that Preston's 'Christ is dead for him' could be merely expressing what elsewhere he teaches, namely, that to the extent to which Christ is preached to all, in that sense Christ "belongeth to all without exception" in terms of a "general Covenant."[34] That is to say, in terms of a conditional, outward covenant, if any man without exception believes on Christ he shall be saved. However, the examination of Preston's theology of the death of Christ so far would provide no real grounds for limiting the phrase to this less likely interpretation.

Boston quoted other places in *The Breast-plate* in an attempt to demonstrate that Preston was not grounding the gospel call in a universal atonement.[35] Yet another passage that Boston and Lachman might have used in

31. David C. Lachman, *The Marrow Controversy 1718-1723: An Historical and Theological Analysis* (Edinburgh: Rutherford House Books, 1988), p. 27; cf. Archibald A. Hodge, *Outlines of Theology* (Grand Rapids, MI: Eerdmans, 1949), p. 417; Louis Berkhof, *Systematic Theology* (Grand Rapids, MI: Eerdmans, 1953), p. 394. Andrew McGowan and Sinclair Ferguson interpret this expression in the same way (Andrew T. B. McGowan, *The Federal Theology of Thomas Boston* [Carlisle, UK: Paternoster Press, 1997], p. 44).

32. Daniel, "Hyper-Calvinism and John Gill," p. 532 (summarising David C. Lachman, "The Marrow Controversy 1718-1723: An Historical and Theological Analysis" [Ph.D. Dissertation, St Andrew's University, 1979]).

33. William J. U. Philip, "The Marrow and the Dry Bones, Ossified Orthodoxy and the Battle for the Gospel in Eighteenth-Century Scottish Calvinism," *SBET* 15 (1997): 27-37, p. 31. Schaefer and Song also see nothing remarkable in these words (Paul R. Schaefer Jr., "The Spiritual Brotherhood on the Habits of the Heart: Cambridge Protestants and the Doctrine of Sanctification from William Perkins to Thomas Shepard" [D.Phil. Dissertation, University of Oxford, 1994], p. 203; Yong Jae Timothy Song, *Theology and Piety in the Reformed Federal Thought of William Perkins and John Preston* [Lewiston, NY: Edwin Mellen Press, 1998], p. 200).

34. Preston, *Riches of Mercy,* p. 425.

35. Fisher, *The Marrow of Modern Divinity,* p. 128. These three quotations read as follows: "Christ hath provided a righteousnesse and salvation, that is his worke that he hath done already. Now if you will beleeve, and take him upon those termes that he is offered, you shall be saved. This, I say, belongs to all men. This you have thus expressed in the Gospel in many places: 'If you will beleeve, you shall be saved': as it is in Marke 16. 'Goe and preach the Gospel to every creature under Heaven: he that will beleeve shall be saved'" (Preston, *The Breast-plate,* I:32); "you must first have Christ himselfe before you can partake of those benefits by him: and that I

support of their case, but did not, is found in Preston's treatise entitled *A heavenly Treatise of the Divine Love of Christ.* Preston is listing means whereby the sinner can obtain a love for Christ. He then answers various anticipated objections. One of these reads, "But . . . how shall I know that the Lord loves mee and is willing to take mee?" Preston's answer is

> I can say *nothing but this, and that is sufficient, thou hast his generall promise made to all,* Mark 16. Goe preach the Gospel to every creature. There is a generall mandate given to Ministers to preach the promise to all, and why wilt thou make exceptions where God hath made none, and enterline [*sic*] his promises? Wee are commanded to offer Christ to all, every one that will come and drinke of this water of life freely. The offer is generall, though but some imbrace it.[36]

The words "nothing but this, and that is sufficient" might suggest that Preston argued that nothing should be added as a basis for the warrant to believe other than a universally proclaimed promise.[37] However, this and the three

---

take to be the meaning of that in Mar. 16. 'Goe and preach the Gospel to every creature under heaven; He that beleeves and is baptized, shall be saved': that is, he that will beleeve that Jesus Christ is come in flesh, and that he is offered to mankind for a Saviour, and will be baptized, that will give up himselfe to him, that will take his marke upon him" (Preston, *The Breast-plate,* I:46); "Goe and preach the Gospel to every creature: goe and tell every man under heaven that Christ is offered to him, he is freely given to him by God the Father, and there is nothing required of you but that you marry him, nothing but to accept of him: here is a word sure enough if there were nothing else but this" (Preston, *The Breast-plate,* I:75).

36. Preston, *Love of Christ,* p. 65 (emphasis added); cf. Preston, *The Breast-plate,* I:248; Preston, *The golden Scepter,* I:262; Preston, *A liveles Life,* I:76.

37. A full treatment of the warrant to believe as found in Preston's theology is intentionally omitted from this study. Schaefer's recent treatment of Preston adequately clears him and the other members of his 'brotherhood' from the common but simplistic charge of preparationism in this connection. See Schaefer, "The Spiritual Brotherhood," *passim;* Norman Pettit, *The Heart Prepared: Grace and Conversion in Puritan Spiritual Life,* 2nd ed. (Middletown, CT: Wesleyan University Press, 1989), pp. 76-79; Peter H. Lewis, "John Preston (1587-1628): Puritan and Court Chaplain" in *Light from John Bunyan and other Puritans: Being Papers Read at the 1978 Westminster Conference* (London: The Westminster Conference, 1979), pp. 34-52; R. T. Kendall, *Calvin and English Calvinism to 1649,* 2nd ed. (Carlisle, UK: Paternoster Press, 1997), pp. 119-24; cf. below, pp. 127, 129, 236. A good place to start in examining Preston's thought in this connection is Preston's court sermon, *Plenitudo Fontis.* Some of Preston's nineteenth-century editors seem to have winced at his arguably preparationist tendencies. For example, qualifications regarding requisite levels of humility or desire before coming to Christ were expunged by the Religious Tract Society (Preston, *The golden Scepter,* I:262, 273; Preston, *The golden Sceptre held forth to the Humble,* pp. 223, 232). However, in Wesleyan quarters it was felt that Preston presented Christ without sufficient qualifications and did not emphasise preparation for con-

quotations Boston uses which relate to Mark 16:15 do nothing to prove that when Preston *did* employ the words "Christ is dead for him," he was not grounding the gospel call *on that particular occasion* in a universal satisfaction. Boston is able to show that Preston did not *always* explicitly ground the gospel call in a universal satisfaction, but this can hardly be used to prove that he *never* explicitly did so.

The argument that claims Preston is teaching, not that Christ died for all men without exception, but that he *is* dead for (i.e., available to) all men without exception, largely hangs upon the premise that in seventeenth-century English 'Christ is dead for' is distinct from 'Christ died for' and that consequently Preston could not or would not have meant the latter. However, it will now be shown that the line taken by Boston, Lachman, and Philip in order to vindicate Preston from the charge of hypothetical universalism remains unconvincing. Preston once preached a sermon on Romans 8:34 later entitled "The Buckler of a Believer." Romans 8:34 in the Geneva Bible reads:

> Who shall condemne? It is *Christ* which *is dead:* yea, or rather, which is risen againe, who is also at the right hand of God, and maketh request also for us.

The printed version of this sermon is headed with the Genevan text almost *verbatim:*

> Who shall condemn? It is *Christ* that *is dead,* yea rather which is risen again, who is also at the right hand of God, and maketh request also for us.[38]

The words "Christ which is dead" in the Geneva version are a translation of "χριστὸς ὁ ἀποθανών." This is an aorist active participle, that is to say, not a complex past participle but a simple participle standing for a completed action. Preston's Authorised Version renders the significant phrase in Romans 8:34 as follows: "It is *Christ that died,* yea rather that is risen again." That Preston understood this to be the case is indisputably clear from his subsequent exposition of Romans 8:34, where he uses remarkably similar language to that of "Christ is dead for him." Because "the Lord Jesus out of his love and free fa-

---

version enough. Implying, as was claimed, that faith conceptually preceded repentance, Preston's "way of speaking" was "dangerous to the souls of men," and led "to the grossest antinomianism" (John Wesley, ed., *A Christian Library: Consisting of Extracts from and Abridgements of the choicest Pieces of practical Divinity which have been published in the English Tongue,* ed. A. G. Jewitt [London: T. Cordeux for T. Blanshard, 1819-27], V:324-27, 340).

38. Preston, *Riches of Mercy,* p. 143 (emphasis added).

vour" has "undertaken for the poor believer" paying "his debt," Preston echoes the apostle and asks, "Who then can condemn this poor Believer?" Of course the answer is no one can, and Preston explains how this can be the case: "Because *Christ* our Surety *is* not onely *dead for us,* and so hath paid our debt, but also is risen again to make the poor believer more sure, he hath paid the debt."[39] Thus Preston has explained for himself his own use of the phrase "Christ is dead for him." It is synonymous with "Christ died for him"; it means Christ "hath paid his debt"; and it can be freely employed with reference to the elect as well as to "every man without exception."[40]

Nor was Preston being subtle in his use of language, as Boston, Lachman, and Philip have implied. Preston's use of language at this point is in no way idiosyncratic. A reading of the Geneva Bible in comparison with the Authorised Version gives evidence that the phrase 'is dead for' was used in translation to mean 'died for.' First Thessalonians 4:14 in the Geneva Bible reads "if we beleeve that *Jesus is dead,* and is risen." The Authorised Version renders the same verse "if we believe that *Jesus died* and rose again." The Greek translated here 'is dead' or 'died' is ἀπέθανεν, an indicative, active aorist which was translated either way in the sixteenth and seventeenth centuries. The popular use of the English participle as synonymous with the simple past tense is also clear from the Geneva Bible's heading for Isaiah 53. It is stated that Christ "is our righteousnesse" and "*is dead* for our sinnes." Preston freely employed both these Bible translations, and it is unwarranted to suppose he was making the proposed distinction.[41]

Furthermore, the interchangeability of the two phrases is also evident in other theological literature of the period. Even in the context of the extent of Christ's satisfaction, Hugh Ince translated "Christus mortuus est pro omnibus" as both Christ "died for all" and also "is dead for all," evidently without seeking to convey any distinction by the variation in the English rendering.[42] Thomas

39. Preston, *Riches of Mercy,* pp. 148-49 (emphasis added).

40. Preston, *The Breast-plate,* I:8. Interestingly, even if 'is dead for' did mean only 'available for,' the modern Reformed theologian Louis Berkhof still deemed this language to be inconsistent with orthodox Reformed particularism (Berkhof, *Systematic Theology,* p. 394).

41. For Preston's critical use of both translations see Preston, *The golden Scepter,* I:251; II:55; Preston, *The New Covenant,* pp. 35-36, 277, 549; cf. p. 87; John Preston, *Sermons preached before His Majestie,* pp. 59-60; Preston, *Riches of Mercy,* p. 386.

42. Jacobus Kimedoncius, *De Redemtione generis Humani Libri tres: Quibus copiosè traditur Controversia, de Redemtionis et Gratiæ per Christum universalitate, et Morte ipsius pro Omnibus. Accessit tractatio finitima de divinia Prædestinatione, uno Libro comprehensa* (Heidelberg: Abraham Smesmann, 1592), pp. 94-95; Jacobus Kimedoncius, *Of the Redemption of Mankind. Three Bookes: Wherein the Controversie of the Universalitie of Redemption and Grace by Christ, and of his Death for all Men, is largely handled. Hereunto is annexed a Treatise of Gods Predestination in one Booke,* trans. Hugh Ince (London: Felix Kingston, 1598), p. 49; cf. pp. 193, 318, 328.

Taylor, another Cambridge preacher, disciple of Perkins, and contemporary of Preston's, contrasted Christ's 'being dead for' sinners, not with Christ 'dying for' them, but with his rising again for them: "We must not content our selves with common people, that Christ is dead for all and no more; but fasten our eyes upon his resurrection so much the more diligently, by how much it is easier to beleeve that hee was dead, than that hee rose againe."[43] William Ames, the notable Puritan and particular redemptionist, took Christ being "pro omnibus mortuus" or "dead for us" to refer only to Christ's effectual death for the elect.[44] Baxter and Jean Daillé were therefore not without justification in citing this sermon of Preston's in support of their own universal redemptionism,[45] and the Wesleyan-Methodist edition of Preston's *Breast-plate* was not in fact guilty of misrepresenting Preston when the editorial pen, presumably that of A. G. Jewitt, reproduced Preston's words as "Christ hath died for him."[46]

43. Thomas Taylor, *Japhets first publique Perswasion into Sems Tents: Or, Peters Sermon which was the first generall Calling of the Gentiles preached before Cornelius. Expounded in Cambridge by Thomas Taylor, and now published for the further Use of the Church of God* (Cambridge?: By Cantrell Legge for Raph Mab, 1612), p. 155.

44. William Ames, *Medulla S.S. Theologiæ ex sacris Literis* (London: Apud Robertum Allottum, 1630), p. 95; William Ames, *The Marrow of sacred Divinity, drawne out of the Holy Scriptures* (London: Edward Griffin for Henry Overton, 1642), pp. 78-79.

45. Richard Baxter, *Plain Scripture Proof of Infants Church-membership and Baptism* (London: For Robert White, 1651), p. 275; John Daillé, *Apologia pro duabus Ecclesiarum in Gallia Protestantium Synodis Nationalibus* (Amsterdam: Joannis Ravesteynii, 1655), pp. 1183-87. Daillé begins his extended Latin translation of Preston with *The Breast-plate*, I:7, and therefore also saw significance for his own position in Preston's doctrine, already noted, of a universal donation of the righteousness of God "to every man" without exception. Daillé's Latin rendering of Preston, *The Breast-plate*, I:8 is as follows: "Ite & dicite unicuique hominum sine exceptione, quod faustus fit ipsi nuntius; quod *Christus fit pro eo mortuus*, quodque si velit eum admittere, atque de ejus justitia accipere, habebit" (Daillé, *Apologia*, p. 1184; emphasis added). Interestingly, this section of Preston on the free offer is also exploited in a manuscript on predestination dating from the early 1630s. This lengthy, anonymous treatise opposes Calvin and Elizabethan particularism on the one hand, and the doctrines of the Remonstrants on the other. Instead, a middle way is advocated, along which even the too "rigid" Dr Preston failed to walk, who was rightly opposed by Francis White and Richard Montagu at the York House Conference (ECL MS. 44, ff. 32r, 35v, 39r, 84v). For more on the York House Conference see Ch. 6.

46. Wesley, ed., *A Christian Library*, V:324; cf. XXX:377. In the edition published in John Wesley's lifetime, however, the original reading was retained, despite Wesley's readiness to "correct . . . mistakes" in the selected material (John Wesley, ed., *A Christian Library. Consisting of Extracts from and Abridgements of the choicest Pieces of practical Divinity, which have been publish'd in the English Tongue* [Bristol, UK: Felix Farley and E. Farley, 1749-55], IX:233, I:v). For further examination of John Wesley's abridgements of works by Preston see Robert C. Monk, *John Wesley: His Puritan Heritage* (Lanham, MD: Scarecrow Press, 1999), Chs. 3-5. Sadly, however, Monk completely ignores the eighteenth-century edition of *A Christian Library*.

The hypothetical universalism behind Preston's notion that "Christ is dead for every man" becomes increasingly clear as his sermons are further examined. Elsewhere Preston can be found basing his invitation to sinners to come to Christ on the fact that Christ has already paid for their sins in particular.

> The Proclamation of pardon brings the Rebels in, and what greater motive can wee use than this, that whatever your sinnes are or have beene, never so great in themselves and aggravated with never so many circumstances, yet if you will come in and humble your selves, and turne to God, God will bee mercifull to you. No matter what thy sinnes have beene . . . they have not gone beyond that price which hath beene paid for them.[47]

Such theology leads logically to the doctrine that salvation is genuinely and in a very real sense possible for all upon their believing, and not only hypothetically so. We have already seen how, concerning fallen humanity, Preston says that God "might have left us, as he left the Angells that fell without any possibility of salvation," but that in fact "he gave his Sonne to redeem us," thereby granting to all mankind "the advantage of the possibility of being saved." Most men lose this advantage because left to themselves, but in God's chosen people he works faith to appropriate this advantage and brings them home.[48] As we shall see in Chapter 7, the concept of 'possibilities' of being saved is a favourite with the proponents of hypothetical universalism, and that Preston was such a proponent has become increasingly clear.

In the same treatise as his phrase "Christ is dead for him," Preston shortly afterwards implies that before a man can be expected to believe the gospel he has to believe that Christ died for him in particular. Given that "there is a certaine justice of [*sic*] righteousness that Christ hath prepared or purchased for men, though they be ungodly," it follows for Preston that "he that will beleeve God that he hath prepared this *for him,* and will receive it, it is enough to make him a righteous man in Gods acceptation."[49] It is therefore not just full assurance of faith that involves knowing that Christ died for you in particular. This emphasis in Preston's sermons seems to flow from the fact

---

47. Preston, *The golden Scepter,* I:273.

48. Preston, *The golden Scepter,* I:180; cf. Preston, *The Breast-plate,* I:9.

49. Preston, *The Breast-plate,* I:32-33 (emphasis added). The second edition has "justice *or* righteousness" (John Preston, *The Breast-plate of Faith and Love. A Treatise wherein the Ground and Exercise of Faith and Love, as they are set upon Christ their Object, and as they are expressed in good Workes, is explained,* ed. Richard Sibbes & John Davenport [London: W. Jones & George Purslowe for Nicholas Bourne, 1630 (1631)], I:39).

that rather than merely seeing the authoritative call to believe itself as being the means of quickening the dead — a doctrine Preston did hold[50] — Preston also wants to emphasise the wooing power of the gospel and reflect the alluring beauty of Christ to attract the sinner. Christ must be presented therefore not only as "propitious" to his people, but to all hearers of the gospel without exception.[51] Nothing less than this constitutes Preston's presentation of the gospel.

Covenantal Formulations

The universal call of the gospel, grounded in part on a universal atonement, also takes on a covenantal structure in Preston's thought, as we have already seen, particularly within the visible church. In terms of the universal gospel call, Preston speaks of "the freenesse of the covenant which God hath made with mankind." Here "the tenour of the covenant runnes"; "if any man will come, let him come and drink of the waters of life freely."[52] That is to say, the covenant that "belongs to all men" is "expressed in these termes, Christ hath provided a righteousnesse and salvation, that is his worke that he hath done already. Now if you will beleeve, and take him upon those termes that he is offered, you shall be saved." This is the "conditionall Covenant of Grace, which is common to all."[53] The gospel almost even becomes a new law to Preston. Making an explicit parallel with the prelapsarian covenant of works with Adam, Preston asserts that "we are offered Christ, and to be heirs of heaven upon condition of obedience to the Law of faith."[54] Preston also seems to have held that this conditional covenant was a form of grace to all hearers, saying that this covenant is "indefinitely propounded unto all men & such universal grace we grante." Thus the reprobate are judged because they have "despised so gracious an offer."[55]

Addressing those who are "outside the covenant," by which Preston means unregenerate,[56] Preston says "you may (if you will consider it) come to the assurance of his love towards you." This love is manifest in that "the Lord

---

50. Preston, *Riches of Mercy*, p. 424.
51. Cf. Preston, *The Breast-plate*, II:15-16.
52. Preston, *The golden Scepter*, I:262.
53. Preston, *The Breast-plate*, I:32.
54. Preston, *Riches of Mercy*, p. 431.
55. Preston, *Summe*, f. 4; Preston, *Riches of Mercy*, p. 421.
56. Preston, *The Breast-plate*, II:142, 145; cf. Preston, *Riches of Mercy*, p. 405. Preston did *not* teach baptismal regeneration, contrary to Pettit (Pettit, *The Heart Prepared*, p. 78).

hath made knowne his owne willingnesse to take you to marriage. There are but two that are to give their consent, the Father to give his Sonne, and the Sonne to give his owne consent." But the Father "hath given his consent" by giving his Son, and the Son has given his consent by giving himself. Consequently, Preston can say to those outside the covenant that "therefore you cannot doubt but that hee is willing to marry with you, to take you, and to receive you if you will come in." Although they are church members here who are being addressed as unregenerate, once again Preston's preaching still suggests an accommodation to a hypothetical universalist system in that this offer of Christ's hand in marriage is made to the unregenerate outside of the absolute Covenant but within the conditional general covenant on the basis that "the Son gave himselfe to thee."[57]

In terms of the church and this "double" covenant of grace, the reprobate are only baptised into "a general covenant propounded without exception."[58] The call goes out to these baptised reprobate: "Let whosoever will come and believe in Christ he shall be saved," for this "general Covenant belongeth to all without exception." However, "there is another Covenant of grace which belongeth peculiarly to the elect," or "is proper onely to the Elect," and in this covenant God "promiseth to give them ability to believe" and so fulfil the conditions of this general covenant. It is thus "absolute and peculiar," not "conditionall."[59] Certainly, as Schaefer observes, with regard to the covenant of grace, Preston "recognized both conditional and unconditional elements working side by side."[60] Schaefer and Woolsey rightly dismiss Trinterud's somewhat crude claim of a sharp chronological discontinuity between a unilateral covenant and a bilateral covenant.[61] However, it should not be implied that there is no change at all, even if it be only in emphasis. Veninga's thesis, although flawed, was provoked by significant change in formulation. Indeed, Schaefer himself, even while arguing for continuity,

---

57. Preston, *The Breast-plate,* II:142-43.

58. Preston, *Riches of Mercy,* p. 425. Interestingly, the proof that Preston gives for this assertion that "none are excluded out of this general Covenant," is that "Baptism the seal of the Covenant is to be administered to all within the Church, to infants though afterwards they do not actually and visibly believe" (Preston, *Riches of Mercy,* p. 425). This is yet more evidence for the subconscious influence of a state church context upon Preston's theology.

59. Preston, *Riches of Mercy,* p. 425; Preston, *The Breast-plate,* I:32.

60. Schaefer, "The Spiritual Brotherhood," p. 203.

61. Schaefer, "The Spiritual Brotherhood," p. 45; Andrew A. Woolsey, "Unity and Continuity in Covenantal Thought: A Study in the Reformed Tradition to the Westminster Assembly" (Ph.D. Dissertation, University of Glasgow, 1988), II:227; Leonard J. Trinterud, "The Origins of Puritanism," *CH* 20 (1951): 37-57, *passim; cf.* John von Rohr, *The Covenant of Grace in Puritan Thought* (Atlanta, GA: Scholars Press, 1986), pp. 24-25.

does acknowledge Preston's "emphasis on bilateralism."[62] Thus, although Perkins was happy to speak of the covenant of grace as a compact,[63] we see here that Preston has considerably developed the conditional covenant motif, multiplied the number of covenants, and increased their scope. In Chapter 7 we shall see more of the significance of this universal covenant with mankind.

The Gospel Promise

With the universal gospel call formulated as a conditional, general covenant partly based on a universal atonement, Preston's system needs to be explored further in order to find out the answers to two questions. The first question concerns the nature of the promise of the gospel in relation to this universal call. What exactly does Preston mean when he speaks of "the promises wherein Christ is offered"?[64] The second question concerns how God deals with the reprobate within these structures.

As we have already seen, Preston is quite clear that the gospel promise can, in one sense, be said to be general.[65] Another example of God's "generall promise" is "Whosoever will beleeve, shall be saved." To the extent that Christ is thus "offered to every creature" so far do the promises "belong unto him."[66] Thus what Preston is at pains to communicate by saying "Gods promises are generall," or with the phrase "a generall pardon," is that it is "without exception of persons, or sinnes."[67] The "generalitie of the promise" then, is that it "is offered to all, none excepted."[68] This is the sense in which Baxter understood Preston to teach that "the promise and offer of Christ is generall."[69] It is not meant to imply that God conditionally promises to the reprobate to save them. This would tie in with the concept of a

---

62. Schaefer, "The Spiritual Brotherhood," p. 185; cf. von Rohr, *The Covenant of Grace in Puritan Thought*, pp. 25, 32. Song, overlooking Preston's hypothetical universalism, tries his best to minimise the differences with Perkins in the area of bilateralism (Song, *Theology and Piety*, pp. 207-12).

63. E.g., Perkins, *Workes*, I:164; II:243.

64. Preston, *The Breast-plate*, I:47.

65. See p. 119.

66. Preston, *A liveles Life*, I:74; Preston, *Remaines*, p. 298; Preston, *The Breast-plate*, I:150.

67. Preston, *Saints Qualification*, I:122; III:43; cf. III:23.

68. Preston, *The Breast-plate*, I:81; cf. Preston, *The New Covenant*, p. 400; Preston, *Saints Qualification*, I:122-23.

69. Richard Baxter, *Aphorismes of Justification* (The Hague: Abraham Brown, 1655), p. 287.

universal gospel covenant. However, while Preston is happy to have the gospel *covenant* as something contractual and conditional, he saw this as something the gospel *promise* could never be, lest even the salvation of the elect be made meritorious or uncertain. It is therefore inadequate to say that in Preston's thought, God uses the free offer "to provide comfort in a general promise sealed by the blood of Christ."[70] Furthermore, Preston insists that the gospel promise is "free without any condition," in that it is wrong to "looke for sorrow and holinesse before thou takest Christ." This opposition to preparationism[71] flows from his reasoning that if "godly sorrow and grace were required, it were not free; godly sorrow and grace followes [*sic*] faith, but are not required before it." The promise is therefore absolute because unconditional.

However, as if fearing antinomian deductions from the unconditionality of the promise, Preston immediately in this same passage qualifies this unconditionality. It is not that the sinner is to be presented with no conditions whatsoever, but rather that these conditions are to be understood as duties that are to *follow* faith. He insists that "there be conditions following after, though not going before faith." These conditions are, "you must serve him in all his commands, and leave all your sinnes."[72] The gospel promise is unconditional, but final salvation is conditioned upon progressive sanctification. This side of the coin "is another part [of the gospel]" and constitutes the covenant of grace expressed conditionally.[73] Thus when we

> come to a beleever going out of the world, and aske him what hope hee hath to be saved, and what ground for it? he will be ready to say, I know that Christ is come into the world, and that he is offered, and I know that I am one of them that have a part in him; I know that I have fulfilled the conditions, as that I should not continue willingly in any knowne sinne, that I should love the Lord Jesus, and desire to serve him above all; I know that I have fulfilled these conditions, and for all this I have the word for my ground, if the ground whereon our faith is builded be the Word, then it is builded on a sure rocke.

Elsewhere Preston qualifies the unconditionality of the gospel promise even further by pointing out that, in reality, because only those humbled for sin will take this promise seriously, the gospel is "sometimes," but not always, to

---

70. Schaefer, "The Spiritual Brotherhood," p. 204.
71. Cf. above, p. 119.
72. Preston, *A liveles Life*, I:76.
73. Preston, *Saints Qualification*, III:16; Preston, *Summe*, f. 4.

be preached "with the condition."[74] Thus while it is arguably true to say that Preston taught "God's universal, conditional promise," this lacks clarity.[75] Preston himself shyed away from the notion of a divine *promise* being conditional, but not so for a divine *covenant*.

That this is so becomes clear when, despite his hypothetical universalism and reluctance to depart totally from the language of conditionality in the context of the gospel call, Preston describes the gospel promise in strictly particular terms.[76] This is because Preston is still desirous to defend the "irresistible working" of "quickning Grace." Indeed, in the face of a rising Arminianism, Preston, in his treatise *Irresistiblenesse of converting Grace*, goes so far as to say that in one sense "quickning Grace" is not even "offered to any, but those in whom it is effectuall."[77] Before the promises can therefore be said to belong to us we must first "have Christ," lay hold on his Promises, and make them our own.[78] This is because the promise is made to all that come and "onely" to those who are convicted of sin.[79] The gospel promise is not impotent in a universal conditionality but is itself effectual and therefore made to the elect alone, although announced in the hearing of all. In the light of Preston's simultaneous holding to a universal, conditional gospel covenant, the concepts of covenant and promise are here being prised apart and being made to serve different soteriological purposes, the one immanent, the other transcendent. As for the gospel promise, it is at once both universal and particular — almost paradoxically so.

The Reprobate and the Gospel Call

Given that "the gift of faith is a fruit of election," and "God gives faith & repentance, and ability to receive him, where he pleaseth,"[80] Preston was compelled — if not for his own satisfaction's sake then certainly in the face of his anti-Calvinist opponents — to deal with the difficult question of how God can sin-

---

74. Preston, *Life eternall*, I:72; Preston, *Remaines*, p. 192.

75. James I. Packer, "The Redemption and Restoration of Man in the Thought of Richard Baxter: A Study in Puritan Theology" (D.Phil. Dissertation, University of Oxford, 1954), p. 211.

76. Preston, *The Breast-plate*, I:192; Preston, *A liveles Life*, I:76.

77. John Preston, *Irresistiblenesse of converting Grace*, p. 14.

78. Preston, *Love of Christ*, p. 6; Preston, *Sinnes Overthrow*, p. 150; cf. Preston, *The Breast-plate*, I:150.

79. Preston, *Love of Christ*, p. 66; Preston, *A liveles Life*, I:44-45; cf. I:69-70; Preston, *Sinnes Overthrow*, pp. 149-50.

80. Preston, *The Breast-plate*, I:10.

cerely invite the doomed reprobate to come to him for salvation, while having no intention according to his secret will of enabling them to come. For although "God offers Salvation to all (as it is true none is excepted) yet he lookes to none with a gracious eye to save him indeed, but him that is poore and contrite in heart, and trembles at his Word."[81] Of course, in Preston's theology, it is the revealed will of God that any given sinner should come to Christ and be saved. None can hold back under the apprehension that God does not demand his conversion, or that he is not 'poor and contrite' enough.[82] Indeed, "[t]he Gospell is nothing but this . . . that God the Father is willing to give you his Sonne."[83] But what does this revealed will actually reveal about God's disposition towards the reprobate specifically? Does he really desire to save them? How else could the offer be sincere? But if such a desire in God be granted, then how can portraying a frustrated God be avoided? In short, what exactly is happening when "God offereth Christ . . . to the reprobate"?[84]

Preston was not slow to see the dangerous potential for the incubation of Arminianism around such questions. Certainly he condemned the Arminians for implying a frustrated desire in God to save the reprobate:

> For according to Arminius, though God did heartily desire the conversion of such a man, and offered him al the meanes of Grace that could be, yet it is stil in the free choise of his wil to convert, or not to convert; Their onely answer here is, that seeing God hath made a Decree, that man shal be a free Agent, though he doe most earnestly desire the conversion of such and such men, yet because he cannot disannul his Decree, he doth, and must leave it to the liberty of the Creature to doe contrary to even that himselfe desires. But what is this else but to put God into such streights as Darius was in, who would faine have saved Daniel, but because of his Decree he could not? . . . [W]hat is this else but to attribute griefe unto God, and so to detract from his Blessednesse?[85]

In this anti-Arminian spirit, Preston could happily occupy the Reformed high ground, teaching that God does not so desire the salvation of the reprobate that the world will exist any longer than it takes for the last one of the elect to

81. Preston, *Saints Qualification*, I:18.

82. Cf. Preston, *The Breast-plate*, I:10, 12-13, 33-34, 192; II:143-44; John Preston, *Plenitudo Fontis*, pp. 8-13; Preston, *A liveles Life*, I:76; Preston, *Love of Christ*, pp. 65-67; Preston, *Irresistiblenesse of converting Grace*, p. 14.

83. Preston, *Love of Christ*, p. 6; cf. pp. 80-81.

84. Preston, *Riches of Mercy*, p. 423.

85. Preston, *Plenitudo Fontis*, pp. 9-10. This anti-Arminian passage was expunged from the 1640 edition (Preston, *The Fulnesse of Christ*, p. 14; see below, pp. 238-39).

be converted.[86] Futhermore, the gospel is primarily preached for the salvation of the elect, and since "God hath commanded us, 'not to cast Pearles before Swine' . . . will hee himselfe doe it?"[87] From the preacher's perspective, ministers preach the gospel to clear themselves of the blood of their perishing listeners.[88] The elect clearly take priority in Preston's mind, and he instinctively recoiled from the portrayal of a mutable, impotent, and frustrated God vainly longing that the reprobate might save themselves.

However, be that as it may, Preston the hypothetical universalist was now also committed to other tenets. He asks, "for to what purpose, or what comfort is it to see that there is such a righteousnesse, if it be nothing to us? But it is so revealed, that it is also offered." Preston was still therefore opposed to the idea that the call of the gospel was merely "a bare offer," and not also a serious command and an earnest beseeching on the part of God.

> God doth not only or merely offer Christ, but he sendeth out his Ministers and Ambassadors, 'beseeching' us to be 'reconciled', he doth not only tell us that there is a marriage of his Son, and that whosoever will come may come, but he sendeth messengers to beseech, and to use an holy violence and earnest persuasion.[89]

Employing the same text of 2 Corinthians 5:20, Preston insists that

> wee use all the perswasions, and motives that we can; we exhort, rebuke, instruct you, and all to this end to make you willing to receive Christ; nay wee doe not onely beseech you, but with those in the Gospel wee compell you to come in, that is, wee perswade you often against your wils, to receive Christ.[90]

While it is the ministers who say this, they are not out of step with God himself, who also "beseecheth and compelleth men to come and believe."[91] The

---

86. Preston, *Saints Qualification*, I:287.

87. Preston, *Foure Treatises*, p. 169; cf. Preston, *Riches of Mercy*, p. 7.

88. Preston, *The Breast-plate*, I:29.

89. Preston, *The Breast-plate*, I:14; Preston, *Riches of Mercy*, p. 420; cf. pp. 55, 426; Preston, *Love of Christ*, p. 6; Preston, *Remaines*, p. 89.

90. Preston, *Remaines*, p. 297; cf. Preston, *Saints Qualification*, II:186 and Anthony Tuckney's catechism delivered in Emmanuel College Chapel in the year of Preston's death (ECL MS. 181, f. 2). This is to be contrasted with Perkins' understanding of 2 Corinthians 5:20. Due to its immediate context, Perkins sees the apostolic injunction — "be ye reconciled to God" — to refer to believers who have already repented, and not to the unregenerate (Perkins, *Workes*, III[i]:139; III[ii]:301).

91. Preston, *Riches of Mercy*, p. 420.

"great God beseecheth us to be reconciled to him . . . hee desires to bee at peace with us, and to be friends with us."[92] "God offereth Christ to all, and beseecheth them and persuadeth them, and commandeth men to come in and believe."[93] With much longsuffering <u>God waits for the reprobate</u> to repent, for "he is a patient God" and "<u>waits for their conversion.</u>"[94]

At first it might appear that all Preston means by this is that there is an undeniable congruity between a sinner repenting — even a reprobate sinner hypothetically repenting — and God's own nature. One reason Preston gives for the free offer is "because it is acceptable to God that the Gospel should be obeyed, that is, that men should believe that they might live and not die; and therefore he saith he desireth not the death of a sinner." Preston is thinking of Deuteronomy 5:29 and Ezekiel 18:31; 33:11 — the latter being one of Harsnett's 'proof texts.'[95] By this Preston means that "it is a thing very pleasing to God that men should not perish, but that they come in and believe, and live for ever."[96] That is to say, the reprobate's repentance is consistent with God's attributes and in that sense acceptable and even delightful to him. Indeed, "You can do nothing so acceptable to God as to 'believe on his Son.'"[97] Sometimes, Preston allows his language to become even stronger, stating that "the Lord hath an exceeding great desire, [and] earnestly longs to save soules of men."[98] Preston always sees this *desire* as conceptually prior to the *command* of the gospel call. He does not teach the earnest beseeching as the ultimate form of the gospel offer, but always sees the command to believe as the ultimate revelation that God is serious in the gospel call.[99] Although "he saith not that he will give every one grace to come in," this <u>does mean that for whoever does 'come in' the Lord stands "ready to forgive him."</u>[100] This might be all Preston meant when he said, "The Gospel comes and tells you that the Lord Jesus is willing to be your Redeemer, is willing to be your Lord, he is content to be yours. If you will take him, you shall have

---

92. Preston, *The Breast-plate,* II:43; cf. I:93.

93. Preston, *Riches of Mercy,* p. 423.

94. Preston, *Sinnes Overthrow,* p. 88; cf. p. 159. Paradoxically, however, God simultaneously tarries for the reprobate so that they will be without excuse (Preston, *A liveles Life,* II:15).

95. See above, p. 58.

96. Preston, *Riches of Mercy,* p. 421.

97. Preston, *Riches of Mercy,* p. 432.

98. Preston, *Saints Qualification,* III:20.

99. E.g., Preston, *The golden Scepter,* II:51; Preston, *Riches of Mercy,* p. 420. Neither is it "a bare command, but hee adds a threatening; if they will not take him, they shall bee damned" (Preston, *The golden Scepter,* II:51).

100. Preston, *Saints Qualification,* III:20.

him and all his."[101] Preston is well aware that he is getting himself into deep water at this point. Yet he is confident that he can make "stand together" the fact that on the one hand "God desires that men should believe and live" and "expresseth in . . . Scripture such an earnest desire to have men live and not die," while on the other hand, although "he hath it in his power to make them to believe . . . yet will not."

Preston's solution consists in two considerations. Firstly,

> the scope of all [such] places in Scripture is, to show that if men will come in, there shall be no impedient [*sic*] upon God's part, and they show that he is full of mercy and compassion, the fault shall be in their own stubborness and contempt, and these declare that it is more acceptable to God to save them, than to condemn them, and that he is full of mercy and ready to forgive, that he hath such a disposition as was in the father of the Prodigal.[102]

The parable of the prodigal son "expresseth how willing God is to receive Sinners."[103] Secondly, "there is a double consideration of the will of God." Considered "simply," "God being Holy and pure must needs be delighted in the faith and repentance and obedience of his creature." This follows from the fact that "it cannot be but when any object is put into the will of any, if it be suitable and agreeable to the will, it must needs be well-pleasing to it." Therefore "it is acceptable to God to have men to believe." It is "agreeing to him . . . because of the conformity the thing itself hath with his will." Yet this is overruled by "a *secret* will of God," whereby "for reasons best known to himself" he has mercy on some and hardens others.[104] Nevertheless God does pursue the salvation of the reprobate in the free offer. Preston asks "to what end" God declares "the riches of his mercie" to those who "refuse them?" It is so "that you may come in and partake of them."[105] God

> sends his messengers to declare to the sonnes of men, to let them know their estate by nature, and to tell them that he hath given them his Sonne to save them from their sinnes, and to reconcile them to himselfe, to give them title to the kingdome, from the hope of which they were fallen.[106]

---

101. Preston, *The Breast-plate*, II:13; cf. II:14.

102. Preston, *Riches of Mercy*, p. 421. I have supplied the word "such" to make sense of what seems to be a printing error in both editions.

103. Preston, *Sermons preached before His Majestie*, p. 149; cf. Preston, *Saints Qualification*, III:42, 45.

104. Preston, *Riches of Mercy*, pp. 421-22.

105. Preston, *Riches of Mercy*, p. 4.

106. Preston, *Saints Qualification*, III:16.

There is no contradiction here, "as if God should will the damnation and salvation of Judas both at one time," for Preston is adamant that "it is most possible for a man to will and nill one and the same thing upon the same object if it be in different respects." Preston gives the following example: "A man may will his friends departure from him, and yet not will it. He wills his departure out of a desire he hath of his friends good, and yet will [*sic*] it not out of a love he hath of his friends company." Thus it follows that although God "willeth that all men should be saved, and therefore he beseecheth men to believe," nevertheless "he will not use all means to bring this to pass." For example,

> A father will not have his son drunk, if he tie him up in a chamber he will not be drunk, yet he will not take such a course, though he hath a will his son should not be drunk, so God though he do will that men should believe and repent and be saved, yet he will not be said to use all means for the effecting of it in all men, because he will glorify his justice as well as his mercy.[107]

Preston does not deal with obvious objections against this argument from analogy, such as the friend's frustration or 'lack of blessedness,' and the father's lack of omnipotence. It does appear clear from this, however, that Preston teaches a desire in God to save the reprobate but that this desire is subordinated to other desires.[108]

The next objection that Preston had to answer was the possibility that his doctrine of the gospel call to the reprobate attributed to God "some collusion and deceit." Preston denied the charge and asserted that

> God may seriously offer and give a thing, and yet know aforehand that the party to whom it is offered will not receive it out of the stubborness and refractoriness of his own will. A Prince may offer and give a pardon to a rebel, and yet know aforehand that the rebel to whom it is offered, out of pride and contempt will not receive it; so I say when God offereth Christ, he offereth him in good earnest, here is no deceit, what he promiseth he will perform, he offereth him to the reprobate.[109]

---

107. Preston, *Riches of Mercy*, p. 422. Preston has implicitly adopted Harsnett's interpretation of 1 Timothy 2:4 over against that of Perkins.

108. Cf. Preston, *Riches of Mercy*, pp. 32, 33 (quoted above, p. 80). Of course, no matter how incomprehensible this may appear, this is not to be understood to compromise God's immutability (cf. above, p. 72).

109. Preston, *Riches of Mercy*, p. 423.

Again, Preston does not deal with the obvious objection to this analogy that the elect also would refuse the offer "out of pride and contempt" were it not for prevenient grace and a prior decree to give them a compliant heart — something anteriorly denied to the reprobate. However, Preston was adamant that this argumentation proved that the gospel call to the reprobate is utterly sincere. He was adamant that "when Christ offereth himself unto you, you must beleeve that there is such a thing, and that God intendeth it really."[110] Preston sought to uphold a desire in God to save the reprobate on a level that secured the sincere earnestness of the gospel call, but without compromising or undermining the divine, double decree.

However, his success in this venture is debatable. Although he attacks Arminius for detracting from God's blessedness by implying a frustrated will in God, Preston, inconsistently or otherwise, is found doing the very same thing. He states that "Christ offers himselfe, we make offer of him, when we preach the Gospell, in the Sacrament he is offered, he is made like a common dole, all may come that will, and certainly all that hunger doe come." However, some do not respond to this offer, and to such Preston says, referring to Matthew 23:37, "thou art one of them, whom he would gather, and thou wilt not." Preston pleads, "let it not be in vaine unto you when you heare those patheticall speeches . . . 'He came to his owne, and his owne received him not:' And againe, 'Oh Jerusalem, Jerusalem, how oft would I have gathered thee.'" Preston then applied this to his hearers as follows: "Thou takest the Grace of God in vaine, thou tramplest the blood of Christ under-foot, as a common thing, thou doest what thou canst, that the death of Christ should be of no effect, thou recompencest to the Lord evill for good."[111] The reprobate within the visible church who reject the free offer "take the grace of God in vain" by "frustrating the end of" the "manifestation" of God's riches.[112] In this we see a markedly different handling of Matthew 23:37 from that of John Dove.

In the face of growing anti-Calvinist accusations, Preston's desire to reinstate the impression of full human responsibility under the gospel call led him to give considerable prominence to the imagery of Christ as suitor. Continuing to develop 2 Corinthians 5:20, Preston portrays Christ as suing for the sinner's response. Not only does Christ beseech us, "hee becomes a downeright suter." "Nay beloved, more than this, hee is not a cold, but an im-

110. Preston, *The Breast-plate,* I:44.

111. Preston, *Saints Qualification,* III:44; cf. III:93; Preston, *The Breast-plate,* I:93; Preston, *The New Covenant,* p. 582; Preston, *Sinnes Overthrow,* p. 150. Preston also uses Matthew 23:37 to undergird the free offer in Preston, *The New Covenant,* p. 422.

112. Preston, *Riches of Mercy,* p. 5.

portunate earnest suter."[113] Again, it is through his ministers by the Spirit that Christ is a suitor. "Christ he is a suter by his Spirit, and we are his friends to perswade you to match with him. . . . And therefore, take heede of deferring."[114] Preston told his hearers that Christ

> hath made knowne that he is thine, and that he is willing to become thy familiar friend; God hath given him in marriage to thee. . . . And Christ himselfe hath shewne sufficiently his love unto thee. He hath spent his blood for thee, yea, he continually speakes to his Father in thy behalfe, yea, hee sues to thee for love, he loves thee first, and sues to thee, as the man doth to the woman; thou maiest be perswaded therefore that he loves thee.[115]

Preston held that it was the ministers of the gospel who were "Christs spokesmen to wooe for Christ." Through them Christ "sues to thee for thy love," and when "such a God shall ask thy love, sue for it, shall he be denied?" Such passages from Preston could easily be multiplied.[116]

The imagery of suiting that Preston employs in presenting the free offer naturally leads on to another dominant theme in his sermons, namely presenting the free offer in terms of an invitation to marry Christ.[117] Preston explains this emphasis of his. "When we preach the Gospell, and offer Christ, we are friends of the Bridegroom: our businesse is, to present you as a pure Virgin to Christ."[118] What this means is that "Christ comes and tels a man, I will have thee . . . I am willing to marry thee. When this is done on the holy Ghosts part, & we on our part come to resolve to take him, now the match is made betweene us, and this is faith indeed."[119] Yet this leads Preston into an unstated dilemma. He states that "[t]he great match is made in Baptisme,"[120] but through infant baptism all his hearers are thus married to Christ already. Yet his evangelical theology tells him that this is not truly the case with most

113. Preston, *The golden Scepter,* II:51; cf. Preston, *The Breast-plate,* II:20; Preston, *Plenitudo Fontis,* p. 2; Preston, *Love of Christ,* p. 10.

114. Preston, *The golden Scepter,* II:68; cf. II:35 (quoted above, p. 110).

115. Preston, *Love of Christ,* pp. 64-65.

116. Preston, *Love of Christ,* pp. 46-47; cf. Preston, *The golden Scepter,* II:41, 50; Preston, *The mysticall Match,* p. 17.

117. Cf. Preston, *The Breast-plate,* I:12-14, 75; II:14, 20; Preston, *The golden Scepter,* title-page, II:2-3, 7, 36, 51; Preston, *Love of Christ,* pp. 6, 67, 81; Preston, *Saints Qualification,* I:78; II:7, 72, 185, 198; III:24, 45, 98.

118. Preston, *The golden Scepter,* II:36.

119. Preston, *The Breast-plate,* I:197-98.

120. Preston, *The golden Scepter,* II:69.

Englishmen.[121] Although the Lord's Supper is "the renewing of the Nuptials, and new Actes of taking and receiving Christ,"[122] for many it will be for the first time. Thus Preston shifts the focus of the gospel call from baptism to the Lord's Supper.[123] The result is that the gospel call is sometimes seen in terms of an offer to the visible church. Perhaps it was this ecclesiological environment that made Preston, despite his particularist heritage, more open to the idea of undergirding the free offer with a universal atonement. Of course, in terms of the godly remnant within the state church, Christ had died 'effectually' only for them. But on the judicial, sacramental, and ecclesiastical levels Christ could easily be said to have died for the whole nation head for head — indeed 'for all.' A universalism within the (national) covenant community, especially by way of increasingly external and conditional covenantal structures, could easily be developed unnoticed by most, and would not shock rigorous particularists the way that blatant anti-Calvinism would.[124]

Another feature of Preston's formulations on the gospel call to the reprobate, again germinated in the context of the English state church, is the decisive rejection by the reprobate of an *internal* work of the Holy Spirit. Those who finally prove to be reprobate are nevertheless "invited to come to Christ Jesus, either by the preaching of the Word, or by the secret motions of the Spirit."[125] They are to be those who "would not put off the motions of the spirit, but . . . would strike while the Iron is hot, and grinde while the wind blowes."[126] It is in this connection that Preston plays on the imagery of Revelation 3:20 where Christ knocks on the door. Preston asks,

> God awakens sinners, but what kinde of awakening is it? With such awakening that they fall asleepe againe. God may send many messengers of wrath to knocke at the doore of their hearts, which perhaps disquiets and

---

121. Preston was convinced that "the greatest part of . . . common Protestants, neglect the Gospell," and that consequently out of a whole "Church full of people" only "a few of them shall be saved" (Preston, *Saints Qualification*, I:12; Preston, *Riches of Mercy*, p. 56; cf. Preston, *Remaines*, p. 90).

122. Preston, *The golden Scepter*, II:69.

123. E.g. Preston, *The Breast-plate*, I:73-74; Preston, *The golden Scepter*, II:69; Preston, *Saints Qualification*, I:25; III:15, 24, 39, 44, 45; Preston, *Riches of Mercy*, pp. 208-9.

124. Cf. Preston, *Riches of Mercy*, p. 425. To this day, scholarly treatments of Preston's covenant theology have suffered from an overlooking of the important relationship between Preston's covenantal formulations, his hypothetical universalism, and his ecclesiastical context (e.g., Song, *Theology and Piety*, pp. 21, 145-226).

125. Preston, *The golden Scepter*, II:36.

126. Preston, *Riches of Mercy*, p. 56; cf. Preston, *Remaines*, p. 90.

troubles them a little, but they return to their rest againe. And this God may not onely doe outwardly, but he may cast many sparkes of his displeasure into their hearts, which may there lye glowing for a time, but they last not, they goe out in the end. And this is the condition of most men.[127]

Under preaching God may "knocke at the doore of thy heart, and by his Spirit suggest many good motions in thee to come home."[128] This imagery of opening the door is sometimes combined with the one of suting. For example, "when thou findest the Holy Ghost a suter to thee, and that Christ speakes to thy heart, take heede of refusing, his Spirit shall not alwayes strive with men: if he knocke but once, open to him, perhaps he will knocke no more."[129] But when "wee cannot deny his knocking at our doores, and yet wee will not come in," then in his wrath he will destroy such, saying "I would have purged thee, and thou wouldest not be purged, therefore thou shalt never be purged till my wrath light on thee."[130] It is then that "God with-drawes from a man his Spirit and speciall providence, because he loathes him." Thereafter, "though wee would give a world to have but one motion of the spirit againe, one moment of repentance, one offer of grace," yet it will be denied us. "How many thousand are now in Hel who thought to have repented, and did not because they neglected those breathings of the Spirit where they were offered?"[131] These "enlightnings and good motions they have from the Spirit" only finally serve to "encrease their condemnation."[132] While loathing the god of the Arminians, therefore, Preston was not afraid of almost giving the dis-

127. Preston, *Saints Qualification,* I:22; cf. Preston, *Plenitudo Fontis,* p. 13; Preston, *The New Covenant,* p. 422; Preston, *Riches of Mercy,* pp. 137-38. In great contrast to this, Perkins insisted that Revelation 3:20 is addressed only to those already converted (Perkins, *Workes,* II:638; but cf. I:731). Indeed, Preston himself on another occasion took this text to be referring to a subjective experience of the seal of the Spirit in those already regenerate (Preston, *The New Covenant,* pp. 388, 403).

128. Preston, *Saints Qualification,* I:21; cf. John Preston, *Saints Infirmities,* pp. 59, 76; Preston, *Saints Qualification,* II:100 ("he knocks at thy heart againe and againe").

129. Preston, *The golden Scepter,* II:68. Genesis 6:3 is similarly used in Preston, *Plenitudo Fontis,* p. 15; Preston, *The golden Scepter,* II:68.

130. Preston, *Saints Qualification,* I:21; this is Preston's own translation of Ezekiel 24:13.

131. Preston, *Sinnes Overthrow,* p. 59; Preston, *Remaines,* p. 295; Preston, *Plenitudo Fontis,* pp. 12-13.

132. Preston, *Saints Qualification,* II:205-6; cf. Preston, *The Breast-plate,* I:22-23, 24, II:20, 208-10; Preston, *Foure Treatises,* pp. 60-61, 170, 178-79; Preston, *The golden Scepter,* II:34-5; Preston, *A liveles Life,* I:10; Preston, *Love of Christ,* pp. 11, 50, 85-86; Preston, *Saints Qualification,* I:9-10, 76, 99-100, 146-48, 194; Preston, *The mysticall Match,* p. 9; Preston, *Riches of Mercy,* pp. 4, 191, 295, 430-31.

tinct impression of a frustrated work of the Holy Spirit. In his treatise *Irresistiblenesse of converting Grace* Preston quotes the following words of Arminius in order to prove the Dutch theologian's heresy: "Grace . . . is so described in Scripture, as that it may be resisted, received in vaine, that man may hinder his assent unto it, deny to co-operate with it, and therefore an irresistible power, and working, is not to be attributed unto Grace."[133] Preston's condemnation of this central tenet of Arminianism must therefore be taken in the context of his own theology of the gospel call. Perhaps his doctrine of an internal work of the Spirit in the reprobate flows from his Trinitarian theology. Having asserted a reference to the reprobate in the death of Christ, Preston is not in a position to deny to the saving work of the Holy Spirit any reference to the reprobate. Trinitarian parallels must be maintained, even as the Father gave the Son with an eye to the reprobate. Whatever the case may be, Preston can fiercely uphold human inability in the context of the gospel call, with words such as these:

> For the heart of every man by nature is so shut up against Christ, that it will give no entrance to him; he may stand and knock long enough, unlesse God himselfe shake off the bolts, and open the gates, and break open these 'everlasting doors, that the King of glory may come in,' we will not admit him, but keepe him out.[134]

Yet at the same time, Preston does not shy away from giving a somewhat different impression with the words, "open thy heart and let him in."[135]

In conclusion, therefore, although "Ministers are not to goe a begging in offering the Gospell, but are as Ambassadors of the Lord of Heaven,"[136] nevertheless there is in Preston's thought a genuine desire in God to save the reprobate.[137] This must not be presented in such a way as to imply divine frustration and detract from God's blessedness, but neither must the sovereignty of God be so stressed that the immediacy and urgency of the gospel call be lost or presented as a cold and bare command to believe. Neither must the full responsibility of the reprobate to believe be undermined, nor

133. Preston, *Irresistiblenesse of converting Grace*, pp. 1-2.
134. Preston, *The Breast-plate*, I:160; cf. I:166.
135. Preston, *Riches of Mercy*, p. 177.
136. Preston, *Love of Christ*, p. 84.
137. This will not surprise Seán Hughes, who sees a universal saving will in God as the distinctive mark of hypothetical universalism (Seán F. Hughes, "The Problem of 'Calvinism'": English Theologies of Predestination c.1580-1630" in *Belief and Practice in Reformation England: A Tribute to Patrick Collinson from his Students*, ed. Susan Wabuda & Caroline Litzenberger [Aldershot, UK: Ashgate Publishing Company, 1998], 229-49, p. 244).

their ability freely and actively to reject the grace offered be obscured. It seems that Preston, with his particularist heritage, was now becoming more sensitive to Arminian criticisms and, endeavoring to follow that *via media* of least offence, was losing the stark simplicity of Elizabethan formulations. Certainly, Preston was now caught on the horns of an unsolvable paradox, for he also taught that the very same sincere and earnest beseeching of the reprobate to be reconciled to God was simultaneously designed "to increase their condemnation." Preston held that "we Ministers come not only to convert the soules of men . . . but to harden mens hearts to hate the Truth."[138] God therefore desires to save the reprobate through the free offer, but simultaneously purposes to increase their damnation through that very same offer. It is through the free offer that God "showeth" "his love" "to the wicked," but at the same time it is in order "that the glory of his justice might appear in their damnation, when they shall see that they have . . . despised so gracious an offer."[139]

While Schaefer and Song are content to observe unresolved paradoxes in Preston's theology,[140] it could possibly be that at least some of these apparent contradictions, in addition to those already outlined with regard to the gospel promise, are actually indicative of Preston's own doctrinal development. There is a small amount of evidence that Preston was once at home with a more Perkinsian system, a system which, perhaps despite himself, continued to live on alongside his newly found hypothetical universalism. After a careful reading of Hildersham's manuscript on John 4, Preston was asked by Hildersham to give an assessment. In a letter dated 28th November, 1615, Preston was full of praise and urged Hildersham to publish it.[141] Yet these lectures, delivered around 1610, teach a rigorous particularism and give a distinctly 'Perkinsian' interpretation of passages such as John 4:42; 17:9; 1 Corinthians 8:11; 2 Corinthians 5:19; 1 Timothy 2:4; Titus 2:11; Hebrews 2:9; and 1 John 2:2. The donation of Christ is said to be to the elect only, and Hildersham is convinced that "in many places of Scripture the benefit of Christ's death is restrained, and limitted to a peculiar and choise company." Therefore "Christ is not the Saviour of all mankinde," and "Christ desired not that . . . most men in the world, should have benefit by his death." In short, the

---

138. Preston, *Saints Qualification*, I:147; cf. I:193-94, II:202; Preston, *Life eternall*, I:149.

139. Preston, *Riches of Mercy*, p. 421.

140. Schaefer, "The Spiritual Brotherhood," pp. 187, 203; Song, *Theology and Piety*, pp. 160, 176, 197, 222, 232.

141. Samuel Clarke, *A general Martyrologie, containing a Collection of all the greatest Persecutions which have befallen the Church of Christ, from the Creation, to our present Times* (London: For William Birch, 1677), II:121.

notion "that Christ dyed for all men" is a "conceit."[142] Preston originally thought that these lectures contained *"nihil quod amputem,"* and he hoped they would "be a good help to Ministers."[143] It seems that Preston must have embraced hypothetical universalism sometime after 1615. This conversion will be investigated in Chapter 7. But first, it is time to see the mature Preston in action in his historical context.

142. Arthur Hildersham, *CVIII Lectures upon the fourth of John. Preached at Ashby-Delazouch in Leicestershire* (London: George Miller for Edward Brewster, 1632), pp. 14, 137, 249, 328-30.
143. Clarke, *A general Martyrologie,* II:121.

CHAPTER 6

Defender of the Faith at the York House Conference

"[T]he worser the times are the better the Saints should be: the starres are most needed in the darkest night."[1]

Introduction

Behind closed doors in the Duke of Buckingham's London residence a select number of clergy and nobility were meeting to do serious and urgent business. The date was 11th February, 1626; the venue, York House in the Strand; the subject, heresy. This York House Conference was convening within a year of the accession to the throne of Charles I and five days after the commencement of his second parliament. A number of historians have positioned the conference at a watershed period in the changing face of the Church of England. Nicholas Tyacke sees this conference "as poised between two worlds." The first world was "Calvinist England" and the second, one of "overtly competing sects and churches." Tyacke argues that if "in the long term such a development was inevitable, the York House meeting hastened the process." These "competing sects" were to be dominated by a rising anti-Calvinism. The York House Conference "also marked the approximate point at which the circle of clerics patronized by Bishop Neile of Durham emerged as the effective spokesmen of the English Church."[2] A closer look at the proceedings

---

1. John Preston, Lincoln's Inn, February 1623 (John Preston, *Foure Treatises*, p. 231).

2. Nicholas R. N. Tyacke, *Anti-Calvinists: The Rise of English Arminianism c.1590-1640*, 2nd ed. (Oxford: Clarendon Press, 1990), p. 180; cf. Irvonwy Morgan, *Puritan Spirituality: Illustrated from the Life and Times of the Rev. Dr. John Preston* (London: Epworth Press, 1973), p. 31; Joseph B. Gavin, "The York House Conference, 1626: A Watershed in the Arminian-Calvinist-Puritan Debate over Predestination" in *Trinification of the World: A Festschrift in Honor of Fred-*

of this conference would therefore seem to promise a better understanding of the state of the Jacobean Church before power was transferred to the rulers of the 'new world.' And it is at this conference that we find John Preston playing a key role — a key role that has hitherto not been properly understood, due to a lack of awareness of Preston's true theological position outlined in the previous chapters. Before the York House Conference is presented as simply a clash between Calvinists and anti-Calvinists, Preston must be recognised as a mediating hypothetical universalist, and not a promoter of the old-school, Elizabethan particularism which he had left behind. The purpose of this chapter is therefore twofold. Firstly, the correctness of the preceding interpretation of Preston's works is confirmed by additional manuscript evidence. Secondly, this clarification of Preston's theological position is applied to recent interpretations of the York House Conference, enabling a reassessment of what was happening at this conference in terms of a 'Calvinistic consensus' and the rise of anti-Calvinism.

The Background

For over sixty years, Reformed English churchmen had been forced to be content with the Thirty-Nine Articles of 1562 as their official confession of faith. While in those early days many an English churchman rejoiced that such doctrinal progress had been made in the direction of truth and reformation, increasingly it was becoming clear to many that more precise articles were needed. This was in order to keep at bay a growing clamour of new assertions, which, while seeming to be diametrically opposed to the religion that had developed during Elizabeth's reign, were nevertheless claiming to be the 'true' voice of the Church of England. Examining their full compatibility with one possible interpretation of the Thirty-Nine Articles

---

erick E. Crowe in Celebration of His 60th Birthday, ed. Thomas A. Dunne & Jean-Marc Laporte (Toronto: Regis College Press, 1978), 280-311, pp. 281, 308; Patrick Collinson, The Religion of Protestants: The Church in English Society, 1559-1625 (Oxford: Clarendon Press, 1982), pp. 34, 282; Kevin Sharpe, "Parliamentary History, 1603-29: In or Out of Perspective?" in Faction and Parliament: Essays on Early Stuart History, ed. Kevin Sharpe (London: Methuen, 1985), 1-42, p. 22; Derek Hirst, Authority and Conflict: England 1603-1658 (London: Edward Arnold, 1986), pp. 141, 167; Barbara Donagan, "The York House Conference Revisited: Laymen, Calvinism and Arminianism," BHR 64, no. 155 (1991): 312-31, p. 313; Peter White, Predestination, Policy and Polemic: Conflict and Consensus in the English Church from the Reformation to the Civil War (Cambridge: Cambridge University Press, 1992), p. 238; John Spurr, ed., English Puritanism, 1603-1689 (London: Macmillan, 1998), p. 82.

could easily prove this. These articles did not unmistakably condemn the tenets that were soon to be known as 'Arminianism.' Neither was the undeniably Reformed bent to the articles so expressed as to commit the subscriber to a full-blown Reformed soteriology. Other interpretations were available. In short, the Thirty-Nine Articles did not clinch the victory for the English reformation.[3]

In the light of this felt need there had been preparatory moves to produce a revision of or at least an explanatory appendix to the Thirty-Nine Articles. The nine Lambeth Articles of 1595 were developed under the supervision of William Whitaker and his advisors. Although arguably softened a little by the influence of Archbishop Whitgift,[4] these articles unmistakably teach an absolute and unconditional predestination to life and uphold a rigorous Reformed soteriology on the further points of total depravity and certainty of perseverance.[5] On the latter doctrine in particular the Thirty-Nine Articles were weak,[6] but the Lambeth Articles filled up the breach. However, the articles were not drawn up with royal authority. At Lambeth on 20th November, 1595, they were formally approved by Whitgift and Matthew Hutton (Archbishop of York), with Richard Fletcher (Bishop of London), Richard Vaughan (Bishop elect of Bangor), and some other prelates. Yet they never became fully authoritative in the Church of England.[7] Queen Elizabeth repudiated them and James, although allegedly of-

3. Cf. Richard Baxter, *An Apology for the Nonconformists' Ministry* (London: Thomas Parkhurst and D. Newman, 1681), p. 122; Benjamin B. Warfield, *Studies in Theology* (New York: Oxford University Press, 1932), pp. 138-42; Jan Rohls, *Reformed Confessions: Theology from Zurich to Barmen* (Louisville, KY: Westminster John Knox Press, 1998), p. 26; Carl R. Trueman, *The Claims of Truth: John Owen's Trinitarian Theology* (Carlisle, UK: Paternoster Press, 1998), p. 17.

4. Harry C. Porter, *Reformation and Reaction in Tudor Cambridge* (Cambridge: Cambridge University Press, 1958), pp. 367-71; Peter G. Lake, *Moderate Puritans and the Elizabethan Church* (Cambridge: Cambridge University Press, 1982), pp. 224-25.

5. But they are neither supralapsarian, contrary to Clausen's claim, nor infralapsarian, contrary to Tyacke's revised suggestion, and omit to address this debate (Sara J. Clausen, "Calvinism in the Anglican Hierarchy, 1603-1643: Four Episcopal Examples" [Ph.D. Dissertation, Vanderbilt University, 1989], p. 46; Nicholas R. N. Tyacke, "Anglican Attitudes: Some Recent Writings on English Religious History, from the Reformation to the Civil War," *JBS* 35 [1996]: 139-67, p. 150; cf. Tyacke, *Anti-Calvinists*, p. 31; Peter Heylyn, *Aerius Redivivus: Or, the History of the Presbyterians* [Oxford: John Crosley for Thomas Baffet, 1670], p. 344).

6. Article 16 (Philip Schaff, ed., *The Creeds of Christendom, with a History and Critical Notes* [Grand Rapids, MI: Baker Books, 1993], III:496); cf. Albert Peel, ed., *The seconde Part of a Register: Being a Calendar of Manuscripts under that Title intended for Publication by the Puritans about 1593, and now in Dr Williams's Library, London* (Cambridge: Cambridge University Press, 1915), I:197; White, *Predestination, Policy and Polemic*, pp. 96, 196-98, 220.

7. Schaff, ed., *Creeds of Christendom*, I:660-61; III:523.

fering to consider their official sanctioning at the Hampton Court Conference in 1603, never did so.[8]

The Irish Articles of Religion of 1615, which incorporated the Lambeth Articles and were destined one day to be "the chief source" of the Westminster Confession of Faith,[9] were similarly influential as a rallying point for English Calvinists in the early seventeenth century. However, these also failed to gain establishment status in the Church of England, and James revealed no sympathy for them.[10] By 1626 all attempts from British soil to clarify the official testimony of the established church had still been unsuccessful. Meanwhile the new king was giving much cause for concern, and hostility to the old Elizabethan religion was mounting.

Yet there was one last hope for Reformed English churchmen: the Canons of the Synod of Dort. James had sent a delegation of British theologians to this international, ecumenical Reformed Synod in 1618. This delegation signed the resulting Contraremonstrant canons, thereby demonstrating their harmony with the established doctrine of the Church of England.[11] In early 1624 Bishop Carleton had sought to persuade Arch-

---

8. William Laud, *The Works of the most reverend Father in God, William Laud*, ed. William Scott & James Bliss, Library of Anglo-Catholic Theology (Oxford: John Henry Parker, 1847-60), VI:246; Roland G. Usher, *The Reconstruction of the English Church* (London: D. Appleton and Co., 1910), II:344-45; Patrick Collinson, Sarah Bendall, & Christopher N. L. Brooke, *A History of Emmanuel College, Cambridge* (Woodbridge, UK: Boydell Press, 1999), p. 41. Heylyn characteristically denied that James had any sympathy for the Lambeth Articles (Peter Heylyn, *Cyprianus Anglicus: Or the History of the Life and Death, of the most reverend and renowned Prelate William* [London: For A. Seile, 1668], p. 205; Peter Heylyn, *Historia Quinqu-Articularis: Or, a Declaration of the Judgement of the Western Churches, and more particularly of the Church of England, in the five controverted Points, reproached in these last Times by the Name of Arminianism* [London: E. C. for Thomas Johnson, 1660], III:100-101; but cf. Heylyn, *Aerius Redivivus*, p. 389). Porter has unsuccessfully questioned the Calvinism of these articles, saying that they do not represent a clear statement of Calvinist doctrine. Lake has responded to this weak argumentation (Porter, *Reformation and Reaction*, pp. 366-71, 376; Lake, *Moderate Puritans*, pp. 224-26; cf. Tyacke, *Anti-Calvinists*, p. 31; Richard A. Muller in *OER*, III:336).

9. Schaff, ed., *Creeds of Christendom*, III:526; cf. Alexander F. Mitchell & John Struthers, eds., *Minutes of the Sessions of the Westminster Assembly of Divines* (Edinburgh: William Blackwood and Sons, 1874), pp. xlvii-xlix; Alexander F. Mitchell, *The Westminster Assembly: Its History and Standards Being the Baird Lecture for 1882* (London: James Nisbet & Co., 1883), pp. 379-84; Benjamin B. Warfield, *The Westminster Assembly and Its Work* (New York: Oxford University Press, 1931), pp. 124, 148-51, 169-75.

10. Tyacke, *Anti-Calvinists*, p. 155.

11. However, they studiously avoided subscribing to the ecclesiastical polity advocated by the Synod. See George Carleton, John Davenant, Walter Balcanqual, Samuel Ward, & Thomas Goad, "A joynt Attestation avowing that the Discipline of the Church of England was not impeached by the Synode of Dort" in *An Examination of those Things wherein the Author of the late*

bishop Abbot to have the Canons of Dort adopted by convocation, but James was not willing.[12] James died without ever having ratified the Canons of Dort as the official teaching of the Church of England. By early 1626 many of 'the godly' were wishing more than ever that he had done so. Yet they did not stop at a mere nostalgic glance back to the olden days. Rather they moved into action and attempted to consolidate the English Reformation upon the attainments of the Synod of Dort.[13]

The strategic focus of the English Reformed was upon the most powerful Court personality, the great Favourite himself, George Villiers the Duke of Buckingham. Hitherto the Duke had been most favourable to Reformed churchmen, including to Preston himself as we have seen.[14] However, as early as 1622 he was associated with Arminianism, and from approximately December 1624, William Laud "seems to have been more in the Duke's religious confidence than was Preston."[15] But particularly since the death of James, the Duke's allegiance to 'the godly' seemed to be wavering and it was increasingly unclear to which side of the growing division he was going to give himself. In fact, "the Duke was in a great strait, & knew not what to doe."[16] It became clear to the Reformed that it was vital to force the Duke to a public renewing of his allegiance to Reformed principles or else, as seemed more likely, to a public disowning of them. The latter scenario would at least enable 'the godly,' and especially the Duke's client Preston, to know who their real friends were and to reorganise themselves for the power struggle ahead.

Although many of Puritan persuasion expected and even, in order to gain time, desired the Duke to be divorced from the more Reformed wing,[17] the York House Conference can still be seen as a last attempt "to try to bring the Favourite to declare Calvinism to be the true theological position of the Church of England."[18] In the unlikely event that this should actually happen, it was envisaged that the Duke could then be pressured into openly supporting the conclusions of the Synod of Dort as the definitive interpretation of

---

Appeale holdeth the Doctrines of the Pelagians and Arminians, to be the Doctrines of the Church of England, by George Carleton (London: M. Flesher for R. Mylbourne, 1626), II:1-26.

12. Tyacke, *Anti-Calvinists*, p. 105.

13. Cf. Peter White, "The Rise of Arminianism Reconsidered," *Past and Present* 101 (1983): 34-54, p. 50.

14. See pp. 7, 10.

15. Tyacke, *Anti-Calvinists*, pp. 166, 167.

16. Thomas Ball, *The Life of the Renowned Doctor Preston,* ed. Edward W. Harcourt (Oxford: Parker and Co., 1885), p. 118.

17. Ball, *Life of Preston,* p. 118.

18. Morgan, *Puritan Spirituality,* p. 28.

the soteriology of the Thirty-Nine Articles. From there "it would be easy enough then to get it through Parliament."[19] This would leave the Duke once more fully committed to the cause of 'the godly' and alienate him from the growing anti-Calvinist party.

It would be wrong, however, to portray the York House Conference as occurring entirely upon the initiative of the English Calvinists, and especially only of those who wanted further to reform the Church of England's confession of faith. The Calvinist ranks also included those who, as shall be seen, were not at all interested in increasing confessional union between the Church of England and the continental Reformed churches. Such men were rather spurred into action in an attempt to maintain the *status quo* amidst the furore caused by Richard Montagu, who can be described as the catalyst behind the York House Conference. Montagu, as Canon of Windsor and Archdeacon of Hereford, had sought to defend the catholicity of the English church over against the claims of Rome in two books, *A new Gagg* and *Appello Caesarem*. The origins of these books can be traced as far back as 1619, when Montagu discovered a number of Papists seeking to proselytise his parishioners of Standford Rivers in Essex. In their own defence these Papists had resorted to, among other things, the tract of Papist John Heigham, *The Gagge of the Reformed Gospel*.[20] Montagu's *A new Gagg* was an answer to this tract. In it he sought to refute Heigham's attack on Protestantism, and in particular the Church of England, by saying that what he really was attacking was Puritanism, to which faithful Protestants were also opposed.[21] In his own words, he sought "to stand in the gapp against Puritanisme and Popery, the Scilla and Charybdis of antient piety."[22]

Yet because the 'Puritanism' that Montagu attacked sounded remarkably similar to plain 'Calvinism,' he gave the impression to many that he was an anti-Calvinist. Montagu would not admit to charges of 'heresy' but rather sought in his second book, *Appello Caesarem*, to vindicate *A new Gagg*.[23] He

19. Irvonwy Morgan, *Prince Charles's Puritan Chaplain* (London: George Allen & Unwin Ltd, 1957), p. 158; cf. Morgan, *Puritan Spirituality*, p. 29.

20. Richard Montagu, *A Gagg for the new Gospell? No: A new Gagg for an old Goose* (London: Thomas Snodham for Matthew Lownes & William Barret, 1624), To the Reader, pp. ii, v-vi; John Heigham, *The Gagge of the Reformed Gospell. Briefly discovering the Errors of our Time. With the Refutation by expresse Textes of their owne approoved English Bible* (St Omer: Charles Boscard, 1623). This book was printed under the pseudonym of Matthew Kellison.

21. Montagu, *A Gagg*, pp. 323-24; cf. Tyacke, *Anti-Calvinists*, p. 126.

22. John Cosin, *The Correspondence of John Cosin, D.D. Lord Bishop of Durham: Together with other Papers illustrative of his Life and Times*, ed. George Ornsby (Durham, UK: Andrews & Co., 1869-72), I:21.

23. Richard Montagu, *Appello Caesarem. A just Appeale from two unjust Informers* (London: For Matthew Lownes, 1625).

again attempted to demonstrate that the Church of England occupied the only safe ground between Popery (superstition) on the one hand, and Puritanism (anarchy) on the other.[24] The publication of this book only seemed to increase the evidence against him, and Montagu became a marked man, an advocate of 'Arminianism' and 'Popery' emerging from the ranks of Elizabeth and James's Protestant and Reformed church. Numerous attacks on his books immediately poured from the presses.[25] In July 1625 he had to be placed under the personal protection of King Charles, and the matter was serious enough to merit the attention of the House of Commons. The House had just begun to meet, and seemed intent on prosecuting him. The York House Conference therefore, from the Puritan point of view, can be seen as a private dress rehearsal in order to determine how easy it would be to prosecute Montagu in the Commons and to influence and ascertain the Duke's attitude toward him. If they could succeed in demonstrating that Montagu and his supporters stood in contradiction to the Thirty-Nine Articles, then it might be a natural development to establish the Canons of Dort as the authoritative interpretation of the Thirty-Nine Articles. Montagu's ecclesiastical position could then be thoroughly denounced, and his open followers silenced.[26]

In the light of this it was the strongly Protestant Earl of Warwick and Viscount Saye who finally made a move to initiate a conference on behalf of the English Calvinists. They swiftly put forward an "importunate suit unto the duke and to his majesty, that their two champions might be but admitted to shew their valour against the heresies, blasphemies, treasons, apostacies, that were pretended to be in [Montagu's] books."[27] In doing this they were

---

24. Cf. Tyacke, *Anti-Calvinists*, pp. 125-26.

25. See, for example, Henry Burton, *A Plea to an Appeale: Traversed Dialogue wise* (London: W. I., 1626); George Carleton, *An Examination of those Things wherein the Author of the late Appeale holdeth the Doctrines of the Pelagians and Arminians, to be the Doctrines of the Church of England* (London: For William Turner, 1626); Daniel Featley, *Pelagius redivivus. Or, Pelagius raked out of the Ashes by Arminius and his Schollers* (London: For Robert Milbourne, 1626); Daniel Featley, *A Second Parallel together with a Writ of Error sued against the Appealer* (London: J. Haviland for Robert Milbourne, 1626); Anthony Wotton, *A dangerous Plot discovered. By a Discourse, wherein is proved, that, Mr Richard Montague, in his two Bookes; the one, called A new Gagg; the other, A just Appeale: laboureth to bring in the Faith of Rome, and Arminius* (London: For Nicholas Bourne, 1626); John Yates, *Ibis ad Cæsarem. Or, a submissive Appearance before Cæsar; in Answer to Mr Montagues Appeale in the Pointes of Arminianisme and Popery, maintained and defended by him, against the Doctrine of the Church of England* (London: For R. Mylbourne, 1626).

26. From the point of view of Buckingham, however, the aim was probably to rally enough support for Montagu amongst the influential lords present, so that the House of Lords would be able to defeat any prosecution of Montagu by the House of Commons (Tyacke, *Anti-Calvinists*, p. 166).

27. John Cosin, *The Works of the Right Reverend Father in God, John Cosin*, Library of

"encouraged by some orthodox & very learned Bishops."[28] Charles and Buckingham agreed to this confrontation, and Tyacke suggests that this was possibly because they "hoped to drive a religious wedge between Pembroke and the other more politically radical peers such as Warwick and his ally Viscount Saye."[29] Whatever the motives, the stage had now been set.

The Participants

Before the details of the conference debates are examined it is necessary to examine the list of those who were present. On the side of English Calvinism there were two speakers. The first was the Bishop of Lichfield and Coventry, Thomas Morton. During his 'Puritan' regime as Master of St John's,[30] Cambridge, Whitaker had personally picked Morton to be Fellow. Subsequently as Rector of Long Marston near York, Morton had acquired a formidable reputation in public disputations with Roman Catholics, and by 1626 he had already published a number of learned and rigorous attacks against the Roman Church.[31] In the favourable climate of James's reign, Morton had attained to the See of Lichfield and Coventry having been bishop of Chester. However, although he never revealed any sympathy with the views of William Laud, Morton was by no means an ecclesiastical Puritan. He had already dedicated to the Duke of Buckingham a treatise in defence of surplices, the signing of the cross at baptism, and kneeling at the Eucharist.[32] However, he now came

Anglo-Catholic Theology (Oxford: John Henry Parker, 1843-55), II:21-22, 73-74; cf. Laud, *Works*, III:182; Heylyn, *Cyprianus Anglicus*, p. 147. Saye seems to have been more zealous against Montagu than Warwick. Cf. Cosin, *Works*, II:69; Thomas Fuller, *The Church-History of Britain* (London: For John William, 1655), XI:124-25.

28. Ball, *Life of Preston*, p. 118.

29. Tyacke, *Anti-Calvinists*, p. 168.

30. See Lake, *Moderate Puritans*, pp. 169-200.

31. Thomas Morton, *Apologia Catholica ex Meris Jesuitarum Contradictionibus conflata, in qua Paradoxa, Hæreses, Blasphemiæ, Scelera, quæ a Pontificiis obijci Protestantibus solent, ex ipsorum Pontificiorum Testimoniis diluuntur omnia* (London: George Bishop, 1605); Thomas Morton, *A full Satisfaction concerning a double Romish Iniquitie; hainous Rebellion, and more than heathenish Æquivocation* (London: Richard Field for Edmond Weaver, 1606); Thomas Morton, *A Catholike Appeale for Protestants, out of the Confessions of the Romane Doctors* (London: George Bishop and John Norton, 1609). Nor did he stop after the York House Conference.

32. *ODNB*; Thomas Morton, *A Defence of the Innocencie of the three Ceremonies of the Church of England. Viz. The Surplice, Crosse after Baptisme, and Kneeling at the receiving of the Blessed Sacrament* (London: For William Barret, 1618). This substantial work against nonconformists was reprinted in 1619. Furthermore, Morton was later to write in defence of episcopacy: Thomas Morton, *Confessions and Proofes of Protestant Divines of Reformed Churches, that Epis-*

to York House determined, as he saw it, to stamp out any tendencies to exploit this moderation and take the Church of England back to Rome. In this stand Morton "almost certainly had" Archbishop Abbot's "tacit approval."[33] John Preston, with whose views on predestination and grace we are now more familiar, seconded Morton at the request of certain influential friends.

In addition to the two Reformed protagonists there were also present several aristocrats who acted as political leaders for 'the godly.' The first of these were the hard-line Protestants Saye and Sele and Warwick, already mentioned. Warwick was given the title "the temporal head of the puritans" by Lord Conway in a letter to Laud, and Tyacke sees 'Puritan' as a suitable label for both these men.[34] Saye was an "honourable and faithful" friend of Preston's,[35] and Warwick was "the intimate friend" of Sibbes.[36] These two political Puritans were joined by William the third Earl of Pembroke and the Lord Chamberlain. Pembroke was one of the richest of the English nobility, and his allegiance to the Calvinist cause appears to have owed relatively little to personal religious convictions.[37] Yet in practical terms his promotion of Reformed churchmanship was in no way softened as a result. Four months after this conference, as Chancellor of Oxford University, Pembroke secured for the university a respite from the 1626 proclamation, which at Cambridge had been used immediately to silence Calvinism under Buckingham.[38] Sir John Coke, the Secretary of State, was another Calvinist present at the conference. He "enjoyed a certain popularity as being a sound protestant" and was even "accounted a puritan." He was also the only one of the nine laymen present who was not a member of the House of Lords.[39]

---

copacy is in Respect of the Office according to the Word of God, and in Respect of the Use the best. Together with a briefe Treatise touching the Originall of Bishops and Metropolitans (Oxford: Henry Hall, 1644); Thomas Morton, Επισκοπος Αποστολικος, The Episcopacy of the Church of England justified to be apostolical, from the Authority of the ancient primitive Church: And from the Confessions of the most famous Divines of the Reformed Churches beyond the Seas (London: For J. Collins, 1670).

33. Tyacke, *Anti-Calvinists*, p. 171.

34. PRO SP 16/456/43; Tyacke, *Anti-Calvinists*, p. 169. See also William A. Hunt Jr., *The Puritan Moment: The Coming of Revolution in an English County* (Cambridge, MA: Harvard University Press, 1983), p. 166.

35. PRO, PROB. 11/154, f. 102v.

36. *DNB.*

37. Tyacke, *Anti-Calvinists*, p. 168; *ODNB.*

38. Nicholas R. N. Tyacke, "Puritanism, Arminianism & Counter-Revolution" in *The Origins of the English Civil War*, ed. Conrad Russell (London: Macmillan, 1973), 119-43, p. 133; Tyacke, *Anti-Calvinists*, p. 168.

39. *DNB*; Tyacke, *Anti-Calvinists*, p. 166.

In defence of Montagu at the Conference were three churchmen of an allegedly 'Arminian' persuasion. The first was the Bishop of Rochester John Buckeridge. As Foundation Fellow of St John's, Oxford, Buckeridge had already instilled into his pupil and future life-long friend William Laud his anti-Calvinistic, high-church convictions.[40] He was consecrated Bishop of Rochester in 1611 when Lancelot Andrewes and Richard Neile were among the assisting prelates.[41] Twice he had written to the Duke of Buckingham in support of Montagu — on 2nd August, 1625, with Laud and Howson, and again on 16th January, 1626, with Laud, Andrewes, Neile, and Montaigne — and now he was to defend him in person.[42] The second defendant was Dr. Francis White, Dean of Carlisle. White was soon to be made Bishop of Carlisle in December, when Neile and Buckeridge would be among those performing the consecration, and John Cosin would preach the consecration sermon.[43] As well as assisting Montagu in the writing of his *Appello Caesarem*, White had written in 1624 'The Approbation' for the same book, in which he had stated with approval that the book contained nothing "but what is agreeable to the Publick Faith, Doctrine and Discipline established in the Church of England."[44] White had therefore come to the Conference as much to defend himself as to defend Montagu. The last of this 'Arminian' trio was the young John Cosin, Canon of Durham. As secretary to Bishop Overall, Cosin was already involved in continental Arminianism, and his sermons of 1625 reveal a certain amount of chafing against predestinarianism.[45] Montagu's *Appello Caesarem* was the product of a close literary partnership with Cosin, and parts inserted by Cosin can be detected when Montagu is referred to in the third person.[46] Although this was secret knowledge at the time, Cosin was therefore another who had come to the Conference as much to defend himself as to defend Montagu. In addition to these active participants, there were also a few other laymen present who do not appear to have had any vocal role

40. However, whether Laud was an 'Arminian' as such is a subject of debate. See Kevin Sharpe, "Archbishop Laud," *HT* 33 (1983): 26-30; Tyacke, *Anti-Calvinists*, pp. x-xi, 266-70.

41. *DNB; ODNB.*

42. Laud, *Works,* VI:244-46, 249.

43. Cosin, *Works,* I:85-105.

44. White, *Predestination, Policy and Polemic,* p. 224. For White's own defence of this approbation and his comments on the supportive stand he took towards Montagu see Bod Rawlinson MS. C.573, ff. 21r-92r; ECL MS. 95a, ff. 1-176.

45. Tyacke, *Anti-Calvinists,* p. 172; Cosin, *Works,* I:66, 78-79.

46. Thomas Birch, ed., *The Court and Times of Charles the First. Illustrated by authentic and confidential Letters, from various public and private Collections* (London: Henry Colburn, 1848), I:449; Cosin, *Correspondence,* I:xiii; White, *Predestination, Policy and Polemic,* p. 223.

in the proceedings.[47] Presiding over all these was the chairman, the Duke of Buckingham.

The Evidence

No account of the proceedings at York House was published at the time, but a number of manuscript reports were produced. Thomas Fuller noted that these reports were all "differently related" with some "makeing it a clear conquest on one, some on the other side, and a third sort a drawn battail betwixt both."[48] Of the latter group it would appear that no copies are now extant. Perhaps it was this more balanced type of account that was present at the Company of Stationers on 2nd September, 1645, but was evidently never finally printed.[49] Of the first group the margin cites Ball's 'Puritan' account, which forms part of Preston's biography. Also to be included under Fuller's first group are the several accounts made by Preston himself in order to vindicate himself before those who, as we shall see later, were disappointed at reports of his performance. At least three of these manuscripts survive and it is likely that Ball relied primarily, though not exclusively, on Preston's manuscripts.[50] Of Fuller's second group, namely those clearly biased towards the 'Arminian' side, the manuscript account of John Cosin survives.[51] Francis White made corrections and additions to Cosin's draft, but these eyewitness reports were not published until 1845. Clausen sees Cosin's account as having been "more influential" than Preston's, but argues that the 'Arminian' reports of Morton's contribution at the conference cannot be accurate as some of his reported statements concerning baptism do not tally with his 1618 defence of ceremonies.[52] However, even

47. These included Edmund Sheffield the first Earl of Mulgrave, John Egerton the first Earl of Bridgewater, and Lord Dorset (all of whom only attended the second session), as well as the Earl of Lincoln, James Hay the first Earl of Carlisle, who was possibly sympathetic to Popery (*DNB; ODNB*), and possibly one or two others (Morgan, *Prince Charles's Puritan Chaplain*, p. 160).

48. Fuller, *Church-History of Britain*, XI:125.

49. Company of Stationers, *A Transcript of the Registers of the worshipful Company of Stationers: From 1640-1708 A.D.* (London: Private publication, 1913), I:190; cf. II:239-40.

50. BL Harleian MS. 6866, ff. 73-81; BL Burney MS. 362, ff. 86r-95r; Bod Tanner MS. 303, ff. 46-47. It seems as if one of these manuscripts later fell into 'enemy' hands. The editor of Laud's diary, Henry Wharton declared in 1693 that, "An account of this Conference is in my hands, but wrote very partially, in favour of Dr. Preston and prejudice of Dr. White" (Laud, *Works*, III:182).

51. Bod Tanner MS. 303, ff. 32-46.

52. Clausen, "Calvinism in the Anglican Hierarchy," pp. 97, 313; Morton, *A Defence of the Innocencie of the three Ceremonies of the Church of England*.

if this were so, this assumes, perhaps without warrant, that Morton's opinions had not changed over the course of eight years. Donagan, however, has satisfactorily established the general reliability and accuracy of these sources for our purposes, despite their partisan origins.[53]

The Proceedings

The first point to be noted is Preston's reluctance to attend the conference in the first place. Preston himself tells us that at midday on Saturday, 11th February, he received clear notice concerning the conference to begin at 4 o'clock,[54] and Warwick and Saye came to Morton's lodging at about 2 o'clock and from there sent for him.[55] However, Preston did not "enter the chamber" until "a quarter of an houre before the Conference was ended: for which time hee stood by as an hearer."[56] He had "refused for some reason to goe: as judging it inconvenient," but had later changed his mind because he was "doubting how his absence might bee taken by some, and fearing lest he should seeme to discredit ye cause."[57] The Duke would have been more surprised with Preston's final attendance than with his absence, for he had warned the Duke that he would not attend. Ball explains Preston's reticence in terms of both his and the Duke's unwillingness "to open a breach," loving as they did "to temporize & wait upon events." Preston did not want to do anything that might endanger his relationship with the Duke, and, if their close association was noticeably dissolving, it was not his purpose to hasten the process by an open wrangle. In this he was clearly set against the strategy of 'the godly' who had organised the York House Conference with its express purpose being "to cause a clear breach between the Duke and Preston's cause."[58] Ball tells us

53. Donagan, "The York House Conference Revisited," Appendix. Donagan finds only "minor" variations between the manuscripts in Preston's group, and even these "mostly arise from copying." Even when the narratives from the two rival groups are compared, Donagan finds "few significant discrepancies," and argues for their reliability from, among other things, the fact that they "were sufficiently plausible to be circulated," and that neither side "could hope to get away with seriously misleading narratives."

54. BL Harleian MS. 6866, f. 73r; Ball, *Life of Preston*, p. 119.

55. Ball, *Life of Preston*, p. 119. Preston himself gives the time as 3 o'clock (BL Harleian MS. 6866, f. 73r).

56. BL Harleian MS. 6866, f. 73r; cf. Cosin, *Works*, II:30, 51. Ball says he "sat by as a hearer silent, untill all was done" (Ball, *Life of Preston*, p. 119).

57. BL Harleian MS. 6866, f. 73r. Ball puts it this way: "fearing his absence might betray the cause, & give encouragement unto the other side" (Ball, *Life of Preston*, p. 119).

58. Ball, *Life of Preston*, p. 118.

how Preston was finally to change his mind. Preston had hesitated to go as he had previously been thinking that, no matter how shaky the relationship might be, the Duke was still on his side. According to Ball the Duke "had sent to Doctor Preston to decline this clashing conference, and assured him that he was as much his friend as ever, & would have stopt it if he could, but the Bishops had overruled it."[59] Because Preston had initially believed this, he delayed to attend the confrontation. When he finally did arrive at York House, however, "he saw the confidence of Dr. White and his companion" and consequently "doubted the sincerity of that assurance."[60]

Perhaps Preston was still shaken by such doubts for the remainder of the first session of the conference. He cannot have regretted his silence, however, because thus far the accusations by Morton against Montagu had been embarrassingly trivial and "needless," and even Pembroke said that his charges were to "stretch and wrest a well-meaning man's words too far."[61] Montagu's books had escaped condemnation in any point. It was then, however, that Lord Saye's great confidence in Preston's theological acumen became apparent. Unhappy that proceedings should end without some words from the Master of Emmanuel, and ignoring the fact that the other Lords were arising from the table to depart, Saye urged that they had not yet discussed "the chiefest matter," namely "falling away from grace, and the definitions of the synod of Dort against Arminianism." He announced that Preston would now speak to the question "and manifest Mr. Montague's errors."[62] Yet although the lords delayed their departure, it seems that even after this attempt by Saye to involve Preston that he remained silent.[63]

It was up to Morton therefore to attempt to refute White, which he began to do. Soon they were embroiled in a dispute over possible objective and subjective states of justification. At this point, pressed once again by Lord Saye, Preston finally spoke up, undoubtedly to the great relief of Saye.[64] Preston "began very soberly to declare that it was none of his desire to say any thing; but yet seeing it pleased their lordships to have it so, he would endeavour to answer Dr. White's objections, and to make the matter as clear and evident as might be."[65] Preston argued that one could not lose one's state

59. Ball, *Life of Preston*, pp. 122-23.

60. Ball, *Life of Preston*, p. 123. Morgan misreads Ball here (Morgan, *Prince Charles's Puritan Chaplain*, p. 160).

61. Cosin, *Works*, II:35, 52.

62. Cosin, *Works*, II:56.

63. BL Harleian MS. 6866, f. 73r; Cosin, *Works*, II:56-59.

64. Cosin, *Works*, II:59.

65. Cosin, *Works*, II:59.

of justification or sonship, although one could become a son under chastisement. White thought Preston's comments "most absurd," and Buckeridge rejected Preston's reasoning outright.[66] However, by this time it was "growing late" and the conference soon dispersed, breaking into groups of heated dispute as they left.[67]

After this first session Preston was "informed that there had bin a meeting at the Countess of Denbigh's," at which the Duke "had promised to leave him." Knowing now therefore that the Duke "doubled with him," Preston found "resolution and encouragement against the second conference" and "was less fearfull to offend him."[68] The Duke was now well and truly committed to 'the other side' and had openly become "the great protector of the Montagutians."[69] Discussion at the second session on 17th February was therefore much more involved and pertinent than that of the first. This time Montagu himself was present to answer in person the accusations made against him. According to Cosin every single one of these charges was "defended and freely answered," Montagu replying "with perspicuous brevity and delight to all that were present."[70] Whether this was the case or not, the focus did extend beyond general nit-picking concerning Montagu's ambiguous printed statements, to more of the larger theological controversies of the day in their own right.

Proceedings began with a debate between Preston and Montagu on questions arising from Mountagu's *A new Gagg* concerning the authority of ecclesiastical tradition. It was not long, however, before Preston switched his line of attack. He raised the issue of divine election, provoked by some dubious comments on the subject in Montagu's books.[71] These were interpreted by his opponents as to mean "that he held election out of foresight or to be a respective conditionall decree."[72] White, who was "very fierce & eager to engage,"[73] sought to focus attention on the decree of reprobation, on which the Thirty-Nine Articles were silent, and affirmed that it was "but a privat fancy of some to

66. BL Harleian MS. 6866, ff. 73r, 73v; Cosin, *Works*, II:60.

67. BL Harleian MS. 6866, f. 74v.

68. Ball, *Life of Preston*, p. 123.

69. Dr Meddus to Joseph Mead on 22nd May, 1626. Quoted in W. Brown Patterson, *King James VI and I and the Reunion of Christendom* (Cambridge: Cambridge University Press, 1997), p. 285.

70. Cosin, *Works*, II:73, 74.

71. Ball, *Life of Preston*, p. 126; Montagu, *A Gagg*, p. 179; Montagu, *Appello Caesarem*, pp. 58, 64.

72. BL Harleian MS. 6866, f. 77r.

73. Ball, *Life of Preston*, p. 127.

saie absolutely that Judas was condemned without respect to sinne," and was certainly "not the doctrine of the Church of England." It would be interesting to know who these "some" were to whom White was referring. Certainly he cannot have rightly included Perkins or Preston in this misrepresentation of Reformed soteriology.[74] Preston was therefore not willing to "charge Mountague with yt [i.e., that] point of the decree, but with the other, yt Election is no absolute but respective decree: grounded uppon ye foresighte of faith & obedience." This was an unmistakable charge of Arminianism and White, no doubt seeing this, "[g]ave in" and "left Mr Mountague to him selfe to defend it," having on his own part "nothing to saie" in objection to Preston.[75]

This was the beginning of a clever stratagem from Preston to divide his opposition. Willing further to alienate White from Montagu, Preston informs us that he did not turn to Montagu immediately as White had motioned, but continued to interrogate White. He forced White into admitting that saving grace was "ye fruite of Election," and then argued that where the fruit or effect was, there must also be the cause, namely election. The inescapable conclusion was that "whoseover hath saving grace is elected, and whosoever is elected cannot falle away." White was now found contradicting his own position taken at the first session concerning falling from grace, although this he denied.[76]

Montagu, observing that White "forsooke him in the point of respective Election," was not sure which line to take.[77] He attempted to defend conditional election "as if the doctrine of the Church of England had exprest nothing against the opinion of respective Election ex previsa fide." Preston pointed out that the 17th Article did in fact oppose such a notion. Having whispered with "one of the Lords," Montagu realised he was trapped, and admitted that "indeed he had not considered some things set doune by him in those points of Arminianisme."[78] He confessed that he had written his book "somwhat more neclygently [sic] against an aduersary" and had not realised that it "shoulde bee brought to so strickt examination by friends." Somewhat feebly he promised the conference that "he would write a booke to ye contrary to explaine himselfe better and yt he would doe it with butter & honny."[79]

Saye and Coke then motioned "to the duke's Grace, that he would be a means to bring in the synod of Dort, and to get it established here by author-

74. See above, pp. 34, 78-79.
75. BL Harleian MS. 6866, f. 77v.
76. BL Harleian MS. 6866, ff. 77v-78r; cf. Ball, *Life of Preston*, p. 126.
77. BL Harleian MS. 6866, f. 78r; cf. Ball, *Life of Preston*, p. 129.
78. BL Harleian MS. 6866, f. 78r; Ball, *Life of Preston*, p. 130.
79. BL Harleian MS. 6866, f. 78r. Montagu never did publish such a sequel.

ity in the Church of England."[80] Their reasons were simple: "All these matters would be quieted if the Synod of Dort might be established here in England" for, after all, James's British delegation had "approved" the Canons.
White was not at all impressed with this suggestion, having little respect for
the work of that Synod, and exhorted the conference with the words, "let us
have none of that, for neither our Church nor state may bear it."[81] By this
comment White seems to have been referring both to the discipline *and* doctrine of the Church of England.[82] He continued: "I beseech your lordships
. . . that we of the Church of England be not put to borrow a new faith from
any village in the Netherlands."[83] Buckingham was similarly unequivocal:
"away with it; we have nothing to do with that synod."[84] He said that this was
"not the first motion that hath been made for the synod of Dort," and repeated White's concern, having "been assured by divers grave and learned
prelates, that it can neither stand with the safety of this Church nor state to
bring it in."[85]

White "produced divers reasons against the admission and establishing"
of the Canons of Dort, and, interestingly for our own purposes, one of these
reasons was the extent of Christ's satisfaction and the gospel call. White knew
that Dort "either apertly or covertly denied the universality of man's redemption per pretii solutionem pro omnibus, nemine excepto, pro mortem
Christi." He saw that such teaching "opposeth the Church of England, and
taketh away all preaching to such as are not absolutely elected."[86] White
claimed that the Synod "either plainly or involvedly" had

80. Cosin, *Works*, II:63.
81. Cosin, *Works*, II:38; Ball, *Life of Preston*, p. 130.
82. BL Harleian MS. 6866, f. 78v; cf. White's comments on the Synod of Dort in ECL MS.
95a, ff. 83-85.
83. Cosin, *Works*, II:63.
84. Cosin, *Works*, II:38. Buckingham was echoing precisely the view that Buckeridge,
Howson, and Laud had expressed to him by letter the previous August (Laud, *Works*, VI:246).
85. Cosin, *Works*, II:63.
86. Cosin, *Works*, II:38; cf. White's understanding of Calvinist doctrine in Bod Rawlinson
MS. C.573, f. 28. It is likely that the reference is to Article 8 of the Second Head of the Canons,
which reads: "It was the will of God, that Christ by the blood of the cross . . . should effectually
redeem out of every people, tribe, nation and language, all those, *and those only,* who were from
eternity chosen to salvation, and given to him by the Father; that he should confer upon them
faith, which, together with all the other saving gifts of the Holy Spirit, he purchased for them by
his death" (Schaff, ed., *Creeds of Christendom*, III:587; emphasis added). The Latin reads: "voluit
Deus, ut Christus per sanguinem crucis . . . ex omni populo, tribu, gente, et lingua, eos omnes *et
solos,* qui ab æterno ad salutem electi, et a Patre ipsi dati sunt, efficaciter redimeret" (Schaff, ed.,
Creeds of Christendom, III:562). Cosin says White was referring to "the second Article" (Cosin,
Works, II:63).

established a doctrine repugnant to the faith of our Church. The Dortists (as appeareth by their several expositions of that Article) have denied that Christ died for all men. But our Church, in the Catechism, and many other places, hath taught us to believe that Christ died for all, 'and hath redeemed me and all mankind,' that is, paid the ransom and the price for all without exception; and that if any man be damned, it is not because Christ died not for him, but because the fruit of Christ's death, by that man's own fault, is not applied unto him. Adding hereunto, that a great and manifest mischief it was, to have our people taught that Christ died not for them all.[87]

The words must have hung in the air for Preston, who was suddenly faced with the troubled question of the extent of Christ's satisfaction and its relation to the universal gospel call. While Preston hesitated, some of the Lords were not reticent to offer their own opinion. Pembroke and Carlisle took a middle path, saying, "Let the synod of Dort bind them that have submitted themselves unto it, in England we have a rule of our own." Buckingham continued to distance himself even more from 'the godly,' saying openly, "We have nothing to do with that synod; it is all about the hidden and intricate points of predestination, which are not fit matters to trouble the people withal." Morton objected to this comment in that the Thirty-Nine Articles also "speak of predestination." Cosin rejoindered that "the conclusion of that Article is, that predestination is so to be taught, as that the general promises of the Gospel be not destroyed by it."[88] But *did* the particularity of grace exhibited in the Canons of Dort 'destroy' the promises of the gospel? If not, wherein exactly lay the offensive nature of the Canons over against the Thirty-Nine Articles? Cosin does not seem to have been interested in pursuing this investigation further, as his account does not cover this part of the conference. Yet Preston's version, revealing an acute sensitivity to this subject, provides detailed coverage. Preston's first tactic was to try to deny that there was any such tension. After all, he himself could subscribe to both formularies, since the doctrine of the Synod was "most sound." To reinforce this statement Preston threw out a challenge: "If you thinke good to oppose any parte of it I will defend it."[89] The gauntlet had been thrown down by the highly es-

---

87. Cosin, *Works*, II:63. White also expressed these same views in his defence of Montagu in ECL MS. 95a, f. 83; cf. Bod Rawlinson MS. C.573, ff. 70v-71r. White is referring to the Church of England Catechism of 1549, where the catechumen is to state his belief "in God the Son, who hath redeemed me and all mankind" (Schaff, ed., *Creeds of Christendom*, III:518).

88. Cosin, *Works*, II:64.

89. BL Harleian MS. 6866, f. 78v. At this point Preston also bolstered his authority by de-

teemed leader of 'the godly.' White could not resist this opportunity to drive a wedge between the narrow theology of the continental Reformation and the catholic faith of the Church of England.

White immediately took up Preston's gauntlet by selecting the death of Christ for discussion. White claimed that it was "universall & for all," which Dort denied. Preston did not defend Dort's statements at this point. Rather, he responded indirectly by asking White whether he held that "the decree of giving Christ to all" preceded or followed "the decree of Election and reprobation."[90] White asserted that it preceded it. Preston expressed disagreement with the implication of this, namely, that "Gods intention in giuing Christ did alike respect Elect and reprobate." White remained adamant that Christ was "giuen alike to all in Gods intention and decree."[91] Preston could not accept this, although he was willing to acknowledge before White a twofold donation of Christ, in that Christ is given to the elect and the reprobate in different senses.[92] However, if there was no discrimination at all, as White envisaged, "then the greatest loue yt God ever shewed to mankind, and ye best gift yt ever he gaue, is a like intended to ye saints in heauen, and to the damned in hell." Preston, as we have already come to expect, saw this as "contrary to ye scriptures, which are frequent in setting forth Gods peculiar Grace." Preston saw White's position as "absurd" for then the elect are "no more behoulding unto God for the peculiar mercy of giving his owne sonne: than ye Reprobate: and shall haue no more cause to giue him thankes for it in harte [*sic; lege* heaven], than they in hell." But White had not actually said this, and he too could see a particular aspect to God's love: "The particulernes of Gods loue though it appeare not in the decree of giuing Christ, who was intended to all; yet it appeareth in ye particulation of Christ yt he giues faith to some & not to others." This subtle distinction stems from constructing a clear difference in scope between the death of Christ and the application of the benefits of that death. Christ did not give faith to all those for whom he died.

---

claring that he had spoken personally about such matters with certain members of the British delegation to Dort. One of these divines would undoubtedly have been his intimate friend Bishop Davenant. For an examination of Davenant's hypothetical universalism see Ch. 7. Furthermore, if Preston did not personally own a copy of the Synod's proceedings, he would have been able to consult the copies in his college's library (Sargent Bush Jr. & Carl J. Rasmussen, *The Library of Emmanuel College, Cambridge, 1584-1637* [Cambridge: Cambridge University Press, 1986], pp. 119, 147).

90. BL Harleian MS. 6866, f. 78v. A marginal note at this point reads, "For this is the touchstone to know whether it be Arminious opinion or no."

91. BL Harleian MS. 6866, f. 79r.

92. Ball, *Life of Preston*, p. 132.

Alarmingly for Preston, White's 'Arminianism' was coming to sound remarkably like his own brand of hypothetical universalism at this point. It is not surprising that in Preston's account he immediately seeks to push White back into a fully 'Arminian' position and distance himself from any notions of universal redemption. He asked White if he did not "hold universall grace running along with [his] universall redemption." Preston suspected he might, "because none hould ye one without the other." White freely admitted that he did. Preston thought that this admission that "all haue a sufficiency of grace to take Christ" undermined White's alleged doctrine of particularity of grace. White's teaching that Christ gave faith only to the elect was mere rhetoric, because clearly in his system what finally "makes the difference betweene peter [*sic*] & Judas" is "mans free will." Preston concluded that the lords present would be able to "see how this doctrine of universall redemption opposeth Gods peculiar free grace" and "takes it away."[93]

According to Preston, White did not answer this point, "but was willing to leaue this question of universall grace & to retourne againe unto ye point of Christ dying for all." White clearly knew how to avoid being diverted from his agenda and now made it more explicit, "abruptly" asking Preston, "did Christ dye for all or not?" It seems from Preston's account that in the presence of such strict Calvinists as Lord Saye, who had initiated this conference on behalf of English Calvinists and who was later to sit in on the Westminster Assembly, Preston now had to be extremely careful. He began by saying that this "question must be answered with a distinction." While happy to resort to fine distinctions himself, White appears, however, to have had little patience with others who might seek the same refuge. He replied, "What need any distinction, answer directly: did Christ die for all or no?" That White pressed this question so urgently indicates that he expected English Calvinists, Preston included, to deny this and then be made to appear out of step with the Thirty-Nine Articles.[94] However, Preston insisted that distinctions were in fact necessary at this point concerning "in what sence he died for all" and "in what not," and were standard practice "with diuines on both sides." This may well have been true, but White was determined to get a straight answer from Preston: "But can you not say I, or noe?" Preston replied, "If you will need haue it so answered: I will answer affirmatiuely, yt he did die for all: because yt agrees with the words of Scrip-

93. BL Harleian MS. 6866, ff. 79r, 79v.

94. Nor was White pursuing an irrelevant, obscurantist point for the sheer fun of it (cf. Julian E. Davies, *The Caroline Captivity of the Church: Charles I and the Remoulding of Anglicanism, 1625-1641* [Oxford: Clarendon Press, 1992], p. 92). Rather, this controversy had been troubling leading English divines for many years (cf. James Ussher, *The whole Works of the most Rev. James Ussher,* ed. Charles R. Erlington [Dublin: Hodges and Smith, 1847-64], XII:553).

ture."[95] While for decades the Reformed had been seeking to explain that Scripture's numerous references to 'all' in relation to the death of Christ did not in fact mean 'all without exception' but 'all without distinction' or alternatively 'all of the elect,' Preston was prepared to admit that they must be accepted in the sense of the plainest meaning. In his manuscript account of the conference, Preston is clearly at pains to stress the circumstances under which he was pressured to make such a statement. But as we have already seen, Preston was in fact uttering no more than the unmistakable undercurrent of his regular preaching ministry, and, on more than one occasion, his own explicit teaching.

Tyacke therefore misreads the situation when he sees in these words of Preston "the conventional Calvinist distinction between the sufficiency of Christ's death for all and its efficacy to the elect alone."[96] Although Preston later does go on to speak of a "distinction of sufficiency and efficacy: id est, yt it is sufficient for all, both elect and reprobate: effectuall to some, id est, the elect only,"[97] he does not mean this in the sense that a 'conventional' Calvinist would. Preston did not now qualify his statement with the familiar interpretation of 'all' meaning 'all sorts' or 'all the elect.' Rather, his hypothetical universalism is articulated in the very manuscripts of Preston from which Tyacke quotes. Preston continued by pleading, "I must add the distinction afterwards in what sence I afferme it."[98] He proceeded to explain that

> though his intention be not to saue the Reprobate: yet it was to make them *saluabiles* in regarde of the suffitiency of Christ's death to saue them: though they bee not *saluabiles* in regarde of there [sic] inabillitie to apprehend it. And this is to put them into another condition than deuells are in, for Christs death hath no suffitiency to saue the divells: but to saue those it hath.[99]

The sufficiency of Christ's satisfaction is here no longer being linked with the hypostatic union of the two natures, but with one aspect of the salvific will of God. Peter White therefore considerably underestimates Preston's position at the conference when he describes this as "a merely cosmetic adjustment to the doctrine of limited Atonement."[100] Dewey Wallace also hardly offers us an adequate summary of Preston's teaching on the atonement at York House

---

95. BL Harleian MS. 6866, f. 79v.
96. Tyacke, *Anti-Calvinists*, p. 180.
97. BL Harleian MS. 6866, f. 80r.
98. BL Harleian MS. 6866, f. 79v.
99. BL Harleian MS. 6866, f. 80r.
100. White, *Predestination, Policy and Polemic*, p. 230.

when he presents it merely as the belief that "the elect alone benefit from Christ's death."[101] Preston himself seems to have felt some vulnerability through his statement, and in his account is eager to explain how he differed from the Arminian doctrine of universal atonement:

> ye decree and purpose of God in giuing Christ did followe the decree of Election & reprobation; and not goe before it, as in order of nature the disease goeth before the Remedy or medicine: after this manner after God had chosen some to life out the masse of man kind, passing by others: he secondly decreed to giue Jesus Christ to them as a mediator, & meanes to bring them to euerlasting life . . . so that Gods decree & purpose of giuing Christ proceedeth out of a peculiar Loue to the Elect, not of a generall Loue to all which is one difference of[102] the Arminians and us, in this point for they afferme yt the intention of God in giuing Christe, is equall to saue all one as well as an other.[103]

The *ordo decretorum* with regard to predestination and redemption, and not the nature of redemption itself, was therefore crucial to Preston in distinguishing his own position from Arminian formulations.

More evidence for Preston's hypothetical universalism is also found in Ball's account of the proceedings. It must be remembered that Preston's own manuscript reports of the York House Conference, as we shall see later, were occasioned by considerable disappointment in his performance from 'the godly.' It is thus likely that Preston is seeking to put as favourable a construction on what he said as possible so as to placate the high Calvinists amongst them. But it seems as if Ball, writing after Preston's decease, was less con-

---

101. Dewey D. Wallace Jr., *Puritans and Predestination: Grace in English Protestant Theology, 1525-1695* (Chapel Hill, NC: University of North Carolina Press, 1982), p. 88. Wallace also seems unaware of the distinct hypothetical universalist position when he asserts that the "English delegates at Dort agreed that . . . atonement was limited to the elect," and that Ussher also taught "limited atonement" (Wallace, *Puritans and Predestination*, pp. 81, 97). Cf. Clausen, "Calvinism in the Anglican Hierarchy," pp. 148, 163, 285, 355.

102. The word "betweene" is written above the text at this point in what appears to be the same hand. This may have been supplied from BL Burney MS. 362, f. 94v, which reads "difference betweene."

103. BL Harleian MS. 6866, ff. 79v-80r. In passing we may note here further evidence of Preston's infralapsarian schema. Preston does not explicitly say here that the decree of election and reprobation followed the decree of the fall. However, he does state that humanity having fallen is subject to the decree of election and reprobation in which some are selected to life and the remainder merely 'passed by' and left to themselves in their sin. Secondly, due to the evidence presented above on pp. 113-16, Preston's words are to be taken in the sense of "not *merely* of a general love to all *only*."

cerned to placate such men and provides us with further evidence of Preston's hypothetical universalism. Concerning the English Catechism's statement of belief "in God the Son, who hath redeemed me and all mankind," Preston is reported to have defined 'redemption' there as meaning

> only . . . the freeing of mankind from that inevitable ruine the sin of Adam had involved them in, and making them savable upon conditions of another covenant. Jn. 3:16, 17. So that now salvation was not impossible, as it was before the death of Christ; but might be offered unto any man, according to the tenour of that commission, Mk. 16:15, 16. This could not however be applied unto the Divels, if they were left in that forlorn condition whereunto their sin & disobedience put them.[104]

White insisted "earnestly" to the contrary "that Christ dyed for all alike in God's intention and decree; for Cain as well as Abel; for Saul as well as David; for Judas as much as Peter; for the reprobate & damned in Hell as well as for the elect and saints in Heaven."[105] Preston conceded that

> Christ was indeed a ransome for all, 1 Tim. 2:6 yet the Saviour only of his body, . . . he redeemed all, but called, justified, & glorified, whom he knew before, & had predestinated to be formable to the image of his Son.[106]

Here we see that 'ransom' and 'redemption' are said to be larger in scope than the elect of God, and the 'all' of 1 Timothy 2:6 is taken to be referring to all without exception.[107] What makes the difference is the intercession of Christ, which, as we have already seen in Preston's works, is limited to the elect, unlike the death of Christ. Whereas "in Adam all men were lost," and by Christ's death were made "savable upon conditions of another covenant," nevertheless it was "such as had not Christ's intercession" who "could not recover."[108]

Although Francis White presented Preston with statements that would have made Tyacke's 'conventional Calvinists' shudder, Preston was far more accommodating to White's attack on his position. White asserted that

---

104. Schaff, ed., *Creeds of Christendom*, III:518; Ball, *Life of Preston*, p. 131. Preston's linking with Mark 16:15 the salvability of all men due to Christ's death reinforces the interpretation made in Ch. 5 of Preston's controversial phrase in connection with the same text, "Christ is dead for him."

105. Ball, *Life of Preston*, p. 132.

106. Ball, *Life of Preston*, p. 132.

107. Note how Preston has therefore granted to the likes of Harsnett full exegetical rights to their use of 1 Timothy 2:4.

108. Ball, *Life of Preston*, pp. 133, 131, 134.

Christ had tasted death for every man; Heb. 2:9 he dyed for those who might notwithstanding perish, 1 Co. 8:11 and bought those that yet might bring upon themselves swift damnation, 2 Pet. 2:1 because they did not husband & improve ye favour offered to them.[109]

According to Ball, Preston's only answer was that "Christ was in himselfe sufficient to save all; and might be said to be provided for that end & use; as a medicine is to cure infected persons, though it cures none actually but those that drinke it."[110] In support of this notion, Preston quotes Prosper of Aquitaine, where Prosper, opposing Vincent of Lérins, is quoted as saying of Christ's death that, "Habet in se quod omnibus prosit, sed si non bibitur non medetur."[111] The implication is that Christ was provided to save all men without exception, and that the reason why "many did not thus apply Christ" was, as Preston says, "because they had him not so offered & exhibited as others had." Moses' serpent "was in itselfe sufficient to cure those that were bitten, Num. 21:8, 9 yet cured none but only those who looked on it." Rather than tracing the reason why some do not apply Christ to the particularity of redemption in God's decree, Preston was at pains to stress human responsibility for failure to fulfil the terms of the conditional covenant. After all, "God had done all that they could challenge of Him."[112]

109. Ball, *Life of Preston*, pp. 134-35.

110. Ball, *Life of Preston*, p. 135.

111. Thomas Ball, "The Life of Doctor Preston, who dyed Anno Christi 1628" in *A general Martyrologie, containing a Collection of all the greatest Persecutions which have befallen the Church of Christ, from the Creation, to our present Times*, ed. Samuel Clarke (London: For William Birch, 1677), II:75-114, II:105. There appears to be a printing omission at this point in Harcourt's 1885 edition (Ball, *Life of Preston*, p. 135). Interestingly, Baxter later highly recommended Prosper and Preston as part of a whole string of books for the financially "poorer" sort of library, being "[t]heological Disputations and Treatises which I take to be extraordinary clear and sound, escaping the extreams which many err in, and opening the Reconciling truth." Baxter's leaning towards universal redemption is evident in this list, which includes salient works by Davenant, Camero, Amyraut, Daillé, and Ussher as well as highly recommending the British delegation to Dort (Richard Baxter, *Richard Baxter's Catholick Theologie: Plain, pure, peaceable: For Pacification of the dogmatical Word-Warriors* [London: Robert White for Nevill Simmons, 1675], I:922, 924). At the risk of seeming to imply an *argumentum ad hominem,* and while recognising that Prosper was a favourite with Perkins, it is interesting to note that Prosper, while initially an Augustinian predestinarian, "finally rejected Augustine's position . . . believing God willed to save all men" (Steinmetz in *NIDCC*, pp. 1019-20). Preston possibly derived this quotation from Ussher (see below, p. 177).

112. Ball, *Life of Preston*, pp. 135, 136. An additional word about the reliability of sources is necessary at this point (additional, that is, to Donagan's satisfactory treatment cited on p. 152). This is because Lachman seeks to downplay the importance of this evidence for Preston's hypothetical universalism. According to Lachman, this evidence is merely "a manuscript transcript of a

Francis White now followed his attack on Preston's view of the extent of Christ's satisfaction with a consideration of the gospel call. In response to Preston's refusal to admit that Christ died equally for all men, White goes on to try to prove that this, in the context of human inability, removes all sincerity from the gospel call to believe and repent.[113] Preston had already maintained earlier that it was the death of Christ rendering all men without exception "savable upon conditions of another covenant" which undergirded salvation being "offered unto any man." Preston was now forced to give some ground to White's contention that God desired to save all equally and that it was human resistance to the divine will that resulted in some being finally lost. White argued that those who are finally lost "rejected the counsel of God against themselves." Preston saw it as a particularly "Popish" phenomenon to ask "to what end are offers made, & exhortations used," if men are totally unable to respond of themselves.[114] This ability was possessed at one time by all

---

disputation between Preston and Dr Francis White. Recorded by one of Preston's pupils and not examined by Preston himself for infelicitous, misleading or erroneous expressions, this dialogue is between a Calvinist and an Arminian and as such is not intended to speak to the point in question." A number of observations must be made at this point. The claim that it was merely "recorded by one of Preston's pupils" is incorrect or at least pure conjecture. It is true that Ball was the author of the manuscript biography of Preston to which Baxter was referring and which contains this account. However, it is unlikely in the extreme that Ball would have been admitted to York House, and in the absence of any positive evidence, we can safely assume he was not. Secondly, Lachman assumes that because Ball's biography is dated in its title-page to 1628, Ball's account of the conference was "not examined by Preston himself for infelicitous, misleading or erroneous expressions." However, this claim is also very weak. It is likely that Ball, who obviously knew of the existence of Preston's manuscript reports of the conference, was able to use one or more of these accounts written in Preston's own hand. He would have been able therefore to include in his biography the very words Preston employed in his debate with Dr White, or at least the words for which Preston wished to be remembered. It is unlikely that Ball would have been satisfied with trusting the reports written by Preston's opponents. Thirdly, Lachman entirely overlooks the three manuscript accounts that survive with Preston as the attributed author, in which explicit hypothetical universalist statements also occur. Furthermore, Lachman's claim that "this dialogue is between a Calvinist and an Arminian and as such is not intended to speak to the point in question" is also suspect. These comments from Preston are provoked by a challenge to his predestinarianism made by White from the Catechism, which teaches the pupil to believe "in God the Son, who hath redeemed me, and all mankind." It is hard to see how Lachman can view a debate arising from the nature of an alleged universal redemption as 'not speaking to the point in question.' Furthermore, it is not true that White was an Arminian in the classic sense. He was much nearer to Preston than was Montagu. Therefore, Lachman's implying that it was a 'straightforward' Arminian versus Calvinist debate is also inaccurate (David C. Lachman, *The Marrow Controversy 1718-1723: An Historical and Theological Analysis* [Edinburgh: Rutherford House Books, 1988], p. 27).

113. Ball, *Life of Preston*, p. 137.
114. BL Harleian MS. 6866, f. 80v.

men in Adam, but now forfeited. Meanwhile in the gospel God "had done what he could without reversing & rescinding his decree," but "had other ends, Ro. 9:17 and attributes, Ro. 9:22 which he was willing to discover, Prov. 16:4."[115] With regard to the elect, Preston could contend that the gospel call is not an empty, insincere command but is the very means of saving them. The "call & command of Christ is the vehiculum & conduit pipe of strength & power." Therefore "God, by bidding men & commanding them to take Grace, doth thereby fit and enable them ye more to doe it."[116] Yet Preston had avoided the problem of the reprobate under the preaching of the gospel, and White was not going to let him get away with that: "If God . . . were not ready to the utmost of his power to give them grace, he could not be excused from dissembling & double dealing." Preston rejected the validity of this objection by arguing that 'dissembling' only occurs when "they refuse to give when the required condition is performed," and God has never done this. The reprobate *cannot* come because they *will* not come. It is this rebellious will that God punishes.[117] Therefore "God doth not pretend one thinge and intend another: and thoughe they cannot take, yet he makes an offer, to shew their stubornes, and to leaue them inexcusable."[118] White's system was altogether too anthropocentric for Preston's liking, for "if it fall but that, in the illustration & exercise of those his glorious attributes & excellencyes, some creatures smart, yet he delights not in their smart & sufferings, but in ye demonstration of his omnipotency."[119] Preston tells us that "[f]urther he said not anything to explaine him selfe in this point: for it beeing very late they bracke off."[120]

We have, therefore, in these manuscripts a record of Preston setting forth a sophisticated form of hypothetical universalism. He seeks to keep the offensive implications of particular grace to the minimum, and to locate the cause of the eternal state of the reprobate entirely within themselves. This is fully consistent with the low Calvinism found above in Preston's works. It is remarkable, therefore, that Donagan should describe Preston's speech at York House concerning the scope of Christ's death as "inept" and "unsympathetic in its apparent lack of charity and justice." Rather than detecting the hypothetical universalist connotations inherent in the term 'salvibiles,' Donagan

---

115. Ball, *Life of Preston*, p. 136.

116. Ball, *Life of Preston*, p. 138.

117. Ball, *Life of Preston*, p. 139. Preston in his own manuscript adds, "(to this purpose he spake) whether he used that very word dissemble or not I remember not" (BL Harleian MS. 6866, f. 79v).

118. BL Harleian MS. 6866, f. 80v.

119. Ball, *Life of Preston*, p. 140.

120. BL Harleian MS. 6866, f. 80v.

sees this as part of "Preston's ruthless response" to the plight of the reprobate. Peter Lake has similarly misinterpreted Preston when he styles him as defending at the York House Conference "a fairly harsh and uncompromising version of Calvinist orthodoxy."[121] It was undoubtedly a lot less 'harsh' than the Elizabethan Calvinism we have seen, and consequently, as we shall see, Preston endangered not a few of his friendships amongst 'the godly.' Preston was promoting the tenets of a new and much softer brand of Calvinism.[122]

The Verdicts — Past and Present

Although the second session of the York House Conference lasted "about six hours, till past eight at night," there was little remaining time and a lack of willingness to discuss the intricacies of predestination, which might have revealed the alleged dangerous divergences between the two parties.[123] As it happened, the meeting was adjourned somewhat inconclusively. Preston had failed in his commission to prove Montagu guilty of Arminianism.[124] Although Heylyn reports that attendees from both camps claimed a victory, given that the purpose of the initiators of the conference had been to expose Montagu and his allies of Arminian if not blatantly popish aberrations from the Thirty-Nine Articles, the York House Conference must be seen as a failure.[125] In the words of Fuller, "the success of these meetings, answered neither the commendable intentions, nor hopefull expectations, of such who procured them."[126] More recently, Peter White is even stronger in his language, seeing the conference as an occasion when "[d]octrinal Calvinists" were "humiliated in front of Buckingham."[127]

---

121. Donagan, "The York House Conference revisited," p. 321; Peter G. Lake, "Calvinism and the English Church 1570-1635," *P&P* 114 (1987): 32-76, p. 41.

122. For an investigation of the newness of Preston's position, see Ch. 7.

123. Cosin, *Works*, II:74; BL Harleian MS. 6866, ff. 80r-80v.

124. This was in spite of the fact that Montagu did in fact hate Calvin's Calvinism. Montagu could write of the "execrable impiety" of "Calvin's opinion concerning the antecedent immutable decree of predestination" (Archbishop Marsh's Library, Dublin, MS. Z4.2.10 ff. 151v-52; quoted in Tyacke, "Anglican Attitudes," p. 154). Only after the mists of time had fallen could Thomas Hill safely style Preston as a conquering Calvinistic hero at this conference (William Fenner, *The Works of the learned and faithful Minister of Gods Word, Mr William Fenner* [London: T. Maxey for John Rothwell, 1651], p. A4v).

125. Heylyn, *Cyprianus Anglicus*, p. 147.

126. Fuller, *Church-History of Britain*, XI:125.

127. White, *Predestination, Policy and Polemic*, p. 2; cf. White, "The Rise of Arminianism Reconsidered," pp. 50, 35. Clausen sees it as "a subtle victory for the English Arminian party" (Clausen, "Calvinism in the Anglican Hierarchy," p. 98).

The Montagu case certainly never came before the House of Lords,[128] and what is more, Preston seems to have alone received the blame. According to his loyal biographer,

> t]here were few present of Dr. Preston's friends; &, accordingly, this conferrence was represented & reported with all the disadvantage that could be to him; insomuch, that many Parliament men that were his friends were much offended at it. This occasioned Dr. Preston, as soone as he came to Cambridge, to write severall passages of his disputation, & send them to those friends that were unsatisfied.[129]

Donagan would have us believe that this disappointment arose amongst the moderate Calvinist laymen at the conference who were offended by Preston's high and extreme Calvinism.[130] Yet this theory does not fit the evidence. Firstly, as we have seen, Preston's position was not at all a high Calvinism but an accommodating brand of hypothetical universalism. Secondly, Joseph Mead gives further light on this disappointment with Preston in a letter to Sir Martin Stuteville dated 4th March, 1626, where he writes:

> What good they have done, I know not, but Montague's party talk much of the success on their side; and that he that was brought in as a kind of challenger [i.e., Preston] on the contrary side, to undertake Dr. White, was far short in satisfaction and in the expectation of these lords, who were supposed to have thrust him upon the business.[131]

These 'great Lords' as we have seen were the hard-line Calvinists Warwick and Saye, whom Cosin saw as the two fiercest opponents of Montagu.[132] Furthermore, as Donagan admits, "Bridgewater, Manchester, and Mulgrave . . . belonged to the Elizabethan Protestant generation, and may well have been recruited as sympathetic by fellow committee members Warwick, Saye, and Morton." Dorset too belonged to this "old-line English Calvinist component."[133] It is far more likely therefore that this disappointment with Preston came from some of these more strict Calvinists feeling betrayed by Preston's advocacy of a far more moderate soteriology, which was unable roundly to confute a rising Arminianism.

---

128. Tyacke, *Anti-Calvinists*, p. 180.
129. Ball, *Life of Preston*, p. 141.
130. Donagan, "The York House Conference Revisited," p. 327.
131. Birch, ed., *The Court and Times of Charles the First*, I:86.
132. Cosin, *Works*, II:73-74.
133. Donagan, "The York House Conference revisited," pp. 316, 315.

Some might want to argue that the lords' disappointment with Preston was solely because he failed to discredit Montagu. However, if this were so, then Preston's own manuscript defence of his role at the conference would concentrate on Montagu and the allegations of popery. However, the overwhelming focus in his account is on his soteriological disputes with Francis White. This indicates the areas of his performance at which Preston felt the accusations were aimed. Additionally, although this would be an argument from silence, it should be noted that, as far as we know, Morton was not accused of a poor performance at the conference, whereas it was he who had made the big blunders in the first session against Montagu. What Morton had not done, however, was reveal any leanings towards hypothetical universalism.[134] Although Fuller reports that "William Earle of Pembroke was heard to say, that none returned Arminians thence, save such who repaired thither with the same opinions,"[135] nevertheless it seems evident that Preston's softer Calvinism had not proven any more attractive. Cosin ends his narration of the proceedings with a triumphant comment to the effect that Charles now "swears his perpetual patronage of our cause."[136] Soon afterwards the Duke of Buckingham ceased to be Preston's patron.[137]

This study of manuscripts concerning Preston's performance at the York House Conference confirms the preceding analysis of Preston's works. At York House we have seen Preston display an interest in the *ordo decretorum* and commend an infralapsarian perspective. We have seen him advocate a twofold donation of Christ, the hypothetical redemption and salvability of the reprobate (in comparison with demons), and a ransom paid by Christ for the reprobate. We have also seen him teach that although the gospel call is itself an effectual means of awakening the dead, there is a universal conditional covenant made with the reprobate, founded upon the death of Christ. This teaching was accompanied by advocating universal redemption in contrast with limited intercession, as well as a universal redemption providing sincerity to the universal gospel call. Certainly Preston's apparent enthusiasm in 1615 for the particularism contained in Hildersham's *Lectures* is nowhere to be

---

134. That is not to say, however, that previously Morton had never shown any interest at all in making concessions to Arminianism. In December 1618, while the Synod of Dort was underway, Morton confided to Ussher his hope that a holding to universal grace in the sense that "no soul can be said particularly to be excluded" might "sufficiently qualify the violence of oppositions" (Ussher, *Works*, XV:143).

135. Fuller, *Church-History of Britain*, XI:125.

136. Cosin, *Works*, II:74.

137. Tyacke, *Anti-Calvinists*, p. 166.

seen by 1626.[138] If the federal thought of Perkins and Preston is largely identical, as Song argues, this cannot be extended to their formulations of the death of Christ.[139] The implications of this for the often furious debate between historians such as Nicholas Tyacke, Peter Lake, and Peter White will be discussed later as one of the final conclusions. Before that, the next chapter will examine whether it is possible to know from whom Preston learned his hypothetical universalism.

138. See above, pp. 139-40.

139. Yong Jae Timothy Song, *Theology and Piety in the Reformed Federal Thought of William Perkins and John Preston* (Lewiston, NY: Edwin Mellen Press, 1998), p. 226.

Preston's Mentors

CHAPTER 7

Bishops James Ussher and John Davenant

"The true intent and extent [of Christ's death and satisfaction upon the Cross], is Lubricus locus to be handled, and hath, and doth now much trouble the Church."[1]

Introduction

Having ascertained Preston's distinct divergence from late Elizabethan Reformed theology, and seen him defend his position at York House, it remains to investigate, using both circumstantial and textual evidence, how Preston came to these convictions and to what extent he was alone or part of a wider concerted effort amongst Jacobean Calvinists to remould soteriological formulations in the light of rising theological conflicts. Happily, Baxter offers us a clear lead in our investigation. In his posthumously published autobiography, Baxter seeks to find ecclesiastical credentials for his own highly controversial opinions on redemption. As we have already noted, Baxter was fond of citing Preston as an advocate of his own view of universal redemption.[2] But he also cited the two illustrious divines, James Ussher (1581-1656), Archbishop of Armagh, and John Davenant (1572-1641), Bishop of Salisbury.[3] It is in this context that Baxter elucidates an important connection between these men.

---

1. Ussher writing in 1618 (James Ussher, *The Judgement of the late Archbishop of Armagh* [London: For John Crook, 1657], I:1).

2. See above, pp. 96-97.

3. See, for example, Richard Baxter, *The Saints Everlasting Rest: Or, a Treatise of the blessed State of the Saints in their enjoyment of God in Glory* (London: Robert White for Thomas Underhil & Francis Tyton, 1650), p. A4v; Richard Baxter, *Plain Scripture Proof of Infants Church-membership and Baptism* (London: For Robert White, 1651), p. 275; Richard Baxter, *Certain Dis-*

But first we must begin with Dr George Kendall. Kendall was a strict particular redemptionist, and consequently a fierce opponent of Baxter. In the mid-1650s they published furiously against each other before they happened to meet each other in London.[4] Kendall "was so earnest to take up the Controversy" that he urged Richard Vines to persuade Baxter to allow Archbishop Ussher to "determine it." It is not clear why Kendall asked Ussher to mediate nor whether he knew what he was embarking upon, but Baxter was delighted with the result when they met at Ussher's lodgings at the Earl of Peterborough's House in Martin's Lane. In Baxter's own words, "I quickly yielded to Bishop Ussher's Arbitriment, who owned my Judgment about Universal Redemption, Perseverance &c. but desired us to write against each other no more."[5] In another account of the same London meeting, Baxter adds that "when the Bishop had declared his Judgment for that Doctrine of Universal Redemption," he "gloried that he was the Man that brought Bishop Davenant and Dr Preston to it."[6] Baxter had already made this public in 1657, when in a preface to one of his books, he appealed to Kendall for support in his contention concerning universal redemption that Ussher had "intimated that Dr Davenant and Dr Preston were minded of it by him," which he is reported to have said "rejoycing that hee sooner owned it."[7] If Baxter is to be trusted here,[8]

---

putations of Right to Sacraments and the true Nature of Visible Christianity (London: William Du-Gard for Nevil Simmons, 1657), pp. B2r, B2v, C2r; Richard Baxter, Richard Baxter's Catholick Theologie: Plain, pure, peaceable: For Pacification of the dogmatical Word-Warriors (London: Robert White for Nevil Simmons, 1675), IV:50, 52.

4. George Kendall, Θεοκρατια: Or, a Vindication of the Doctrine commonly received in the Reformed Churches concerning Gods Intentions of special Grace and Favour to his Elect in the Death of Christ (London: Thomas Ratcliffe and Edward Mottershed, 1653); Richard Baxter, Richard Baxter's Apology against the modest Exceptions of Mr T. Blake (London: T. Underhill and Francis Tyton for Jos. Nevil and Jos. Barbar, 1654), Pt II; George Kendall, Sancti Sanciti. Or, The common Doctrine of the Perseverance of the Saints (London: Thomas Ratcliffe and Edward Mottershed, 1654); cf. CCRB I:117.

5. Richard Baxter, Reliquiae Baxterianae: Or, Mr Richard Baxter's Narrative of the most memorable Passages of his Life and Times, ed. Matthew Sylvester (London: For T. Parkhurst, J. Robinson, J. Lawrence and J. Dunton, 1696), I:110.

6. Baxter, Reliquiae Baxterianae, I:206.

7. Baxter, Certain Disputations, p. C2r. Note what Baxter is claiming here: the final theological position of Davenant and Preston concerning these matters was not that of their early days as Reformed divines, extremely well read as they were. Furthermore, they had to be taught this new system. It did not effortlessly present itself to them upon 'a plain reading of Scripture,' nor from a nostalgic pilgrimage back to the writings of Calvin or other Reformers.

8. Baxter's constantly self-vindicating autobiographical writings should always be used with the utmost caution. See Tim Cooper, Fear and Polemic in Seventeenth-Century England: Richard Baxter and Antinomianism (Aldershot, UK: Ashgate Publishing Company, 2001), pp. 198-201.

a thorough examination of the formulations of both Ussher and Davenant on the death of Christ and the gospel call should therefore shed light on Preston's own position and help set him in theological context.

Ussher's Theology of the Death of Christ

According to Baxter, Ussher was already well known in his own time for his hypothetical universalism. With regard to Ussher's relationship to "Amyraldus Method," Baxter asserted that it was "well known that hee owned the substance of [Amyraldus'] doctrine of Redemption." Indeed, "his Judgement hath been commonly known in the world about this 30 years to bee . . . for the middle way."[9] It so happens that Ussher has left to posterity a succinct statement of this 'middle way.' This letter on "the true Intent and Extent of Christ's Death" was written in March 1618 on the eve of the Synod of Dort, and in response to enquiries from his friend Ezekiel Culverwell.[10] Copies of this letter were "in many mens hands" in the mid-seventeenth century, and Baxter intended to have it printed.[11] It is unlikely that Ussher would have consented to this in his lifetime, as he is on record as lamenting that "without [his] privity" it had "come to so many men's hands."[12] Nicholas Bernard claimed that it even found its way to the Synod of Dort without Ussher's knowledge, at which Synod objections to his doctrine were collated and sent back to him, resulting in a second letter defending the first.[13] However, there appears to be no sup-

9. Baxter, *Certain Disputations*, pp. C1v, C2r.

10. James Ussher, *The whole Works of the most Rev. James Ussher*, ed. Charles R. Erlington (Dublin: Hodges and Smith, 1847-64), XII:566. Baxter is almost certain that he remembered hearing Ussher say it was written to Culverwell. However, he thought he might have said it was to Culverwell's opponent, William Eyre of Salisbury (Baxter, *Certain Disputations*, p. C2r). Jasper Heartwell's letter to Ussher clears any uncertainty and confirms that Ussher first wrote these words to Culverwell (Ussher, *Works*, XVI:356). I concur with George H. Williams, "Called by Thy Name, Leave Us Not: The Case of Mrs. Joan Drake, a formative Episode in the pastoral Career of Thomas Hooker in England," *Harvard Library Bulletin* 16 (1968): 278-303, pp. 283-84 in identifying Ussher's correspondent here as Jasper Heartwell.

11. Baxter, *Certain Disputations*, p. C2r. Baxter was himself first given a manuscript copy of this letter in 1651 (Baxter, *Plain Scripture Proof*, p. 275).

12. Ussher, *Works*, XII:563. Heartwell had informed Ussher in a letter of July 1618 that "there are now many copies of it scattered abroad, and it is much divulged, by some liked, and by some not" (Ussher, *Works*, XVI:356).

13. Bernard in Ussher, *The Judgement*, I:A3v. Samuel Ward would have been the most likely member of the Synod to have taken this letter with him. Ward corresponded regularly with Ussher and wrote to him about the Synod immediately upon his return to Cambridge (Ussher, *Works*, XV:144-45).

porting evidence for this amongst the manuscripts relating to the Synod itself. It is far more likely that Ussher's second letter arose from the fact that Culverwell gave Ussher's first letter to John Forbes at Middelburg, who promised to write a refutation of it.[14] It was in the years immediately following Ussher's death that these letters were first published, edited by Bernard.[15] Ussher's other biographer, Richard Parr, also published them in 1686.[16] Both these essays were reprinted twice in the nineteenth century.[17]

In this work, Ussher carefully outlines a coherent statement of hypothetical universalism. Well aware of the theological climate, Ussher, the predestinarian, is careful to make clear that he agrees with particular redemptionists up to a point. He acknowledges that "the principal end" of Christ's death was the salvation of the elect, and that therefore "Christ in a special manner died for these." He even states that "forgiveness of sins is not by our Saviour impetrated for any unto whom the merit of his death is not applied in particular."[18] Furthermore, while affirming the all-sufficiency of the atonement, Ussher denied that in his death Christ "intended" to apply "this all-sufficient remedy . . . to make it effectual unto [the reprobate's] salvation . . . or to procure thereby actual pardon for the sins of the whole world."[19]

However, Ussher was aware that in his day good men were being driven to make extreme statements in the heat of controversy with Arminius' followers, and it is to this source that he traced the "extreme absurdity" of the doctrine of definite atonement. This latter position Ussher defined as teaching

14. Ussher, *Works*, XVI:356. A garbled version of this incident may have been what led to Bernard's claim. I am grateful to Anthony Milton for helping to clarify this point.

15. Ussher, *The Judgement*, I:A4r; James Ussher, *The Judgement of the late Archbishop of Armagh* (London: For John Crook, 1658). Baxter reports that Ussher told him "not long before his death" that this doctrine was his settled conviction (Baxter, *Certain Disputations*, p. C2r).

16. Richard Parr, *The Life of the most reverend Father in God, James Usher, late Lord Archbishop of Armagh, Primate and Metropolitan of all Ireland. With a Collection of three hundred Letters* (London: For Nathanael Ranew, 1686), III:46-53.

17. William Dodsworth, *General Redemption, and limited Salvation. To which is added, a Reprint of Archbishop Usher's Treatise on the true Intent and Extent of Christ's Death and Satisfaction on the Cross* (London: James Nisbet, 1831), pp. 77-119; Ussher, *Works*, XII:551-71. Erlington calls them "dissertations rather than letters" (Ussher, *Works*, XV:iii). For additional notes by Ussher on the satisfaction of Christ, see Bod Rawlinson MS. C.849, ff. 286r-92r, and on the gospel call, Bod Rawlinson MS. C.849, f. 283r. For a sermon by Ussher largely concerning the free offer of the gospel, see Ussher, *Works*, XIII:159-74, and for notes on another see CUL MS. Mm.6.55 ff. 46v-47v.

18. Ussher, *Works*, XII:567, 564.

19. Ussher, *Works*, XII:559; cf. James Ussher, *Immanuel, Or, The mystery of the Incarnation of the Son of God* (London: William Hunt, 1658), p. 11.

"that Christ died only for the elect, and for others *nullo modo*."[20] It could be that Ussher had in mind a manuscript found amongst his theological papers in which the unidentified writer gives no fewer than fourteen reasons why "[t]he rejected of god have no interest in Christ, either sanctification of their corrupt nature or sanctification [*sic; lege* satisfaction] for sinne." The writer jealously guards against any teaching that might appear to imply that Christ "dyed in vaine and to noe purpose, and that the efficacye of Christs death colde be made vide [*sic*] by man." Interestingly, his strict doctrine of definite satisfaction was partly grounded on the premise that Christ "makes no intercession for the reprobate." These reprobate "can have noe intrest in the sanctifying and satisfying Saviour, who from eternity were preparred for the curse and ever lasting fyer, prepared for the Divell and his angells." He asserted that "the flock of God which is his Church is only purchased by his bloud."[21] Ussher deemed it foolish to come to such an extreme position from the admittedly particular aspect to Christ's work. Christ died "in a special manner" for the elect, "but to infer from hence, that in no manner of respect he died for any others, is but a very weak collection."[22]

In essence, Ussher's position consists in a qualified condemnation of the notion that the commonly received doctrine of 'the sufficiency of Christ's merits' must be understood to mean "a bare sufficiency" intrinsically considered, which would be "a cold comfort."[23] Rather, a fundamental change had occurred even in reprobate man's state due to Christ's death. The sufficiency of Christ's satisfaction is an 'active' not a merely hypothetical sufficiency, bringing into operation a conditional but very real relationship between God and all men without exception. In Ussher's system it does this in two main ways. In Christ's death a medicine is provided that firstly renders God placable and, secondly, renders all sins now pardonable.

Interestingly, Ussher borrows from Prosper the quotation that we have seen Preston use in a sermon, and at the York House Conference, namely, "habet quidem in se ut omnibus prosit, sed si non bibitur non medetur."[24]

---

20. Ussher, *Works*, XII:564, 565.

21. Bod Rawlinson MS. C.849, ff. 284r-85r. John 17:9 is cited to prove limited intercession.

22. Ussher, *Works*, XII:567. Ussher was consciously condemning the Conference at The Hague of 1611 in this regard, the precursor to the Synod of Dort which was to assemble eight months after Ussher's letter (Ussher, *Works*, XII:563-64). Ussher interpreted the position espoused at The Hague as implying eternal justification or reconciliation. For an account of this conference see Gerard Brandt, *The History of the Reformation and other Ecclesiastical Transactions in and about the Low-Countries* (London: T. Wood for John Childe, 1720-23), II:93-95.

23. Ussher, *Works*, XII:568; XIII:128.

24. Ussher, *Works*, XII:570. See above, pp. 110, 163. In light of Baxter's comments on the

Ussher frequently employs elsewhere this imagery of the merits of Christ being like medicine stored up with potential efficacy. Christ came "to prepare a
medicine for the sins of the whole world," but as yet, it has actually achieved
nothing, nothing that is, save from a change in the status of both God and
man toward each other and in their potential relationship.[25] In the first place,
God is made placable. His justice now being satisfied, "God is made placable
unto our nature," although he is "not actually appeased with any, until he
hath received his son."[26] This means that in terms of satisfaction for sin nothing more need be done to save the reprobate, for "the former impediment
arising on God's part is taken away." Thus, "if it were not for" unbelief, "there
were no let, but all men might be saved."[27]

Intimately related to God's placability is the pardonable nature of all
sins, or, as Preston would say, man's salvability. Christ's death as the Incarnate
One has made "the nature of man which he assumed, a fit subject for mercy."[28]
The "general satisfaction of Christ," according to Ussher, "prepares the way for
God's mercy, by making the sins of all mankind pardonable," or "fit for pardon," and thereby "puts the sons of men only in a possibility of being justified."
Thus, "all the sins of mankind are become venial, in respect of the price paid
by Christ."[29] Using the same imagery as Preston, Ussher states that Christ's
death therefore "hath procured a jubilee for the sons of Adam" which constitutes a "general grant" of liberty. All may go free if they will.[30] It is important to
note that in Ussher this is not just theoretically true when the atonement is
considered in the abstract. Rather, what Christ "intended" to do and had in
mind upon the cross, among other things, was to render men salvable.[31]

---

derivation of Preston's views it could well be that Preston was informed by Ussher of this place
in Prosper, rather than by a direct reading of Prosper himself. Preston never cites Prosper in his
published works. However, Prosper's complete works had been in the library of Emmanuel College since at least 1597 (Sargent Bush Jr. & Carl J. Rasmussen, *The Library of Emmanuel College,
Cambridge, 1584-1637* [Cambridge: Cambridge University Press, 1986], pp. 9, 152).

25. Ussher, *Works*, XII:559, 567, 570, 571; XIII:160-61; CUL MS. Mm.6.55 ff. 53r, 60r-60v.

26. Ussher, *Works*, XII:555.

27. Ussher, *Works*, XII:568-69.

28. Ussher, *Works*, XII:567; cf. XII:568.

29. Ussher, *Works*, XII:554, 569; cf. CUL MS. Mm.6.55 ff. 60r-60v where Ussher expounds
Hebrews 2:9.

30. Ussher, *Works*, XII:556; cf. John Preston, *Saints Qualification*, I:19-20.

31. Ussher, *Works*, XII:567. Carl Trueman concludes from the book *Body of Divinitie* that
Ussher was a rigorous particularist (James Ussher, *A Body of Divinitie, or the Summe and Sub-
stance of Christian Religion, catechistically propounded, and explained, by way of Question and
Answer* [London: M. F. for Thomas Downes and George Badger, 1645], p. 173; Carl R. Trueman,
The Claims of Truth: John Owen's Trinitarian Theology [Carlisle, UK: Paternoster Press, 1998],
p. 200). However, even if the evidence in this book had been compelling, it is not relevant, for

The main tenets of Ussher's hypothetical universalism have now been outlined. The question now arises as to how Ussher defended this position within the framework of Reformed soteriology, and guarded himself from possible semi-Pelagian or Arminian implications.[32] A number of distinctive

---

Ussher was not in fact its author and was displeased at its publication under his name, even expressing disagreement with some of its content (Ussher, *The Judgement*, II:23-25; Nicholas Bernard, *The Life & Death of the most reverend and learned Father of our Church Dr. James Ussher* [London: E. Tyler for John Crook, 1656], pp. 41-42; Samuel Clarke, *A general Martyrologie, containing a Collection of all the greatest Persecutions which have befallen the Church of Christ, from the Creation, to our present Times* [London: For William Birch, 1677], II:283; Parr, *The Life of the most reverend Father in God, James Usher*, I:62; Ussher, *Works*, I:248-50). Breward is another who, on the basis of this book, mistakenly attributes to Perkins a strong influence upon Ussher's thought (Ian Breward, ed., *The Work of William Perkins* [Abingdon, UK: Sutton Courtenay Press, 1970], p. 102). I am grateful to Alan Ford for clarification on this point.

32. Allegedly "some Arminian Divines" interpreted Ussher's stand for "Universal Satisfaction" as nothing less than Arminianism (Baxter, *Certain Disputations*, pp. C1v, C2v; Ussher, *Works*, XII:563). Thus, in July 1618 Heartwell informed Ussher that "the universalists . . . now are glad that, as they conceive of it, you draw a little towards them" (Ussher, *Works*, XVI:356). It is not unreasonable to suppose that Preston quickly became aware of this interpretation of Ussher's position, which would further explain Preston's rhetorical caution at York House (see Ch. 6). In a Court sermon in June 1626, feeling the pressure from the group of men that opposed Preston at the York House Conference, Ussher condemned the "new doctrine" of "those five points that disturb the Low Countries" and stood with "King James." Thus, faced with the threat of Arminianism, Ussher was willing to stand as a 'five-point Calvinist' or at least a 'five-point Counter-Remonstrant' (Ussher, *Works*, XIII:348-50). Nevertheless, shortly after his death some, including Bishop Brian Walton, claimed that Ussher finally renounced the doctrines of Geneva, came to deny absolute reprobation, and held to resistible saving grace in the manner of Bishop Overall (Ussher, *The Judgement*, I:41-72; Ussher, *Works*, I:289-95; Henry Hammond, *Nineteen Letters*, ed. Francis Peck [London: For T. Cooper, 1739], pp. 17-24; Henry John Todd, *Memoirs of the Life and Writings of the Right Rev. Brian Walton* [London: For F. C. & J. Rivington and Longman, Hurst, Rees, Orme & Brown, 1821], I:203-9; Josiah Allport, "Life of Bishop Davenant" in *An Exposition of the Epistle of St Paul to the Colossians by the Right Rev. John Davenant* [London: Hamilton, Adams, and Co., 1831], I:ix-lii, I:xlvii-xlviii; cf. Thomas Pierce, *The divine Philanthropie defended against the declamatory Attempts of certain late-printed Papers* [London: For Richard Royston, 1657], I:77-78; Thomas Pierce, *Εαυτοντιμορουμενος, or, the Self-revenger exemplified in Mr. William Barlee* [London: R. Daniel for Richard Royston, 1658], pp. 125-63; and Bernard's reply to Pierce in James Ussher, *The Judgement of the late Arch-Bishop of Armagh* [London: For John Crook, 1659], pp. 359-80). There is some truth in Clausen's conclusion that Ussher's position was "often ambiguous and of a sophistication that too easily lent itself to misinterpretation," but these contemporary 'deathbed conversion' claims are most likely fictitious (Sara J. Clausen, "Calvinism in the Anglican Hierarchy, 1603-1643: Four Episcopal Examples" [Ph.D. Dissertation, Vanderbilt University, 1989], p. 359; Alan Ford, personal communication). In correcting Erlington's 1627 date for Ussher's Court sermon, just mentioned, I follow Peter White, *Predestination, Policy and Polemic: Conflict and Consensus in the English Church from the Reformation to the Civil War* (Cambridge: Cambridge University Press, 1992), p. 244; Alexandra

motifs are emphasised by Ussher to this end. In the first place, Ussher puts much weight on the implications of the incarnation for formulations on the extent and intent of Christ's death. This he does by contrasting man's condition with that of the fallen angels. The "possibility of being justified" is "a thing denied to the nature of fallen angels." Without an incarnate suffering Saviour, "God would not have come unto a treaty of peace with us, more than with the fallen angels." The angels have no provision of a saviour, and no propitiation. But man *does*, even reprobate man.[33]

But by far the most important distinctive undergirding Ussher's theology of the death of Christ is the radical separation he makes between the two branches of Christ's priestly work. He ascribes different scopes to the two "divers parts of his priesthood." The first priestly work of satisfaction is "the preparation of the remedy," whereas Christ's second priestly work of intercession "brings with it an application" of the remedy. In the second place Christ's satisfaction "doth properly give contentment to God's justice," whereas Christ's intercession "doth solicit God's mercy."[34] So disconnectedly can Ussher make these two works function, that he can describe the application of the atonement as merely "an appendant" which finally "produceth this *potentia in actum,* that is, procureth an actual discharge from God's anger."[35] This enables Ussher to conclude that Christ's satisfaction "may well appertain to the common nature" or mankind in general, whereas his intercession is limited to the elect.[36] He rejects the particular redemptionist conclusion

---

Walsham, "Vox Piscis: Or The Book-Fish: Providence and the Uses of the Reformation Past in Caroline Cambridge," *EHR* 114 (1999): 574-606, p. 596; and David R. Como, "Puritans, Predestination and the Construction of Orthodoxy in Early Seventeenth-Century England" in *Conformity and Orthodoxy in the English Church, c.1560-1660*, ed. Peter G. Lake & Michael C. Questier (Woodbridge, UK: Boydell Press, 2000), 64-87, p. 76.

33. Ussher, *Works,* XII:569, 555; cf. Ussher, *Immanuel, passim.* The motif of the plight of fallen angels being used in this way is nothing new, still less, distinctive of hypothetical universalism. It is mentioned here merely because it is a key concept in Ussher's thought, and even more so, as shall be seen below, in Davenant's thought.

34. Ussher, *Works,* XII:558-59.

35. Ussher, *Works,* XII:569.

36. Ussher, *Works,* XII:559. Ussher appears to have held to this distinction in the scope of the two branches of Christ's priestly work throughout his ministry, for in 1648 at Lincoln's Inn, he is recorded as having preached that Christ's "Satisfaction is indefinite, Tis, not only Sufficient, but is proposed as a comon Remedy to all men. . . . Every Body is invited: But Intercession is more restrayned: Intercession, for those, whome God hath given him" (CUL MS. Mm.6.55 f. 53r). Later that year, from the same pulpit, Ussher again argued that "Satisfaction was the preparation of the medecine, appliable [*sic*] to all the Sonnes of Adam: But Intercession hath the Application of it. Intercession is not of that large Extent, as the Passion. . . . A medicine cures not by being prepared, but by beinge Applyed" (CUL MS. Mm.6.55 f. 60r; cf. f. 60v). Then in 1654

drawn from John 17:9 that "he *prayed* not for the world, therefore he *payed* not for world."[37] Different aspects of the work of redemption can therefore be ascribed to two separate priestly works. For example, impetration is "a fruit, not of his satisfaction, but intercession."[38] Christ's satisfaction did not impetrate anything for anyone.

Implicit in this application of Christ's twofold priestly work is another key doctrine in Ussher's system, namely, that not only a clear conceptual distinction, but also a firm disjunction, must be made between "the satisfaction of Christ absolutely considered, and the application thereof to every one in particular."[39] Responding to critics of his original letter, Ussher in his *Answer* denies that his doctrine of only 'pardonable' sins dishonours Christ's satisfaction. All must confess that no one is actually cleansed until the blood is applied.[40] That is to say, God is "not actually appeased with any, until he hath received his son."[41] Ussher is here formulating in embryo what John Davenant, as we shall see, was later to develop into his doctrine of a two-staged reconciliation. There is no 'golden chain' or irresistible causal link between propitiation having been made and its application in time in the lives of the elect. Any link at all is not a necessary one, but rests solely in the will of God, abstracted from any explicit reference to a *pactum salutis*.

Consistent with this, Ussher's exegetical treatment of the word 'world' stands in contrast to that of the Elizabethan particularists.[42] When the Scriptures speak of Christ being "the Lamb of God, which taketh away the sin of the world,"[43] rather than focus on the definition of 'world' as Reformed exegetes had traditionally done, Ussher prefers to soften what it means to 'take away.' Thus, the Lamb of God "doth not *actually* take away all the sins of the world, but *virtually*. It hath power to do it *if* it be rightly applied, the sacrifice hath such virtue in it, that *if* all the world would take it, and apply it, it *would* expiate, and remove the sins of the whole world."[44] Thus Christ on the cross did not actually expiate or take away the sins of anybody at all.

Ussher published a catechetical summary of Christian doctrine in which this same view is also discernible (Ussher, *Works*, XI:209-11).

37. Ussher, *Works*, XII:558 (emphasis added).

38. Ussher, *Works*, XII:564.

39. Ussher, *Works*, XII:554.

40. Ussher, *Works*, XII:569-70.

41. Ussher, *Works*, XII:555.

42. See Ch. 1.

43. John 1:29.

44. Ussher, *Works*, XIII:160-61 (emphasis added). Cf. Ussher's Lincoln's Inn sermon of 1648 where he is recorded as having said, "The Lambe of Gode that taketh away the Sinnes of the world: As Ruberb purgeth Choller: not that it purgeth away all choller from a cholerick man,

A vital subordinate purpose involved in Christ's satisfaction, though not its "principal end," is "to make way for God's free liberty in shewing mercy."[45] And this liberty is indeed most free. Due to the "venal" [*sic; lege* venial] nature of all men's sins, God "in shewing mercy upon all, if so it were his pleasure, his justice should be no loser."[46] Thus Ussher teaches a sovereign God who is now empowered by a general atonement to bestow forgiveness freely at will. Divine sovereignty is being divorced from the *pactum salutis* and exalted over any notion of intrinsic justice. The impression is given that this selection of men to forgive might just as well occur conceptually after Christ's death as before it, as if election followed and did not precede propitiation in the decree of God. In conclusion, Ussher could summarise his position in scholastic terms of causality, being happy that Christ "be counted as a kind of universal cause of restoring of our nature, as Adam was of the depraving of it." In plainer, yet more equivocal English, we must believe in summary that "in one respect he may be said to have died for all, and in another respect not to have died for all."[47]

Ussher's Theology of the Call of the Gospel

According to Ussher, one other 'intention' of Christ on the cross was to procure a universal offer of the gospel.[48] Ussher could go so far as to say that without a universal atonement the universal call of the gospel would be an impossibility.[49] It would at least lack sincerity since "a man should be bound in conscience to believe that which is untrue, and charged to take that wherewith he hath nothing to do."[50] This is consistent with Baxter's claim that Ussher had maintained "that wee cannot rationally offer Christ to sinners on other grounds."[51] In these letters, Ussher does not seek to prove his premise here, namely, that the gospel is a declaration that Christ died for the hearer. Nevertheless, what is clear is that for Ussher, a bare setting forth of a proposi-

---

but when it is applyed, cureth him of abundance of choller. Had this bene applyed to Judas, it would have taken away his Sinne." And again, "The death of Christ takes away the Sinnes of the world By way of medicine, if it bee Applyed" (CUL MS. Mm.6.55 ff. 60r, 60v).

45. Ussher, *Works*, XII:567, 569.
46. Ussher, *Works*, XII:554; cf. XII:569. Ussher, *The Judgement*, I:4 reads "venial."
47. Ussher, *Works*, XII:559.
48. Ussher, *Works*, XII:567-68.
49. Ussher, *Works*, XII:565.
50. Ussher, *Works*, XII:554.
51. Baxter, *Certain Disputations*, pp. C2r-C2v.

tional statement — that satisfaction has been provided for certain sinners considered in the abstract — does not constitute true gospel preaching. Christ died "to prepare a sovereign medicine that should not only be a sufficient cure for the sins of the whole world, but also should be laid open to all, and denied to none, that indeed do take the benefit thereof." Furthermore, assurance of salvation is also at stake through the doctrine of definite atonement, for "he is much deceived that thinks a preaching of a bare sufficiency is able to yield sufficient ground of comfort to a distressed soul."[52] Ussher illustrates this claim in a sermon, lamenting that

> Many talk of the extent of Christ's death and passion, saying he died sufficiently for us, which is an improper speech: for what comfort were this, that Christ was offered for us, if there were no more? A bare sufficiency in Christ serves not the turn: this were a cold comfort: as if a man were in debt, and afraid of every serjeant and every sheriff, should be told, Sir, there is money enough in the king's exchequer to discharge all your debts. This is very true, but what is that to him? What comfort hath he by it, unless the king make him an offer to come, and take freely for his discharge? And a cold comfort were it to us to know Christ to be sufficient for us, unless he invite us to take freely of the waters of life.[53]

In his letters, in order that there be no ambiguity as to his meaning, Ussher spells out how the offer of the gospel should be worded if it is to be "a true tender." The preacher is to declare:

> What Christ hath prepared for thee, and the Gospel offereth unto thee, that oughtest thou with all thankfulness to accept, and apply to the comfort of thy own soul. . . . Christ by his death and obedience hath provided a sufficient remedy for the taking away of all thy sins, and the Gospel offereth the same unto thee.[54]

The true gospel therefore "presents [the sinner] with the medicine at hand, and desireth him to take it."[55] Using this phrase, "desireth him to take it," with all the conceivable implications of a frustrated desire in God to save the reprobate, Ussher had to guard carefully against those who would put a semi-Pelagian or Arminian gloss on his writings.[56] He avows that "the universality

---

52. Ussher, *Works*, XII:568.
53. Ussher, *Works*, XIII:128-29.
54. Ussher, *Works*, XII:558, 555; cf. XII:557.
55. Ussher, *Works*, XII:571; cf. I:291, 293.
56. Ussher, *Works*, XII:557. That Ussher held to a desire in God to save the reprobate is

of the satisfaction derogates nothing from the necessity of the special grace in the application."[57] However, although he also explicitly states that spiritual awakening issues "from the execution of the prophetical, and kingly office of our Redeemer,"[58] and that it does not rest "in the free will of every one to receive, or reject" salvation,[59] there is a tendency to portray faith as a condition to be met, lying outside of salvation itself. It is not clear whether the gospel promise is *to* faith or *includes* faith.[60] Ussher was consciously steering "a middle course" between the "two extremities" of an actual universal reconciliation, and a limited satisfaction that leads to justification before the exercise of faith.[61]

At this point a comment concerning the Irish Articles is in order. According to a longstanding tradition, Ussher was 'the author' of these robustly

---

also suggested when, in the context of the infinite value of the blood of Christ, he declares that "God sendeth continually unto us by the preaching of the word, private and public means, desiring us to be reconciled and come unto him" (Ussher, *Works*, XIII:484-85). Ussher also links Matthew 23:37, as well as Jesus weeping over Jerusalem in Luke 19:41, with the free offer (Bod Rawlinson MS. C.849, f. 283r; Ussher, *Works*, XIII:171). At any rate he was certainly aware at some point in his theological investigations that some of his followers were implying this desire in God. This is clear from his careful annotation of this same undated manuscript of Ezekiel Culverwell concerning the "general offer of salvation." By 1618 Ussher had brought Culverwell to be convinced of his own hypothetical universalism (Ussher, *Works*, XII:565-66). Perhaps Culverwell was finally to go beyond his teacher, for the manuscript, which is addressed to Laurence Chaderton, advocates that "although God in his decree have ordayned, some to lyfe, some to death, yet his revealed will is he would have many to believe & to be saved who by their owne fault perish, & that God loves thees and offers his sonn to them, that they might thereby be moved to accept his mercye offred, & bee saved" (Bod Rawlinson MS. C.849, ff. 282v-83r). If in fact, however, this manuscript was written before 3rd March, 1618, then it could be that Ussher was in fact happy with this formulation of Culverwell's. Certainly he was happy in 1618 to stand by Culverwell in a common espousal of hypothetical universalism. Ussher tells us that Culverwell had been accused of teaching a universal actual reconciliation — an 'extreme' position which Ussher explicitly rejects (Ussher, *Works*, XII:553). Ussher doubted whether Culverwell ever held this, and if he did once, he no longer did so. Ussher explains that "after [Culverwell] had well weighed what I had written [i.e., *The Judgement* of 1618], he heartily thanked the Lord and me, for so good a resolution of this question, which for his part he wholly approved, not seeing how it could be gainsayed" (Ussher, *Works*, XII:565-66).

57. Ussher, *Works*, XII:558.

58. Ussher, *Works*, XII:568; cf. XII:569.

59. Ussher, *Works*, XII:564-65.

60. Cf. CUL MS. Mm.6.55 ff. 47r, 74r.

61. Ussher, *Works*, XII:553-54. Although Ussher's position is articulated in private correspondence and not spoken publicly or published in his lifetime, given the semi-public nature of seventeenth-century discursive correspondence, it is perhaps also possible that Ussher was being affected by James I's ban, mentioned immediately below.

Reformed articles of 1615,[62] which drew heavily on the particularism of the Lambeth Articles. Whereas the second English Article stated that Christ died "not only for originall gylt, but also for all actuall sinnes of men," the thirtieth Irish Article stated that it was "not only for original guilt, but also for all our actual transgressions."[63] It is hard to rule out a conscious revision of the Thirty-Nine Articles at this point in a particularist direction, replacing a bold, unqualified universal statement with the voice of the church.[64] The deeply ingrained association of Ussher with these 'Puritan' Irish Articles has led many, including the likes of Peter Lake, to describe Ussher as a "high Calvinist."[65] The question might naturally arise, therefore, as to the relationship between the Irish Articles of 1615 and Ussher's two privately circulated letters defending hypothetical universalism just three years later. Could the same man have been the author of these two productions? The resolution of this potential dilemma is to be found in the fact that the Irish Articles were in fact the product

---

62. Bernard, *The Life & Death of Ussher*, pp. 49-50; Bernard in Ussher, *The Judgement*, I:67; Nicholas Bernard, *Clavi Trabales; Or, Nailes fastned by some great Masters of Assemblyes confirming the Kings Supremacy* (London: R. Hodgkinson for R. Marriot, 1661), p. 62; Peter Heylyn, *Cyprianus Anglicus: Or the History of the Life and Death, of the most reverend and renowned Prelate William* (London: For A. Seile, 1668), p. 206; Peter Heylyn, *Historia Quinqu-Articularis: Or, a Declaration of the Judgement of the Western Churches, and more particularly of the Church of England, in the five controverted Points, reproched in these last Times by the Name of Arminianism* (London: E. C. for Thomas Johnson, 1660), III:101; Peter Heylyn, *Aerius Redivivus: Or, the History of the Presbyterians* (Oxford: John Crosley for John Baffet, 1670), p. 394; William Laud, *The Works of the most reverend Father in God, William Laud*, ed. William Scott & James Bliss, Library of Anglo-Catholic Theology (Oxford: John Henry Parker, 1847-60), VII:75; Philip Schaff, ed., *The Creeds of Christendom, with a History and Critical Notes* (Grand Rapids, MI: Baker Books), 1993, I:663; III:526; R. Buick Knox, *James Ussher: Archbishop of Armagh* (Cardiff: University of Wales Press, 1967), pp. 16-26; Thomas F. Torrance, *Scotttish Theology from John Knox to John McLeod Campbell* (Edinburgh: T. & T. Clark, 1996), pp. 125-26; Jan Rohls, *Reformed Confessions: Theology from Zurich to Barmen* (Louisville, KY: Westminster John Knox Press, 1998), p. 26; John V. Fesko, *Diversity within the Reformed Tradition: Supra- and Infralapsarianism in Calvin, Dort, and Westminster* (Greenville, SC: Reformed Academic Press, 2001), pp. 248-52; Richard A. Muller, *Post-Reformation Reformed Dogmatics: The Rise and Development of Reformed Orthodoxy, ca. 1520 to ca. 1725* (Grand Rapids, MI: Baker Academic, 2003), II:91.

63. Schaff, ed., *Creeds of Christendom*, III:438, 531.

64. The 'all' of the second English Article was omitted from 1630 onwards, and was expunged by the Westminster Assembly in their revision of the Thirty-Nine Articles (Schaff, ed., *Creeds of Christendom*, III:438; Peter Hall, *The Harmony of Protestant Confessions: Exhibiting the Faith of the Churches of Christ, Reformed after the pure and holy Doctrine of the Gospel, throughout Europe* [London: John F. Shaw, 1842], p. 505).

65. Peter G. Lake, *Moderate Puritans and the Elizabethan Church* (Cambridge: Cambridge University Press, 1982), p. 225.

of the Irish Convocation as a whole, of which Ussher was just one member.[66] While Ussher as Professor of Theological Controversies at Trinity College Dublin doubtless was an authoritative contributor to the process of producing this confession of faith[67] — even to the point of his own catechism being foundational for many of the articles — there is no reason to believe that his own preferences were never overruled during the editing process by a majority pushing in another direction. There is no reason therefore to believe that the Articles reflect *verbatim* Ussher's own preferred formulations.[68] Consequently, the commonly perceived need to account for Ussher's shift from high Calvinism to moderate Calvinism becomes considerably less urgent.

According to Baxter, Ussher's views represent "the same middle way as Davenant." Bernard also stated that Ussher "concurred with Bishop Davenant" in this matter.[69] Both Baxter and Bernard were notoriously biased, however, and so the extent to which this is true will now be investigated.

---

66. See Alan Ford, *The Protestant Reformation in Ireland, 1590-1641*, 2nd ed. (Dublin: Four Courts Press, 1997), pp. 157-59, 166; *ODNB*.

67. Cf. Elizabethanne Boran, "An early friendship Network of James Ussher, Archbishop of Armagh, 1626-1656" in *European Universities in the Age of Reformation and Counter-Reformation*, ed. Helga Robinson-Hammerstein (Dublin: Four Courts Press, 1998), 116-34, p. 130.

68. Capern defends the traditional view of Ussher's authorship on the grounds that the wording of the Articles "bears remarkable correspondence to Ussher's early catechistical work at Trinity College Dublin" (Amanda Capern, "The Caroline Church: James Ussher and the Irish Dimension," *HJ* 39 [1996]: 57-85, p. 72). Capern is referring to Ussher, *Works*, XI:197-220. Cf. Amanda Capern, "'Slipperye Times and dangerous Dayes': James Ussher and the Calvinist Reformation of Britain" (Ph.D. Dissertation, University of New South Wales, 1991), p. 113, cited in Ford, *The Protestant Reformation in Ireland*, p. 16. However, it is still one thing to draw up a first draft, but quite another not to be overruled by a wider body in the subsequent (and significant) revision of that document. Even if Nicholas Bernard was correct in understanding Ussher to have been "appointed by the Synode as a principal person to draw them up" and in later life to have been still happy to recommend them (Bernard in Ussher, *The Judgement*, I:67-68), this still places a sufficient explanatory distance between Ussher and the precise text of the Articles. Capern also states that Prynne, in his book *Anti-Arminianisme*, "claimed Ussher for an ally because of the Irish Articles" (Capern, "The Caroline Church," p. 62). However, although in this book Prynne does cite Ussher as a Reformed authority, this is not at any time "because of the Irish Articles" but because of his published treatises (William Prynne, *Anti-Arminianisme. Or, the Church of Englands old Antithesis to new Arminianisme* [London: Eliz. Allde for M. Sparke, 1630], pp. a4r, 100, 112, 186, 216, 217). In the chapter in which Prynne reproduces and evaluates the Irish Articles, Ussher's name is nowhere to be seen, and Prynne states that "most of our Irish Bishops who composed these Articles, were English Divines" (Prynne, *Anti-Arminianisme*, p. 20; cf. p. 217) — and Ussher was born in Dublin and spent most of his life in Ireland.

69. Baxter, *Certain Disputations*, p. C2r; Ussher, *The Judgement*, I:A4v.

Davenant's Theology of the Death of Christ

In Cambridge, shortly after the Synod of Dort, Davenant gave a lengthy series of lectures on the subject of the extent of the atonement, but the political situation prevented them from being published during his lifetime.[70] His nephew, Edward Davenant, sent the manuscripts to Ussher to edit for publication, but in the end it was Ussher's acquaintance Thomas Bedford who edited them in 1650 in the form of a 106-page Latin folio, which was later reprinted in a more convenient form in 1683.[71] Josiah Allport translated this work into English in 1832. Another important source for both Davenant's views and immediate polemical context is found in John Hales' *Golden Remains.*[72] Hales was present at the Synod in the capacity of chaplain to the ambassador, Sir Dudley Carleton. This book contains his reports to Carleton from Dort, as well as an undated document entitled *Doctour Davenant touching the Second Article, discussed at the Conference at the Haghe, of the Extent of Redemption.*[73] This essay deals with the second Remonstrant article of 1610, which asserted that Christ died for every man without exception.

70. Cf. Ussher, *Works,* XVI:521. It is not absolutely clear whether these lectures were delivered after the Synod of Dort and not just before (John Davenant, *Dissertationes duæ: Prima de Morte Christi, quatenus ad omnes extendatur, quatenus ad solos Electos restringatur. Altera de Prædestinatione & Reprobatione,* ed. Thomas Bedford [Cambridge: Roger Daniel, 1650], Preface; John Davenant, *Dissertatio de Morte Christi,* 2nd ed. [Cambridge: Roger Daniel, 1683], Preface; John Davenant, "A Dissertation on the Death of Christ, as to its Extent and special Benefits: containing a short History of Pelagianism, and shewing the Agreement of the Doctrines of the Church of England on general Redemption, Election, and Predestination, with the Primitive Fathers of the Christian Church, and above all, with the Holy Scriptures" in *An Exposition of the Epistle of St Paul to the Colossians,* trans. Josiah Allport [London: Hamilton, Adams, and Co., 1832], II:309-569, II:313-14). However, the first edition of 1650 contains references to publications arising from the Synod, so these lectures must have been at least revised — whether by Davenant or Thomas Bedford — after the middle of 1620 (e.g., Davenant, *Dissertationes duæ,* I:25, 40, 43, 44, 46, 58). It is certainly more natural to see these lectures as the fruit of Davenant's deliberations at the Synod. Whatever the case, the lectures were "ready for ye presse" by 4th November, 1628 (Bod Tanner MS. 72, f. 298v). Anthony Milton's research favours a delivery date in the early 1620s (personal communication).

71. Allport, "Life of Bishop Davenant," I:xlviii-xlix; cf. Ussher, *Works,* XV:581. Yet it was still Ussher who was considered the cause of their being published (Ussher, *The Judgement,* I:A4v).

72. The 1673 edition is used here as it contains considerably more material than the first edition of 1659.

73. John Hales, *Golden Remains of the ever memorable Mr. John Hales,* 2nd ed. (London: Thomas Newcomb for Robert Pawlet, 1673), II:186-90. This essay also exists, with only negligible variations, amongst Ussher's papers at Bod Rawlinson C.849 ff. 278r-81v. Davenant's propositions were first printed in 1620 as part of "Sententia Theologorum Magnæ Britanniæ, De

Like Ussher, Davenant, the infralapsarian double predestinarian,[74] agreed with the particular redemptionists in affirming a particular aspect to

---

Articulo secundo" (*Acta Synodi Nationalis, in Nomine Domini nostri Jesu Christi, autoritate D.D. Ordinum generalium Fœderati Belgii Provinciarum Dordrechti habitæ anno 1618 et 1619. Accedunt plenissima, de quinque Articulis, theologorum judicia* [Dordrecht: Isaac Joannid Canin, 1620], II:100-106). Contrary to numerous assertions, Hales remained sympathetic to the theology of the Synod and was glad to see the Remonstrants defeated (W. Robert Godfrey, "John Hales' Good-Night to John Calvin" in *Protestant Scholasticism: Essays in Reassessment*, ed. Carl R. Trueman & R. Scott Clark [Carlisle, UK: Paternoster Press, 1999], pp. 165-80).

74. Neither Davenant nor Ussher was supralapsarian, contrary to Clausen's claims (Clausen, "Calvinism in the Anglican Hierarchy," pp. 118, 156, 164, 230, 285, 355, 358). According to Baxter, Davenant was neither supralapsarian nor infralapsarian, regarding the whole debate as forbidden speculation (Baxter, *Catholick Theologie*, IV:44). However, although Davenant initially ventured only very cautiously and even reluctantly into this area (see, for example, Davenant, "A Dissertation," II:515), this is most certainly not the case. By 1634 Davenant was willing to defend at length the proposition that "Subjectum divinæ prædestinationeis est homo lapsus" (John Davenant, *Determinationes Quæstionum quarundam Theologicarum* [Cambridge: Thomas & John Buck and Roger Daniel, 1634], pp. 119-23; translated into English in John Davenant, *A Treatise on Justification, or the Disputatio de Justitia habituali at actuali . . . translated from the original Latin, together with Translations of the Determinationes*, trans. Josiah Allport [London: Hamilton, Adams, & Co., 1844-46], II:354-59). Then in 1641 Davenant published an entire book explicitly defending the infralapsarian position over against the Arminian and supralapsarian positions (John Davenant, *Animadversions written by the Right Reverend Father in God John, Lord Bishop of Salisbury, upon a Treatise intitled Gods love to Mankind* [Cambridge: Roger Daniel, 1641]). Curt Daniel's attempt to establish that Davenant espoused a neat Amyraldian view of the *ordo decretorum*, does not even fit the scanty evidence he cites, let alone these larger and more pertinent publications that he entirely overlooks (Curt D. Daniel, "Hyper-Calvinism and John Gill" [Ph.D. Dissertation, University of Edinburgh, 1983], p. 526). Davenant not only explicitly and at great length defended an infralapsarian position, but, contrary to Michael Thomas' recent assertions, he also explicitly rejected what was later to become known as an Amyraldian view of the decree (Bod Tanner MS. 71, f. 37r; G. Michael Thomas, *The Extent of the Atonement: A Dilemma for Reformed Theology from Calvin to the Consensus* [Carlisle, UK: Paternoster Press, 1997], pp. 151, 165). John Fesko builds his whole case for Ussher being a supralapsarian on Ussher, *Works*, XI:203. However, this page does not even speak to the question, and, if any inference may be drawn at all, it would be that Ussher was infralapsarian due to the repeated references to mercy and justice in the context of God's 'choosing out' some and not others (Fesko, *Diversity within the Reformed Tradition*, pp. 247-48). More alarming still are the lengths to which Fesko then goes in attempting to explain how "the supralapsarian Ussher" could have subsequently "composed" the "infralapsarian" Irish Articles (Fesko, *Diversity within the Reformed Tradition*, pp. 246, 248-52). Similar mishandling of the evidence occurs throughout Fesko's book. For Ussher's infralapsarian double predestinarianism, and his preference for the term 'preterition' over against 'reprobation,' see Ussher, *Works*, XVII:xxiv; CUL MS. Mm.6.55 ff. 2v, 219r. Cf. Ussher, *Works*, I:clvii; Ussher, *The Judgement*, 1659, p. 364. Ussher was nevertheless a rigorous predestinarian and, by way of a covert promotion of predestinarianism in the hostile climate of the 1630s, he published a lengthy treatment of the predestinarian theol-

Christ's work with regard to the elect, but objected to deducing from this fact the doctrine of particular redemption. He lamented that "some persons so totally apply themselves to the contemplation of the eternal and secret will and foreknowledge of God, that they admit hardly any thing else into their minds." The salvation of the elect is *not* the "only or sole end" of Christ's death. Davenant insisted that "[w]e ought not . . . so to urge the special good pleasure of God towards the elect, that we should deny that the ransom of Christ was ordained by God to reconcile and deliver all mankind individually." Rather we should be content to affirm that "Christ himself merited, and offered his merits, in a different way for different persons."[75]

A main concern of Davenant was to preach predestination and electing grace without doing despite to "that common loving-kindness of God, of which the Scripture testifies." The gospel as expressed in the well-known text of John 3:16 is part of "the design of God embracing all mankind promiscuously."[76] Too often the Reformed had seen the gospel as a manifestation only of God's special love, despite the fact that to deny "[t]he generall love of God towards mankind" is "plain blasphemie." However, "God in sending the Redeemer was willing to manifest to the world both these kinds of love; namely, that common love of the human race, which we call philanthropy, and that special and secret love, which we call good pleasure."[77] It is not only that a general love of God must be upheld, but that the provision of "the blood of his Son," must also be seen as an outflowing from this "more common providence" or "common philanthropy of God," as opposed to "the grace of Christ."[78] This general love does not manifest itself in the salvation of all, but it does manifest itself in a general donation of Christ to all without exception. For "although salvation or eternal life is every where promised to be given under the condition of faith," we "no where read in the Scriptures, that Christ, or the death or sacrifice of Christ, was given or promised conditionally to the human race."[79] Thus we must not imply that John 3:16 reads in fact, "So God loved the world, that he would

---

ogy of the ninth-century monk, Gottschalk (James Ussher, *Gotteschalci, et Prædestinatianæ Controversiæ ab eo motæ, Historia* [Dublin: Societatis Bibliopolarum, 1631]; Ussher, *Works*, IV:1-233).

75. Davenant, "A Dissertation," II:437, 396, 389, 557; cf. John Davenant, *One of the Sermons preached at Westminster* (London: Richard Badger, 1628), p. 50; Hales, *Golden Remains*, II:185.

76. Davenant, "A Dissertation," II:365, 521.

77. Davenant, *Animadversions*, p. 1; Davenant, "A Dissertation," II:388. Again John 3:16 is cited.

78. Davenant, "A Dissertation," II:370, 566; cf. II:354, 358.

79. Davenant, "A Dissertation," II:385.

give his Son for it if it should believe." Rather, Christ "was given absolutely to all from the love of God to man."[80]

A second main concern of Davenant was that already expressed by Ussher in 1618, namely, that the sufficiency of the atonement was not a bare or "mere sufficiency."[81] Davenant fully accepted that "the ransom paid by Christ is in itself of sufficient and superabundant value to take away the sins, not only of men, but of fallen angels."[82] However, he lamented that

> some persons in such a way concede that Christ died for all men, that with the same breath they assert that he died for the elect alone, and so expound that received distinction of Divines, 'That he died for all sufficiently, but for the elect effectually,' that they entirely extinguish the first part of the sentence.[83]

By this Davenant meant that Christ cannot "be truly said to have died for all men sufficiently," if by the sufficiency of the atonement is meant only "the intrinsic value of the ransom."[84] Rather, to this "mere sufficiency" must be added what Davenant called an "ordained sufficiency."[85] This is because the Scriptures "speak of the death of Christ so as to refer its universal efficacy not to the mere dignity of the sacrifice offered, but to the act and intention of the offering."[86] As in Ussher's thought, therefore, the sufficiency of the atonement involves the will of God and not just christological considerations.

Like Ussher and Preston, Davenant also drew on the imagery of the death of Christ as medicine.[87] Even though no one should take this medicine and benefit from it, the very existence of the medicine has changed the relationship between God and man. This is because Christ's death has "so far rendered God the Father pacified and reconciled to the human race, that he can be truly said to be ready to receive into favour any man whatever, as soon as he shall believe in Christ."[88] Davenant even went so far as to say that there is "an universal propensity in God to save every man, if he should believe in Christ."[89] This willingness "to be reconciled to any man who believes,"

80. Davenant, "A Dissertation," II:384.
81. Davenant, "A Dissertation," II:412; cf. II:401.
82. Davenant, "A Dissertation," II:386.
83. Davenant, "A Dissertation," II:401.
84. Davenant, "A Dissertation," II:407; cf. II:378, 409.
85. Davenant, "A Dissertation," II:408. See also II:402-3.
86. Davenant, "A Dissertation," II:410-11.
87. E.g., Davenant, "A Dissertation," II:460, 513, 522.
88. Davenant, "A Dissertation," II:440.
89. Davenant, "A Dissertation," II:566.

Davenant styles as the "efficacy of the death of Christ." For Davenant this fact is undeniable, since "God would not be actually pacified and reconciled to any man, as soon as he should believe, that is, on the performance of the condition of faith, unless he were placable and reconcilable to any man before he should believe."[90]

Again, as in Ussher and Preston, the parallel doctrine to the achieved placability of God is the attained salvability of man. In Davenant's system "the death of Christ is presupposed to be applicable to all men according to the ordination of God."[91] This means that as a result of Christ's universal atonement all men without exception have "a common right" or "an universal right" to salvation.[92] Thus salvation "neither is, nor ought to be conceived by us to be altogether impossible to any person living."[93] Rather "salvation is procurable" for all without exception, and "his sins are expiable."[94] In concrete terms this means that the death of Christ "was capable of application to Judas, if Judas had repented and believed in Christ," and was genuinely applicable to non-elect Cain before Christ died in history.[95]

But Davenant was not content merely to assert that Christ's satisfaction was *applicable* to the non-elect. To a certain extent, and to at least some of the non-elect, Christ's death was actually *applied*. Davenant boldly asserted that "the meritorious efficacy of the death of Christ is not to be restricted to the elect alone, but is applicable to others from the ordination of God, and is actually applied as to certain effects."[96] Nor was Davenant merely asserting what strict particularists were happy to concede, namely that because of the death of Christ in history, the whole course of Christian civilisation brings innumerable outward benefits to the non-elect. Davenant is instead referring to "sundry initial preparations tending to Conversion, merited by Christ . . . and wrought by the Holy Ghost in the hearts of many" of the unregenerate, non-elect in the church. Such internal works of the Holy Spirit in the non-elect include illumination, a sense of sin, and a fear of punishment.[97] In this,

90. Davenant, "A Dissertation," II:427; 442-43.

91. Davenant, "A Dissertation," II:396.

92. Davenant, "A Dissertation," II:411, 427; cf. II:473.

93. Davenant, "A Dissertation," II:429; cf. II:475.

94. Davenant, "A Dissertation," II:372.

95. Davenant, "A Dissertation," II:342 (Davenant again cites John 3:16 [II:343]), 368.

96. Davenant, "A Dissertation," II:354; cf. II:352.

97. Hales, *Golden Remains,* II:187. Among Ussher's papers in Bod Rawlinson C.849 f. 279r, the examples of such internal works are not in the main text but in the margin, and are thus perhaps not part of Davenant's original, but constitute Ussher's own annotation. Some testimonies have been gathered to indicate that Ussher did come to hold to this tenet (Ussher, *Works,* I:289-95; cf. XIII:227-28). Culverwell, Ussher's disciple in these matters, certainly held to it in an-

Davenant was merely asserting what the British delegation to Dort as a whole were happy to confess. These men believed in "some fruits of Christ's death, not comprised in the Decree of Election, but afforded more generally, yet confined to the Visible Church." By this they meant "true and spiritual Graces accompanying the Gospel, and conferred upon some *non-electi*."[98] Granted that "Christ does not confer anything upon men which he hath not first merited for them by his obedience," it follows for Davenant that, "[w]hatever supernatural grace is given through Christ to any man, is given from the merit of Christ." Christ must therefore have died for the non-elect in a way far more than theoretical.[99]

Davenant could even go so far as to concede that, because of Christ's universal satisfaction, there is "an universal capacity of salvation in all persons living in this world." It was therefore vital that he explain himself more fully, and clear himself of any associated semi-Pelagian implications. The way he goes about doing this is very similar to Ussher, but also more elaborate. Firstly, the incarnation is stressed even more than in Ussher, and is primarily used to set the non-elect in a state denied to fallen angels. Unlike the non-elect, the demons do not have "a common right of obtaining pardon through faith," simply "because he did not in any way die for them."[100]

More important to Davenant's defence of hypothetical universalism is his arguable dislocation of the satisfaction of Christ, not from Christ's work of intercession, as in Ussher, but from the Father's role in redemption.

---

other manuscript that Ussher annotated (Bod Rawlinson MS. C.849, f. 282v). In stark contrast, Perkins had denied any internal work of the Holy Spirit in the reprobate. Any conviction of sin they might feel was merely due to the external work of the law (William Perkins, *The Workes of that famous and worthy Minister of Christ in the Universitie of Cambridge, Mr. William Perkins* [London: John Legatt & Cantrell Legge, 1616-18], I:638).

98. Hales, *Golden Remains*, II:185. Samuel Ward reported to Ussher that the delegation held that "sundry effects" of Christ's oblation were "offered *serio*, and some really communicated to the reprobate" (Ussher, *Works*, XV:145).

99. Davenant, "A Dissertation," II:353. Davenant felt able to walk out on what, in his own theological climate, was very thin ice, due to patristic support. The belief of the early Fathers that every infant baptism removed original sin from the child, led Davenant to conclude that therefore the Church Fathers also held that the death of Christ was applied to some non-elect (Davenant, "A Dissertation," II:353-54). For Davenant's own views on baptismal regeneration see John Davenant, *Baptismal Regeneration and the final Perseverance of the Saints: A Letter of the Right Rev. John Davenant, D.D., Late Bishop of Salisbury, to Dr. Samuel Ward, Lady Margaret's Professor at Cambridge in the Reign of King James*, trans. Josiah Allport (London: William Macintosh, 1864) and below, p. 195. Cf. Davenant, *An Exposition of the Epistle of St Paul to the Colossians*, I:448-49; Davenant, *Treatise on Justification*, I:20; Ussher, *Works*, XV:482.

100. Davenant, "A Dissertation," II:566, 411. For other appeals to the fallen angels in support of his case see Davenant, "A Dissertation," II:342, 368, 369, 373, 374, 386, 412, 414.

Davenant grapples with the particular redemptionist argument that the work of redemption has the same extent for each member of the Trinity. He admits that "the predestination of God, and effectual vocation, which depends upon it, embraces no one not elected." However, he asserts that, nevertheless, "the oblation of Christ on the cross, is of wider extent," as wide "as the offering of Christ in the Gospel." This leads Davenant to argue that Christ had different things in mind for different people when he was dying on the cross. He does this by constructing a 'double will' in the suffering Saviour:

> there was in Christ himself a will according to which he willed that his death should regard all men individually; and there was also a will according to which he willed that it should pertain to the elect alone. He willed that it should regard all the posterity of Adam who should be saved, and that it should actually save them all, provided they should embrace it with a true faith. He willed that it should so pertain to the elect alone, that by the merit of it all things which relate to the obtaining of salvation, should be infallibly given to them.

It was only in this latter sense that Davenant could "confess that the oblation of Christ is of the same extent as the predestination of God."[101] But he denied that he was setting up a Son who was out of redemptive step with his Father, since this larger purpose was also "conformed to the ordination of the Father."[102] Christ dying for a man therefore does not necessarily save him. It all depends what Christ was intending to do in dying for him: to make him salvable, or to save him indeed.[103]

It is of considerable interest that Davenant, unlike Preston, explicitly refuses to follow Ussher's resort of dislocating Christ's satisfaction from his intercession, and only limiting the latter in scope. Because Davenant resorted to a 'double will' in the suffering Saviour, he was not forced to split Christ's two-fold priestly work in the manner that Ussher had done. Perhaps Davenant also felt more than Ussher the force of the particular redemptionist polemic that universal redemption destroys the unity and simplicity of Christ's high priestly work. Whereas Ussher conceded to the particularists that Christ did not intercede for all, and that therefore the satisfaction of Christ stands alone as universal in scope, Davenant argued that "not only . . . the death, but the resurrection and intercession of Christ regards [the non-elect], as to the possibility of their enjoying these benefits, the condition of faith being pre-

---

101. Davenant, "A Dissertation," II:379-80.
102. Davenant, "A Dissertation," II:398; cf. II:518, 530, 542.
103. Davenant, "A Dissertation," II:423.

supposed." Thus Davenant refused to "put asunder those things which God hath joined together"; and professed that "we teach, that the death, resurrection, and intercession of Christ are joined together in indissoluble union, but in a different way."[104] Thus, for Davenant, both the death and intercession of Christ are applicable to all. Christ died for all on condition that they believe, and he will intercede for all if only they believe.

A third major characteristic of Davenant's developed position, but by no means exclusive to hypothetical universalism, is the doctrine of a two-staged reconciliation. Put briefly, Davenant maintained that no one is actually reconciled to a reconcilable God until they believe. Davenant's formulation proceeds from his doctrine of divine placability outlined above, and hangs on his definition of reconciliation. Reconciliation has two steps. Firstly, God is made willing to be reconciled to man upon "the performance of some certain condition"; and secondly, man is actually reconciled when that condition is met. The first is universal, and the second limited in scope.[105] Redemption therefore is "a payment of the just price due for us captives, not that we should be actually delivered on the payment of the price, but that we should be delivered as soon as we believe in the Redeemer."[106] No one is actually reconciled "by the work of Christ alone." Rather, "it is necessary, before he obtains this actual reconciliation, to add the act or work of the man himself believing in Christ the Redeemer, and applying the merit of his death to himself individually by faith."[107] Thus

> it is not impossible to cut off some from salvation for whom [Christ] did die, because it was not appointed by God that the death of Christ alone, by the act of his oblation, should render God propitious to all, and should save all, but that it should 'be a propitiation, through faith in his blood.'[108]

Davenant's concern in all this is to guard against the doctrine of eternal justification that he sees as inherent, if not always actually expressed, in the particular redemptionist system.[109]

104. Davenant, "A Dissertation," II:373; cf. Paul Helm, *Calvin and the Calvinists* (Edinburgh: Banner of Truth Trust, 1998), p. 37.

105. Davenant, "A Dissertation," II:441.

106. Davenant, "A Dissertation," II:388.

107. Davenant, II:442; cf. II:446.

108. Davenant, "A Dissertation," II:382. Traces of this formulation of a two-stage reconciliation can be detected in Preston (John Preston, *The golden Scepter*, II:26, 41; John Preston, *Love of Christ*, p. 8; John Preston, *Saints Qualification*, II:196; III:61).

109. Davenant, "A Dissertation," II:447-58, 463-72. However, the price Davenant pays for

We have already seen how Davenant emphasises that Christ's satisfaction rendered God placable and the sins of all without exception pardonable. This enabled Davenant to assert that the death of Christ "is a ransom from the ordination of God applicable to all men individually." This is far more than the particular redemptionist's hypothetical construct that the death of Christ is theoretically applicable to anyone. Rather, in a very real sense it "is applicable to all from the Divine loving-kindness to man," even to the non-elect who are still in this world.[110]

To deny that Christ's death is applicable to all would make Christ "only a partial Redeemer and Saviour," and would mean that Christ "could not claim for himself any supreme dominion over each and every man in right of his death."[111] The important point to grasp here is that Davenant is at pains to stress that the application of an applicable atonement is by no means necessary or intrinsically guaranteed. Christ's death is applicable but God is not bound to apply it to anyone, its application remaining "in his own most free power."[112]

Davenant stresses how there is as much intrinsic reason why the satisfaction of Christ should save any angel as any human. This is because "the

---

this formulation is a different mode of salvation for infants and those who lack the intellectual faculties necessary for adult faith (Davenant, "A Dissertation," II:440-41, 446-47). In keeping with his belief in baptismal regeneration, Davenant taught that all baptised infants without exception are, by "the goodwill of God," "absolved from the guilt of Original Sin" and also justified, regenerated, and adopted into God's family. However, their justification, regeneration, and adoption "is not exactly the same" as that of adult believers, as it can be lost. "The justification, regeneration and adoption of baptized Infants brings them into a state of salvation as far as they are capable," but nevertheless, "the Christian Infant who is regenerated in Baptism acquires another regeneration, when as an Adult he believes the Gospel." Although God is "embracing them with His favour," baptised children "do not continue justified, regenerated or adopted as Adults unless by repentance, faith, and the renunciation promised, they fulfil their vow taken upon them at baptism" (Davenant, *Baptismal Regeneration*, pp. 14, 19-21, 25, 27; cf. *CCRB*, I:110). It is with this in mind, therefore, that Davenant's comments above concerning being 'cut off from salvation' should be understood. It is no rare or hypothetical matter, but a common and very real and final fall from being in a "truly justified" state before God. In this Davenant was following the lead of his intimate friend and fellow hypothetical universalist at the Synod of Dort, Samuel Ward, who also held similar controversial views on baptismal regeneration, but who was counseled by Davenant to keep them quiet so as not to give the Arminians a foothold (Samuel Ward & Thomas Gataker, *De Baptismatis Infantilis Vi & Efficacia Disceptatio* [London: Roger Daniel, 1653]; Morris Fuller, *The Life, Letters and Writings of John Davenant* [London: Methuen, 1897], p. 329).

110. Davenant, "A Dissertation," II:361, 358, 432.
111. Davenant, "A Dissertation," II:360, 359.
112. Davenant, "A Dissertation," II:371.

death of Christ is not a remedy applicable to expiate the sins of any one, except according to the ordination and acceptation of God." For

> although the ransom paid by Christ is in itself of sufficient and superabundant value to take away the sins, not only of men, but of fallen angels, yet, on account of the want of its ordination and acceptation as to angels, we deny that Christ ought to be said to have died for them in any way.

In contrast,

> [t]here is no one who is a partaker of the same human nature which the Redeemer deigned to assume, for whom Christ did not deliver up himself as a price of redemption, applicable according to the ordination and acceptation of God, for remission of sins, to be obtained by faith in his blood.[113]

The extent of the atonement is therefore seen to depend solely on the will of God, and not on its intrinsic nature or place in an eternal covenant of redemption. Thus "if God had deigned to grant this right in the death of Christ to angels, it would also be applicable for the redemption of angels."[114] The atonement, therefore, means just what God wills it to mean, and it could have meant many other things than what it has finally come to mean. In summary it can be said that

> what Christ merited for any one, he merited according to the appointment and acceptance of his Father: Therefore, according to the will and appointment of the Father, the death of Christ pertains to the elect in some special way, in which it is not extended to others.[115]

In Davenant's system it is therefore a separate decree of predestinating grace which makes the final difference between the relationship of the non-elect and the elect to Christ's satisfaction. It is not the effect of propitiation itself that brings about faith in the elect, as in Perkins' *A golden Chaine*. Although Christ's death is not equally for all, nevertheless propitiation does not, strictly speaking, carry with it its own application, since it is not, strictly speaking, linked with the covenant of redemption. Davenant acknowledged that faith "is given *on account of* the merits of Christ, to all those to whom it is actually given."[116] How-

---

113. Davenant, "A Dissertation," II:386-87.
114. Davenant, "A Dissertation," II:413.
115. Davenant, "A Dissertation," II:547.
116. Davenant, "A Dissertation," II:552 (emphasis added).

ever, he rejected the notion that "in the death of Christ himself is included also the infallible application of his death," maintaining that "the oblation of Christ considered merely in itself, altogether obtains from God, that every individual who is willing to believe in Christ shall be saved."[117] Thus, "the certainty of the application depends, as to the primary cause, on the secret and eternal act of God in predestinating, and not only on the act of Christ in offering up himself for men."[118]

However, despite subordinating Christ to predestination, Davenant pursues a high degree of christocentricity, and avoids the abstractions of later Grotian formulations on the application of redemption. He does this by emphasising that although it is God's separate decree that makes the atonement effectual, Christ himself, while suffering on the cross, affirmed this decree and to that extent participated in its own application. Davenant's Reformed heritage can permit him no other option. For how else could Christ have "exhibited himself as conformed to the eternal appointment of his Father, if, in his saving passion, he had not applied his merits in a peculiar manner infallibly to effect and complete the salvation of the elect?" Thus, "to the price of his death, which was most sufficient in itself," Christ himself "added moreover the most effectual and special intention of his will, in order to effect the salvation of these elect persons."[119] Christ therefore is intimately involved in, though still subordinated to, the separate decree that gives meaning to his own death. Davenant in this way seeks to steer well clear of Arminian, as well as anti-Trinitarian, notions of the merit of Christ's death.[120]

Although the satisfaction of Christ is general and applicable to all according to God's good pleasure, nevertheless salvation is not to be understood as being uncertain when considered in the death of Christ alone, since "[t]he blood of Christ . . . could not flow in vain, because by the price of his blood, according to the decree of God, he merited for the elect the beneficial application of that price."[121] Davenant once again displays his genius for pursuing a middle way between the rocks of both Perkinsian Calvinism and Remonstrantian Arminianism, albeit by a most tortuous route. It is the pre-

---

117. Davenant, "A Dissertation," II:397-98; cf. II:343.

118. Davenant, "A Dissertation," II:398.

119. Davenant, "A Dissertation," II:542, 543.

120. Davenant, "A Dissertation," II:534-35. Davenant argues that "the death of Christ, according to the appointment of God merited this for Judas, that on the condition of faith he might attain to eternal life; but it obtained in addition for Peter, that on account of the merit of Christ he should receive persevering faith and all other spiritual benefits which are required in order infallibly to obtain eternal life" (Davenant, "A Dissertation," II:534-35).

121. Davenant, "A Dissertation," II:527.

destinating and most free will of God that takes a general atonement and applies it how he wills. Christ had a special eye to the elect as he died on the cross, although that does not strictly belong to his work of satisfaction.

Finally, like Ussher, Davenant also avoided semi-Pelagian overtones from being read into his doctrine of universal atonement by resorting to scholastic structures of causality. Christ is to be seen as "the Redeemer and Saviour of all men causally, as the Schoolmen say."[122] This means, as Ussher also taught, that when it is said that Christ "died for all men sufficiently," we are to understand that the "death of Christ is the universal cause of the salvation of mankind."[123] This does not mean that all mankind are actually saved (the efficient cause), but only that "Christ was so offered on the cross for all men, that his death is a kind of universal remedy appointed for all men individually."[124] By Christ's death being "the universal cause of salvation," Davenant meant that "this remedy is proposed indiscriminately to every individual of the human race for salvation," and "of itself it can cure and save all and every individual."[125] This appears to be the replication of Ussher's notion of an "all-sufficient remedy" outlined above.

Davenant's Theology of the Call of the Gospel

Intimately connected with Davenant's formulations on the intent and extent of Christ's satisfaction is his presentation of the doctrine of the universal call of the gospel. Where many had been driven to extremes, and hence glaring inconsistencies, Davenant was determined to demonstrate the biblical harmony of his own system. The context in which he laboured puts it beyond all doubt that a prime concern in his complex elaboration of the doctrine of the gospel call was the refutation of the Remonstrants' "odious imputation of illusion in the general propounding of the Evangelical Promises."[126] Davenant sought to

122. Davenant, "A Dissertation," II:360.
123. Davenant, "A Dissertation," II:401; also II:440, 565.
124. Davenant, "A Dissertation," II:513.
125. Davenant, "A Dissertation," II:341.
126. Hales, *Golden Remains*, II:185; cf. George Carleton, John Davenant, Samuel Ward, Thomas Goad, & Walter Balcanqual, *Suffragium Collegiale Theologorum Magnae Britanniae de quinque Controversis Remonstrantium Articulis, Synodo Dordrechtanae exhibitum Anno M.DC.XIX* (London: R. Young for R. Milbourne, 1626), pp. 29, 43-44; The Remonstrants, *The Confession or Declaration of the Ministers or Pastors, which in the United Provinces are called Remonstrants, or Arminians, concerning the chief Points of Christian Religion* (London: For Francis Smith, 1676), p. 201.

address all apparent tensions and vindicate the sincerity of the universal proclamation of the Reformed gospel.

As in Ussher, a universal satisfaction is vital to the call of the gospel. Davenant did not ground the universal call merely in the naked divine command, but argued that "there is a title to eternal life, founded on the death of Christ, indifferently regarding every individual under the condition of faith."[127] He argued that if the infinite intrinsic sufficiency which particular redemptionists concede is not genuinely offered to the non-elect, then it is a useless concept.[128] He therefore condemned those Reformed theologians who rested only in a hypothetical or "mere" sufficiency and could not acknowledge an "ordained sufficiency," a sufficiency actually intended for the non-elect with "some wish to offer" it.[129] Thus in Davenant's thought, it is the first (universal) stage of his two-staged scheme of reconciliation that lays "the foundation of every future offering, by which he is offered to men in the Gospel," namely an unconditional and absolute, general satisfaction. However, although Christ "was given absolutely to all from the love of God to man," this only profits people "conditionally, . . . if they should believe." Thus, a "condition indeed is annexed in the preaching of the Gospel," but the preaching is based on an unconditional, universal satisfaction.[130]

Furthermore, a universal satisfaction was also vital to Davenant if the gospel was to be preached properly, as only in this way can it be said that "the death or merit of Christ is the object of faith." He maintained that "the death or merit of Christ, in his infinite mercy, ought to be considered as a thing determined on and destined for men before faith is destined for any individual persons." Davenant's reasoning was as follows: "To what purpose would have been the gift of faith to Peter or Paul, unless a saving remedy had first been ordained applicable to any one through faith?" He concluded that "in the order of the Divine decrees, the death of Christ precedes the faith of every Christian."[131] In this way, a universal gospel call and a universal satisfaction become inextricably linked in Davenant's system.

As already noted, a chief concern for Davenant was to evade the allega-

127. Davenant, "A Dissertation," II:378.
128. Davenant, "A Dissertation," II:402.
129. Davenant, "A Dissertation," II:403.
130. Davenant, "A Dissertation," II:384.
131. Davenant, "A Dissertation," II:363; cf. II:364, 555-56. Of course, for Davenant this was still only a conceptual order and not "a real precedence or succession of views or decrees in the Divine mind and will" (Davenant, *Treatise on Justification,* II:354). It was deemed safer in this "thorny question" to acknowledge that these various decrees "with respect to God himself consist of an equable eternity of infinity" (Davenant, "A Dissertation," II:515).

tions of the Remonstrants that the call of the Reformed gospel to the reprobate was insincere. At this point, while adamantly anti-Remonstrantian,
Davenant was inclined to agree with the Remonstrants over against a strict
particular redemptionist scheme, and that on two grounds. Firstly, the reprobate under the particular redemptionist scheme are not "bound to gratitude"
for the death of Christ. Secondly, the reprobate must know they will be saved
if they meet the condition of faith. Davenant wants to formulate a system of
"conditional grace" in which the non-elect can truthfully say, "If I believe I
shall be saved."[132] Yet because particular redemptionism denies "that Christ
died for some persons, it will immediately follow, that such could not be
saved by the death of Christ, even if they should believe."[133] Similarly, "it does
not follow from the declaration, That God by the death of Christ confirmed a
covenant concerning the salvation of all the elect through faith; Therefore, If
Cain should believe, he shall be saved."[134] Consequently it is impossible to offer Christ sincerely to the non-elect: "Take away the regard to the death of
Christ which is present to the mind of God and which embraces the human
race, and there is nothing serious, solid or true in promises of this kind [i.e.,
Ezek. 38:21] as to the non-elect."[135] In contrast to this,

> the Scriptures clearly teach, that Christ by dying obtained for each and
> every man this grace, that, under the condition of faith, they might now
> hope for and obtain remission of sins and salvation.[136]

The only possible conclusion for Davenant from all this was that

> since this conditional promise, 'If thou shalt believe' . . . flows from the
> gracious kindness of God towards men, it cannot have its foundation
> elsewhere than in the death and merit of Christ the Mediator.

The atonement, therefore, "is as far applicable as it is announceable," and if it
were not applicable, it would not be announceable.[137]

The quest for a 'sincere' offer of the gospel along the lines of meeting
Remonstrantian objections naturally led Davenant into the area of whether
there is a desire in God to save the reprobate. 'Sincerity' must be more than
the setting forth of a naked, abstract, conditional salvation. Rather, God must

132. Davenant, "A Dissertation," II:359, 383, 406; cf. II:373.
133. Davenant, "A Dissertation," II:358.
134. Davenant, "A Dissertation," II:421.
135. Davenant, "A Dissertation," II:427.
136. Davenant, "A Dissertation," II:383; cf. II:421.
137. Davenant, "A Dissertation," II:418, 380.

be presented as, in some sense at least, desiring that the reprobate hearers respond in faith to the preaching. Davenant's doctrine of a universal or general love of God leading to a universal satisfaction flows naturally into a desire in God actually to save the reprobate. Given that Davenant in this context defines love, with Aristotle before him, as "to wish good things to another,"[138] this seems a natural corollary of his system. We have seen that the salvation of the elect was not the "only or sole end" of the death of Christ in Davenant's theology.[139] In fact,

> God sent his Son into the world, and willed that he should die, not only that he might effectually save the elect, but also that remission of sins and eternal life might be brought to and also conferred upon mankind generally in the Gospel, if they should believe.[140]

Davenant therefore sees the gospel call as involving preachers saying to "any individual," "God hath so loved thee, that he gave his only begotten Son, that if thou shouldest believe in him, thou shalt not perish but have everlasting life."[141] Davenant is willing to affirm that "the will of Christ is never without conformity to that of his Father,"[142] and is quick to assert that "it is certain, and admitted by all sound Divines, That God does not will the salvation of all, in the same way as he wills the salvation of some."[143] Yet although the "gracious and saving will of God towards sinners" has a particularist aspect, it can also be seen "as appointing sufficiently for all, of his common philanthropy, the means of saving grace, applicable to all for salvation, according to the tenor of the covenant of grace."[144] Davenant accommodated this doctrine systematically by drawing on the traditional distinction of a twofold will in God. Excluding God's "determinate will," God can be said 'to will' things in

---

138. Davenant, "A Dissertation," II:395. Although Davenant elsewhere echoes Aristotle's definition more fully — namely, that "'to love' is to wish good things to any one, *and to confer them*" — he seems willing also to embrace the shorter definition as equally valid (Davenant, "A Dissertation," II:394; emphasis added). However, elsewhere, Davenant is happy to endorse the scholastic definition "that the love of God must be understood according to *effect*, rather than to *affection*" (Davenant, *Treatise on Justification*, I:10). For Aristotle's definition of love, see Aristotle, *Aristotle with an English Translation: The 'Art' of Rhetoric*, The Loeb Classical Library (London: William Heinemann, 1926), II.4.2.

139. See p. 189.

140. Davenant, "A Dissertation," II:396.

141. Davenant, "A Dissertation," II:344; cf. Davenant, *An Exposition of the Epistle of St Paul to the Colossians*, I:324 (on 1 Timothy 2:4).

142. Davenant, "A Dissertation," II:530.

143. Davenant, "A Dissertation," II:532.

144. Davenant, "A Dissertation," II:563. Davenant cites John 3:16 at this point.

the sense that he providentially appoints to certain ends certain things. For example, if God gives a man eyes, he wills him to see, but this alone does not guarantee that the man cannot be blind.[145] At first appearance, Davenant might seem to be teaching no more than the traditional distinction between the revealed and secret will of God. In his treatment of 1 Timothy 2:4, Davenant rejects the Augustinian (and Perkinsian) interpretation of 'all sorts of men,' in preference for just this distinction. Concerning this *voluntate signi* or "approbative will" that all men be saved, Davenant notes that it "is not always fulfilled, because it is not formally and essentially in God." "God is, therefore, said to will, by his *visible will,* the salvation of all, to whom he proposes and offers the Gospel, which is the ordinary means of effecting salvation."[146] It is to be noted that here it is the existence of gospel preaching which undergirds the *voluntate signi* and not a *habitus* in God. However, whether or not this exhausts what Davenant means when he states that "God, with a general intention, wills life to all men, inasmuch as he willed the death of Christ to be the foundation and cause of life to all men individually, according to the tenor of the evangelical covenant,"[147] can only be ascertained with an examination of his doctrine of this 'evangelical covenant.'

Central to Davenant's system of hypothetical universalism, but not mentioned in this context by Ussher, are covenantal formulations. We see in Davenant a considerable development of the covenant motif, so common in Elizabethan Reformed soteriology, but, it will be seen, considerably modified by Davenant to suit his new polemical context. The main function of the first universal stage in Davenant's scheme of two-staged reconciliation is to furnish a new covenantal relationship between God and all men without exception in the form of what Davenant usually styles as the "Evangelical covenant,"[148] and very occasionally by the term "the covenant of the Gospel."[149] By infusing rich covenantal structures into Ussher's notion of applicability of salvation, Davenant is able further to develop the relationship between a universal satisfaction and the gospel call, for it was Christ's "Oblation once made" which "did found, confirm, and ratifie the Evangelical Covenant."[150]

145. Davenant, "A Dissertation," II:564-65.

146. Davenant, *An Exposition of the Epistle of St Paul to the Colossians,* I:324; cf. I:93.

147. Davenant, "A Dissertation," II:565.

148. References to this 'Evangelical covenant' are legion: Davenant, "A Dissertation," II:357, 375, 381, 396, 398, 399, 401, 404-5, 417-29, 439, 440, 442, 449, 473, 478, 511, 512, 525, 554-55, 556, 557; Hales, *Golden Remains,* II:187; Davenant, *Treatise on Justification,* I:289; II:144.

149. Davenant, "A Dissertation," II:389, 512; Davenant, *Treatise on Justification,* I:288, 298.

150. Hales, *Golden Remains,* II:187. Bod Rawlinson C.849 f. 278v in Ussher's hand has at this point a marginal reference to John 3:16, perhaps added by Ussher himself.

Davenant was probably not being original here, as there is evidence that he was clearly indebted to Bishop John Overall at this point.[151] Overall was "apparently the only English bishop who dared to defend the Dutch Arminians on the eve of the Synod of Dort."[152]

The two main characteristics of Davenant's 'Evangelical covenant,' a "covenant concerning the grant of remission of sins,"[153] are its universality and its conditionality. It is a "universal covenant of salvation under condition of faith."[154] Firstly, it is a "a kind of universal covenant"[155] which "embraces the whole human race"[156] and has "regard to every man"[157] as a man, in distinction from being among "the fallen angels."[158] Secondly, it is "general or conditional" in character.[159] Davenant infuses into this conditional covenant highly contractual notions. Through the Evangelical covenant, for example, "a right accrued to all men individually, on condition of faith, of claiming for themselves remission of sins and eternal life." Consequently, "through the death of Christ having been accepted by God as a ransom, now it is lawful for any man indiscriminately to ascend into heaven by believing."[160] As in Preston, the gospel almost becomes a new law, for the universal Evangelical covenant consists in the command, "'Believe, and thou shalt live,' and is opposed to the legal command, 'Do this and thou shalt live.'"[161] Davenant sees faith as

151. White, *Predestination, Policy and Polemic,* pp. 191-92. White shows from Exeter College, Oxford MS. 48 that Overall taught that "the general promise was to be understood 'to be by virtue of the Gospel covenant.'" Davenant took this manuscript of Overall's with him to the Synod of Dort.

152. Nicholas R. N. Tyacke, *Anti-Calvinists: The Rise of English Arminianism c.1590-1640,* 2nd ed. (Oxford: Clarendon Press, 1990), p. 127; cf. p. 142; White, *Predestination, Policy and Polemic,* pp. 165-66; Seán F. Hughes, ""The Problem of 'Calvinism'": English Theologies of Predestination c.1580-1630" in *Belief and Practice in Reformation England: A Tribute to Patrick Collinson from his Students,* ed. Susan Wabuda & Caroline Litzenberger (Aldershot, UK: Ashgate Publishing Company, 1998), 229-49, pp. 241, 245.

153. Davenant, "A Dissertation," II:418. The use of the word 'grant' in this context is perhaps significant in the light of the way hypothetical universalist Ezekiel Culverwell used the same word (Ezekiel Culverwell, *A Treatise of Faith* [London: I. L. for William Sheffard, 1623], p. 14).

154. Davenant, "A Dissertation," II:368.

155. Davenant, "A Dissertation," II:511; cf. II:442.

156. Davenant, "A Dissertation," II:368; cf. II:428, 511.

157. Davenant, "A Dissertation," II:473.

158. Davenant, "A Dissertation," II:368; cf. II:373, 512, 556; Hales, *Golden Remains,* II:187.

159. Davenant, "A Dissertation," II:396; cf. II:357, 399, 401, 405, 428, 442.

160. Davenant, "A Dissertation," II:473, 404. Davenant cites Romans 3:21-26.

161. Davenant, "A Dissertation," II:404. This was common teaching at Emmanuel College by the year of Preston's decease (ECL MS. 181, f. 1).

"subserving" the gospel and "not as comprising or constituting the covenant itself," but nevertheless faith still is annexed as a "condition of works."[162]

In connection with this apparent 'legalising' of the gospel, and in the light of the recent scholarly controversy over the origin and implications of the prelapsarian covenant of works in Reformed theology, it is interesting to note that Davenant self-consciously derives support for his Evangelical covenant formulations from this very doctrine of a prelapsarian covenant of works or "covenant of nature" made by God with Adam as "the federal head of all his posterity."[163] In this covenant

> salvation was procurable by Adam and all his posterity under the condition of obedience to be paid to the law of nature, and to the express commandment of God; so in the covenant of grace . . . salvation is also understood to be procurable for all men under the condition published in the Gospel, that is, of faith.

Davenant also uses this prelapsarian covenant to clear himself of the objection that his 'Evangelical covenant,' having no explicit textual support in its nomenclature, is merely a product of theological speculation. The prelapsarian covenant of works and the Evangelical covenant stand or fall together and so the argument, for Davenant, is settled.[164]

Another area of difference is the nature of the gospel promise. Whereas Perkinsian Elizabethan theology proclaimed universally a particular promise, the gospel promise in Davenant's system has become explicitly universal.[165] This is linked in Davenant's mind again with the need to demonstrate sincerity in the gospel call to the reprobate. Davenant held that eternal life is "promised" to the non-elect "under the condition of faith,"[166] for God has "in the Gospel . . . promised eternal life to all men individually, on account of the merits of Christ, if they believe."[167] Of course, this does not mean that God has "promised to any unbeliever, that he would give to him, on account of the merits of Christ, infallibly and perseveringly to believe," nor that the promise to the elect is not absolute, but it does involve

---

162. Davenant, *Treatise on Justification*, I:289; cf. II:46. Of course, Davenant would still not see faith as meritorious in any way (Davenant, *Treatise on Justification*, II:144).

163. Davenant, "A Dissertation," II:364, 485.

164. Davenant, "A Dissertation," II:364. Davenant also argues that the prelapsarian Adam could have obtained "eternal life" (Davenant, "A Dissertation," II:381, 535).

165. Davenant, "A Dissertation," II:418-21.

166. Davenant, "A Dissertation," II:429; cf. II:420; Hales, *Golden Remains*, II:188.

167. Davenant, "A Dissertation," II:556; cf. II:419, 551.

Davenant in the proclamation of a promise that is simultaneously conditional and unconditional.[168]

Davenant's system therefore involves a number of significant differences from the late Elizabethan divinity examined in Chapter 2. Firstly, and in the language of later Reformed orthodoxy, we find that the gospel or covenant of grace now subsists in two forms, a conditional form and an unconditional form. This latter covenant is what actually saves the elect, in contrast to the conditional Evangelical covenant which in reality saves nobody.[169] Davenant styles this "absolute covenant" as God's "secret covenant which comprehends some certain individual persons known only to God," and calls it "the new covenant."[170] Significantly, Davenant repeatedly states that this second covenant "is more properly understood to be established between God and [the Mediator than between God and] men."[171] It is therefore "known to Christ alone, nor can it be opened to any one by the ministers of Christ, as to the individual persons whom it embraces."[172] It seems that from the perspective of later Reformed orthodoxy, what Davenant is engaged in here is the merging into one of the *pactum salutis* and the *foedus gratiae*.

Secondly, Davenant allows his infralapsarianism and covenant theology to permeate his portrayal of the conceptual order in the divine mind concerning the gospel call. Conceptually, the absolute new covenant, though eternal, comes after the conditional, Evangelical covenant with the purpose of ensuring that salvation becomes a reality. Davenant reasons that

> lest the blood of the Son of God should flow, and through the fault of the human will the same should happen in the second covenant which had happened in the first [prelapsarian covenant], namely, that no one should enjoy the benefit of it, God resolved with Himself a more deep and secret

---

168. Davenant, "A Dissertation," II:556 (cf. II:383); Davenant, *Treatise on Justification*, II:143.

169. Davenant, "A Dissertation," II:405.

170. Davenant, "A Dissertation," II:404, 405; cf. II:525; Davenant, *Treatise on Justification*, I:289.

171. Davenant, "A Dissertation," II:405; cf. II:404. The bracketed words are my own translation of Latin words erroneously unrepresented in Allport's translation, which does not make sense in terms of Davenant's theology at this point. Allport's translation was evidently based on the 1683 edition which reads, "Absque hoc posteriore fœdere quod magìs propriè inter Deum & Homines stabilitum intelligitur . . ." (Davenant, *Dissertatio de Morte Christi*, p. 203). However, this is a printer's error as the first Latin edition more naturally reads, "Absque hoc posteriore fœdere quod magìs propriè inter Deum & *Mediatorem quam inter Deum &* Homines stabilitum intelligitur . . ." (Davenant, *Dissertationes duæ*, I:39; emphasis added).

172. Davenant, "A Dissertation," II:405.

counsel, and determined of His mere and special mercy to give to some persons the ability and will to fulfil the aforesaid condition of faith, and further, that they should actually and infallibly fulfil it.[173]

Even more explicitly, Davenant is prepared to say that "this special intention of God" to save the elect is

> a kind of special design subordinate to the infallible fulfilment of this universal compact. . . . Lest, therefore, this universal compact should not bring the effect of salvation to any one, God, by a special and secret intention, hath taken care that the merit of the death of Christ should be applied to some for the infallible obtaining of faith and eternal life.[174]

In this divine decree the provision of salvation for all precedes the infallible decreeing of salvation for the elect.

A third distinguishing characteristic appears when Davenant seeks to refute the particular redemptionist argument against universal satisfaction, which states that God is presented as exacting a 'double payment' from the reprobate in hell. Davenant saw no injustice in damning those for whom Christ died. He argued that

> since God himself of his own accord provided that this price should be paid to himself, it was in his own power to annex conditions, which being performed, this death should be advantageous to any man, nor being performed it should not profit any man. Therefore no injustice is done to those persons who are punished by God after the ransom was accepted for the sins of the human race, because they offered nothing to God as a satisfaction for their sins, nor performed that condition, without the performance of which God willed not that this satisfactory price should benefit any individual.[175]

Here we see that for Davenant ultimate salvation does not rest on Christ's satisfaction for sin, but rather on the sinner's 'meeting the condition of faith.' Davenant does not deal with the problem for this scheme arising from the fact that the absence of the condition of faith merely constitutes the sin of unbelief, a sin for which "perfect satisfaction"[176] has surely been made. Yet Davenant does not feel the force of such logic. Because God has decreed that

173. Davenant, "A Dissertation," II:364.
174. Davenant, "A Dissertation," II:555-56.
175. Davenant, "A Dissertation," II:376; cf. II:461.
176. Davenant, "A Dissertation," II:376.

salvation is conditional on faith *and* that Christ's satisfaction does not procure faith for all those for whom he made satisfaction, no more questions need be asked. We see in Davenant, therefore, the development of a conditional salvation that is not dependent on the death of Christ *per se*. In terms of a desire in God to save the reprobate, this desire must be covenantally and decretally understood. Under the anterior and conditional Evangelical covenant God desires their salvation, but not under the posterior and absolute new covenant. In terms of the practical preaching of the gospel, God does desire the salvation of all the hearers, since it is primarily the Evangelical and not the 'new' covenant which is to be presented.[177]

The whole thrust of such a system swings in a potentially Arminian or semi-Pelagian direction. If the focal cause of salvation is no longer Christ, but on meeting the condition of faith, then the cause of differentiation amongst men might be sought in the sinner himself. But any such notions were abhorrent to Davenant, and therefore much time in his treatise and his debates at Dort is given over to asserting his Reformed credentials and condemning all forms of Pelagianism.[178] Yet it must be acknowledged that Davenant advocated a much 'softer' Calvinism than his Elizabethan forbears. He maintained that the "efficacy of the death of Christ as to all men individually ought to be acknowledged, and to be preached to all promiscuously" with "the unreasonable speculation of election and reprobation being set aside."[179] This led Davenant to downplay the active divine hardening of the reprobate under the preaching of the gospel. Whereas Romans 9:18 reads God "hath mercy on whom he will have mercy, and whom he will he hardeneth," Davenant more than once paraphrases the text as God "hath mercy upon whom he will, and whom he will he *leaves hardened*."[180] This passivity on the part of God is frequently emphasised by Davenant, stating, for example, that it is because of "his non-pleasure" that God withholds faith from some.[181] God is almost merely a spectator when it comes to the response of the reprobate to his Word, for he "neither will nor can work in those to whom he deigns to grant

177. Davenant, "A Dissertation," II:404, 443.

178. Davenant, "A Dissertation," II:381, 390, 406, 444, 475, 488, 512, 536; Hales, *Golden Remains*, II:185. See also Davenant's attack on the Arminian, but former Calvinist, Samuel Hoard (Davenant, *Animadversions, passim*).

179. Davenant, "A Dissertation," II:443.

180. Davenant, "A Dissertation," II:392 (emphasis added); also II:434; cf. II:397. Davenant's original Latin reads "quem vult induratum relinquit" (Davenant, *Dissertationes duæ*, I:33). However, elsewhere Davenant did quote this text *verbatim, i.e.,* "quem vult indurat" (Davenant, *Dissertationes duæ*, I:73; cf. Davenant, "A Dissertation," II:482).

181. Davenant, "A Dissertation," II:445.

the means of grace, a contempt or abuse of these means."[182] The gospel is rejected by some because of "the common unbelief of mankind," whereas "that it is received by some proceeds from the special compassion of God."[183]

Doubtless linked in Davenant's mind with this desire to emphasise the moral responsibility and freedom of the non-elect, is the breadth he is prepared to give to his definition of "the grace of Christ, or saving grace." Arguing that "whatever is graciously granted by God to men, may in some sense be called grace," Davenant maintains that 'saving grace' is given to the non-elect who finally despise it. He defines 'saving grace' as

> benefits and supernatural gifts . . . which are directly ordained for obtaining salvation through Christ, but not infallibly: such as the preaching of the Gospel; the illumination of the minds of men in the mysteries of the faith, and, in one word, whatever supernaturally tends to unite men to Christ and place them in a state of salvation, yet does not of itself unite them to him, or translate them from a state of death to a state of salvation.[184]

This resistible 'saving grace' is in distinction from "other supernatural gifts which place those who have them in a state of salvation, such as a good Will, Faith, Conversion, Regeneration, and, in short, those which belong only to men who are ingrafted into Christ and reconciled to God."[185] Such formulations are a far cry from Perkins' chart in *A golden Chaine*, in which there are no lines connecting the work of Christ to the experience of the reprobate under the sound of the gospel call.[186] Although, therefore, Davenant was unequivocally and wholly opposed to any form of semi-Pelagianism, he is not willing to deny that from the human point of view salvation is entirely conditional upon faith, which is a very real possibility for all, and that some finally perish for whom Christ in a very real sense did make satisfaction for sin, and who experienced a measure of his saving grace.

Summary and Analysis

It should by now be apparent that Preston, Davenant, and Ussher embraced a remarkably similar system of theology with regard to predestination, the

182. Davenant, "A Dissertation," II:568.
183. Davenant, "A Dissertation," II:397.
184. Davenant, "A Dissertation," II:497; cf. II:383.
185. Davenant, "A Dissertation," II:498.
186. See above, p. 39.

death of Christ, and the call of the gospel, in distinction from the system of Perkins and his Elizabethan brethren. So similar are certain distinctive aspects of their system, even down to key citations from the Church Fathers and particular arguments, illustrations, motifs, and use of key biblical texts, that Baxter's claim that Ussher had in fact introduced both Preston and Davenant to this new school of hypothetical universalism does seem plausible. Allport's denial that Ussher brought about a change in Davenant's theology is based on the unsupported claim that Davenant was not acquainted with Ussher until after the Synod of Dort, where Davenant was already skilful in his articulation of hypothetical universalism.[187] In favour of this claim it could be said that Ussher did occasionally speak in such glowing terms of Davenant's writings on Christ's satisfaction that a relationship with Ussher as the pupil might be inferred. For example, Ussher confesses that, concerning "the Arminian Question, I desire never to read more than my Lord of Salisbury's [i.e., Davenant's] Lectures touching Predestination and Christ's death." "They are excellent, learnedly, soundly, and perspicuously performed." By this it is clear that he agreed, at least substantially, with Davenant's position, for he follows this praise with the words, "I hope [they] will do much good here for the establishing of our young divines in the present truth."[188] However, these words could still be those of a mentor rejoicing to see how a pupil has run with the baton. Furthermore, the way in which Ussher came by Davenant's treatise (a loan extracted from his regular correspondent and hypothetical universalist Samuel Ward) suggests that he was already in agreement with its contents.[189] Allport's concerns appear to be

187. Allport, "Life of Bishop Davenant," I:xlviii. Godfrey recognises Davenant's apparent development of Ussher's position, but follows Allport in assuming that "Davenant and Ussher did not know each other before the Synod." Godfrey thus wrongly concludes there was no intellectual inheritance between Ussher and Davenant (W. Robert Godfrey, "Tensions within International Calvinism: The Debate on the Atonement at the Synod of Dort, 1618-1619" [Ph.D. Dissertation, Stanford University, 1974], p. 129; W. Robert Godfrey, "Reformed Thought on the Extent of the Atonement to 1618," *WTJ* 37 [1975]: 133-71, p. 170). Packer rightly highlighted Allport's mistake in 1954 (James I. Packer, "The Redemption and Restoration of Man in the Thought of Richard Baxter: A Study in Puritan Theology" [D.Phil. Dissertation, University of Oxford, 1954], p. 225).

188. In letters to Samuel Ward in the mid 1630s (Ussher, *Works*, XV:542, 583; XVI:9-10; cf. XVI:46). The thread of this correspondence means that Erlington's date of 28th July, 1631, for the letter of Ussher (*Works*, XV:542-43) cannot be accurate. More realistic would be 28th July, 1634, as this would be when a response to Ward's loan of the manuscript in June 1634 could be most expected (Ussher, *Works*, XV:581).

189. Ussher requested a transcript of Davenant's lectures from Samuel Ward in December 1630. Despite having alerted Ussher to their existence in the first place, Ward was not forth-

wholly hagiographic, and, despite his knowledge that this claim conflicts with Baxter's testimony, he produces no evidence for his counter-claim that "not a shadow of change occurred in [Davenant's] opinions."[190] The fact is, Ussher first met Davenant in London in 1609, well before the Synod of Dort, and when both Davenant and Preston were Fellows at Queens' College, Cambridge.[191]

It should not surprise us if these men strongly influenced each other, with Ussher as the leader. Bernard tells us that when Ussher was in London "[t]welve of the most eminent Divines" of that city "were wont . . . to apply themselves to him as a Father . . . between whom and him there was a most entire affection." Preston was among these admirers who "wrote then unto [Ussher] for his direction of them in a body of *Practical Divinity,* which he returned them accordingly."[192] Furthermore, Ussher's wide-ranging theological correspondence demonstrates the tremendous extent to which he was revered as a learned mentor. This correspondence included Preston, who prayed daily for Ussher. Interestingly, Preston seems to have discussed with Ussher the very question of the gospel call, writing to him in about 1621 with the request, "I wish you would put down something concerning the manner of propounding of Christ, and concerning humiliation, which you mentioned at Coventry." This appears in a letter in which Preston is declining Ussher's personal invitation to accept the post of Professor of Theological Controversies in Dublin.[193] Clearly the admiration was mutual. Ussher and Preston possibly also communicated later over the case of Joan Drake between 1624 and 1625, as both men had visited her in the capacity of experienced physicians of the soul.[194] The two men also once formed a preaching duo for a public

---

coming, and Ussher repeated his request in April 1634. Ward finally lent him his own copy in June 1634 (Ussher, *Works,* XV:540, 500, 578, 581).

190. Allport, "Life of Bishop Davenant," I:xlvii-xlviii.

191. Ussher, *Works,* I:29.

192. Bernard, *The Life & Death of Ussher,* p. 83; also without attribution in Clarke, *A general Martyrologie,* II:292. Cf. Tom Webster, *Godly Clergy in Early Stuart England: The Caroline Puritan Movement, c.1620-1643* (Cambridge: Cambridge University Press, 1997), pp. 257-58.

193. Ussher, *Works,* XVI:370-73, 372; see above, p. 6.

194. Jasper Heartwell, *The Firebrand taken out of the Fire. Or, The Wonderful History, Case, and Cure of Mrs Drake, sometimes the wife of Francis Drake of Esher in the County of Surrey Esq. Who was under the Power and severe Discipline of Satan for the Space of ten Yeares; and was redeemed from his Tyranny in a wonderfull Manner a little before her Death, by the great mercy of God; and (instrumentally) by the extraordinary Paines, Prayers and Fasting, of foure Reverend Divines, whose Names are here subscribed, viz. B. Usher, M. Hooker, D. Preston, M. Dod* (London: For Thomas Mathewes, 1654), p. 68 (for Ussher) and pp. 153, 158, 160-61, 163 (for Preston). For more on Drake, see above, p. 23.

thanksgiving at the Barrington home at Hatfield Broad Oak in Essex in December 1625.[195] At least once Preston thanked Ussher "for your great love."[196] Similarly, Davenant was "on close terms of intimacy" with Ussher, who admired him as second to none in certain aspects of polemical theology.[197] In return, Davenant had a high respect for Ussher, seeing him as a "man of singular Piety, abounding with all manner of Learning."[198]

The influence that Ussher exerted upon the thinking of Preston and Davenant on Christ's satisfaction was likely to have been reinforced by the strong relationship existing between these two men in their own right. Preston enjoyed an endearing life-long friendship with Davenant. It was Preston, who as Fellow of Queens' College, had cunningly secured for Davenant the post of Master of the college in 1614.[199] It was therefore understandable that subsequently "it was commonly said in the Colledge that every time when Master Preston plucked off his hat to Dr. Davenant . . . he gained a chamber or study for one of his pupils."[200] Later, in 1621, Davenant's "leaving of ye college troubled" Preston, for "Doctor Davenant had bin his constant & faithfull friend, & given countenance upon all occasions to him and all his pupils."[201] In 1625 it was to Davenant that Preston went for advice about Montagu's writings, and it could well be that Davenant, in response, was one of the bishops who instigated the York House Conference.[202] It should not be altogether surprising, therefore, to find a strong interrelationship between these three leading churchmen in their systemisation of the death of Christ and the gospel call, at a crucial time in the development of this doctrine in the context of the Remonstrant threat and the Synod of Dort.

Although neither Davenant nor Preston anywhere mention their indebtedness to Ussher for their thinking on redemption, Baxter's claims are still borne out by the internal evidence, even if it is granted that on this question "Davenant's ideas were not identical to those of Ussher."[203] Even more

---

195. ERO, Barrington Papers, D/DBa/F5/1.

196. Ussher, *Works*, XVI:373.

197. Fuller, *Life, Letters and Writings of John Davenant*, p. 5; Allport, "Life of Bishop Davenant," I:xlv.

198. Clarke, *A general Martyrologie*, II:301.

199. Thomas Ball, *The Life of the Renowned Doctor Preston*, ed. Edward W. Harcourt (Oxford: Parker and Co., 1885), pp. 36-39; Irvonwy Morgan, *Prince Charles's Puritan Chaplain* (London: George Allen & Unwin Ltd, 1957), pp. 20-21.

200. Thomas Fuller, *The History of the Worthies of England* (London: J. G. W. L. and W. G., 1662), II:291.

201. Ball, *Life of Preston*, pp. 76, 71.

202. Ball, *Life of Preston*, pp. 114, 118.

203. Godfrey, "Tensions within International Calvinism," p. 129; Godfrey, "Reformed

certain is Preston's reliance upon Ussher's teaching. A line of intellectual inheritance may therefore be tentatively suggested as follows. Perkins' outspo-
ken and rigorous defence of supralapsarian particular redemptionism provoked a series of attacks on Reformed soteriology as a whole. Although
Ussher's first religious impressions at the age of ten were received partly from
Perkins,[204] Ussher came to believe that the Perkinsian system mitigated
against the universal gospel call and assurance, and unnecessarily provoked
hostility to Reformed doctrine and threatened ecclesiastical unity. It is clear
that Ussher consciously believed that his resultant position of hypothetical
universalism was a new position for his contemporaries, and not generally
held at that time. Without wanting to go into print with his concerns, he
counseled ministers through an extensive correspondence and sought
through his immense personal influence quietly to win the next generation of
theologians to a more balanced position. Culverwell was one thus influenced,
but Davenant was Ussher's key convert.

Yet as an official representative of James I and the Church of England at
the troubled international Synod of Dort, Davenant could not similarly keep
his position discreetly concealed among friends. The hostile scrutiny to which
his hypothetical universalism was subjected by some of the divines connected
with the Synod of Dort — both Remonstrant and Contraremonstrant — led
to Davenant, under the influence of Overall, considerably developing and re-
fining the views of Ussher his mentor, and pushing them into new subtleties
of formulation. Davenant also did much to ground hypothetical universalism
in the patristic evidence. Like Ussher, Davenant, with his similar episcopal re-
sponsibilities, studiously pursued a unifying *via media* position, a position
that in the face of numerous counter-attacks required an ever-increasing
treatment of the wider ramifications of his new formulations. It is into this
context that Preston, the alleged 'militant Puritan,' comes. Initially seemingly
happy with 'Perkinsian' particularism as articulated by Hildersham, Preston
learned his hypothetical universalism from Ussher. He then became convinced not only that it was biblical, but that it was vital to the struggle for the
unity of the Church of England based on the Thirty-Nine Articles in the light
of a rising anti-Calvinism. Then, conversant with the debates at Dort, and as a
personal friend of Davenant's, he also embraced Davenant's elaboration of
Ussher's central tenets. Meanwhile Davenant, as well as significantly softening

---

Thought," p. 170. Godfrey does recognise that "[c]learly some common concerns, however, mo-
tivated both of them as they thought about the atonement" (Godfrey, "Reformed Thought,"
p. 170).

204. Bernard, *The Life & Death of Ussher*, p. 23.

the final form of the Canons of Dort,[205] had, along with Ward, considerably influenced the other members of the British delegation away from their initial defence of particular redemptionism.[206] With theologians as influential and respected as this British delegation now commending Bishop Ussher's hypothetical universalism, the credibility and attraction of the position became a widespread reality in the Jacobean church.

205. Godfrey, "Tensions within International Calvinism," pp. 263-64.

206. Hales, *Golden Remains,* II:101; Baxter, *Certain Disputations,* pB2v; White, *Predestination, Policy and Polemic,* pp. 187, 190. Ward was not only an intimate friend of Davenant but of Ussher also (*ODNB;* see above, pp. 175, 210). The three other delegates were George Carleton, Bishop of Llandaff, Thomas Goad, and the Scottish delegate Walter Balcanqual. Their cooperation with Davenant and Ward at this point was possibly, however, a mere tactical decision rather than the fruit of a full conversion (Anthony Milton, personal communication).

SECTION V

Conclusions

Conclusions

"The Divell knowes that as Labans sheepe have conceived by the eye; so men have beene apt peremptorily to conclude from the opinions of their great Masters."[1]

The terms 'hypothetical universalism' and 'Amyraldianism' are often used interchangeably by scholars of the seventeenth century, and consequently a certain amount of confusion exists as to what exactly is or should be denoted by these terms.[2] We find men like Ussher[3] and Davenant[4] being styled as Amyraldians, and Moyse Amyraut himself described as a hypothetical universalist.[5] This study would suggest that the two terms are better reserved for

1. John Stafford (John Preston, *The Fulnesse of Christ*, pp. A3r-A3v).

2. Some in the Reformed tradition have even used 'Hypothetical Universalism' as a catch-all term to include Pelagianism and Arminianism (A. Craig Troxel, "Amyraut 'at' the Assembly: The Westminster Confession of Faith and the Extent of the Atonement," *Presbyterion* 22 (1996): 43-55, p. 46; cf. Benjamin B. Warfield, *Studies in Theology* [New York: Oxford University Press, 1932], p. 288).

3. E.g., W. Robert Godfrey, "Tensions within International Calvinism: The Debate on the Atonement at the Synod of Dort, 1618-1619" (Ph.D. Dissertation, Stanford University, 1974), pp. 128-29; W. Robert Godfrey, "Reformed Thought on the Extent of the Atonement to 1618," *WTJ* 37 (1975): 133-71, p. 169. Strangely, this is done at the same time as defending Davenant from the charge of Amyraldianism (Godfrey, "Tensions within International Calvinism," pp. 182-85).

4. E.g., Brian G. Armstrong, *Calvinism and the Amyraut Heresy: Protestant Scholasticism and Humanism in Seventeenth-Century France* (Madison, WI: University of Wisconsin Press, 1969), p. 99; James I. Packer, *A Quest for Godliness: The Puritan Vision of the Christian Life* (Wheaton, IL: Crossway Books, 1990), p. 346; Paul Helm, *Calvin and the Calvinists* (Edinburgh: Banner of Truth Trust, 1998), p. 37.

5. E.g., Philip Schaff, ed., *The Creeds of Christendom, with a History and Critical Notes* (Grand Rapids, MI: Baker Books, 1993), I:770; Godfrey, "Tensions within International Calvin-

two distinct theologies — one for the theology of Amyraut and his close followers, and *universalismus hypotheticus* for those who retain, or at least do not oppose, the Reformed orthodox *ordo decretorum* in either a supralapsarian or infralapsarian form, but who hold that Christ died for everyone, head for head, procuring for them a conditional salvation in case they do believe. Both of these terms can be seen as subsets of the more generic 'universal redemptionism,' to which, in all its forms, theologians like Perkins were opposed. In contrast, Amyraldianism places the decree of election after the decree to give Christ and thus constitutes a far more radical, and one might say speculative, revision of particularism, not just in the *locus* of the work of Christ but also in the *ordo decretorum*. The object of predestination becomes, in effect, redeemed mankind and not merely unfallen or fallen mankind as in the supralapsarian and infralapsarian schemas.[6]

There are, of course, similarities between the two systems, but this is to be seen more as a function of their sharing the same broad polemical context, than of any significant cross-fertilisation. Ussher was espousing hypothetical universalism before John Cameron had even arrived at Saumur, and Ussher had brought Davenant to embrace this system well before Cameron's own teaching first became widely known through the Synod of Dort. Although at this time Davenant became familiar with Cameron's thought, he carefully distanced himself from aspects of it.[7] It should also be remembered that

---

ism," pp. 183, 185; Mark W. Karlberg, "The Mosaic Covenant and the Concept of Works in Reformed Hermeneutics: A Historical-Critical Analysis with Particular Attention to Early Covenant Eschatology" (Th.D. Dissertation, Westminster Theological Seminary, 1980), p. 199; Richard A. Muller, *The Dictionary of Latin and Greek Theological Terms Drawn Principally from Protestant Scholastic Theology* (Grand Rapids, MI: Baker Book House, 1985), pp. 319-20; Bost in *EP,* p. 30; Yong Jae Timothy Song, *Theology and Piety in the Reformed Federal Thought of William Perkins and John Preston* (Lewiston, NY: Edwin Mellen Press, 1998), p. 202; Jan Rohls, *Reformed Confessions: Theology from Zurich to Barmen* (Louisville, KY: Westminster John Knox Press, 1998), p. 28; Richard A. Muller, "Reformed Confessions and Catechisms" in *The Dictionary of Historical Theology,* ed. Trevor A. Hart (Grand Rapids, MI: Eerdmans, 2000), 466-85, p. 485; Richard A. Muller, *Post-Reformation Reformed Dogmatics: The Rise and Development of Reformed Orthodoxy, ca. 1520 to ca. 1725* (Grand Rapids, MI: Baker Academic, 2003), I:76; cf. Richard A. Muller, "Found (No Thanks to Theodore Beza): One 'Decretal' Theology," *CTJ* 32 (1997): 145-53, p. 147.

6. G. Michael Thomas, *The Extent of the Atonement: A Dilemma for Reformed Theology from Calvin to the Consensus* (Carlisle, UK: Paternoster Press, 1997), pp. 190-91, 212. Cf. Armstrong, *Calvinism and the Amyraut Heresy;* Frans P. Van Stam, *The Controversy over the Theology of Saumur, 1635-1650: Disrupting Debates among the Huguenots in Complicated Circumstances* (Amsterdam & Maarssen: APA-Holland University Press, 1988).

7. John Davenant, "A Dissertation on the Death of Christ, as to its Extent and special Benefits: containing a short History of Pelagianism, and shewing the Agreement of the Doc-

Amyraut himself did not publish his seminal work until 1634, six years after Preston's death and sixteen years after the Synod of Dort. Furthermore, Davenant and Preston both rejected what was later to be known as an Amyraldian view of the decree.[8] Thus, while avoiding all unnecessary multiplication of categories, it is argued here that hypothetical universalism is best seen as a relatively independent, earlier development, distinct from Amyraldianism and 'the Saumur theology' and worthy of its own place in the history of Christian doctrine, especially given the central place which the death of Christ occupies in the Christian system. If anything, its origins were neither Scottish (Cameron) nor French (Amyraut), but Irish (Ussher).

If, however, Amyraldianism must continue to be seen as a branch of *universalismus hypotheticus,* then at least *universalismus hypotheticus anglicus* should be recognised as another distinct and older branch. It is this contention, coupled with the significant implications for political interpretations of early Stuart England, which justifies this highly focused study of Preston's theology. While having much in common with later Amyraldianism, it was a convenient oversimplification on the part of Baxter, perhaps fuelled by his "great love and zeal to the name of Davenant,"[9] to merge English hypothetical universalism and Amyraldianism into what he saw as a united and coherent testimony to the correctness of his own version of 'the middle way.' In fact

---

trines of the Church of England on general Redemption, Election, and Predestination, with the Primitive Fathers of the Christian Church, and above all, with the Holy Scriptures" in *An Exposition of the Epistle of St Paul to the Colossians,* trans. Josiah Allport (London: Hamilton, Adams, and Co., 1832), II:309-569, II:561-69. It has been said that Davenant "felt no theological affinity with Cameron" on the grounds of his statement, given upon request from the troubled French Reformed churches, that "the opinion of [Master] Cameron was here badly expressed" or "malè hîe fuisse expressam" (Davenant, "A Dissertation," II:568; John Davenant, *Dissertationes duæ: Prima de Morte Christi, quatenus ad omnes extendatur, quatenus ad solos Electos restringatur. Altera de Prædestinatione & Reprobatione. . . . Quibus subnectitur ejusdem D. Davenantii Sententia de Gallicana Controversia: sc. de Gratiosa & Salutari Dei erga Homines Peccatores voluntate,* ed. Thomas Bedford [Cambridge: Roger Daniel, 1650], I:250; Godfrey, "Tensions within International Calvinism," p. 182). But this particular piece of evidence is not compelling. Not only is this said in the immediate context of why some men are not saved, and not of Cameron's system as a whole, but also Davenant may still have sympathised with Cameron's actual position on this point, but not with the "badly expressed" summary of his beliefs provided by the French Reformed churches.

8. See above, pp. 158, 161, 188. A note from the Hartlib Papers for 1634 compares only one feature of Preston's (and Thomas Goodwin's) anthropology to that of Cameron: "Dr Prestons et Goodin Opinio. Quod voluntas sequitur Intellectum sicut etiam Cameron" (SUL Hartlib MS. 29/2/21b).

9. Richard Baxter, *Plain Scripture Proof of Infants Church-membership and Baptism* (London: For Robert White, 1651), p. 289; cf. p. 332.

there were a number of middle ways, some more 'middle' than others, and some more likely to end up on 'the other side.'

Another area concerning which profitable conclusions may be drawn from this close examination of Preston's thought is the ever-persistent historiographical paradigm of 'Calvin versus the Calvinists.' Interestingly for us, Kendall, in the archetypal monograph of this school, enlists Preston as one of the characters to perform for him in this drama of apostasy from Calvin. Thomas rightly points out that if only Kendall had enlisted Ussher or Davenant, they "might have significantly affected [his] conclusions."[10] But if Kendall had only studied more carefully a man he *did* select, namely John Preston, the same effect would have been seen. The demonstration of Preston's hypothetical universalism is therefore embarrassing for Kendall's thesis. Having styled 'limited atonement' as a key determinative doctrine in a subsequent 'distortion' of Calvin's theology into the 'rigid' and 'legalising' system of the experimental predestinarians, we now find that the doctrine of universal redemption could be firmly embraced by one of Kendall's own experimental predestinarian case studies without, it seems, any alteration to the doctrine of conversion and assurance in that tradition. If Calvin was in fact a universal redemptionist, then in Kendall's central dogma there is actually direct continuity between Calvin and Preston. On the other hand, if Calvin was in fact a particular redemptionist, then English Calvinism in certain ways represented a loosening of Calvin's system, at least amongst certain leading theologians.[11] Furthermore, doubt is cast on the importance of the doctrine of 'limited atonement' — as opposed to a broad Augustinianism — in producing the distinctives of the experimental predestinarian tradition. There seems to be no surviving attack on Preston for holding to a broader conception of Christ's work of redemption, but neither did his hypothetical universalism liberate him from having one of the strongest doctrines of preparation for conversion out of all the divines Kendall examines.[12] Clearly, the extent of Christ's satisfaction is not the touchstone issue that Kendall

10. G. Michael Thomas, "Calvin and English Calvinism: A Review Article," *SBET* 16 (1998): 111-27, p. 112.

11. Certainly Preston cites Luther far more than any other author, and hardly mentions Calvin at all.

12. Ironically, out of Perkins, Sibbes, Baynes, and Preston, all of whom Kendall treats in his thesis, Schaefer considers that it is Preston who places the most emphasis on covenantal bilateralism and preparation for conversion, and who is most open to the charge of "a new moralism" (Paul R. Schaefer Jr., "The Spiritual Brotherhood on the Habits of the Heart: Cambridge Protestants and the Doctrine of Sanctification from William Perkins to Thomas Shepard" [D.Phil. Dissertation, University of Oxford, 1994], p. 200).

maintains.[13] Although 'Calvin *equals* the Calvinists' is, of course, also a misguided paradigm, when a theory backfires to this degree, it is time to rethink one's basic assumptions.

One such assumption involves viewing scholasticism as somehow determining someone's theological position.[14] In such historiography, 'scholasticism' is often used as a pejorative term, explaining the 'rigid' particularism of seventeenth-century orthodoxy in contrast to the golden 'dynamism' of the sixteenth-century humanist Reformers. Yet scholasticism is actually a method and not a result.[15] Preston was no particular redemptionist, but not because he had been 'delivered' from scholasticism. We have already seen how Preston delighted in Aristotle, and this has even led to the notion that Preston brought a rationalism into Reformed divinity.[16] But Preston's 'Aristotelianism' seems to boil down to little more than

13. R. T. Kendall, "The Nature of Saving Faith from William Perkins (d.1602) to the Westminster Assembly (1643-1649)" (D.Phil. Dissertation, University of Oxford, 1976), pi; cf. Thomas, "Calvin and English Calvinism: A Review Article," pp. 126-27. For further reflection on the implications of the case of John Preston for Kendall's thesis, see Jonathan D. Moore, "Calvin versus the Calvinists? The Case of John Preston (1587-1628)," *RRR* 6 (2004): 327-48.

14. Cf. Armstrong, *Calvinism and the Amyraut Heresy*, p. xi; Stephen A. Strehle, "The Extent of the Atonement within the Theological Systems of the Sixteenth and Seventeenth Centuries" (Th.D. Dissertation, Dallas Theological Seminary, 1980), *passim*; Alan C. Clifford, *Atonement and Justification: English Evangelical Theology, 1640-1790: An Evaluation* (Oxford: Clarendon Press, 1990), pp. 95-110.

15. Richard A. Muller, *After Calvin: Studies in the Development of a Theological Tradition* (New York: Oxford University Press, 2003), pp. 75-78, 81-83; Richard A. Muller, "The Problem of Protestant Scholasticism: A Review and Definition" in *Reformation and Scholasticism: An Ecumenical Enterprise*, ed. Willem J. van Asselt & Eef Dekker (Grand Rapids, MI: Baker Academic, 2001), pp. 45-64; Carl R. Trueman, *The Claims of Truth: John Owen's Trinitarian Theology* (Carlisle, UK: Paternoster Press, 1998), pp. 1-101; Carl R. Trueman, "John Owen's *Dissertation on Divine Justice:* An Exercise in Christocentric Scholasticism," *CTJ* 33 (1998): 87-103; Carl R. Trueman, "Richard Baxter on Christian Unity: A Chapter in the Enlightening of English Reformed Orthodoxy," *WTJ* 61 (1999): 53-71, p. 71; cf. Richard A. Muller, *God, Creation and Providence in the Thought of Jacob Arminius: Sources and Directions of Scholastic Protestantism in the Era of Early Orthodoxy* (Grand Rapids, MI: Baker Book House, 1991), pp. 275-77; U. Sebastian G. Rehnman, "Theologia Tradita: A Study in the Prolegomenous Discourse of John Owen (1616-1683)" (D.Phil. Dissertation, University of Oxford, 1997), pp. 80-83.

16. See p. 5; Perry Miller, *The New England Mind: The Seventeenth Century* (Cambridge, MA: Harvard University Press, 1954), p. 200; William Haller, *The Rise of Puritanism, or the Way to the New Jerusalem as Set Forth in Pulpit and Press from Thomas Cartwright to John Lilburne and John Milton, 1570-1643* (New York: Harper & Brothers, 1957), p. 334; Irvonwy Morgan, *Prince Charles's Puritan Chaplain* (London: George Allen & Unwin Ltd, 1957), pp. 45, 205-6; Everett H. Emerson, *English Puritanism from John Hooper to John Milton* (Durham, NC: Duke University Press, 1968), p. 241.

that at Lincoln's Inn Preston could be heard declaring that "to understand what an accident is, you consider the subject, the author, and efficient, and the extent thereof; so consider you these three things, and then you shall know what this Truth is."[17] But this was nothing more than the intellectual environment of all divines of his day, right across the theological spectrum, be it semi-Pelagianism or high supralapsarianism. If Preston was scholastic, Calvin also freely employed Aristotelian categories, and can in some ways also be seen as scholastic.[18] Ironically, Preston's embracing of hypothetical universalism actually involved the multiplication of the very scholastic categories that allegedly produce increasing rigidity in doctrinal formulation.[19] Scholastic categories were also relied upon in Ussher and Davenant's defences of their respective positions.[20] The case of Preston, occupying at once as he does both the circles of radical puritans such as Cotton and the circles of establishment figures such as bishops Ussher and Davenant, also challenges the standard, and often anachronistic, generalisations about the relationships between 'Puritan' and 'Anglican' divinity.[21] The temptation to oversimplification is great, and indeed, if we are to say anything at all, a certain amount of generalisation is not only necessary, but vital. However, one area that will not endure a sloppy shorthand is the area of 'scholasticism' and so-called 'rationalism' as an explanatory motif in studying the relationships between Reformation and Post-Reformation orthodoxy.

Another common, implicit assumption is that the sixteenth-century Reformers and the seventeenth-century orthodox can be the subject of com-

17. John Preston, *Saints Qualification*, I:128.

18. Trueman, *The Claims of Truth*, p. 38; David C. Steinmetz, "The Scholastic Calvin" in *Protestant Scholasticism: Essays in Reassessment*, ed. Carl R. Trueman & R. Scott Clark (Carlisle, UK: Paternoster Press, 1999), pp. 16-30.

19. Out of Perkins, Sibbes, Baynes, and Preston, Schaefer holds that it was Preston who was "probably the one who had imbibed scholastic methodology the most" (Schaefer, "The Spiritual Brotherhood," p. 195). This would support Rainbow's contention, that it was in fact the universal redemptionists who availed themselves most of scholastic distinctions, whereas it was the strict particular redemptionists who upheld an Augustinian simplicity in their soteriology (Jonathan H. Rainbow, *The Will of God and the Cross: An Historical and Theological Study of John Calvin's Doctrine of Limited Redemption* [Allison Park, PA: Pickwick Publications, 1990], pp. 47, 185). Truly, "Preston was a very exact schoolman" (SUL Hartlib MS. 29/2/62b).

20. See above, pp. 182, 198.

21. This is particularly the case since one thing that links Cotton, Preston, Ussher, and Davenant together was a common espousal of hypothetical universalism. For Cotton's hypothetical universalism, see David R. Como, "Puritans, Predestination and the Construction of Orthodoxy in Early Seventeenth-Century England" in *Conformity and Orthodoxy in the English church, c. 1560-1660*, ed. Peter G. Lake & Michael C. Questier (Woodbridge, UK: Boydell Press, 2000), 64-87, pp. 76-77, 80, 86.

parative studies without reference to their differing polemical and historical contexts. Preston was well aware of how a different polemical context affected one's formulation of doctrine and relative emphasis.[22] Yet often the fact that men like Preston faced the new Remonstrant challenge and new mediating theological options is overlooked. However, even more important for English Calvinism is the historical context. We have already noted that the directions of King James may well have caused Preston to tone down his public statements on predestination and irresistible grace.[23] However, an historical factor less dramatic than any effects of the Palatinate unrest, but more pervasive, is often overlooked. Once the fact is reckoned with, that England and Scotland were the only kingdoms in the sixteenth century in which the Reformed faith was established as the national religion, simple comparisons become impossible between seventeenth-century parish preachers in the English state church and sixteenth-century continental Reformers in their gathered congregations surrounded by the false church of Antichrist. Along with Scotland, England was an island in covenant with God. Citizenship and church membership were but two sides of one coin, and choice and persecution were involved in neither. For the 'experimental predestinarian' pastor, his congregation was coextensive with a state parish. Through infant baptism all his parishioners were 'in covenant' with God, yet his evangelical impulse persuaded him that the real church was in fact a far smaller number than his parish. In short, the dilemma of an unconverted community of the baptised was pressed strongly upon him. He could not escape the fact that he was faced with an ungodly godly nation. We have already seen how in practice this ecclesiastical context not only caused Preston in practice to make the Lord's Supper and not baptism the sacrament of initiation and focal point of the free offer, but also facilitated the development of the covenantal and soteriological structures of the hypothetical universalism that he shared with Ussher and Davenant.[24] The resultant inclusive particularism, to the delight of King James, then served as an ideal mediating position between the more strict Reformed orthodox, and the Lutherans.[25] Any study of English particularism must take into account this formative context of an inclusive national church, although few seem to do so.[26]

22. Preston, *Saints Qualification*, III:66.

23. See p. 82.

24. See pp. 135-36.

25. Cf. W. Brown Patterson, *King James VI and I and the Reunion of Christendom* (Cambridge: Cambridge University Press, 1997), *passim* but especially pp. 260-92.

26. Yet the sacramental dilemma for a comprehensive national Church produced by the doctrine of particular redemption was felt keenly by contemporaries. Francis White at the York

A third major area in which profitable conclusions can be drawn from the life and thought of John Preston is the controversial area of an alleged 'Calvinistic consensus' in the Jacobean Church, and the implications of this for the causation of the English Civil War. There is no reason to doubt Hill's claim that Perkins was "the dominant influence in Puritan thought for the forty years after his death."[27] However, certain qualifications are needed at this point. The first has been made by Breward who states that "although Perkins was one of the most widely quoted authors prior to 1660, his users normally used him as they used the fathers and the schoolmen — to support their own opinions and to provide a further link in the chain of argument."[28] Personal piety aside, therefore, Perkins' influence at the intellectual level was often superficial, and his readers were not allowing Perkins' theology to mould their own system, but merely using him, when convenient, as an authority. A second, and related qualification is that in the decades following Perkins' death, not only did a considerable diversity of opinion thrive amongst English Reformed divines, but also progressive and reactionary changes away from Perkinsian particularism were discernible over time.

It is important to recognise this considerable diversity of opinion. A regrettable aspect of the influence of Tyacke's seminal work concerning an English 'Calvinistic consensus' has been a tendency amongst scholars who have embraced Tyacke's thesis, to replace the unhelpful dualism of 'Puritanism and Anglicanism' with yet another simplistic dualism of two homogenous warring parties comprising 'Calvinists and Arminians.' The example of Preston is a

---

House Conference, for example, protested that "if this [doctrine] were once admitted . . . how could we say to all communicants whatsoever, 'The Body of our Lord which was given for thee,' as we are bound to say? Let the opinion of the Dortists be admitted, and the tenth person in the Church shall not have been redeemed" (John Cosin, *The Works of the Right Reverend Father in God, John Cosin,* Library of Anglo-Catholic Theology [Oxford: John Henry Parker, 1843-55], II:63-64). Regrettably, right from the outset, although acknowledging their relevance, Kendall excluded ecclesiological and sacramental factors from his thesis (Kendall, "The Nature of Saving Faith," p. 2). This confession does not appear in the published editions, but clears Kendall from Horton's conjecture (Michael S. Horton, "Thomas Goodwin and the Puritan Doctrine of Assurance: Continuity and Discontinuity in the Reformed Tradition, 1600-1680" [Ph.D. Dissertation, University of Coventry, 1998], p. 413).

27. Christopher Hill, *Puritanism and Revolution: Studies in Interpretation of the English Revolution of the Seventeenth Century* (London: Secker & Warburg, 1958), p. 216.

28. Ian Breward, ed., *The Work of William Perkins* (Abingdon, UK: Sutton Courtenay Press, 1970), p. 102; cf. Norman Pettit, "The Heart Renewed: Assurance of Salvation in Puritan Spiritual Life" in *Transatlantic Encounters: Studies in European-American Relations. Presented to Winfried Herget,* ed. Udo J. Hebel & Karl Ortseifen (Trier, Germany: Wissenshaftlicher Verlag Trier, 1995), 14-28, p. 15.

timely reminder of the heterogeneity of English Calvinism,[29] and a supporting case study for the work of Milton, Hughes, and Como who have called for considerable refinement to Tyacke's thesis.[30] Indeed, Preston's example takes it even further, in that it identifies a clear trend amongst the inheritors of late Elizabethan divinity to develop a distinct and more sophisticated defence of particular grace in the face of new threats from both home and abroad. Whereas Harsnett and Baro received a resounding 'No,' we have seen how Montagu and the Remonstrants received a less resounding 'Yes and no.' This new option of hypothetical universalism was a highly complex phenomenon with no one definitive formulation or uniformity of explanation. Nevertheless certain core concerns and fundamental tenets go to establish it as an important mediating position in the doctrinal debates in seventeenth-century England and Europe. In histories of the period a hasty application of the rigid label 'Calvinist' should be avoided, since underneath this label lay a whole spectrum of predestinarian beliefs, and only when such a spectrum is acknowledged can the language of a 'Calvinist consensus' be helpfully employed.

Concerning the progressive changes away from Perkinsian particularism discernible in Jacobean England, and particularly in Cambridge, the pulse of the nation, the move away from supralapsarianism to infralapsarianism by the 1610s has already been recognised, including by Tyacke.[31] What also appears to

---

29. For a study illustrating the diversity that could exist amongst predestinarians at the local, ecclesiological level — in this case, that of Preston's own Diocese of Peterborough — see A. John Fielding, "Arminianism in the Localities: Peterborough Diocese, 1603-1642" in *The Early Stuart Church, 1603-1642*, ed. Kenneth Fincham (London: Macmillan Press, 1993), pp. 93-113, 237, 262-64.

30. Anthony Milton, "Review of Nicholas Tyacke's "Anti-Calvinists: The Rise of English Arminianism," *JEH* 39 (1988): 613-16; Anthony Milton, "The Laudians and the Church of Rome c.1625-1640" (Ph.D. Dissertation, University of Cambridge, 1989); Anthony Milton, "The Church of England, Rome and the True Church: The Demise of a Jacobean Consensus" in *The Early Stuart Church, 1603-1642*, ed. Kenneth Fincham (Stanford, CA: Stanford University Press, 1993), pp. 187-210; Anthony Milton, *Catholic and Reformed: The Roman and Protestant Churches in English Protestant Thought, 1600-1640* (Cambridge: Cambridge University Press, 1995); Seán F. Hughes, "'The Problem of "Calvinism"': English Theologies of Predestination c. 1580-1630," in *Belief and Practice in Reformation England: A Tribute to Patrick Collinson from His Students*, ed. Susan Wabuda & Caroline Litzenberger (Aldershot, UK: Ashgate Publishing Company, 1998), pp. 229-49; Como, "Puritans, Predestination and the Construction of Orthodoxy." See Nicholas R. N. Tyacke, *Aspects of English Protestantism, c.1530-1700* (Manchester, UK: Manchester University Press, 2001), pp. 9-11 for Tyacke's own critique of his seminal 1973 essay, with the benefit of twenty-eight years more study.

31. Lynne C. Boughton, "Supralapsarianism and the Role of Metaphysics in Sixteenth-Century Reformed Theology," *WTJ* 48 (1986): 63-96, pp. 82, 83; David M. Hoyle, "'Near Popery Yet No Popery': Theological Debate in Cambridge 1590-1644" (Ph.D. Dissertation, University of Cam-

have been happening is a general softening of Reformed distinctives on other fronts as well, especially that of the extent of Christ's satisfaction and the nature of the gospel call to the reprobate. From Perkins' stark supralapsarian particularism, we move to Ussher's conservative, qualified condemnation of the concept of 'bare sufficiency.' This is then taken up by Davenant and infused with covenantal structures to create a highly complex mediating system that enables a growing number of preachers like Preston to retain in one system paradoxes such as a simultaneous hardening of and desiring to save the reprobate under gospel preaching, and a gospel covenant that is both universal and conditional, and particular and unconditional. Rigorous Perkinsian logic which sought out and eliminated all possible internal contradictions had given way to a more irenic and sophisticated divinity that pursued mediation, and instead sought to eliminate all possible causes of unnecessary offence. The fact that Preston, as a hypothetical universalist, was widely regarded as the spiritual figurehead of 'the godly,' suggests that mainstream English Calvinism itself had undergone considerable internal modification from the time of Elizabeth's reign and in particular from the predominant position of the 1590s. William Perkins, with his popular, supralapsarian, particular redemptionism, may perhaps be seen, at least in this respect, as more the end of an era than, as is more usually stated, the beginning of a new one. If a rise of anti-Calvinism was partly to blame for the outbreak of the Civil War, it was not before the 'Calvinistic consensus' itself had undergone significant internal modification. Even the Reformed were distancing themselves from some of the excesses of their Elizabethan forefathers. In short, by this intermediate position that weakened the emphasis on absolute predestination and the unconditional particularity of grace, the Jacobean Calvinists themselves had paved the path of change. It is therefore clear that not only must a 'Calvinistic consensus' be allowed to embrace a significant spectrum of beliefs, it must also allow for modification within this consensus over time. It also follows that if by the phrase 'Calvinistic consensus' our thoughts turn immediately to views on predestination and grace, then we are likely to underestimate the role of actual forms of worship and polity, rather than theology proper, in fostering sentiments that fuelled the Civil War.[32] The

---

bridge, 1991), p. 102; Nicholas R. N. Tyacke, "Anglican Attitudes: Some Recent Writings on English Religious History, from the Reformation to the Civil War," *JBS* 35 (1996): 139-67, pp. 145, 149.

32. This is not, of course, to deny that there were other causative factors which may be seen as more political and legal in nature, not least Charles I's own clumsy pursuit of divine-right monarchy (see Julian E. Davies, *The Caroline Captivity of the Church: Charles I and the Remoulding of Anglicanism, 1625-1641* [Oxford: Clarendon Press, 1992]). But for those who continue to demote the role of religion altogether in understanding the causation of the Civil War, the following words of Reventlow are reserved: "modern secularized thought-patterns often

'Calvinistic consensus' was not so much on a specific formulation of predestination and redemption, as on a firm conviction that salvation is by predestinating grace and not the grace of sacramentalism, and that therefore the Church of Rome is to be abhorred, and every resurgence of its ceremonialism to be fiercely resisted. The term 'Reformed consensus' is therefore preferable.[33]

Our revised interpretation of the proceedings of the York House Conference also show Peter White's thesis to be flawed.[34] White would have us believe in an 'Anglican *via media*' throughout Elizabeth's and James's reigns to the extent that both the Puritan Calvinists and Montagu were extremists on the unacceptable fringe of the English Church. Concerning Preston's position at the York House Conference, we have already seen how White thinks that it was "a merely cosmetic adjustment to the doctrine of limited Atonement."[35] He asserts therefore that "Preston's doctrine was no longer typical of English Calvinism," for "he had been left behind by the adjustments made to the moderate English Calvinist position evident at Dort." Nothing could be further from the truth. In Chapter 7 we saw that Preston was himself intimately involved in these 'adjustments.' White has no grounds for saying that at the York House Conference there "was no cleric of the subtlety of Davenant to state a moderate Calvinist position."[36] Preston held just such a position. Thus, if even a 'subtle' moderate Calvinist such as John Preston found the position of Montagu, White, Buckeridge, and Cosin so objectionable, then it can be no myth that something quite new was arising amongst the English clergy.[37]

---

lead to complete incomprehension of the deeper motives of the thought and action of a period in which faith and the world were still closely connected and theology could assert its central position unassailed" (Henning Graf Reventlow, *The Authority of the Bible and the Rise of the Modern World*, trans. John Bowden [London: SCM Press, 1984], p. 92). For how this might work out in practice, see, for example, John S. Morrill, "The Religious Context of the English Civil War," *TRHS* 34 (1984): 155-78.

33. Cf. Alister E. McGrath, *Historical Theology: An Introduction to the History of Christian Thought* (Oxford: Blackwell, 1998), p. 161.

34. For more general exposures of Peter White's thesis see Seán F. Hughes, "Review of Peter White's 'Predestination, Policy and Polemic: Conflict and Consensus in the English Church from the Reformation to the Civil War,'" *JTS* 45 (1994): 403-9; Peter G. Lake, "Predestinarian Propositions," *JEH* 46 (1995): 110-23; Tyacke, "Anglican Attitudes."

35. See above, p. 160; cf. Peter White, "The *via media* in the Early Stuart Church" in *The Early Stuart Church, 1603-1642*, ed. Kenneth Fincham, pp. 211-30, 243-44, 285-89.

36. Peter White, *Predestination, Policy and Polemic: Conflict and Consensus in the English Church from the Reformation to the Civil War* (Cambridge: Cambridge University Press, 1992), pp. 228, 230.

37. Montagu was also too much even for Baxter, who saw him as the first heterodox bishop of the Reformed Church of England (Richard Baxter, *Five Disputations of Church-Government and Worship* [London: R. W. for Nevil Simmons and by Thomas Johnson, 1659], p. 6).

Furthermore, this quartet was equally opposed to Preston's moderate position. It should not be altogether surprising therefore, that Preston's contemporaries perceived this rising theology to be none other than Arminianism. Margo Todd has helpfully reminded us that whether or not there was in fact a distinct romanizing 'Arminian party' taking over the English Church in the late 1620s and 1630s, it is these contemporary perceptions that are crucial. And we have seen at York House that there can be no doubt concerning this "evident perception of contemporaries that there *were* two warring parties, and that the theological stakes were very high."[38]

In closing, one qualification must be made so as to avoid possible misunderstanding. I have not argued that there were no moderates in late Elizabethan England, nor that Perkinsian particularism was the only option for mainstream Elizabethan divines. I freely acknowledge that Perkins endured many "reproaches" cast upon "the 'Calvinists' doctrine," and that it was necessary for him to try and "mitigate and appease the mindes of some of our Brethren, which have bin more offended at it than was fit."[39] But I also maintain that Perkins was still mainstream — in the 'higher' half of the mainstream maybe, but mainstream nonetheless — and that he not only shaped the Elizabethan mainstream, but embodied it. Furthermore, given Perkins' position as a patriarch of the spiritual brotherhood, Perkinsian divinity was 'Preston's heritage' in an even greater sense. However, I have not sought to demonstrate that Perkins' divinity was 'authentic Calvinism,' whereas that of his successors was a 'treacherous departure' from it. Such a question, if valid and useful at all, lies beyond the scope of this study. In theory at least, it is possible to argue that Perkins was part of a counter-productive theological extremism that his 'moderate' successors rejected, returning to the balance of Calvin and the early English Reformers. These successors would be unprecedentedly united in distancing themselves from any hint of the rigors of Elizabethan particularism, because they had witnessed both at home and abroad the severity of the associated anti-Calvinist backlash. On the other hand, it could be argued that due to this increasing but unavoidable anti-Calvinist polemic, such primitive simplicity was now simply not possible for Perkins, if he was to preserve intact the theological attainments of the Reformation. At the same time, the hypothetical universalists responded by developing an entirely new system to such an extent that they considerably muddied the waters

38. Margo Todd, "'All One with Tom Thumb': Arminianism, Popery, and the Story of the Reformation in Early Stuart Cambridge," *CH* 64 (1995): 563-79, p. 578.

39. William Perkins, *The Workes of that famous and worthy Minister of Christ in the Universitie of Cambridge, Mr. William Perkins* (London: John Legatt & Cantrell Legge, 1616-18), II:605.

of the sixteenth-century Reformation testimony, and compromised fundamental principles of the Reformed theology of grace. However, I have sought to avoid falling into this all-too-common trap of the futile 'loyalty' versus 'betrayal' paradigm. I have sought, rather, to unfold the significant differences in the doctrine of Christ's satisfaction and its proclamation, which existed amongst late Elizabethan and Jacobean divines, and let those facts speak for themselves.

Whatever might be said about the nature of doctrinal modifications within the ranks of the Jacobean Reformed, what cannot be denied is that a marked theological change and shift in the balance of power had occurred within the ranks of the established church by the time of Preston's death. Harsnett's blistering attack on particular grace in 1594 was examined in Chapter 2.[40] At that point he was severely rebuked by the Archbishop of Canterbury for disturbing the peace of the Church, and roundly refuted at Paul's Cross by Dr John Dove. However, despite being charged with Popery by the House of Commons in 1624,[41] Harsnett was made Archbishop of York in 1628. A year later he was found condemning Davenant's Court sermon before Charles I because towards the end it contained a brief defence of the doctrine of election.[42] With even the theology of grace propounded by hypothetical universalists being too strict for Harsnett, it comes as no surprise that at this time Harsnett also banned the sale of Perkins' works.[43] Preston's heritage as well as Preston's new mentors were *all* under attack. It was time for even 'the godly' to go to war.

---

40. See pp. 58-62.

41. *Journals of the House of Lords*, 19th May, 1624, III:388-89.

42. Bod Tanner MS. 290, ff. 86r-87r; Thomas Fuller, *The Church-History of Britain* (London: For John William, 1655), XI:138-41; cf. Peter Heylyn, *Cyprianus Anglicus: Or the History of the Life and Death, of the most reverend and renowned Prelate William* (London: For A. Seile, 1668), p. 214; James Ussher, *The whole Works of the most Rev. James Ussher*, ed. Charles R. Erlington (Dublin: Hodges and Smith, 1847-64), XVI:512-13. Similarly, having preached against the Durham House clerics and the Remonstrants in a Court sermon in 1626, Ussher knew he would never be invited back (Ussher, *Works*, XIII:350-51; see also above, p. 179).

43. Nicholas R. N. Tyacke, *Anti-Calvinists: The Rise of English Arminianism c.1590-1640*, 2nd ed. (Oxford: Clarendon Press, 1990), pp. 182-83. It was also too strict for Laud's loyal biographer Peter Heylyn (Peter Heylyn, *Respondet Petrus: Or, the Answer of Peter Heylyn D.D. to so much of Dr Bernard's Book entituled, The Judgement of the late Primate of Ireland* [London: For R. Royston and R. Marriot, 1658], pp. 102-4).

Bibliography

A Bibliographical Note on Preston's Works

"It would be a good prevention of manie inconveniences . . . if able men would bee perswaded to publish their owne works in their life time."[1]

Although Preston's own works were not published in his lifetime, he was far from being uninterested in the perpetuation of his influence through the printed word. Perhaps this was only because he knew it was inevitable that his sermons would be published. Whatever the case, at the end of his short life, aware that he would not live to see his sermons "setled & provided for," Preston "desired that they might not come into ye world like vagabonds," and that "those would be carefull whom he named."[2] When Lord Saye visited him on his deathbed, Preston named these chosen men: Richard Sibbes and John Davenport for his Lincoln's Inn sermons *(The Breast-plate, The New Covenant, Saints daily Exercise, Saints Qualification*[3]*)*, and Thomas Goodwin and Thomas Ball for all his other sermons *(Saints Infirmities, The golden Scepter, Life eternall, Sermons preached before His Majestie)*.[4] However, twice as many

---

1. Richard Sibbes and John Davenport (Preface to the Reader, John Preston, *Saints daily Exercise*, p. A2v).

2. Thomas Ball, *The Life of the Renowned Doctor Preston*, ed. Edward W. Harcourt (Oxford: Parker and Co., 1885), p. 173. Goodwin and Ball state that Preston "presaged" that otherwise any unofficial editors might be "lesse carefull" (John Preston, *Sermons preached before His Majestie*, p. A2r).

3. *Saints Qualification*, I:245-305, however, is actually a sermon preached at Oxford before the House of Commons.

4. John Preston, *The New Covenant*, p. A4r; John Preston, *Saints Qualification*, p. ¶4r; Pres-

titles in Preston's name were to come from other editors who lacked this special commission from the author *(The deformed Forme, Foure Treatises, The Fulnesse of Christ, Plenitudo Fontis, The Law, A liveles Life, Love of Christ, Remaines, Saints Submission, Sinnes Overthrow, Life and Death, Lords Supper, Irresistibilitate Gratiæ convertentis, The mysticall Match, Irresistiblenesse of converting Grace, Riches of Mercy).* Nor were the authorised editors entirely happy with this unsolicited competition, as we will see. John Stafford, in one of Preston's unauthorised editions, warned the reader that "[i]t is not . . . alwaies safe to trust posthume writings, and to say, This such a man held, because we finde it in the Books published under his name when hee is dead."[5] Given that this is the case, it is necessary to make enquiry into the reliability of Preston's published works for a study of his thought. First the authorised editions will be considered, and then the unauthorised.

The four official editors did not publish everything that was committed to their charge by Preston, but only what they deemed to be "usefull."[6] According to Grosart, Preston "left all his papers" to Sibbes and Davenport.[7] Some of the material through which the editors sifted, therefore, were manuscripts written by Preston himself. Although he does not seem to have preached from notes, he frequently made copies of what he had said for the benefit of people who could not attend, or to clarify his message for posterity, although he does not appear to have been overly careful in this.[8] The rest of the material would have been notes taken by stenographers. In addition to

---

ton, *Sermons preached before His Majestie*, pp. A2r-A3v; John Preston, *Riches of Mercy*, p. ▲3r. Only Davenport have we not met before in this book. He was involved, with Sibbes, in the Feoffees for Impropriations (see above, p. 18), and later was to become co-founder of New Haven.

5. John Preston, *The Fulnesse of Christ*, p. A3v.

6. Preston, *Sermons preached before His Majestie*, p. A3v. For example, for one reason or another, it appears from Preston, *Saints Qualification*, II:2 that Preston's series of sermons on sanctification made it to the press, whereas his preceding sermons on justification did not. The editors' role was *not*, as Haller claims, simply identifying those sermons of which Preston was the true author, and rejecting the rest as spurious (William Haller, *The Rise of Puritanism, or the Way to the New Jerusalem as set forth in Pulpit and Press from Thomas Cartwright to John Lilburne and John Milton, 1570-1643* [New York: Harper & Brothers, 1957], p. 66). But as could be expected, one part of the work was simply eliminating needless repetition. Goodwin stated that "[i]n Dr Preston MS. much must bee left out, for hee hase often one and the selfe same thing as about the conflict etc. and so that having a forme of godliness et wanting the power brings in all those notions under an upright heart etc. where hee speakes of that" (SUL Hartlib MS. 29/2/56b).

7. Richard Sibbes, *The Complete Works of Richard Sibbes*, ed. Alexander B. Grosart (Edinburgh: James Nichol, 1862-64), I:li. However, in his will of 1618 Preston was to leave Sibbes only one book, and he does not name Davenport at all (PRO, PROB. 11/154, f. 102v).

8. Ball, *Life of Preston*, p. 69. An example of Preston's sermon notes survives at Bod Tanner MS. 283, ff. 202r-202v. The text is Matthew 15:21-28.

sermonic material, Preston left other theological and exegetical writings, but only *Irresistibilitate Gratiæ convertentis* and *Irresistiblenesse of converting Grace* made it to the press, and that without the help of the authorised editors. In 1641 a book by Preston entitled *Questiones duae ad disputandem proposite a Johanne Prestono* was about to be published in both Latin and English. It is unclear whether this was finally split into *Irresistibilitate Gratiæ convertentis* and *Irresistiblenesse of converting Grace,* or never was published at all.[9] Preston's sermons on 2 Peter 1:10, 11 were ready for the press but were never published.[10] Preston's whole Latin commentary or "exact & logical analysis" of the New Testament epistles, or at least the Pauline ones, was never published either, and appears not to have survived.[11] Nor were the authorised editors particularly swift in seeing Preston into print. It was nearly six months after Preston's death when the first book was registered with the Company of Stationers.[12] But neither did they give up easily. On behalf of Nicholas Bourne, Ball was still assiduously trying to acquire more new material by Preston from Preston's surviving relatives as late as 28th November, 1638.[13]

In their dedicatory epistles to the likes of Lord Saye and Sele, Sir Richard Knightley, the Earl of Warwick, the Earl of Pembroke, and Henry Lawrence, Preston's nominated editors all make claims for the faithfulness of their editions. With regard to Preston's legacy from Lincoln's Inn, Sibbes and Davenport resided in London and therefore "were better conversant with those that tooke them from his mouth."[14] In their preface to *The New Covenant,* Sibbes and Davenport assure the reader that "there was very little or no mistake in taking them from his mouth." They write,

> We are not ignorant that it is a thing subject to censure to seem bold and witty in another man's work, and therefore as little is altered as may be.

9. Company of Stationers, *A Transcript of the Registers of the worshipful Company of Stationers: From 1640-1708 A.D.* (London: Private publication, 1913), I:18. It appears again in the *Register* as late as 18th October, 1659 (II:239).

10. William Prynne, *Anti-Arminianisme. Or, the Church of Englands old Antithesis to new Arminianisme* (London: Eliz. Allde for M. Sparke, 1630), p. 212.

11. Ball gives the fact that it was in Latin and Preston's poor handwriting as reasons why it was never published (Ball, *Life of Preston,* p. 73; cf. p. 69). In 1635 it was in the hands of Lord Saye: "Lord Say habet Analyses in omnes Epistolas Pauli Dr Prestons, which were very accurate" (SUL Hartlib MS. 29/3/13b).

12. See below, p. 234.

13. SUL Hartlib MS. 48/3/1a. It would appear that this quest was unsuccessful, since what was to become the last authorised book by Preston, namely *The golden Scepter,* was by this stage already at the press.

14. Preston, *Sermons preached before His Majestie,* p. A2v.

And we desire the reader, rather to take in good part that which is intended for public good, than to catch at imperfections, considering they were but taken as they fell from him speaking.[15]

In their preface to the reader in *Saints daily Exercise* they offer similar assurances:

[W]e let these Sermons passe forth as they were delivered by himselfe, in publicke, without taking that libertie of adding or detracting, which, perhaps, some would have thought meete: for wee thought it best that his owne meaning should be expressed in his owne words and manner, especially considering there is little which perhaps may seeme superfluous to some, but may, by Gods blessing, be usefull to others.[16]

Goodwin and Ball also express basic confidence in the reliability of their own editions of Preston's other sermons, especially in view of the fact that they were often "his Auditors," and "had reason fully to know his Doctrine." Concerning the sermons in *The golden Scepter* they are persuaded that they "may more properly be counted his, than any thing that hitherto hath seene the light."[17] They acknowledge that *Life eternall* is an "unfinished draught," only "at last through many hazards delivered unto us," but this is because Preston died while in the middle of this series.[18] Six out of the eight authorised editions were produced by Nicholas Bourne.[19] Bourne was also responsible for publishing, in 1648 and 1658, William Jemmat's abridgement of Preston's works. Although technically unauthorised, the source material for the abridgment was confined to these six authorised editions.[20]

The actual text of Preston's printed sermons lends support to these editorial claims. They contain occasional circumstantial side-remarks from the

15. Preston, *The New Covenant*, pp. A3r, A4r. In their preface to *Saints Qualification* they similarly acknowledge "some imperfections," but no more than "usually accompany the taking of other mens speeches" (Preston, *Saints Qualification* p. ¶3r).

16. Preston, *Saints daily Exercise*, p. A2v.

17. John Preston, *The golden Scepter*, p. A5r.

18. John Preston, *Life eternall*, pp. A7r, A4r. The manuscript was not, therefore, given personally by Preston to Goodwin and Ball, as Haller claims (Haller, *Rise of Puritanism*, pp. 74, 168; cf. Erasmus Middleton, *Biographia Evangelica* [London: J. W. Pasham for Alex. Hogg, 1779-86], II:478).

19. For more on Bourne, see Leona Rostenberg, *Literary, Political, Scientific, Religious and Legal Publishing, Printing and Bookselling in England, 1551-1700: Twelve Studies* (New York: Burt Franklin, 1965), I:75-96.

20. This was first entered on 25th June, 1642 (Company of Stationers, *Transcript of the Registers*, I:47).

preacher, suggesting both relatively diligent stenography and a reverent editorial policy of maximum preservation.[21] Goodwin and Ball's stated goal was the reverent enshrining of "these living and surviving peeces of his soule" and "vigorous and usefull breathings of his spirit," rather than the creation of literary masterpieces.[22] It seems that the market was as much for authentic records of Preston's ministry, as for volumes of polished theologising. There seems to be no substantial reason to doubt the basic accuracy of Preston's authorised editions any more than any other seventeenth-century posthumous publications.

The unauthorised editions of Preston's works merit their own examination, not least because of the anxious stance taken towards them by Preston's four nominated editors. Ball informs us that throughout his life Preston often "was troubled lest any thinge he had said should be mistaken or misinterpreted."[23] Characteristically, then, Preston had expressed his fears that, after his decease, those who were not his close friends might publish his manuscript legacy. Sibbes and Davenport also seem to have anticipated that this would happen. In their preface to their very first edition of Preston's sermons, before any unauthorised editions had seen the light of day, Sibbes and Davenport took the opportunity to "intreate those, that have any thing of his in their hands, that they would not be hastie, for private respects, to publish them, till we, whom the Author put in trust, have perused them. We purpose (by Gods helpe) that what shall be judged fit, shall come forth."[24] The exact criteria that would be used to determine this 'fitness' were never disclosed. Ball seems to hint that there may well have been material from Preston in circulation in his lifetime which he "had not published according to his mynde."[25] Perhaps this was due to Preston's own personal doctrinal develop-

21. E.g., Preston, *Saints Qualification*, I:30. However, it must be admitted that at least one such side-remark is found in the unauthorised edition but not in the official edition (e.g., John Preston, *Life and Death*, p. 32 and Preston, *Sermons preached before His Majestie*, p. 56). But *Life and Death* is a dubious edition and has been avoided for the reasons outlined below, pp. 235, 237.

22. Preston, *The golden Scepter*, p. A5r.

23. Ball, *Life of Preston*, p. 58.

24. John Preston, *The New Covenant, or the Saints Portion. A Treatise unfolding the All-sufficiencie of God, Man's Uprightness, and the Covenant of Grace. Delivered in fourteene Sermons upon Genesis 17:1, 2. Whereunto are adjoyned foure Sermons upon Ecclesiastes 9:1, 2, 11, 12*, ed. Richard Sibbes & John Davenport, 1st ed. (London: J. Dawson for Nicholas Bourne, 1629), p. A3v. This book was registered on 1st January, 1629 *(STC)*.

25. Ball, *Life of Preston*, p. 150. This is not to be taken as if Preston 'published' anything in his lifetime via the presses (contrary to Everett H. Emerson, *English Puritanism from John Hooper to John Milton* [Durham, NC: Duke University Press, 1968], p. 241), but in the sense of the wide circulation of manuscripts.

ment rather than a slip of the pen, and perhaps he explicitly informed his editors of his worries in this regard. We do not know. What does seem clear is that there was a general fear that certain publishing ventures might present Preston in such a way as he could be 'misinterpreted.'

Whatever the case may be, the following year the stationer Michael Sparke published two editions of a sermon preached by Preston before James at Whitehall in November 1626.[26] Sparke's production was dedicated to Nathaniel Rich, Richard Knightley, and John Pym. William Prynne, another opponent of Montagu, seems to have been behind its publication.[27] The margins are replete with additional patristic and other citations not originating from Preston,[28] but the text differs only very slightly from that published in the same year by Goodwin and Ball, probably just before Sparke's edition.[29] In their 1630 preface Goodwin and Ball declared, "Wee have laboured what we could to discharge the trust by him reposed in us, and desire that others would be pleased to forbeare the putting forth of any thing of his, without acquainting some of us therewith, by him deputed for that worke."[30] But even as they wrote their desires were being frustrated by Sparke.

Meanwhile in the next two years numerous other unauthorised editions appeared from presses in London and Edinburgh, including seven more from an undeterred Sparke.[31] This provoked Sibbes and Davenport in their 1633 preface to their first edition of *Saints Qualification* to lament "the injurious dealing of such as for private gaine have published what they can get, howsoever taken, without any acquainting" of the four chosen editors. "Hereby not

26. Preston, *Life and Death;* John Preston, *A Sermon of spirituall Life and Death. Preached before the King, at White-Hall, November, 1626,* another ed. (London: Thomas Cotes for Michael Sparke, 1630); cf. Ball, *Life of Preston,* pp. 155-56.

27. Preston, *Life and Death,* p. A1r.

28. In a similarly painstaking way Sparke added copious scripture references to the margins of Preston, *Lords Supper.*

29. Cf. Christopher Hill, *Puritanism and Revolution: Studies in Interpretation of the English Revolution of the Seventeenth Century* (London: Secker & Warburg, 1958), pp. 252-53. Nevertheless, it could be, therefore, that *both* editions are suspect, due to a curious note in the Hartlib Papers for 1634, where someone is said to have "counted Prestons of life et death no better than a Pamphlet because it was so unperfectly taken" (SUL Hartlib MS. 29/2/21a). On the other hand, this could be referring to Part 2 of John Preston, *Foure Treatises.*

30. John Preston, *Sermons preached before His Majestie, and upon other speciall Occasions,* ed. Thomas Goodwin & Thomas Ball, 1st ed. (London: Eliot's Court Press and R. Young for Leonard Greene and James Boler, 1630), pp. 27-59, A4r. This was registered on 14th and 22nd January, 1630 *(STC).*

31. The four Edinburgh editions were produced by the stationer John Wreittoun, who had dealings with Sparke (Rostenberg, *Literary, Political, Scientific, Religious and Legal Publishing,* I:185).

onely wrong is done to others but to the deceased likewise, by mangling and misshaping the birth of his braine, and therefore once againe we desire men to forbeare publishing of any thing, until those that were intrusted have the review."[32] But their pleas had little effect. A total of thirty-seven unauthorised editions followed in the next two decades.

There are few clues as to what exactly the official editors feared would come about through unauthorised editions. It is possible that it was no more than that they were seen as inherently disrespectful to the deceased author, given his explicit and emphatic request. However, their allusion to "private gaine" suggests that economic considerations were also involved. Nevertheless, Sibbes and Davenport in their preface to their first edition of *Saints Qualification,* and in an uncharacteristic doctrinal aside, defend the idea of a work of humiliation before regeneration. This may constitute an implicit admission that some of the "imperfections" in the book, about which they speak, entail Preston going too far in some of his phrases concerning this preparatory work. This could have been one area at least where Preston may have been open to misinterpretation through a 'mangled' edition.[33] We cannot entirely exclude the possibility that certain doctrinal motives lay behind the desire to 'review' but not 'mangle' Preston's material for the press. There is no hint at all, however, that the editors' scruples extended to the area of hypothetical universalism.

The unauthorised editions represent a library less even in quality. At least once they merely make available sermons that belonged with series published by the authorised editors. The opening sermon to the series printed as *The golden Scepter* was printed for Francis Eglesfield in 1648, having been registered for over seven years. The shy editor "T. S." explains how this sermon came into his hands after the edition by "those reverend Divines" Goodwin and Ball had been published without it, and, since it was "taken by a skilfull scribe from the Authors mouth," he "thought fit to adde it to the rest, lest the work should seem a body without a head."[34] There is nothing in this sermon that suggests that Goodwin and Ball might have deliberately suppressed it.

At other times the mists of the London underworld raise doubts concerning the reliability of the editions. We have already noted how Sparke pro-

32. Preston, *Saints Qualification,* pp. ¶3v-¶4r.

33. Preston, *Saints Qualification,* pp. ¶3r-¶3v. Preston's *Remaines* is one example of an unauthorised edition containing what sometimes have been termed 'preparationist' sermons. Preston was aware how easy it was to fall into preparationism (Preston, *Saints Qualification,* II:169-70). Cf. above, p. 119.

34. Company of Stationers, *Transcript of the Registers,* I:7; John Preston, *The mysticall Match,* "To the Christian Reader."

duced two editions of a sermon also found in the authorised collection of *Sermons preached before His Majestie,* and that the two versions are almost identical.[35] However, Sparke's editions have generally been avoided in this examination of Preston's theology. *Sermons preached before His Majestie* has always been used in favour of *Life and Death,* and Preston's *Foure Treatises* and *Lords Supper* are quoted or cited only eleven times in total. This is because although Sparke's marginal annotations suggest he was a very conscientious editor, he was often imprisoned, pilloried, and fined for a somewhat flippant attitude towards the legalities of the book trade.[36] For that reason, his editions of Preston's works have to be treated with some caution. In 1631, for example, Sparke, using the Oxford-based printer William Turner, produced a pirated edition of 2,000 copies of Goodwin and Ball's *Sermons preached before His Majestie.* Sparke even had the audacity to reproduce their preface with its plea for no unauthorised editions.[37] Nevertheless, it should not be thought that Sparke's editions of Preston are inherently unreliable. The problem was a legal one concerning licensing, and not fraudulent or mutilated text. Prynne had a hand in preparing some of Preston's sermons for the press,[38] and Sparke was Prynne's longstanding publisher. Prynne studied at Lincoln's Inn "where he became a great follower of Preston's, then the Lecturer there."[39] The evidence suggests that at least part of his motivation for promoting the publication of Preston's sermons through Sparke was a great

35. See p. 235.

36. E.g., PRO SP 16/140/15, 16/141/17, 16/142/22, 16/158/49, 16/182/73, 16/185/11, 16/188/13, 16/190/40, 16/190/64, 16/205/102, 16/231/77, 16/530/48, 16/530/49; Greg, *Companion,* 1967, pp. 268-73. The proceedings of Sparke's trial in the Star Chamber in 1634, along with Prynne, may be found at Bod Tanner MS. 299, ff. 123r-134v. For more on Sparke see Rostenberg, *Literary, Political, Scientific, Religious and Legal Publishing,* I:161-202. Sparke's controversial activities were in fact borne out of a principled objection to the printing monopolies of his day. Rostenberg styles him as a "Puritan crusader" and a "Puritan fanatic" (Leona Rostenberg, *The Minority Press & the English Crown: A Study in Repression, 1558-1625* [Nieuwkoop: B. De Graaf, 1971], p. 97). Sparke's son and namesake also published Preston's works (John Preston, *A Preparation to the Lords Supper; preached in three Sermons,* 5th ed. [London: John Dawson for Michael Sparke, 1638]; John Preston, *Grace to the Humble. As Preparations to receive the Sacrament* [London: Thomas Cotes for Michael Sparke, 1639]; Rostenberg, *Literary, Political, Scientific, Religious and Legal Publishing,* I:184).

37. PRO SP 16/190/40. Madan incorrectly identifies this with an edition of Preston, *Saints daily Exercise* (Falconer Madan, *Oxford Books: A Bibliography of printed Works relating to the University and City of Oxford or printed or published there* [Oxford: Clarendon Press, 1912], II:117, 665).

38. Preston, *Life and Death,* p. A2r; cf. Prynne, *Anti-Arminianisme,* p. 212.

39. Peter Heylyn, *Cyprianus Anglicus: Or the History of the Life and Death, of the most reverend and renowned Prelate William* (London: For A. Seile, 1668), p. 156.

respect for the "Reverend, learned, and pious Dr John Preston" himself.[40] This encourages a confidence in the reliability of Sparke's text.

But it is the editions of Preston from the bookseller John Stafford that are the most problematical. Stafford oversaw the publication of Preston's sermon on John 1:16, preached before James, which led to Preston being appointed Chaplain in Ordinary.[41] As far as we know Sparke had nothing to do with these editions, but it is possible that Prynne prepared the manuscript for the press. Prynne once possessed the manuscript, since he cites this sermon on John 1:16 in 1630, and it was not published until 1639.[42] However, Preston made many copies of this sermon — and not "word for word" either — at the request of numerous courtiers, including Prince Charles and Buckingham who had been absent, and so Prynne's involvement is therefore by no means certain.[43] Given Prynne's militant anti-Arminianism, it is certainly out of the question that he deleted Preston's anti-Arminian passages from this sermon. Yet someone did. According to John Stafford, this edition was deceitfully purged to make it appear that Preston had not preached against Arminianism before the king. All this "as if Arminianisme were Englands true Doctrine." At the time Stafford was completely ignorant of this, and even wrote a preface advertising the edition's reliability. Stafford later claimed to have discovered that M. Parsons, the printer of the first edition, had expunged the anti-Arminian sections from the manuscript in 1639 as it went to press. The printer for the 1640 edition, John Okes, had unwittingly reproduced this same mutilated version. It was only in 1644 that the original, full-blown anti-Arminian version of the sermon was recovered and published "without the least diminution [sic]."[44] Or so Stafford claimed. It might be objected that this could have been a double bluff by Stafford to serve his own purposes. But there is evidence that leads us to trust Stafford's claim. Ball informs us that one of the parts of the sermon that had most impressed the king was "that of the Arminians putting God into the same extremity that Darius was put in . . . when he would have saved Daniel but could not."[45] Yet this

---

40. Prynne, *Anti-Arminianisme*, p. 212.

41. See above, p. 16.

42. Cf. Prynne, *Anti-Arminianisme*, p. 212.

43. Ball, *Life of Preston*, p. 69.

44. John Preston, *Plenitudo Fontis*, pp. A2r-A2v. It was also reissued the same year as the fourth part of John Preston, *Sun-beams*. We have already encountered some of the corruptions above, pp. 76, 88, 129.

45. Ball, *Life of Preston*, p. 65. See above, p. 129. Naturally, John Wesley expunged this detail from his edition of Ball's *Life* (John Wesley, ed., *A Christian Library. Consisting of Extracts from and Abridgements of the choicest Pieces of practical Divinity, which have been publish'd in the English Tongue* [Bristol, UK: Felix Farley and E. Farley, 1749-55], IX:207).

passage only appears in *Plenitudo Fontis* and not *The Fulnesse of Christ for us,* indicating that *Plenitudo Fontis* is indeed the more reliable version.[46] Neither sermon has been relied upon in this study, however, and, when it has been sparingly quoted, *Plenitudo Fontis* has been used. It should be noted that, contrary to the impression given by Haller,[47] out of *all* Preston's posthumous sermons, this is the *only* sermon for which there is evidence that one version of it at least is corrupt or spurious.

There is no indication that Preston's unauthorised editions are inherently or generally unreliable, and there is evidence suggesting that some of them at least were as reliable as the authorised editions. For example, Eglesfield was responsible for the publishing of *Riches of Mercy* in 1658, which unwittingly duplicates a sermon in *Remaines* first printed for Andrew Crook in 1637. Yet these two editions of the sermon are almost identical, the differences being almost always only typographical.[48] The preface to *Riches of Mercy* informs us that "this Remainder of Doctor Prestons works was never (heretofore) extant, being the last of His, that are likely to see the light (taken by the same pen that his other works were and no way inferior to those already published)." Furthermore, although "this piece was so long suppressed," because "the age hath doted so much about new lights, that we perceived Old Truths to be neglected and laid aside," Sibbes, one of the authorised editors, "did in his life time own these Treatises by affixing his approbation to them." This approbation reads, "This Treatise hath nothing offensive in it, but contains arguments tending to edification, and may be of singular use and comfort to all true believers."[49] One of these unauthorised editions, therefore, even has a quasi-authorised status.

In conclusion, we can agree with Fuller who in the 1650s recognised that most of Preston's books had been "well brought forth into the World," although some had "not lighted on so good guardians."[50] This study's usage of

46. Preston, *Plenitudo Fontis*, p. 10.

47. Haller, *Rise of Puritanism*, p. 74.

48. Cf. John Preston, *Remaines*, pp. 65-177; Preston, *Riches of Mercy*, pp. 37-120.

49. Preston, *Riches of Mercy*, pp. ♠3r-♠4v. Evidence exists that this material, if not "suppressed," did at least experience considerable delay in being published, having been entered at the Company of Stationers in 1640 and 1641 (Company of Stationers, *Transcript of the Registers,* I:7, 28). Perhaps the manuscript for this book arrived at the press from Sibbes via Lord Saye, since an entry for the year of Sibbes' death (1635) in the Hartlib Papers states that "Lord Say habet MS. Prestonis of the duty of Ministers also divers other" (SUL Hartlib MS. 29/3/14b). This is probably a reference to Preston, *Riches of Mercy,* pp. 269-326 which forms a discrete homiletical treatise within *Riches of Mercy,* entitled "A Pattern of wholesome Words."

50. Thomas Fuller, *The Church-History of Britain* (London: For John William, 1655), XI:131.

Preston's works to reconstruct aspects of his thought reflects this variation in authority. Whether or not the quasi-authorised status of *Riches of Mercy* is accepted, this study still gives the greatest weight to the authorised editions. If *Riches of Mercy* is regarded as authorised, quotations or citations from unauthorised editions constitute well below a third of the total number of references.[51] The unauthorised editions are far from being so unreliable that they can be safely ignored. Rather, they are a valuable *supplementary* resource. In addition to the predominantly sermonic as opposed to systematic nature of Preston's *opera*, a chief reason why Preston's writings have had to be examined at such length in this book lies in these problems with the posthumous primary sources. However, given the extensive influence that Preston exercised both in his life and afterwards through his printed works, it was decided that any limitations in the primary sources should not be allowed to delay any further the first thorough treatment of Preston's thinking on predestination and redemption.

Preston's Works

> "All that we teach you, from day to day, are but conclusions drawn
> from this Covenant."
>
> John Preston, *The New Covenant*, p. 345

Manuscripts and letters by John Preston

In the list below, an asterisk indicates that Preston's authorship of this particular manuscript is not entirely clear. See above, p. 20.

BL Add. MS. 4149, ff. 158r-62v.*
BL Add. MS. 4276, ff. 88r-89v.
BL Add. MS. 18201, ff. 20v-28r.*
BL Add. MS. 22473, ff. 74r-79r.*
BL Add. MS. 40629, ff. 117r-22r.*
BL Burney MS. 362, ff. 86r-95r.
BL Harleian MS. 6866, ff. 73-81.
Bod Tanner MS. 283, ff. 202r-202v.
Bod Tanner MS. 290, ff. 55r-57v.*
Bod Tanner MS. 299, ff. 44r-45v.*
Bod Tanner MS. 303, ff. 46-47.

51. Approximately 129 out of a total of approximately 442.

CUL MS. UA.V.C.Ct.I.9, f. 174r.

CUL MS. UA.V.C.Ct.III.24, f. 88.

CUL MS. UA.Comm.Ct.I.13, f. 15r.

ECL MS. 181.

ERO Barrington Papers, D/DBa/F5/1.

PRO SP 14/115/67.*

PRO SP 14/164/41.

PRO SP 14/165/71.

PRO SP 14/171/15.

PRO SP 84/105/38.

PRO PROB. 11/154, f. 102v.

"Letter CCCLI: Mr. John Preston to Dr. James Ussher." In *The whole Works of the most Rev. James Ussher, D.D., Lord Archbishop of Armagh, and Primate of all Ireland. With the life of the Author, and an Account of his Writings. By Charles Richard Erlington, D.D., Regius Professor of Divinity in the University of Dublin.* 1st ed., Dublin: Hodges and Smith, 1847-64, XVI:370-72.

"Letter CCCLII: Mr. John Preston to Dr. James Ussher." In *The whole Works of the most Rev. James Ussher, D.D., Lord Archbishop of Armagh, and Primate of all Ireland. With the life of the Author, and an Account of his Writings. By Charles Richard Erlington, D.D., Regius Professor of Divinity in the University of Dublin.* 1st ed., Dublin: Hodges and Smith, 1847-64, XVI:373.

The Published Works of John Preston in Chronological Order

Within each year, items are in alphabetical order according to generic title. It seems that Wing STC P3300 and P3301B are ghost entries and are therefore omitted. Also omitted are the funeral sermons by Preston published in the various editions of *Θρηνοικος* (see the bibliography below under Daniel Featley et al.). It is not stated which of these sermons are by Preston, and although the sermon entitled "Deliverance from the King of Feares" could well be Preston's funeral sermon for Joan Drake, this remains inconclusive (cf. George Lipscomb, *The History and Antiquities of the County of Buckingham* [London: J. & W. Robins, 1847], III:154; and above, p. 23). Furthermore, by 'published works' in this bibliography of Preston is meant only volumes in English or Latin. The various Dutch translations of Preston's sermons are beyond the scope of this bibliography, but some are listed in Cornelius W. Schoneveld, *Intertraffic of the Mind: Studies in Seventeenth-Century Anglo-Dutch Translation with a Checklist of Books Translated from English into Dutch, 1600-1700.* Leiden: E. J. Brill, 1983, pp. 227, 229. These include translations of *Saints daily Exercise (De daghelijcksche Oeffeninghe der Heylighen,*

Dort, 1639, 1656) and *The New Covenant* (*Het Nieuwe Verbondt*, Amsterdam, 1649, 1660).

1629

The New Covenant, or the Saints Portion. A Treatise unfolding the All-sufficiencie of God, Man's Uprightness, and the Covenant of Grace. Delivered in fourteene Sermons upon Genesis 17:1, 2. Whereunto are adjoyned foure Sermons upon Ecclesiastes 9:1, 2, 11, 12. Edited by Richard Sibbes & John Davenport. 1st ed., London: J. Dawson for Nicholas Bourne. [STC 20241]

The New Covenant, or the Saints Portion: A Treatise unfolding the All-sufficiencie of God, Mans Uprightnes, and the Covenant of Grace. Delivered in fourteene Sermons upon Genesis 17:1, 2. Whereunto are adjoyned four Sermons upon Ecclesiastes 9:1, 2, 11, 12. Edited by Richard Sibbes & John Davenport. [1629] 2nd Corrected ed., London: J. Dawson, G. Purslowe & W. Jones for Nicholas Bourne. [STC 20241.3]

The New Covenant, or the Saints Portion: A Treatise unfolding the All-sufficiencie of God, Mans Uprightnes, and the Covenant of Grace. Delivered in fourteen Sermons upon Genesis 17:1, 2. Whereunto are adjoyned four Sermons upon Ecclesiastes 9:1, 2, 11, 12. Edited by Richard Sibbes & John Davenport. [1629] 3rd ed., London: J. Dawson, G. Purslowe & W. Jones for Nicholas Bourne. [STC 20241.7]

The Saints daily Exercise. A Treatise concerning the whole Dutie of Prayer. Delivered in five Sermons, upon I Thessalonians 5:17. Edited by Richard Sibbes & John Davenport. 1st ed., London: W. Jones for Nicholas Bourne. [STC 20251]

The Saints daily Exercise. A Treatise concerning the whole Dutie of Prayer. Delivered in five Sermons, upon I Thessalonians 5:17. Edited by Richard Sibbes & John Davenport. [1629] 2nd Corrected ed., London: W. Jones for Nicholas Bourne. [STC 20252]

The Saints daily Exercise. A Treatise unfolding the whole Dutie of Prayer. Delivered in five Sermons, upon I Thessalonians 5:17. Edited by Richard Sibbes & John Davenport. [1629] 3rd corrected ed., London: W. Jones for Nicholas Bourne. [STC 20253]

1630

The Breast-plate of Faith and Love. A Treatise wherein the Ground and Exercise of Faith and Love, as they are set upon Christ their Object, and as they are expressed in good Workes, is explained. Delivered in 18 Sermons upon three severall Texts. Edited by Richard Sibbes & John Davenport. 1st ed., London: W. Jones & George Purslowe for Nicholas Bourne. [STC 20208]

The New Covenant, or the Saints Portion. A Treatise unfolding the All-sufficiencie of God, Man's Uprightness, and the Covenant of Grace. Delivered in fourteene Sermons upon Genesis 17:1, 2. Whereunto are adjoyned foure Sermons upon Ecclesias-

tes 9:1, 2, 11, 12. Edited by Richard Sibbes & John Davenport. [1629] 4th Corrected ed., London: J. Dawson, G. Purslowe & W. Jones for Nicholas Bourne. [STC 20242]

The New Covenant, or the Saints Portion. A Treatise unfolding the All-sufficiencie of God, Mans Uprightnes, and the Covenant of Grace. Delivered in fourteene Sermons upon Genesis 17:1, 2. Whereunto are adjoyned four Sermons upon Ecclesiastes 9:1, 2, 11, 12. Edited by Richard Sibbes & John Davenport. [1629] 5th ed., London: J. Dawson, G. Purslowe & W. Jones for Nicholas Bourne. [STC 20243]

The Saints daily Exercise. A Treatise concerning the whole Dutie of Prayer. Delivered in five Sermons, upon I Thessalonians 5:17. Edited by Richard Sibbes & John Davenport. [1629] 4th ed., London: W. Jones for Nicholas Bourne. [STC 20254]

A Sermon of spirituall Life and Death. Preached before the King at White-Hall, November, 1626. 1st ed., London: Thomas Cotes for Michael Sparke. [STC 20278]

A Sermon of spirituall Life and Death. Preached before the King, at White-Hall, November, 1626. [1630] Another ed., London: Thomas Cotes for Michael Sparke. [STC 20278.5]

Sermons preached before His Majestie, and upon other speciall Occasions: Viz. 1. The Pillar and Ground of Truth. 2. The New Life. 3. A sensible Demonstration of the Deity. 4. Exact Walking. 5. Samuels Support of sorrowfull Sinners. Edited by Thomas Goodwin & Thomas Ball. 1st ed., London: Eliot's Court Press and R. Young for Leonard Greene and James Boler. [STC 20270]

Sermons preached before His Majestie, and upon other speciall Occasions: Viz. 1. The Pillar and Ground of Truth in I Timothy 3:15. 2. The New Life, I John 5:12. 3. A sensible Demonstration of the Deity, Isaiah 64:4. 4. Exact Walking, Ephesians 5:15. 5. Samuels Support of sorrowful Sinners, in I Samuel 12:20, 21, 22. Edited by Thomas Goodwin & Thomas Ball. [1630] Another ed., London: Eliot's Court Press and R. Young for Leonard Greene and James Boler. [STC 20270.5]

1631

The Breast-plate of Faith and Love. A Treatise wherein the Ground and Exercise of Faith and Love, as they are set upon Christ their Object, and as they are expressed in good Workes, is explained. Delivered in 18 Sermons upon three severall Texts. Edited by Richard Sibbes & John Davenport. [1630] 2nd corrected ed., London: W. Jones & George Purslowe for Nicholas Bourne. [The title page incorrectly gives 1630 as the publication date.] [STC 20209]

The Breast-plate of Faith and Love. A Treatise wherein the Ground and Exercise of Faith and Love, as they are set upon Christ their Object, and as they are expressed in good Workes, is explained. Delivered in 18 Sermons upon three severall Texts. Edited by Richard Sibbes & John Davenport. [1630] Another 2nd Corrected ed., London: W. Jones & George Purslowe for Nicholas Bourne. [STC 20210]

The Law out lawed. Or, the Charter of the Gospell, shewing the Priviledge and Prerogative of the Saints by Vertue of the Covenant. Wherein these foure Points of Doc-

trine are properly observed, plainly proved, both by Scripture, and Reason: and pithily applyed. Viz. 1. That he that is in the State of Grace lyeth in no knowne Sinne, no Sinne hath Dominion over him. 2. That Sinne though it doth not raigne in the Saints, yet it doth remaine and dwell in them. 3. That the Way to overcome Sinne, is to get Assurance of the Love, and Grace, and Favour of God, whereby it is forgiven them. 4. That whosoever is under the Law, Sinne hath Dominion over him. 1st ed., Edinburgh: John Wreittoun. [STC 20229]

Life eternall or, a Treatise of the Knowledge of the divine Essence and Attributes. Delivered in 18 Sermons. Edited by Thomas Goodwin & Thomas Ball. 1st ed., London: R. Badger & W. Jones for Nicholas Bourne & Rapha Harford. [STC 20231]

Life eternall or, a Treatise of the Knowledge of the divine Essence and Attributes. Delivered in 18 Sermons. Edited by Thomas Goodwin & Thomas Ball. [1631] 2nd Corrected ed., London: R. Badger for Nicholas Bourne & Rapha Harford. [STC 20232]

The New Covenant, or the Saints Portion. A Treatise unfolding the All-sufficiencie of God, Mans Uprightnes, and the Covenant of Grace. Delivered in fourteen Sermons upon Genesis 17:1, 2. Whereunto are adjoyned foure Sermons upon Ecclesiastes 9:1, 2, 11, 12. Edited by Richard Sibbes & John Davenport. [1629] 6th ed., London: J. Dawson, G. Purslowe, and W. Jones for Nicholas Bourne. [STC 20244]

The Saints daily Exercise. A Treatise unfolding the whole Dutie of Prayer. Delivered in five Sermons, upon I Thessalonians 5:17. Edited by Richard Sibbes & John Davenport. [1629] 5th ed., London: R. Badger for Nicholas Bourne. [STC 20255]

The Saints daily Exercise. A Treatise unfolding the whole Dutie of Prayer. Delivered in five Sermons, upon I Thessalonians 5:17. Edited by Richard Sibbes & John Davenport. [1629] 6th ed., London: W. Jones for Nicholas Bourne. [STC 20256]

Sermons preached before His Majestie, and upon other speciall Occasions: Viz. 1. The Pillar and Ground of Truth in I Timothy 3:15. Page 1. 2. The New Life, I John 5:12. Page 27. 3. A sensible Demonstration of the Deity, Isaiah 64:4. Page 59. 4. Exact Walking, Ephesians 5:15. Page 91. 5. Samuels Support of sorrowful Sinners, in I Samuel 12:20, 21, 22. Page 125. Edited by Thomas Goodwin & Thomas Ball. [1630] Another ed., London: John Beale for James Boler and Joane Greene. [STC 20271]

Sermons preached before His Majestie, and upon other speciall Occasions: Viz. 1. The Pillar and Ground of Truth in I Timothy 3:15. Page 1. 2. The New Life, I John 5:12. Page 27. 3. A sensible Demonstration of the Deity, Isaiah 64:4. Page 59. 4. Exact Walking, Ephesians 5:15. Page 91. 5. Samuels Support of sorrowfull Sinners, in I Samuel 12:20, 21, 22. Page 125. Edited by Thomas Goodwin & Thomas Ball. [1630] Another ed., London: J. Beale for J. Boler and Joane Greene. [STC 20271a]

Sermons preached before His Majestie, and upon other speciall Occasions: Viz. 1. The Pillar and Ground of Truth, I Tim. 3:15. Page 1. 2. Spirituall Life and Death, I John 5:12. Page 1. 3. A sensible Demonstration of the Deitie, Isai. 64:4. Page 31. 4. Exact Walking, Ephes. 5:15. Page 62. 5. Samuels Support of sorrowfull Sinners, I Sam.

12:20, 21, 22. Page 95. [1630] Another ed., London: William Turner for Michael Sparke. [STC 20272]

Three Sermons upon the Sacrament of the Lords Supper. 1st ed., Oxford: W. Turner and H. Curteyn for Michael Sparke. [STC 20280.3]

Three Sermons upon the Sacrament of the Lords Supper. [1631] 2nd variant ed., Oxford: W. Turner & H. Curteyn for Michael Sparke. [STC 20280.5]

Three Sermons upon the Sacrament of the Lords Supper. [1631] Another 2nd variant ed., Oxford: For William Turner & Henry Curteyn, and Michael Sparke. [STC 20280.7]

Three Sermons upon the Sacrament of the Lords Supper. [1631] Another ed., London: Thomas Cotes for Michael Sparke. [STC 20281]

1632

The Breast-plate of Faith and Love. A Treatise wherein the Ground and Excercise of Faith and Love, as they are set upon Christ their Object, and as they are expressed in good Workes, is explained. Delivered in 18 Sermons upon three severall Texts. Edited by Richard Sibbes & John Davenport. [1630] 3rd ed., London: W. Jones & George Purslowe for Nicholas Bourne. [STC 20211]

The deformed Forme of a formall Profession. Or, the Description of a true and false Christian, either excusing, or accusing him, for his pious, or pretended Conversation. Shewing that there is a powerfull Godlynes necessary to Salvation and that many have but the Forme, but not the Power thereof. In handling whereof these three Things are plainely and powerfully explained and applied. What Godlynes is. What the Power of it. What the Reasons why some have but the Forme thereof. Together with the Meanes, and Marks, both how to attaine, and to try ourselves whether we have the Power thereof or not. 1st ed., Edinburgh: John Wreittoun. [STC 20215]

An elegant and lively Description of spirituall Life and Death. Delivered in divers Sermons in Lincolnes Inne, November the 9th MDCXXIII upon John 5:25. 1st ed., London: Thomas Cotes for Michaell Sparke. [STC 20221.5]

Life eternall. Or, a Treatise of the Knowledge of the divine Essence and Attributes. Delivered in 18 Sermons. Edited by Thomas Goodwin & Thomas Ball. [1631] 3rd Corrected ed., London: R. Badger for Nicholas Bourne and Rapha Harford. [STC 20233]

The Saints daily Exercise. A Treatise unfolding the whole Dutie of Prayer. Delivered in five Sermons, upon I Thessalonians 5:17. Edited by Richard Sibbes & John Davenport. [1629] 7th Corrected ed., London: Elizabeth Purslowe for Nicholas Bourne. [STC 20257]

Three godly and learned Treatises. Intituled, I. A Remedy against Covetousnesse. II. An elegant and lively Description of spirituall Death and Life. III. The Doctrine of Selfe-Deniall. Delivered in sundry Sermons. [1632] Another ed., London: B. Alsop and T. Fawcett for Michaell Sparke. [STC 20221.7]

1633

Foure godly and learned Treatises, intituled, I. A Remedy against Covetousnesse. II. An elegant Description of spirituall Death and Life. III. The Doctrine of Selfe-Deniall. IV. Upon the Sacrament of the Lords Supper. Delivered in sundry Sermons. [1632] 3rd ed., London: Thomas Cotes for Michael Sparke. [STC 20222]

The Law out lawed. Or, the Charter of the Gospell, shewing the Priviledge and Prerogative of the Saints by Vertue of the Covenant. Wherein these foure Points of Doctrine are properly observed, plainly proved, both by Scripture, and Reason: and pithily applied. Viz. 1. That he that is in the State of Grace lyeth in no knowne Sinne, no Sinne hath Dominion over him. 2. That Sinne though it doth not raigne in the Saints, yet it doth remaine and dwell in them. 3. That the Way to overcome Sinne, is to get Assurance of the Love, and Grace, and Favour of God, whereby it is forgiven them. 4. That whosoever is under the Law, Sinne hath Dominion over him. [1631] Another ed., Edinburgh: John Wreittoun. [STC 20230]

Life eternall. Or, a Treatise of the Knowledge of the divine Essence and Attributes. Delivered in 18 Sermons. Edited by Thomas Goodwin & Thomas Ball. [1631] 3rd Corrected [variant] ed., London: R. Badger for Nicholas Bourne and Rapha Harford. [STC 20233a]

A liveles Life: Or Mans spirituall Death in Sinne. Wherein is both learnedly and profitably handled these foure Doctrines, The Spirituall Death in Sinne. The Doctrine of Humiliation. Mercy to be found in Christ. Continuance in Sinne, dangerous. Being the substance of severall Sermons upon Ephesians 2:1-3. 'And you hath he quickened, who were dead in trespasses and sins, &c.' Whereunto is annexed a profitable Sermon at Lincolnes Inne, on Genesis 22:14. 1st ed., London: J. Beale for Andrew Crooke. [STC 20235]

A liveles Life: Or, Mans spirituall Death in Sinne. Wherein is both learnedly and profitably handled these foure Doctrines, The Spirituall Death in Sinne. The Doctrine of Humiliation. Mercy to be found in Christ. Continuance in Sinne, dangerous. Being the substance of severall Sermons upon Ephesians 2:1, 2, 3. 'And you hath he quickned, who were dead in trespasses and sins, &c.' Whereunto is annexed a profitable Sermon at Lincolnes Inne, on Genesis 22:14. [1633] 'Last' (2nd) ed., London: E. Purslow for Michael Sparke. [STC 20236]

The New Covenant, or the Saints Portion. A Treatise unfolding the All-sufficiencie of God, Mans Uprightness, and the Covenant of Grace. Delivered in fourteen Sermons upon Genesis 17:1, 2. Whereunto are adjoyned foure Sermons upon Ecclesiastes 9:1, 2, 11, 12. Edited by Richard Sibbes & John Davenport. [1629] 7th ed., London: J. Dawson for Nicholas Bourne. [STC 20245]

The Saints daily Exercise. A Treatise unfolding the whole Dutie of Prayer. Delivered in five Sermons, upon I Thessalonians 5:17. Edited by Richard Sibbes & John Davenport. [1629] 8th Corrected ed., London: Elizabeth Purslow for Nicholas Bourne. [STC 20258]

The Saints Qualification: Or a Treatise I. of Humiliation, in tenne Sermons. II. of Sancti-

fication, in nine Sermons: Whereunto is added a Treatise of Communion with Christ in the Sacrament, in three Sermons. Edited by Richard Sibbes & John Davenport. 1st ed., London: R. Badger for Nicholas Bourne. [STC 20262]

Sins Overthrow: Or, a godly and learned Treatise of Mortification. Wherein is excellently handled; first, the generall Doctrine of Mortification: and then particularly how to mortifie Fornication, Uncleannes, evill Concupiscence, inordinate Affection, and Covetousnes. All being the Substance of severall Sermons upon Colossians 3:5, 'Mortifie therefore your members' &c. 1st ed., London: J. Beale & A. Matthewes for Andrew Crooke. [STC 20275]

Sins Overthrow: Or, a godly and learned Treatise of Mortification. Wherein is excellently handled; first the generall Doctrine of Mortification: and then particularly, how to mortifie Fornication, Uncleannes, evill Concupiscence, inordinate Affection, and Covetousnes. All being the Substance of severall Sermons upon Colos. 3:5, 'Mortifie therefore your members, &c'. [1633] 2nd Corrected and enlarged ed., London: J. Beale for Andrew Crooke. [STC 20276]

1634

The Breast-Plate of Faith and Love. A Treatise, wherein the Ground and Exercise of Faith and Love, as they are set upon Christ their Object, and as they are expressed in good Works, is explained. Delivered in 18 Sermons upon three severall Texts. Edited by Richard Sibbes & John Davenport. [1630] 4th ed., London: R. Young for Nicholas Bourne. [STC 20212]

The deformed Forme of a formall Profession. Or the Description of a true and false Christian, either excusing, or accusing him, for his pious, or pretended Conversation. Shewing that there is a powerfull Godlynes necessary to Salvation and that many have the Forme, but not the Power thereof. In handling whereof these three Things are plainely and powerfully explained and applied. What Godlynes is. What the Power of it. What the Reasons why some have but the Forme thereof. Together with the Meanes, and Marks, both how to attaine, and to try ourselves whether we have the Power thereof or not. [1632] Another ed., Edinburgh: John Wreittoun. [STC 20216]

Life eternall or, a Treatise of the Knowledge of the divine Essence and Attributes. Delivered in 18 Sermons. Edited by Thomas Goodwin & Thomas Ball. [1631] 4th ed., London: E. Purslowe for Nicholas Bourne and Rapha Harford. [STC 20234]

The New Covenant, or the Saints Portion. A Treatise unfolding the All-sufficiencie of God, Mans Uprightnes, and the Covenant of Grace. Delivered in fourteen Sermons upon Genesis 17:1, 2. Whereunto are adjoyned foure Sermons upon Ecclesiastes 9:1, 2, 11, 12. Edited by Richard Sibbes & John Davenport. [1629] 8th Corrected ed., London: J. Dawson for Nicholas Bourne. [STC 20246]

Remaines of that Reverend and Learned Divine, John Preston, Dr in Divinity, Chaplaine in Ordinary to his Majesty, Master of Emanuel Colledge in Cambridge, and sometimes Preacher of Lincolnes-Inne. Containing three excellent Treatises, namely Ju-

das's Repentance. The Saints Spirituall Strength. Pauls Conversion. 1st ed., London: J. Beale for Andrew Crooke. [STC 20249]

The Saints daily Exercise. A Treatise unfolding the whole Duty of Prayer. Delivered in five Sermons, upon I Thessalonians 5:17. Edited by Richard Sibbes & John Davenport. [1629] Another 8th Corrected ed., London: Elizabeth Purslowe for Nicholas Bourne and W. Hope. [STC 20258.5]

The Saints daily Exercise. A Treatise unfolding the whole Duty of Prayer. Delivered in five Sermons, upon I Thessalonians 5:17. Edited by Richard Sibbes & John Davenport. [1629] 9th ed., London: Elizabeth Purslowe for Nicholas Bourne. [STC 20259]

The Saints Qualification: or a Treatise I. of Humiliation, in tenne Sermons. II. of Sanctification, in nine Sermons: whereunto is added a Treatise of Communion with Christ in the Sacrament, in three Sermons. [1633] 2nd Corrected ed., London: R. Badger for Nicolas Bourne. [STC 20263]

The Saints Qualification: or a Treatise I. of Humiliation, in tenne Sermons. II. of Sanctification, in nine Sermons: whereunto is added a Treatise of Communion with Christ in the Sacrament, in three Sermons. [1633] Variant 2nd ed., London: R. Badger for Nicolas Bourne. [STC 20264]

Sermons preached before His Majestie, and upon other speciall Occasions. Viz. 1. The Pillar and Ground of Truth in I Timothy 3:15. Page 1. 2. The New Life, I John 5:12. Page 27. 3. A sensible Demonstration of the Deity, Isaiah 64:4. Page 59. 4. Exact Walking, Ephesians 5:15. Page 91. 5. Samuels Support of sorrowful Sinners, in I Samuel 12:20, 21, 22. Page 125. Edited by Thomas Goodwin & Thomas Ball. [1630] 4th Corrected and amended ed., London: J. Beale for J. Boler and Joane Greene. [STC 20273]

1635

A liveles Life: Or Man's spirituall death in Sinne. Wherein is both learnedly and profitably handled these foure doctrines, The Spirituall Death in Sinne. The Doctrine of Humiliation. Mercy to be found in Christ. Continuance in sinne, dangerous. Being the substance of severall Sermons upon Ephesians 2:1-3. 'And you hath he quickened, who were dead in trespasses and sins.' Whereunto is annexed a profitable Sermon at Lincolnes-Inne, on Genesis 22:14. [1633] 3rd ed., London: J. Beale for Andrew Crooke and D. Frere. [STC 20237]

A Preparation to the Lords Supper. [1631] 4th ed., London: Thomas Cotes for Michael Sparke. [STC 20281a.3]

The Saints daily Exercise. A Treatise unfolding the whole Duty of Prayer. Delivered in five Sermons, upon I Thessalonians 5:17. Edited by Richard Sibbes & John Davenport. [1629] Another 9th ed., London: Elizabeth Purslowe for Nicholas Bourne. [STC 20260a]

Sinnes Overthrow: or, a godly and learned Treatise of Mortification: wherein is excellently handled; first the generall Doctrine of Mortification: and then particularly, how to mortifie Fornication, Uncleanesse, evill Concupiscence, inordinate Affec-tion, and Covetousnesse. All being the Substance of severall Sermons upon Colossians 3:5, 'Mortifie therefore your members'. [1633] 3rd Corrected and en-larged ed., London: Felix Kingston for Andrew Crooke and Daniell Frere. [STC 20277]

Two godly and learned Treatises upon Mortification and Humiliation. [1633] Reissue ed., London: For Andrew Cooke and Daniel Frere. [STC 20282]

1636

The Doctrine of the Saints Infirmities. Deliverd in sundry Sermons. Edited by Thomas Goodwin & Thomas Ball. 1st ed., London: N. and J. Okes for Henry Taunton. [STC 20219]

Foure godly and learned Treatises, intituled, I. A Remedy against Covetousnesse. II. An elegant Description of spirituall Death and Life. III. The Doctrine of Selfe-Deniall. IV. Upon the Sacrament of the Lords Supper. Delivered in sundry Sermons. [1632] 4th ed., London: A. Griffin for Michael Sparke. [STC 20223]

1637

The Breast-plate of Faith and Love. A Treatise wherein the Ground and Exercise of Faith and Love, as they are set upon Christ their Object, and as they are expressed in good Works, is explained. Delivered in 18 Sermons upon three severall Texts. Edited by Richard Sibbes & John Davenport. [1630] 5th ed., London: Robert Young for Nicholas Bourne. [The title page incorrectly gives 1634 as the publi-cation date.] [STC 20213]

The Doctrine of the Saints Infirmities. Delivered in severall Sermons. Edited by Thomas Goodwin & Thomas Ball. [1636] Another ed., London: Nicholas and John Okes for Henry Taunton. [STC 20220]

Remaines of that Reverend and Learned Divine, John Preston, Dr in Divinity, Chaplaine in Ordinary to his Majesty, Master of Emanuel Colledge in Cambridge, sometimes Preacher of Lincolnes-Inne. Containing three excellent Treatises, namely Judas's Repentance. The Saints Spirituall Strength. Pauls Conversion. [1634] 2nd ed., London: R. Badger and J. Legate for Andrew Crooke. [STC 20250]

The Saints Qualification: Or a Treatise I. Of Humiliation, in tenne Sermons. II. Of Sanc-tification, in nine Sermons. Whereunto is added a Treatise of Communion with Christ in the Sacrament, in three Sermons. [1633] 3rd ed., London: R. Badger for Nicolas Bourne and T. Nicholes. [STC 20265]

The Saints Qualification: or a Treatise I. Of Humiliation, in tenne Sermons. II. of Sancti-fication, in nine Sermons. Whereunto is added a Treatise of Communion with Christ in the Sacrament, in three Sermons. Edited by Richard Sibbes & John Davenport. [1633] 3rd Corrected ed., London: R. Badger for Nicolas Bourne and W. Hope. [STC 20265.5]

Sermons preached before His Majestie, and upon other speciall Occasions: Viz. 1. The Pil-lar and Ground of Truth in I Timothy 3:15. 2. The New Life, I John 5:12. 3. A sensi-ble Demonstration of the Deity, Isaiah 64:4. 4. Exact Walking, Ephesians 5:15. 5. Samuels Support of sorrowful Sinners, in I Samuel 12:20, 21, 22. Edited by Thomas Goodwin & Thomas Ball. [1630] 5th Corrected and amended ed., Lon-don: John Norton for Anne Boler. [STC 20274]

1638

The Doctrine of the Saints Infirmities. Delivered in severall Sermons. Edited by Thomas Goodwin & Thomas Ball. [1636] Another ed., London: John Okes for Henry Taunton. [STC 20221]

The Doctrine of the Saints Infirmities. Delivered in severall Sermons. Edited by Thomas Goodwin & Thomas Ball. [1636] Another ed., London: John Okes for Sarah Taunton. [STC 20221.1]

The Doctrine of the Saints Infirmities. Delivered in severall Sermons. Edited by Thomas Goodwin & Thomas Ball. [1636] Another ed., Amsterdam: Richt Right Press [i.e., John Canne] for T. L. [Sprunger, following Van Eeghen, suggests T. L. is Thomas Loof and identifies the printer as John Canne. Flowingburrow is Fluwelen Burgwal (Keith L. Sprunger, *Trumpets from the Tower: English Puritan Printing in the Netherlands 1600-1640* [Leiden: E. J. Brill, 1994], pp. 113, 221)] [STC 20221.3]

The golden Scepter held forth to the Humble. With the Churches Dignitie by her Mar-riage. And the Churches Dutie in her Carriage. In three Treatises. The first deliv-ered in sundry Sermons in Cambridge, for the weekely Fasts, 1625. The two later in Lincolnes Inne. Edited by Thomas Goodwin & Thomas Ball. 1st ed., London: R. Badger and E. Purslow for Nicholas Bourne, and A. Boler and R. Harford. [STC 20226]

The golden Scepter held forth to the Humble. With the Churches Dignitie by her Mar-riage and the Churches Dutie in her Carriage. In three Treatises. The former deliv-ered in sundry Sermons in Cambridge, for the weekely Fasts, 1625. The two latter in Lincolnes Inne. Edited by Thomas Goodwin & Thomas Ball. [1638] Another ed., London: R. Badger for Nicholas Bourne, and Rapha Harford and Francis Eglesfield. [The title page incorrectly gives 1639 as the publication date.] [STC 20227]

Mount Ebal, or a heavenly Treatise of divine Love. Shewing the Equity and the Necessity of his being accursed that loves not the Lord Jesus Christ. Together with the Mo-tives, the Meanes, the Markes of our Love towards him. 1st ed., London: M. Par-sons for John Stafford. [STC 20238]

A Preparation to the Lords Supper; preached in three Sermons. [1631] 5th ed., London: John Dawson for Michael Sparke. [STC 20281a.7]

The Saints Submission, and Sathan's Overthrow. Or, Sermons on James 4:7. 1st ed., Lon-don: J. Dawson for Peter Cole. [STC 20266]

1639

De Irresistibilitate Gratiæ convertentis. Thesis. Habita in Scholis Publicis Academiæ Cantabrigiensis . . . Ex ipsius Manuscripto. 1st ed., Rotterdam: Jacobus Moxon.

The Fulnesse of Christ for us. A Sermon preached at the Court before King James of blessed Memory. 1st ed., London: M. Parsons for John Stafford. [STC 20224]

Grace to the Humble. As Preparations to receive the Sacrament. London: Thomas Cotes for Michael Sparke. [STC 20228]

The New Covenant or the Saints Portion: A Treatise unfolding the All-sufficiencie of God, Mans Uprightnes and the Covenant of Grace, delivered in fourteen Sermons upon Genesis 17:1, 2. Whereunto are adjoyned foure Sermons upon Ecclesiastes 9:1, 2, 11, 12. Edited by Richard Sibbes & John Davenport. [1629] 9th Corrected ed., London: J. Dawson for Nicholas Bourne. [STC 20247]

The onely Love of the chiefest of ten Thousand: Or an heavenly Treatise of the divine Love of Christ. In five Sermons. [1638] 2nd ed., London: For John Stafford. [STC 20239.5]

1640

The Fulnesse of Christ for us. A Sermon preached at the Court before King James of blessed Memory. [1639] Another ed., London: J. Okes for John Stafford. [STC 20225]

A heavenly Treatise of the Divine Love of Christ. Shewing the Motives, the Meanes, the Markes, the Kindes thereof. Delivered in five Sermons. [1638] 3rd ed., London: Thomas Paine for John Stafford. [STC 20240.3]

The onely Love of the chiefest of ten Thousand: Or, an heavenly Treatise of the Divine Love of Christ. Shewing 1. The Motives. 2. The Meanes. 3. The Markes. 4. The Kinds, &c. of our Love towards him. Delivered in five Sermons. [1638] Another 2nd ed., London: For John Stafford. [STC 20240]

1641

The deformed Forme of a formall Profession. Or, the Description of a true and false Christian, either excusing, or accusing him, for his pious, or pretended Conversation. Shewing that there is a powerfull Godlinesse necessary to Salvation, and that many have the Forme, but not the Power thereof. In handling whereof, these three Things are plainely and powerfully explained and applyed. What Godlines is. What the Power of it is. What be the Reasons why some have but the Forme thereof. Together with the Meanes, and Marks, both how to attaine, and to try ourselves whether we have the Power thereof or not. [1632] 2nd ed., London: n.p. [Wing STC P3301C]

A liveles Life: Or Man's spirituall death in Sinne. Wherein is both learnedly and profitably handled these foure doctrines, The Spirituall Death in Sinne. The Doctrine of

Humiliation. Mercy to be found in Christ. Continuance in sinne, dangerous. Being the substance of severall Sermons upon Ephesians 2:1-3. 'And you hath he quickened, who were dead in trespasses and sins.' Whereunto is annexed a profitable Sermon at Lincolnes-Inne, on Genesis 22:14. [1633] 4th ed., London: G. M. for Andrew Crooke. [Wing STC P3302]

Sinnes Overthrow: or, a godly and learned Treatise of Mortification: wherein is excellently handled; first the generall Doctrine of Mortification: and then particularly, how to mortifie Fornication, Uncleannesse, evill Concupiscence, inordinate Affection, and Covetousnesse. All being the Substance of severall Sermons upon Colossians 3:5, 'Mortifie therefore your members &c'. [1633] 4th Corrected ed., London: Richard Badger for Andrew Crooke. [Wing STC P3307]

Two Treatises, viz. The Christian Freedome, and the Deformed Forme of a formall Profession. [1631, 1632] Reprint ed., London: J. N. for John Stafford. [Wing STC P3308]

1644

Sun-beams of Gospel-light, shining clearly from severall Texts of Scripture, opened and applyed. 1. A heavenly Treatise of the Divine Love of Christ. 2. The Christian Freedome. 3. The deformed Forme of a formall Profession. 4. Christs Fulnesse, and Mans Emptinesse. [1631, 1632, 1638, 1639] Reissue ed., London: For John Stafford. [Wing STC P3307A]

1645

Plenitudo Fontis, or Christ's Fulnesse and Man's Emptinesse. A Sermon preached by John Preston. [1639] New ed., London: For John Stafford. [Wing STC P3304A]

1648

An Abridgment of Dr Preston's Works, formerly published by Dr. Sibbs, Mr. Davenport (for Sermons preached at Lincolns Inn), Mr. Goodwin, Mr. Ball (for those at Cambridge) reduced into Order, and contracted thus for the Comfort and Benefit of meaner Christians, who cannot buy, or attend to read the great Volumes. By the industry of William Jemmat, M.A. and Preacher of the Word at Isleworth in Middlesex. As a cordial Friend of the Reverend Author. 1st ed., London: J. L. for Nicholas Bourne. [Wing STC P3298]

The mysticall Match between Christ and his Church . . . The leading Sermon to that Treatise of his called The Churches Marriage. Edited by T. S. 1st ed., London: For Francis Eaglesfield. [Wing STC P3303]

1651

The Breast-plate of Faith and Love. A Treatise wherein the Ground and Exercise of Faith and Love, as they are set upon Christ their Object, and as they are expressed in good Works, is explained. Delivered in 18 Sermons upon three severall Texts. Edited by Richard Sibbes & John Davenport. [1630] 6th ed., London: George Purslow. [Wing STC P3301A]

1652

"De Gratiæ Convertentis irresistibilitate. Thesis exmii tum Pietate, tum Eruditione theologi, D.D. Joannis Præstoni, Collegi Immanuelis in Academia Cantabrig. quondam Præfecti." In *The Lightless-Starre: Or, Mr. John Goodwin discovered a Pelagio-Socinian: and this by the Examination of his Preface to his Book entituled Redemption Redeemed: together with an Answer to his Letter entituled Confidence dismounted. . . . Hereunto is annexed a Thesis of that reverend, pious and judicious Divine, Doctor Preston, sometimes of Immanuel College in Cambridge, concerning the Irresistibility of converting Grace.* Edited by Richard Resbury. [1639] Reprint ed., London: John Wright. N6r-P1v. [Wing STC R1134]

1654

The Position of John Preston, Doctor in Divinity, sometimes Mr. of Emanuel Colledge in Cambridge, and Preacher at Lincolns-Inn; concerning the Irresistiblenesse of converting Grace. 1st English ed., London: J. G. for Nathanial Webb & William Grantham. [Wing STC P3305]

1655

The New Covenant, or the Saints Portion: A Treatise, unfolding the All-sufficiency of God. Man's Uprightnesse, and the Covenant of Grace. Delivered in fourteen Sermons upon Genesis 17:1, 2. Whereunto are adjoined four Sermons upon Ecclesiastes 9:1, 2, 11, 12. [1629] 10th Corrected ed., London: For Nicolas Bourne and William Hope. [Wing STC P3304]

1658

An Abridgment of Dr Preston's Works, formerly published by Dr Sibbs, Mr Davenport (for Sermons preached at Lincolns Inn), Mr Goodwin, Mr Ball (for those at Cambridge) reduced into Order, and contracted thus for the Comfort and Benefit of meaner Christians, who cannot buy, or attend to read the great Volumes. By the industry of William Jemmat, M.A. and Preacher of the Word at Isleworth in Middlesex. As a cordial Friend of the Reverend Author. [1648] 2nd expanded ed., London: J. F. for Nicholas Bourne. [Wing STC P3299]
Riches of Mercy to Men in Misery. Or, certain excellent Treatises concerning the Dignity and Duty of Gods Children. 1st ed., London: J. T. for John Alen. [Wing STC P3306]

Riches of Mercy to Men in Misery. Or, certain excellent Treatises concerning the Dignity and Duty of Gods Children. [1658] Another ed., London: J. T. for Francis Eglesfield. [Wing STC P3306A]

1751

"The Breast-plate of Faith and Love; or, the Ground and Exercise of Faith and Love, as set upon Christ their Object, and express'd in Good Works, explain'd. In three Parts." In *A Christian Library. Consisting of Extracts from and Abridgements of the choicest Pieces of practical Divinity, which have been publish'd in the English Tongue.* Edited by John Wesley. Abridged ed., Bristol, UK: Felix Farley, IX:221-319; X:3-45.

"The New Covenant: Or, the Saints Portion." In *A Christian Library. Consisting of Extracts from and Abridgements of the choicest Pieces of practical Divinity, which have been publish'd in the English Tongue.* Edited by John Wesley. Abridged ed., Bristol, UK: Felix Farley, X:47-97.

1819

"The Breast-plate of Faith and Love. Or, the Ground and Exercise of Faith and Love, as set upon Christ their Object, and expressed in Good Works, explained. In three Parts." In *A Christian Library: Consisting of Extracts from and Abridgements of the choicest Pieces of practical Divinity which have been published in the English Tongue.* Edited by John Wesley. [1751] Abridged ed., London: T. Cordeux for T. Blanshard, V:313-430.

"The New Covenant; or the Saints' Portion." In *A Christian Library: Consisting of Extracts from and Abridgements of the choicest Pieces of practical Divinity which have been published in the English Tongue.* Edited by John Wesley. [1751] Abridged ed., London, VI:3-45.

1832

The Saint's daily Exercise: A Treatise, unfolding the whole Duty of Prayer; in five Sermons upon 1 Thessalonians 5:17. [1629] Reprint ed., Xenia, Ohio: J. H. Purdy.

1836

The golden Sceptre held forth to the Humble. [1638] New ed., London: Religious Tract Society.

1968

"That God is." In *English Puritanism from John Hooper to John Milton.* Edited by Everett H. Emerson. 1st ed., Durham, NC: Duke University Press, pp. 242-50.

1971

"Of Faith." In *In God's Name: Examples of Preaching in England from the Act of Supremacy to the Act of Uniformity, 1534-1662.* Edited by John Chandos. 1st ed., London: Hutchinson & Co., pp. 291-97.

"Of Love." In *In God's Name: Examples of Preaching in England from the Act of Supremacy to the Act of Uniformity, 1534-1662.* Edited by John Chandos, London: Hutchinson & Co., pp. 297-301.

1976

"Natural Theology." In *Introduction to Puritan Theology: A Reader.* Edited by Edward Hindson. 1st ed., Grand Rapids, MI: Baker Book House, pp. 30-41.

The Saints daily Exercise. A Treatise concerning the whole Dutie of Prayer. Delivered in five Sermons, upon I Thessalonians 5:17. The English Experience: Its Record in Early Printed Books published in Facsimile. Vol. 824. [1629] Facsimile ed., Amsterdam: Theatrum Orbis Terrarum Ltd.

1979

The Breast-plate of Faith and Love. A Treatise wherein the Ground and Exercise of Faith and Love, as they are set upon Christ their Object, and as they are expressed in Good Works, is explained. Delivered in 18 Sermons upon three severall Texts. Edited by Richard Sibbes & John Davenport. [(1630) 1637] Facsimile ed., Edinburgh: Banner of Truth Trust.

1980

"Natural Theology." In *Introduction to Puritan Theology: A Reader.* Edited by Edward Hindson. A Canon Press Book. [1976] Reprint ed., Grand Rapids, MI: Baker Book House, pp. 30-41.

1990

The golden Sceptre held forth to the Humble: Six Sermons on II Chronicles 7:14. [1836] Reprint ed., Ligonier, PA: Soli Deo Gloria Publications.

1995

"The Saints' daily Exercise. A Treatise concerning the whole Duty of Prayer. Delivered in five Sermons, upon 1 Thessalonians 5:17." In *The Puritans on Prayer.* Edited by Don Kistler. [1629] New ed., Ligonier, PA: Soli Deo Gloria Publications., pp. 1-125.

Other Primary Sources

". . . the way to get that Grace that will save a man, is to give much attendance to reading and to learning."

Preston, *The New Covenant*, p. 433

Manuscripts

Bodleian Library, Oxford

Tanner 71.
Tanner 72.
Tanner 283.
Tanner 290.
Tanner 299.
Tanner 303.
Rawlinson C.573.
Rawlinson C.849.
Rawlinson 1349.

British Library, London

Additional 4149.
Additional 4276.
Additional 18201.
Additional 22473.
Additional 40629.
Burney 362.
Harleian 389.
Harleian 3142.
Harleian 6037.
Harleian 6866.
Harleian 7038.

Emmanuel College Library, Cambridge

Archive Col. 14.1.
MS. 44.
MS. 95a.
MS. 181.

Essex Record Office, Chelmsford

Barrington Papers, D/DBa/F5/1.

Northamptonshire Record Office, Northampton

MS. 53p/1.

Public Record Office, London

PROB. 11/154.
SP 14/115.
SP 14/148.
SP 14/164.
SP 14/165.
SP 14/170.
SP 14/171.
SP 16/140.
SP 16/141.
SP 16/142.
SP 16/158.
SP 16/182.
SP 16/185.
SP 16/188.
SP 16/190.
SP 16/205.
SP 16/231.
SP 16/456.
SP 16/530.
SP 84/105.

The University Library, Cambridge

UA.Comm.Ct.I.13.
UA.V.C.Ct.I.9.
UA.V.C.Ct.III.23.
UA.V.C.Ct.III.24.
MS. Mm.1.43.
MS. Mm.1.45.
MS. Mm.6.55.
Queens' College Archives, QCV.5.
Queens' College Archives, QCV.6.
Queens' College Archives, QCV.12.

Queens' College Archives, QCV.14.
Queens' College Archives, QCV.24.
Queens' College Archives, QCV.25.
Queens' College Archives, QCV.26.

The University Library, Sheffield

Hartlib Papers 28.
Hartlib Papers 29.
Hartlib Papers 48.

The Wren Library, Trinity College, Cambridge

MS. B/14/9.

Books

Acta Synodi Nationalis, in Nomine Domini nostri Jesu Christi, autoritate D.D. Ordinum generalium Fœderati Belgii Provinciarum Dordrechti habitæ anno 1618 et 1619. Accedunt plenissima, de quinque Articulis, theologorum judicia, Dordrecht: Isaac Joannid Canin, 1620.

Ames, William. *The Marrow of sacred Divinity, drawne out of the Holy Scriptures, and the Interpreters thereof, and brought into Method. . . . Translated out of the Latine, for the Benefit of such who are not acquainted with strange Tongues. Whereunto are annexed certaine Tables representing the Substance and Heads of all in a short View, directing to the Chapters where they are handled. As also a Table opening the hard Words therein contained. A Worke usefull for this Season. . . . Published by Order from the Honourable the House of Commons.* [(1627) 1642] Another English ed., London: Edward Griffin for Henry Overton, 1642.

————. *Medulla S.S. Theologiæ ex sacris Literis, earumque interpretibus, extracta, & methodicè disposita . . . In sine adjuncta est Disputatio de Fidei Divinæ Veritate.* 4th Corrected ed., London: Apud Robertum Allottum, 1630.

Aristotle. *Aristotle with an English Translation: The 'Art' of Rhetoric.* Edited by E. Capps, T. E. Page & W. H. D. Rouse. Translated by John Henry Freese. The Loeb Classical Library, London: William Heinemann, 1926.

Arminius, James. *Iacobi Arminii veteraquinatis Batavi, S. Theologiæ Doctoris eximii, Examen modestum Libelli, quem D. Gulielmus Perkinsius apprimé Doctus Theologus, edidit ante aliquot Annos De Praedestinationis Modo & Ordine, itemque De Amplitudine Gratiæ divinæ. Addita est propter Argumenti Convenientiam Analysis Cap. ix. ad Roman. Ante multos Annos ab eodem ipse D. Arminio delineata. Cum Indice Rerum contentarum,* Leiden: Godefridi Basson, 1612.

Bastingius, Jeremias. *An Exposition or Commentarie upon the Catechisme of Christian*

Religion, which is taught in the Schools and Churches both of the Low Countries, and of the Dominions of the Countie Palatine . . . Translated out of Latine into English. With three Tables. [(1588) 1589] Another ed., Cambridge: John Legat, 1595.

Baxter, Richard. *Aphorismes of Justification, with their Explication annexed. Wherein also is opened the Nature of the Covenants, Satisfaction, Righteousnesse, Faith, Works, &c. Published especially for the Use of the Church of Kederminster in Worcestershire by their unworthy Teacher.* [1649] Another ed., The Hague: Abraham Brown, 1655.

———. *An Apology for the Nonconformists Ministry: Containing I. the Reasons of their Preaching. II. An Answer to the Accusations urged as Reasons for the Silencing of about 2000, by Bishop Morley, Bishop Gunings Chaplain, Dr Saywell, Mr Durel, the nameless Ecclesiastical Politician and Debate-maker, the Counterminer, H. Fowlis, Dr Good, and many others. III. Reasons proving it the Duty and Interest of the Bishops and Conformists to endeavour earnestly their Restoration. With a Postscript upon oral Debates with Mr H. Dodwell, against his Reasons for their Silence. And a Scheme of Interests. Written in 1668, and 1669, for the most of it, and now published as an Addition to the Defence against Dr Stillingfleet, and as an Account to the Silencers of the Reasons of our Practice.* 1st ed., London: Thomas Parkhurst and D. Newman, 1681.

———. *Certain Disputations of Right to Sacraments and the true Nature of Visible Christianity: Defending them against several Sorts of Opponents, especially against the second Assault of that pious, reverend and dear Brother Mr Thomas Blake.* [1657] Another ed., London: William Du-Gard for Nevil Simmons, 1657.

———. *A Christian Directory: Or, a Summ of practical Theologie, and Cases of Conscience. Directing Christians, how to use their Knowledge and Faith; how to improve all Helps and Means, and to perform all Duties; how to overcome Temptations, and to escape or mortifie every Sin. In four Parts, I. Christian Ethicks (or private Duties.) II. Christian oeconomics (or Family Duties.) III. Christian Ecclesiasticks (or Church Duties.) IV. Christian Politicks (or Duties to our Rulers and Neighbours.).* 1st ed., London: Robert White, for Nevill Simmons, 1673.

———. *A Defence of the Principles of Love, which are necessary to the Unity and Concord of Christians; and are delivered in a Book called The Cure of Church-divisions. I. Inviting all sound and sober Christians, (by what name soever called) to receive each other to Communion in the same Churches. II. And where that (which is first desirable) cannot be attained, to bear with each other in their distinct Assemblies, and to manage them all in Christian Love. Written to detect and eradicate all love-killing, dividing, and church-destroying Principles, Passions and Practice, and to preserve the Weak in this Hour of manifold Temptation.* 1st ed., London: For Nevil Simmons, 1671.

———. *Five Disputations of Church-Government and Worship. I. Whether it be necessary or profitable to the right Order or Peace of the Churches of England, that we restore the extruded Episcopacy? Neg. II. Assert. Those who nullifie our present Ministry and Churches, which have not the prelatical Ordination, and teach the*

People to do the like, do incur the Guilt of grievous Sin. III. An Episcopacy desirable for the Reformation, Preservation and Peace of the Churches. IV. Whether a stinted Liturgie or Form of Worship be a desirable Means for the Peace of these Churches? V. Whether humane Ceremonies be necessary or profitable to the Church? 1st ed., London: R. W. for Nevil Simmons and by Thomas Johnson, 1659.

―――. *A Petition for Peace: With the Reformation of the Liturgy. As it was presented to the right reverend Bishops, by the Divines appointed by his Majesties Commission to treat with them about the Alteration of it.* 1st ed., London: n.p., 1661.

―――. *Plain Scripture Proof of Infants Church-membership and Baptism, being the Arguments prepared for (and partly managed in) the publike Dispute with Mr Tombes at Bewdley on the first Day of January, 1649. With a full Reply to what he then answered, and what is contained in his Sermon since preached, in his printed Books, his M.S. on 1 Cor. 7:14 which I saw, against Mr Marshal, against these Arguments. With a Reply to his valedictory Oration at Bewdley, and a corrective for his Antidote. By Richard Baxter a Minister of Christ for his Church at Kederminster. Constrained unavoidably hereto by Mr Tombes his Importunity; by frequent Letters, Messengers, in his Pulpit, and at last in Print, calling out for my Arguments, and charging the Denial upon my Conscience. Hereto is added an Appendix, against the Doctrine in the other Extream, contained in a Tractate of Mr. Th. Bedford's, adorned with the great Names and pretended Concent of famous learned Dr Davenant, and Dr Usher; and with an Epistle of Mr Cramfords, and a Tractate of Dr Wards (on which also some Animadversions are added).* 1st ed., London: For Robert White, 1651.

―――. *Reliquiae Baxterianae: Or, Mr Richard Baxter's Narrative of the most memorable Passages of his Life and Times. Faithfully published from his own original Manuscript.* Edited by Matthew Sylvester. London: For T. Parkhurst, J. Robinson, J. Lawrence and J. Dunton, 1696.

―――. *Richard Baxter's Apology against the modest Exceptions of Mr T. Blake. And the Digression of Mr G. Kendall. Whereunto is added Animadversions on a late Dissertation of Ludiomaeus Colvinus, alias, Ludovicus Molinaeus, M. Dr. Oxon. And an Admonition of Mr W. Eyre of Salisbury. With Mr Crandon's Anatomy for Satisfaction of Mr Caryl,* London: T. Underhill and Francis Tyton for Jos. Nevil and Jos. Barbar, 1654.

―――. *Richard Baxter's Catholick Theologie: Plain, pure, peaceable: For Pacification of the dogmatical Word-Warriours, who, 1. By contending about things unrevealed or not understood, 2. And by taking verbal differences for real, and their arbitrary Notions for necessary sacred Truths, deceived and deceiving by ambiguous unexplained Words, have long been the Shame of the Christian Religion, a Scandal and Hardning to Unbelievers, the Incendiaries, Dividers and Distracters of the Church, the Occasion of State Discords and Wars, the Corrupters of the Christian Faith, and the Subverters of their own Souls, and their Followers, calling them to a blind Zeal, and wrathful Warfare, against true Piety, Love and Peace, and teaching them to censure, backbite, slander, and prate against each other, for things which they never understood. In three Books. 1. Pacifying Principles, about Gods Decrees, Fore-Knowledge, Providence, Operations, Redemption, Grace, Mans Power, Free-Will, Justification, Merits, Certainty of Salvation, Perseverence, &c. II. A pacifying Praxis or Dialogue, about the Five Articles, Justification, &C. Proving that Men here contend almost only about ambiguous Words, and unrevealed things. III. Pacifying Disputations against some real Errors which hinder Reconciliation, viz. About physical Predetermination, original Sin, the extent of Redemption, sufficient Grace, Imputation of Righteousness, &c. Written chiefly for Posterity, when sad Experience hath taught Men to hate theological logical Wars, and to love, and seek, and call for Peace. (Ex Bello Pax.).* 1st ed., London: Robert White for Nevill Simmons, 1675.

————. *The Saints Everlasting Rest: Or, a Treatise of the blessed State of the Saints in their enjoyment of God in Glory. Wherein is showed its Excellency and Certainty, the Misery of those that lose it, the Way to attain it, and Assurance of it; and how to live in the continual delightful Foretasts of it, by the Help of Meditation. Written by the Author for his own Use, in the Time of his Languishing, when God took him off from all publike Imployment; and afterwards preached in his weekly Lecture.* 1st ed., London: Robert White for Thomas Underhill & Francis Tyton, 1650.

————. *A second true Defence of the meer Nonconformists, against the untrue Accusations, Reasonings and History of Dr Edward Stillingfleet, Dean of St Pauls, &c. Clearly proving that it is (not sin but) duty 1. Not wilfully to commit the many sins of Conformity. 2. Not sacriligiously to forsake the Preaching of the Gospel. 3. Not to cease publick worshipping of God. 4. To use needful pastoral Helps for Salvation, though Men forbid it, and call it Schism. Written by Richard Baxter, not to accuse others, but to defend Gods Truth, and the true Way of Peace after near 20 years loud Accusations of the Silencing, prosecuting Clergy and their Sons. With some Notes on Mr Joseph Glanviles zealous and impartial Protestant, and Dr L. Moulins Character.* 1st ed., London: For Nevil Simons, 1681.

————. *A Sermon of Judgement, preached at Pauls before the Honorable Lord Maior and Aldermen of the City of London, Dec. 17 1654. And now enlarged.* 1st ed., London: R. W. for Nevil Simmons, 1655.

————. *A Treatise of justifying Righteousness, in two Books: 1. A Treatise of imputed Righteousness, opening and defending the true Sense, and confuting the false, with many of Dr Tullies Reasonings against Truth, Peace and Me: With an Answer to Dr Tullies Letter adjoyned. II. A friendly Debate with the learned and worthy Mr Christopher Cartwright, containing: 1. His Animadversions on my Aphorisms, with my Answer. 2. His Exceptions against that Answer. 3. My Reply to the Summe of the Controversies agitated in those Exceptions. All published instead of a fuller Answer to the Assaults in Dr Tullies Justificatio Paulina, for the Quieting of censorious and dividing Contenders, who raise odious Reports of their Brethren as Pop-*

ish, &c. who do but attempt reconcilingly to open this Doctrine more clearly than themselves. 1st ed., London: For Nevil Simons and Jonathan Robinson, 1676.

—————. *Universal Redemption of Mankind, by the Lord Jesus Christ: Stated and cleared by the late learned Mr Richard Baxter. Whereunto is added a short Account of special Redemption, by the same Author.* 1st ed., London: For John Salusbury, 1694.

Baynes, Paul. *The Diocesans Tryall. Wherein all the Sinnewes of Doctor Downhams Defence are brought into three Heads, and orderly dissolved. By M. Paul Baynes. Published by Dr. William Amis. The Questions discussed in this Diocesans Tryall are these: 1. Whether Christ did institute, or the Apostles frame any diocesan Forme of Churches, or parishionall onely, pag. 1. 2. Whether Christ ordained by himselfe, or by his Apostles, any ordinary Pastours, as our Bishops, having both Precedency of Order, and Majority of Power over others, pag. 24. 3. Whether Christ did immediately commit ordinary Power ecclesiasticall, and the Exercise of it, to any one singular Person, or to an united Multitude of Presbyters, pag. 78.* [1618] Reprint ed., [London]: n.p., 1621 [i.e., 1644].

Bernard, Nicholas. *Clavi Trabales; Or, Nailes fastned by some great Masters of Assemblyes confirming the Kings Supremacy. The Subjects Duty. Church Government by Bishops. The particulars of which are as followeth. I. Two Speeches of the late Lord Primate Ushers. The one of the Kings Supremacy. The other of the Duty of Subjects to supply the Kings Necessities. II. His Judgement and Practice in Point of Loyalty, Episcopacy, Liturgy, and Constitutions of the Church of England. III. Mr Hookers Judgment of the Kings Power in Matters of Religion, Advancement of Bishops &c. IV. Bishop Andrews of Church Government &c both confirmed and enlarged by the said Primate. V. A Letter of Dr Hadrianus Saravia of the like Subjects. Unto which is added a Sermon of regal Power, and the Novelty of the Doctrine of Resistance. Also a Preface by the right reverend Father in God, the Lord Bishop of Lincoln.* 1st ed., London: R. Hodgkinson for R. Marriot, 1661.

Beza, Theodore. *Ad Acta Colloquii Montisbelgardensis Tubingæ edita Theodori Bezæ Responsionis.* 3rd ed., Geneva: Joannes le Preux, 1589.

—————. *A briefe and pithie Summe of the Christian Faith made in forme of a Confession, with a Confutation of all suche superstitious Errours, as are contrary thereunto, made by Theodore de Beza. Translated out of French.* Translated by R. Filles. 1st English ed., London: Rouland Hall, 1563.

Beza, Theodore & Thomas Wilcox. *Two very learned Sermons of M. Beza, togither with a short Sum of the Sacrament of the Lordes Supper: Whereunto is added a Treatise of the Substance of the Lords Supper, wherin is breflie and soundlie discueed the principall Points in Controversie, concerning that Question, by T.W.* Translated by Thomas Wilcox. 1st ed., London: Robert Waldegrave for T. Man and T. Gubbins, 1588.

The Bible: that is, the Holy Scriptures contained in the Olde and Newe Testament: Translated according to to the Ebrew and Greeke, and conferred with the best Translations in divers Languages. [1560] Reprint ed., London: Robert Barker, 1610.

Birch, Thomas, ed. *The Court and Times of Charles the First. Illustrated by authentic and confidential Letters, from various public and private Collections; including Memoirs of the Mission in England of the Capuchin Friars in the Service of Queen Henrietta Maria. By Father Cyprien de Gamache, Capuchin Preacher and Missionary to the Queen. Edited, with an Introduction and Notes, by the Author of 'Memoirs of Sophia Dorothea, Consort of George I,' 'The Court and Time of James I'*. 1st ed., London: Henry Colburn, 1848. 2 vols.

———, ed. *The Court and Times of James the First; containing a Series of historical and confidential Letters, in which will be found a Detail of the public Transactions and Events in Great Britain during that Period, with a Variety of Particulars not mentioned by our Historians. Transcribed from the Originals in the British Museum, State Paper Office, and private Collections*. 2nd ed., London: Henry Colburn, 1849. 2 vols.

Bridges, John. *A Defence of the Government established in the Church of Englande for ecclesiasticall Matters. Contayning an Answere unto a Treatise called, The learned Discourse of Eccl. Government, otherwise intituled, A briefe and plaine Declaration concerning the Desires of all the faithfull Ministers that have, and do seeke for the Discipline and Reformation of the Church of Englande. Comprehending likewise an Answere to the arguments in a Treatise named The Judgement of a most reverend and learned Man from beyond the Seas, &c. Aunswering also to the Argumentes of Calvine, Beza, and Danæus, with other our Reverend learned Brethren, besides Cænalis and Rodinus, both for the Regiment of Women, and in defence of her Majestie, and of all other Christian Princes supreme Government in ecclesiasticall Causes, against the Tetrarchie that our Brethren would erect in every particular congregation, of Doctors, Pastors, Governors and Deacons, with their severall and joynt authoritie in Elections, Excommunications, Synodall Constitutions and other ecclesiasticall Matters*. 1st ed., London: John Windet for Thomas Chard, 1587.

———. *A Sermon, preached at Paules Crosse on the Monday in Whitson Weeke Anno Domini. 1571*. 1st ed., London: Henry Binneman for Humfrey Toy, 1571.

Burton, Henry. *The Baiting of the Popes Bull. Or, an Unmasking of the Mystery of Iniquity, folded up in a most pernitious Breeve or Bull, sent from the Pope lately into England, to cawse a Rent therein, for his Reentry. With an Advertisement to the Kings seduced Subjects*. 1st ed., London: W. Jones for M. Sparke, 1627.

———. *A Plea to an Appeale: Traversed Dialogue wise*. 1st ed., London: W. I., 1626.

Calvin, John. *Institutes of the Christian Religion*. Edited by John T. McNeill. Translated by Ford Lewis Battles. Library of Christian Classics. Vol. 20 & 21. [1559] New ed., Philadelphia, PA: Westminster Press, 1960. 2 vols.

Capel, Richard. *Capel's Remains. Being an useful Appendix to his excellent Treatise of Tentations. Concerning the Holy Scriptures. Left written by his own Hand*, London: T. R. for John Bartlet, 1658.

Carleton, George. *An Examination of those Things wherein the Author of the late Appeale holdeth the Doctrines of the Pelagians and Arminians, to be the Doctrines of the Church of England. Whereunto also there is annexed a joynt Attestation avowing that the Discipline of the Church of England was not impeached by the Synod of Dort.* 2nd Revised and enlarged ed., London: For William Turner, 1626.

Carleton, George, John Davenant, Samuel Ward, Thomas Goad & Walter Balcanqual. *Suffragium Collegiale Theologorum Magnae Britanniae de quinque Controversis Remonstrantium Articulis, Synodo Dordrechtanae exhibitum Anno M.DC.XIX. Judicio Synodico praevium,* London: R. Young for R. Milbourne, 1626.

―――. "The British Divines at Dort, March 11. 1618. To the Arch-Bishop of Canterbury. Reasons of enlarging Grace beyond Election." In *Golden Remains of the ever memorable Mr. John Hales of Eton Colledge &c. With additions from the Authours own Copy, viz. Sermons and Miscellanies. Also Letters and Expresses concerning the Synod of Dort, (not before Printed), from an authentic Hand.* Edited by John Hales. [London: For T. Garthwait, 1659] 2nd ed., London: Thomas Newcomb for Robert Pawlet, 1673, II:184-86.

―――. "A joynt Attestation avowing that the Discipline of the Church of England was not impeached by the Synode of Dort." In *An Examination of those Things wherein the Author of the late Appeale holdeth the Doctrines of the Pelagians and Arminians, to be the Doctrines of the Church of England. Whereunto also there is annexed a joynt Attestation avowing that the Discipline of the Church of England was not impeached by the Synod of Dort.* Edited by George Carleton. [1626] 2nd Revised and enlarged ed., London: M. Flesher for R. Mylbourne, 1626, II:1-26.

Company of Stationers. *A Transcript of the Registers of the worshipful Company of Stationers: From 1640-1708 A.D.,* London: Private publication, 1913. 3 vols.

Cosin, John. *The Correspondence of John Cosin, D.D. Lord Bishop of Durham: Together with other Papers illustrative of his Life and Times.* Edited by George Ornsby. The Publications of the Surtees Society, established in the Year 1834. Vol. 52 & 55. 1st ed., Durham, UK: Andrews & Co., 1869-72. 2 vols.

―――. *The Works of the Right Reverend Father in God, John Cosin, Lord Bishop of Durham. Now first Collected.* Library of Anglo-Catholic Theology. Oxford: John Henry Parker, 1843-55. 5 vols.

Culverwell, Ezekiel. *A Treatise of Faith: Wherein is declared, how a Man may live by Faith, and finde Releefe in all his Necessities. Applyed especially unto the Use of the weakest Christians.* 1st ed., London: I. L. for William Sheffard, 1623.

Daillé, John. *Apologia pro duabus Ecclesiarum in Gallia Protestantium Synodis Nationalibus; altera alensone, anno 1637: altera verò Carentone, anno 1645 habitis: Adversus Friderici Spanhemii Exercitationes de Gratia universali,* Amsterdam: Joannis Ravesteynii, 1655.

Davenant, John. *Animadversions written by the Right Reverend Father in God John, Lord Bishop of Salisbury, upon a Treatise intitled Gods love to Mankind.* [1641] Another ed., Cambridge: Roger Daniel, 1641.

―――. *Baptismal Regeneration and the final Perseverance of the Saints: A Letter of the Right Rev. John Davenant, D.D., Late Bishop of Salisbury, to Dr. Samuel Ward, Lady Margaret's Professor at Cambridge in the Reign of King James. Translated from the Latin.* Translated by Josiah Allport. 1st English ed., London: William Macintosh, 1864.

————. *Determinationes Quæstionum quarundam Theologicarum . . . publicè Disputatarum.* 1st ed., Cambridge: Thomas & John Buck and Roger Daniel, 1634.

————. "The Determinationes, Or Resolutions of certain theological Questions, publicly discussed in the University of Cambridge." In *A Treatise on Justification, or the Disputatio de Justitia habituali at actuali . . . translated from the original Latin, together with Translations of the Determinationes.* Edited by Josiah Allport. Translated by Josiah Allport. [1634] 1st English ed., London: Hamilton, Adams, & Co., 1846, II:199-539.

————. *Dissertatio de Morte Christi . . . Quibus subnectitur ejusdem D. Davenantii Sententia de Gallicana Controversia: sc. de Gratiosa & Salutari Dei erga Homines peccatores voluntate.* [1650] 2nd ed., Cambridge: Roger Daniel, 1683.

————. "A Dissertation on the Death of Christ, as to its Extent and special Benefits: containing a short History of Pelagianism, and shewing the Agreement of the Doctrines of the Church of England on general Redemption, Election, and Predestination, with the Primitive Fathers of the Christian Church, and above all, with the Holy Scriptures." In *An Exposition of the Epistle of St Paul to the Colossians.* Translated by Josiah Allport. [1650] 1st English ed., London: Hamilton, Adams, and Co., 1832, II:309-569.

————. *Dissertationes duæ: Prima de Morte Christi, quatenus ad omnes extendatur, quatenus ad solos Electos restringatur. Altera de Prædestinatione & Reprobatione. . . . Quibus subnectitur ejusdem D. Davenantii Sententia de Gallicana Controversia: sc. de Gratiosa & Salutari Dei erga Homines Peccatores voluntate.* Edited by Thomas Bedford. 1st ed., Cambridge: Roger Daniel, 1650.

————. "Doctour Davenant touching the Second Article, discussed at the Conference at the Haghe, of the Extent of Redemption." In *Golden Remains of the ever memorable Mr. John Hales of Eton Colledge &c. With Additions from the Authours own Copy, viz. Sermons and Miscellanies. Also Letters and Expresses concerning the Synod of Dort, (not before Printed), from an authentic Hand.* Edited by John Hales. [London: For T. Garthwait, 1659] 2nd ed., London: Thomas Newcomb for Robert Pawlet, 1673, II:186-90.

————. *One of the Sermons preached at Westminster: The fifth of Aprill (being the Day of the Publike Fast;) before the right honourable Lords of the High Court of Parliament, and set forth by their Appointment.* [1628] Variant ed., London: Richard Badger, 1628.

————. *A Treatise on Justification, or the Disputatio de Justitia habituali at actuali . . . translated from the original Latin, together with Translations of the Determinationes.* Translated by Josiah Allport. [1631, (1634) 1639] 1st English ed., London: Hamilton, Adams, & Co., 1844-46. 2 vols.

Dodsworth, William. *General Redemption, and limited Salvation. To which is added, a*

Reprint of Archbishop Usher's Treatise on the true Intent and Extent of Christ's Death and Satisfaction on the Cross, London: James Nisbet, 1831.

Dove, John. *An Advertisement to the English Seminaries, amd [sic] Jesuites: Shewing their loose kind of Writing.* 1st ed., London: N. Okes for S. Waterson, 1610.

———. *A Defence of Church Government. Dedicated to the high Court of Parliament. Wherein is proved that subjects ought to conforme themselves to the state ecclesiasticall. Together with a Defence of the Crosse in Baptisme.* 1st ed., London: T. Creede for H. Rockit and by J. Hodgets, 1606.

———. *Of Divorcement. A Sermon preached at Pauls Crosse the 10. of May 1601.* 1st ed., London: T. Creede, 1610.

———. *A Sermon preached at Paules Crosse, the Sixt of February, 1596. In which are discussed these three Conclusions. 1. It is not the Will of God that all Men should be saved. 2. The absolute Will of God, and his secret Decree from all Eternitie, is the Cause why some are predestinated to Salvation, others to Destruction, and not any Foresight of Faith, or good Workes in the one, or Infidelitie, Neglect, or Contempt in the other. 3. Christ died not effectually for all.* 1st ed., London: T. Creede for R. Dexter, 1597.

Featley, Daniel. *Pelagius redivivus. Or, Pelagius raked out of the Ashes by Arminius and his Schollers.* 1st ed., London: For Robert Milbourne, 1626.

———. *A Second Parallel together with a Writ of Error sued against the Appealer.* 1st ed., London: J. Haviland for Robert Milbourne, 1626.

Featley, Daniel et al. Θρηνοικος *The House of Mourning: furnished with Directions for, Preparations to, Meditations of, Consolations at, the Houre of Death. Delivered in 47 Sermons, preached at the Funerals of divers faithfull Servants of Christ. By Daniel Featley, Martin Day, Richard Sibbs, Thomas Taylor, Doctors in Divinitie. And other Reverend Divines.* Edited by H.W. 1st ed., London: John Dawson for Ralph Mabbe and Philip Nevill, 1640 (1639).

———. Θρηνοικος *The House of Mourning: furnished with Directions for, Preparations to, Meditations of, Consolations at, the Houre of Death. Delivered in 47 Sermons, preached at the Funerals of divers faithfull Servants of Christ. By Daniel Featly, Martin Day, Richard Sibbs, Thomas Taylor, Doctors in Divinitie. And other Reverend Divines.* Edited by H.W. Another first ed., London: John Dawson for Ralph Mabbe and J. Bellamie & R. Smith, 1640.

———. Θρηνοικος *The House of Mourning: furnished with Directions for, Preparations to, Meditations of, Consolations at, the Hour of Death. Delivered in 53 Sermons, preached at the Funerals of divers faithfull Servants of Christ. By Daniel Featley, Martin Day, John Preston, Ri. Houldsworth, Richard Sibbs, Thomas Taylor, Doctors in Divinity. Thomas Fuller. And other Reverend Divines.* Edited by H.W. [1640] 2nd newly corrected and ammended ed., London: G. Dawson for John Williams, 1660.

———. Θρηνοικος *The House of Mourning, furnished with Directions for, Preparations to, Meditations of, Consolations at, the Hour of Death: delivered in 56 Sermons, preached at the Funerals of divers faithful Servants of Christ. By Daniel Featly,*

Martin Day, John Preston, Thomas Taylor, Ri. Houldsworth, Richard Sibs, John Pearson, Christ. Shute, Thomas Fuller, Edm. Barker, Josias Alsop, Doctors in Divinity. And other Reverend Divines. Edited by H. W. [1640] 3rd Newly corrected and amended ed., London: For John Williams, 1672.

Fenner, William. *The Works of the learned and faithful Minister of Gods Word, Mr William Fenner, sometime Fellow of Pembroke-Hall in Cambridg, and Rector of Rochford in Essex, in four Treatises, viz. 1. Wilfull Impenetency, 2. Of Conscience, 3. Of the Affections, 4. Christs Alarm to drowsie Saints. Finished by himself and published by his Over-seers. To which is annexed his Catechism on the Creed, Lord's Prayer, and X. Commandments.* 1st ed., London: T. Maxey for John Rothwell, 1651.

Fisher, Edward. *The Marrow of Modern Divinity: in two Parts. Part I. The Covenant of Works and the Covenant of Grace. Part II. An Exposition of the Ten Commandments.* Edited by Thomas Boston. [1645] New reprint ed., Philadelphia, PA: Presbyterian Board of Publication, 1910.

Gardiner, Samuel R., ed. *The Constitutional Documents of the Puritan Revolution, 1625-1660.* [(1889) 1906] 3rd ed., Oxford: Clarendon Press, 1962.

Goodwin, Thomas. *The Works of Thomas Goodwin D.D.* Edited by John C. Miller. Nichol's Series of standard Divines: Puritan Period. Edinburgh: James Nichol, 1861-67. 12 vols.

Gouge, William. *A learned and very useful Commentary on the Whole Epistle to the Hebrews. Wherein every Word and Particle in the Originall is explained, and the Emphasis thereof fully shewed. The Sense and Meaning of every Verse clearly unfolded. Each Chapter and Verse logically, and exactly Analysed. Genuine Doctrines naturally raised, and applied from the severall Words, and Particles in the whole Epistle. The manifold Types of Christ clearly, and largely unveiled. Divers Cases of Conscience satisfactorily resolved. Severall Controversies pithily discussed. Various Common-places thoroughly handled. Sundry Errors and Heresies substantially confuted. Very many dark and obscure Places of Scripture, which occasionally occur, perspicuously opened. Being the Substance of thirty Years Wednesdayes Lectures at Black-fryers London . . . Before which is prefixed a Narrative of his Life and Death. Whereunto is added two alphabeticall Tables. I. Of the particular Points contained in the whole Commentary. II. Of the severall Greek Words in this Epistle, which are clearly and fully explained.* 1st ed., London: A. M. T. W. and S. G. for Joshua Kirton, 1655.

Hales, John. *Golden Remains of the ever memorable Mr. John Hales of Eton Colledge &c. With Additions from the Authours own Copy, viz. Sermons and Miscellanies. Also Letters and Expresses concerning the Synod of Dort, (not before Printed,) from an authentic Hand.* [London: For T. Garthwait, 1659] 2nd ed., London: Thomas Newcomb for Robert Pawlet, 1673.

Hall, Peter, ed. *The Harmony of Protestant Confessions: Exhibiting the Faith of the Churches of Christ, Reformed after the pure and holy Doctrine of the Gospel, throughout Europe. Translated from the Latin.* Revised and enlarged ed., London: John F. Shaw, 1842.

Hammond, Henry. *Nineteen Letters of the truly reverend and learned Henry Hammond, D.D. (Author of the Annotations on the New Testament, &c.) written to Mr. Peter Staninough and Dr. Nathanael Ingelo: Many of them on very curious Subjects. Now first published from the Originals communicated by the very Reverend Mr. Robert Marsden, B.D. Archdeacon of Nottingham, and the late pious Mr. John Worthington, M.A. and illustrated with Notes by Francis Peck, M.A.* Edited by Francis Peck. 1st ed., London: For T. Cooper, 1739.

Harsnett, Samuel. "A Sermon preached at S. Pauls Cross in London, the 27. Day of October, Anno Reginæ Elizabethæ 26. by Samuel Harsnet then Fellow of Pembroke Hall in Cambridge, but afterwards Lord Arch-Bishop of Yorke." In *Three Sermons preached by the reverend, and learned, Dr. Richard Stuart, Dean of St. Pauls, afterwards Dean of Westminster, and Clerk of the Closset to the late King Charles. To which is added, a fourth Sermon, preached by the right reverend Father in God, Samuel Harsnett, Lord Arch-Bishop of Yorke.* Edited by Richard Steward. 1st ed., London: For Gabriel Bedel and Thomas Heath, 1656, pp. 121-65.

Heartwell, Jasper. *The Firebrand taken out of the Fire. Or, The Wonderful History, Case, and Cure of Mrs Drake, sometimes the wife of Francis Drake of Esher in the County of Surrey Esq. Who was under the Power and severe Discipline of Satan for the Space of ten Yeares; and was redeemed from his Tyranny in a wonderfull Manner a little before her Death, by the great mercy of God; and (instrumentally) by the extraordinary Paines, Prayers and Fasting, of foure Reverend Divines, whose Names are here subscribed, viz. B. Usher, M. Hooker, D. Preston, M. Dod.* [1647] Reprint ed., London: For Thomas Mathewes, 1654.

———. *Trodden down Strength by the God of Strength, or, Mrs Drake revived. Showing her strange and rare Case, great and many uncouth Afflictions, for tenne Years together. Together with the strange and wonderfull manner how the Lord revealed himselfe unto her, a few dayes before her Death. Related by her sometime unworthy Friend Hart On-hi.* 1st ed., London: R. Bishop for Stephen Pilkington, 1647.

Heigham, John. *The Gagge of the Reformed Gospell. Briefly discovering the Errors of our Time. With the Refutation by expresse Textes of their owne approved English Bible.* [1623] 2nd Augmented ed., St Omer: Charles Boscard, 1623.

Heywood, James & Thomas Wright. *Cambridge University Transactions during the Puritan Controversies of the 16th and 17th Centuries.* London: Henry G. Bohn, 1854. 2 vols.

Hildersham, Arthur. *CVIII Lectures upon the fourth of John. Preached at Ashby-Delazouch in Leicestershire.* [1629] 2nd corrected and enlarged ed., London: George Miller for Edward Brewster, 1632.

———. *Lectures upon the fourth of John. Preached at Ashby-Delazouch in Leicestershire.* 1st ed., London: George Miller for Edward Brewster, 1629.

Howes, John. *Real Comforts, extracted from moral and spiritual Principles. Presented in a Sermon, preached at the Funeral of that reverend Divine Mr Thomas Ball late*

Minister of Gods Word at Northampton, upon the 21 Day of June, A.D. 1659. With a Narrative of his Life and Death. 1st ed., London: S. Griffin for R. Royston, 1660.

Keeble, N. H. & Geoffrey F. Nuttall, eds., *Calendar of the Correspondence of Richard Baxter.* 1st ed., Oxford: Clarendon Press, 1991. 2 vols.

Kendall, George. *Sancti Sanciti. Or, The common Doctrine of the Perseverance of the Saints: as who are kept by the Power of God, through Faith unto Salvation. Vindicated from the Attempts lately made against it, by Master John Goodwin in the Digression of his Book, which he was pleased to entitle Redemption Redeemed. Together with two Digressions: The one maintaining special Difference between the Graces of the Saints; and whatsoever is found in Men unregenerate. The other, asserting God to be the sole Authour, of whatever difference of the Saints, from themselves, and others. As also an Appendix in Answer to Master Horne, goring all University-Learning.* 1st ed., London: Thomas Ratcliffe and Edward Mottershed, 1654.

————. *Θεοκρατια Or, a Vindication of the Doctrine commonly received in the Reformed Churches concerning Gods Intentions of special Grace and Favour to his Elect in the Death of Christ: As also his Prerogative, Power, Prescience, Providence, the Immutability of his Nature and Counsels, &c. from the Attempts lately made against it, by Master John Goodwin in his Book entituled Redemption Redeemed. Together with some Digressions concerning the Impossibility of new immanent Acts in God, the Possibility of Faiths being an Instrument of Justification, and the Nature of the Covenants of Works and Grace.* 1st ed., London: Thomas Ratcliffe and Edward Mottershed, 1653.

Kenyon, John P., ed. *The Stuart Constitution, 1603-1688: Documents and Commentary.* [1965] 2nd ed., Cambridge: Cambridge University Press, 1986.

Kimedoncius, Jacobus. *De Redemtione generis Humani Libri tres: Quibus copiosè traditur Controversia, de Redemtionis et Gratiæ per Christum universalitate, et Morte ipsius pro Omnibus. Accessit tractatio finitima de divinia Prædestinatione, uno Libro comprehensa.* 1st ed., Heidelberg: Abraham Smesmann, 1592.

————. *Of the Redemption of Mankind. Three Bookes: Wherein the Controversie of the Universalitie of Redemption and Grace by Christ, and of his Death for all Men, is largely handled. Hereunto is annexed a Treatise of Gods Predestination in one Booke.* Translated by Hugh Ince. [1592] 1st English ed., London: Felix Kingston, 1598.

Larkin, James F. & Paul L. Hughes, eds. *Stuart Royal Proclamations.* 1st ed., Oxford: Clarendon Press, 1973-83. 2 vols.

Laud, William. *The Works of the most reverend Father in God, William Laud, D.D. sometime Lord Archbishop of Canterbury.* Edited by William Scott & James Bliss. Library of Anglo-Catholic Theology. 1st ed., Oxford: John Henry Parker, 1847-60. 7 vols.

Leigh, Edward. *A Systeme or Body of Divinity consisting of ten Books: Wherein the Fundamentals and main Grounds of Religion are opened, the contrary Errours re-*

futed, most of the Controversies between us, the Papists, Arminians, and Socinians discussed and handled, several Scriptures explained and vindicated from corrupt Glosses: A Work seasonable for these Times, wherein so many Articles of our Faith are questioned, and so many gross Errours daily published. 1st ed., London: By A. M. for William Lee, 1654.

Mahaffy, John P. *The Particular Book of Trinity College, Dublin. A Facsimile from the Original, with Introduction and Appendices.* 1st Facsimile ed., London: T. Fisher Unwin, 1904.

Mitchell, Alexander F. & John Struthers, eds., *Minutes of the Sessions of the Westminster Assembly of Divines while engaged in preparing their Directory for Church Government, Confession of Faith, and Catechisms (November 1644 to March 1649) from Transcripts of the Originals produced by a Committee of the General Assembly of the Church of Scotland.* 1st ed., Edinburgh: William Blackwood and Sons, 1874.

Montagu, Richard. *Appello Caesarem. A just Appeale from two unjust Informers.* 1st ed., London: For Matthew Lownes, 1625.

———. *A Gagg for the new Gospell? No: A new Gagg for an old Goose. Who would needs to undertake to stop all Protestants Mouths for ever, with 276 places out of their owne English Bibles. Or, an Answer to a late Abridger of Controversies, and Belyar of the Protestants Doctrine.* 1st ed., London: Thomas Snodham for Matthew Lownes & William Barret, 1624.

Morton, Thomas. *Apologia Catholica ex Meris Jesuitarum Contradictionibus conflata, in qua Paradoxa, Hæreses, Blasphemiæ, Scelera, quæ a Pontificiis obijci Protestantibus solent, ex ipsorum Pontificiorum Testimoniis diluuntur omnia. Eius Libri duo de Notis Ecclesiæ.* 1st ed., London: George Bishop, 1605.

———. *A Catholike Appeale for Protestants, out of the Confessions of the Romane Doctors; particularly answering the mis-named Catholike Apologie for the Romane Faith, out of the Protestants: Manifesting the Antiquitie of our Religion, and satisfying all scrupulous Objections which have bene urged against it.* 1st ed., London: George Bishop and John Norton, 1609.

———. *Confessions and Proofes of Protestant Divines of Reformed Churches, that Episcopacy is in Respect of the Office according to the Word of God, and in Respect of the Use the best. Together with a briefe Treatise touching the Originall of Bishops and Metropolitans.* 1st ed., Oxford: Henry Hall, 1644.

———. *A Defence of the Innocencie of the three Ceremonies of the Church of England. Viz. The Surplice, Crosse after Baptisme, and Kneeling at the receiving of the Blessed Sacrament. Divided into two Parts: In the former whereof the generall Arguments urged by the Non-Conformists; and, in the second Part, their particular Accusations, against these III Ceremonies severally, are answered, and refuted . . . published by Authoritie.* 1st ed., London: For William Barret, 1618.

———. *Επισκοπος Αποστολικος The Episcopacy of the Church of England justified to be apostolical, from the Authority of the ancient primitive Church: And from the Confessions of the most famous Divines of the Reformed Churches beyond the*

Seas. Being a full Satisfaction in this Cause, as well for the Necessity, as for the Just Right thereof, as consonant to the Word of God. . . . Before which is prefixed a Preface to the Reader concerning this Subject: By Sir Henry Yelverton Baronet. 1st ed., London: For J. Collins, 1670.

―――. *A full Satisfaction concerning a double Romish Iniquitie; hainous Rebellion, and more than heathenish Æquivocation. Containing three Parts: The two former belong to the Reply upon the moderate Answerer; the first for Confirmation of the Discoverie in these two Points, Treason and Æquivocation: the second is a Justification of Protestants, touching the same Points. The third Part is a large Discourse confuting the Reasons and Grounds of other Priests, both in the Case of Rebellion, and Æquivocation.* 1st ed., London: Richard Field for Edmond Weaver, 1606.

Parker, Henry. *A Discourse concerning Puritans: A Vindication of those, who unjustly suffer by the Mistake, Abuse, and Misapplication of that Name. A Tract necessary and usefull for these Times.* 2nd ed., London: For Robert Bostock, 1641.

Peel, Albert, ed. *The seconde Part of a Register: Being a Calendar of Manuscripts under that Title intended for Publication by the Puritans about 1593, and now in Dr Williams's Library, London.* 1st ed., Cambridge: Cambridge University Press, 1915. 2 vols.

Perkins, William. *The Workes of that famous and worthy Minister of Christ in the Universitie of Cambridge, Mr. William Perkins. Newly corrected according to his owne Copies. With distinct Chapters, and Contents of every Booke, and two Tables of the whole: one, of the Matter and Questions, the other of choice Places of Scripture.* Corrected ed., London: John Legatt & Cantrell Legge, 1616-18. 3 vols.

Pierce, Thomas. *The divine Philanthropie defended against the declamatory Attempts of certain late-printed Papers intitl'd A correptory Correction. In Vindication of some Notes concerning Gods Decrees, especially of Reprobation.* 1st ed., London: For Richard Royston, 1657.

―――. *Εαυτοντιμορουμενος, or, the Self-revenger exemplified in Mr. William Barlee. By Way of Rejoynder to the first Part of his Reply, viz. the unparallel'd Variety of Discourse in the two first Chapters of his pretended Vindication. (The second Part of the Rejoynder to the second Part of his Reply being purposely designed to follow after by it self, for Reasons shortly to be alledged.) Wherein are briefly exhibited, amongst many other Things, the rigidly-presbyterian both Principles and Practice. A Vindication of Grotius from Mr Baxter, of Mr Baxter from Mr Barlee, of episcopal Divines from both together. To which is added an Appendage touching the Judgment of the right honourable and right Reverend Father in God, James, Lord Primate of Armagh, and Metropolitan of Ireland, irrefragably attested by the Certificates of Dr Walton, Mr Thorndike, and Mr Gunning, sent in a Letter to Doctor Bernard.* 2nd ed., London: R. Daniel for Richard Royston, 1658.

Porter, Harry C., ed. *Puritanism in Tudor England.* 1st ed., London: Macmillan and Co., 1970.

Prynne, William. *Anti-Arminianisme. Or, the Church of Englands old Antithesis to new Arminianisme. Wherein seven Anti-Arminian Orthodox Tenets, are evidently* proved; their seven opposite Arminian (once Popish and Pelagian) Errours, are manifestly disproved, to be the ancient, established, undoubted Doctrine of the primitive and moderne Church of England; (as also of the primitive and present Churches of Scotland, and Ireland:) By the concurrent Testimony of sundry ancient Brittish, English, Scottish, Irish Authours and Records, from the Yeare of our Lord 430 till about the Yeare 1440: and by the severall Records and Writers of these Churches, from the Beginning of Reformation to this present. [1629] 2nd Enlarged ed., London: Eliz. Allde for M. Sparke, 1630.

————. Canterburies Doome. Or the first Part of a compleat History of the Commitment, Charge, Tryall, Condemnation, Execution of William Laud late Arch-Bishop of Canterbury. Containing the severall Orders, Articles, Proceedings in Parliament against him, from his first Accusation therein, till his Tryall: Together with the various Evidences and Proofs produced against him at the Lords Bar, in Justification of the first Branch of the Commons Charge against him; to wit, his trayterous Endeavours to alter and subvert Gods true Religion, by Law established among us; to introduce and set up popish Superstition and Idolatry in liew thereof, by insensible Degrees; and to reconcile the Church of England to the Church of Rome, by sundry Jesuiticall Pollices, Practises: with his severall Answers to those Evidences, Proofs, and the Commons Reply thereunto. Wherein this Arch-Prelates manifold Trayterous Artifices to usher in Popery by Degrees, are cleerly detected, and the ecclesiasticall History of our Church-Affaires, during his pontificall Domination, faithfully presented to the publike View of the World. 1st ed., London: John Macock for Michael Spark Sr, 1646.

Records of the Hon. Society of Lincoln's Inn: The Black Books. Vol. II. from A.D. 1586 to A.D. 1660. Vol. II. 1st ed., London: Lincoln's Inn, 1898.

The Remonstrants. The Confession or Declaration of the Ministers or Pastors, which in the United Provinces are called Remonstrants, or Arminians, concerning the chief Points of Christian Religion. In XXV Chapters. New English ed., London: For Francis Smith, 1676.

Rogers, Thomas. The English Creede, consenting with the true ancient catholique, and apostolique Church in all the points and articles of Religion which everie Christian is to knowe and beleeve that would be saved. The first Parte, in most loyal Maner to the Glorie of God, Credit of our Church, and displaieng of al hærisies, and errors, both olde and newe, contrarie to the Faith, subscribed unto by Thomas Rogers. Allowed by Auctoritie. [1584] Another ed., London: John Windet for Andrew Maunsel, 1585.

Russell, John. The Spy, discovering the Danger of Arminian Heresie and Spanish Trecherie: Written by I. R. 1st ed., Amsterdam: n.p., 1628.

Schaff, Philip, ed. The Creeds of Christendom, with a History and Critical Notes. Edited by David S. Schaff. [1931] 6th Revised reprint ed., Grand Rapids, MI: Baker Books, 1993. 3 vols.

Shepard, Thomas. God's Plot: The Paradoxes of Puritan Piety: Being the Autobiography

& Journal of Thomas Shephard. Edited by Michael McGiffert. The Common-weath Series. [1832] New ed., n.p.: University of Massachusetts Press, 1972.

Sibbes, Richard. *The Complete Works of Richard Sibbes*. Edited by Alexander B. Grosart. Nichol's Series of standard Divines: Puritan Period. Edinburgh: James Nichol, 1862-64. 7 vols.

Taylor, Thomas. *Japhets first publique Perswasion into Sems Tents: Or, Peters Sermon which was the first generall Calling of the Gentiles preached before Cornelius. Expounded in Cambridge by Thomas Taylor, and now published for the further Use of the Church of God*. [1612] Another ed., Cambridge?: By Cantrell Legge for Raph Mab, 1612.

Ussher, James. *A Body of Divinitie, or the Summe and Substance of Christian Religion, catechistically propounded, and explained, by way of Question and Answer: Methodically and familiarly handled. Composed long since by James Usher B. of Armagh. And at the earnest Desires of divers godly Christians now printed and published. Whereunto is adjoyned a Tract, intituled Immanuel, or the Mystery of the Incarnation of the Son of God; heretofore writen and published by the same Authour*. 1st ed., London: M. F. for Thomas Downes and George Badger, 1645.

———. *Gotteschalci, et Prædestinatianæ Controversiæ ab eo motæ, Historia: Unà cum duplice ejusdem Confessione, nunc primùm in lucem editâ*. 1st ed., Dublin: Societatis Bibliopolarum, 1631.

———. *Immanuel, Or, The mystery of the Incarnation of the Son of God*. [1643] Reprint ed., London: William Hunt, 1658.

———. *The Judgement of the late Archbishop of Armagh and Primate of Ireland, 1. Of the Extent of Christs Death, and Satisfaction, &c. 2. Of the Sabbath, and Observation of the Lords Day. 3. Of the Ordination in other Reformed Churches. With a Vindication of him from a pretended Change of opinion in the first; some Advertisements upon the Latter; and, in Prevention of further injuries, a Declaration of his judgement in several other Subjects*. Edited by Nicholas Bernard. 1st ed., London: For John Crook, 1657.

———. *The Judgement of the late Archbishop of Armagh and Primate of Ireland, 1. Of the Extent of Christs Death, and Satisfaction, &c. 2. Of the Sabbath, and Observation of the Lords Day. 3. Of the Ordination in other Reformed Churches. With a Vindication of him from a pretended Change of opinion in the first; some Advertisements upon the Latter; and, in Prevention of further injuries, a Declaration of his judgement in several other Subjects*. Edited by Nicholas Bernard. [1657] Another ed., London: For John Crook, 1658.

———. "The Judgment of the Late Archbishop of Armagh, and Primate of Ireland, of the true Intent and Extent of Christ's Death and Satisfaction upon the Cross. Written in Answer to the Request of a Friend, March 3, 1617." In *General Redemption, and limited Salvation. To which is added, a Reprint of Archbishop Usher's Treatise on the true Intent and Extent of Christ's Death and Satisfaction on the Cross*. Edited by William Dodsworth. London: James Nisbet, 1831, pp. 77-119.

———. *The Judgement of the late Arch-Bishop of Armagh, and Primate of Ireland. Of Babylon (Rev. 18.4) being the present See of Rome. (With a Sermon of Bishop Bedels upon the same Words.) Of Laying on of Hands (Heb. 6.2) to be an ordained Ministery. Of the old Form of Words in Ordination. Of a set Form of Prayer . . . unto which is added a Character of Bishop Bedel, and an Answer to Mr Pierces fifth Letter concerning the late Primate.* Edited by Nicholas Bernard. 1st ed., London: For John Crook, 1659.

———. *The Reduction of Episcopacie unto the Form of synodical Government received in the antient Church: Proposed as an Expedient for the Compromising of the now Differences, and the Preventing of those Troubles that may arise about the Matter of Church-Government. . . . And now published, seriously to be considered by all sober conscientious Persons, and tendred to all the Sons of Peace and Truth in the three Nations, for Recovering the Peace of the Church, and setling its proper Government.* [1656] Another ed., London: T. N. for G. B. and T. C., 1656.

———. *The whole Works of the most Rev. James Ussher, D.D., Lord Archbishop of Armagh, and Primate of all Ireland. With the life of the Author, and an Account of his Writings.* Edited by Charles R. Erlington. New ed., Dublin: Hodges and Smith, 1847-64. 17 vols.

Vermigli, Peter Martyr. *The Common Places of the most famous and renowmed [sic] Divine Doctor Peter Martyr, divided into foure principall Parts: With a large Addition of manie theologicall and necessarie Discourses, some never extant before. Translated and partlie gathered by Anthonie Marten, one of the Sewers of hir Majesties most honourable Chamber. Meliora spero. In the End of the Booke are annexed two Tables of all the notable Matters therein conteined.* Translated by Anthony Marten. [1576] 1st English ed., London: Henry Denham and Henry Middleton, 1583.

Ward, Samuel & Thomas Gataker. *De Baptismatis Infantilis Vi & Efficacia Disceptatio, privatim habita, inter Virum celeberrimum D[omi]num Samuelem Wardum, Theologiæ Sacræ Doctorem, ejusdémqe [sic] in Academiâ Cantabrigiensi Professorem, et Thomam Gatakerum Th. S. B. Ecclesiæq[ue] Londinum propter Rotherhithiensis Pastorem. Ea qibus [sic] Partibus constet, Pagina aversa sigillatim indicabit.* 1st ed., London: Roger Daniel, 1652 (1653).

Wesley, John, ed. *A Christian Library. Consisting of Extracts from and Abridgements of the choicest Pieces of practical Divinity, which have been publish'd in the English Tongue.* 1st ed., Bristol, UK: Felix Farley and E. Farley, 1749-55. 50 vols.

———, ed. *A Christian Library: Consisting of Extracts from and Abridgements of the choicest Pieces of practical Divinity which have been published in the English Tongue.* Edited by A. G. Jewitt. [1749-55] New ed., London: T. Cordeux for T. Blanshard, 1819-27. 30 vols.

Wotton, Anthony. *A dangerous Plot discovered. By a Discourse, wherein is proved, that, Mr Richard Montague, in his two Bookes; the one, called A new Gagg; the other, A just Appeale: laboureth to bring in the Faith of Rome, and Arminius: under the Name and Pretence of the Doctrine and Faith of the Church of England. A Work very necessary for all them which have received the Truth of God in Love, and desire to escape Errour. The Reader shall finde:* 1. *A Catalogue of his erroneous Poynts annexed to the Epistle to the Reader.* 2. *A Demonstration of the Danger of them, cap. 21. num. 7 &c. pag. 178.* 3. *A List of the Heads of all the Chapters contained in this Booke.* 1st ed., London: For Nicholas Bourne, 1626.

Yates, John. *Ibis ad Cæsarem. Or, a submissive Appearance before Cæsar; in Answer to Mr Montagues Appeale in the Pointes of Arminianisme and Popery, maintained and defended by him, against the Doctrine of the Church of England.* 1st ed., London: For R. Mylbourne, 1626.

Secondary Sources

". . . read the books that are most profitable, delight in them above others . . ."

Preston, *Riches of Mercy,* p. 284

Books, Articles, and Theses

Allport, Josiah. "Life of Bishop Davenant." In *An Exposition of the Epistle of St Paul to the Colossians by the right Rev. John Davenant D.D. . . . originally delivered, in a Series of Lectures, before the University. Translated from the original Latin; with a Life of the Author, and Notes illustrative of the Writers and Authorities referred to in the Work . . . to the Whole is added, a Translation of Dissertatio de Morte Christi.* 1st ed., London: Hamilton, Adams, and Co., 1831, I:ix-lii.

Anderson, James William. "The Grace of God and the Non-elect in Calvin's Commentaries and Sermons." Th.D. Dissertation. New Orleans Baptist Theological Seminary, 1976.

Arber, Edward, ed. *A Transcript of the Registers of the Company of Stationers of London, 1554-1640.* 1st ed., London: Private publication, 1875-94. 5 vols.

Armstrong, Brian G. *Calvinism and the Amyraut Heresy: Protestant Scholasticism and Humanism in Seventeenth-Century France,* Madison, WI: University of Wisconsin Press, 1969.

Ball, Thomas. "The Life of Doctor Preston." In *A generall Martyrologie, containing a Collection of all the greatest Persecutions which have befallen the Church of Christ from the Creation to our present Times. Whereunto are added, the Lives of sundry modern Divines, famous in their Generations for Learning and Piety, and most of them great Sufferers in the Cause of Christ.* Edited by Samuel Clarke. 1st ed., London: A. M. for Thomas Underhill and John Rothwell, 1651, pp. 473-520.

———. "The Life of Doctor Preston, who died Anno Christi, 1628." In *A general Martyrologie, containing a Collection of all the greatest Persecutions which have befallen the Church of Christ, from the Creation, to our present Times, both in En-*

gland and all other Nations. Whereunto are added the two and twenty Lives of English Modern Divines, famous in their Generations for Learning and Piety; and most of them great Sufferers in the Cause of Christ. As also the Life of the heroical Admiral of France, slain in the Parisian Massacre, and of Joane Queen of Navar, poisoned a little before. Edited by Samuel Clarke. [1651] Reprint ed., London: Thomas Ratcliffe for Thomas Underhill and John Rothwell, 1660, II:95-143.

———. "The Life of Doctor Preston, who dyed Anno Christi 1628." In *A general Martyrologie, containing a Collection of all the greatest Persecutions which have befallen the Church of Christ, from the Creation, to our present Times; wherein is given an exact Account of the Protestant Sufferings in Queen Maries Reign. Whereunto is added the Lives of thirty-two English Divines, famous in their Generations for Learning and Piety; and most of them Sufferers in the Cause of Christ. Together with the Lives of Gustavus Ericson, King of Sweden; Jasper Coligni, Admiral of France (who was slain in the Massacre of Paris), and Joane Queen of Navarr (who died of Poison a few Dayes before that bloody Massacre). Likewise, of divers other Christians who were eminent for Prudence and Piety. You have also, lively Represented, the divers manners of those cruel, horrid, and inhumane Sufferings, that the People of God have undergone in all Ages and Nations; and the Effigies of some of the eminent Divines, in Copper-plates.* Edited by Samuel Clarke. [1651] Reprint ed., London: For William Birch, 1677, II:75-114.

———. "The Life of Dr John Preston." In *A Christian Library. Consisting of Extracts from and Abridgements of the choicest Pieces of practical Divinity, which have been publish'd in the English Tongue.* Edited by John Wesley. Abridged ed., Bristol, UK: Felix Farley, 1751, IX:195-219.

———. "The Life of Dr John Preston." In *A Christian Library: Consisting of Extracts from and Abridgements of the choicest Pieces of practical Divinity which have been published in the English Tongue.* Edited by John Wesley. [1751] Abridged ed., London: T. Cordeux for T. Blanshard, 1819, V:291-311.

———. *The Life of the Renowned Doctor Preston, writ by his pupil, master Thomas Ball, D.D. Minister of Northampton, in the year, 1628.* Edited by Edward W. Harcourt. [1651] New ed., Oxford: Parker and Co., 1885.

Bangs, Carl. *Arminius: A Study in the Dutch Reformation.* 1st ed., Nashville, TN: Abingdon Press, 1971.

Barkstead, John. *The Speeches, Discourses, and Prayers, of Col. John Barkstead, Col. John Okey, and Mr. Miles Corbet; upon the 19th of April, being the Day of their Suffering at Tyburn. Together with an Account of the Occasion and Manner of their Taking in Holland: As also of their several occasional Speeches, Discourses, and Letters, both before, and in the Time of their late Imprisonment. Faithfully and impartially collected, for a general Satisfaction.* [1662] Another ed., London: n.p., 1662.

Barnard, John. *Theologo-historicus, or the true Life of the most reverend Divine, and excellent Historian Peter Heylyn D.D. Sub-Dean of Westminster,* London: J. S. for Ed. Eckelston, 1683.

Bell, M. Charles. "Calvin and the Extent of the Atonement," *Evangelical Quarterly* 55 (1983): 115-23.

———. *Calvin and Scottish Theology: The Doctrine of Assurance.* 1st ed., Edinburgh: Handsel Press, 1985.

Berkhof, Louis. *Systematic Theology.* [1941] Revised and enlarged ed., Grand Rapids, MI: Eerdmans, 1953.

Bernard, Nicholas. *The Life & Death of the most reverend and learned Father of our Church Dr. James Ussher, late Archbishop of Armagh, and Primate of all Ireland. Published in a Sermon at his Funeral at the Abby of Westminster, Aprill 17, 1656. And now re-viewed with some other Enlargements.* 1st ed., London: E. Tyler for John Crook, 1656.

Bierma, Lyle D. "The Role of Covenant Theology in early Reformed Orthodoxy," *Sixteenth Century Journal* 21 (1990): 453-62.

Boersma, Hans. "Calvin and the Extent of the Atonement," *Evangelical Quarterly* 64 (1992): 333-55.

———. *A Hot Pepper Corn: Richard Baxter's Doctrine of Justification in Its Seventeenth-Century Context of Controversy.* 1st ed., Zoetermeer: Uitgeverij Boekencentrum, 1993.

Boran, Elizabethanne. "An early friendship Network of James Ussher, Archbishop of Armagh, 1626-1656." In *European Universities in the Age of Reformation and Counter-Reformation,* edited by Helga Robinson-Hammerstein. 1st ed., Dublin: Four Courts Press, 1998, pp. 116-34.

Bost, Hubert. "Moyse Amyraut." In *Encyclopédie du Protestantisme,* edited by Pierre Gisel. 1st ed., Paris: Éditions du Cerf, 1995, p. 30.

Boughton, Lynne C. "Supralapsarianism and the Role of Metaphysics in Sixteenth-Century Reformed Theology," *Westminster Theological Journal* 48 (1986): 63-96.

Brandt, Gerard. *The History of the Reformation and other Ecclesiastical Transactions in and about the Low-Countries, from the Beginning of the Eighth Century, down to the famous Synod of Dort, inclusive. In which all the Revolutions that happen'd in Church and State on Account of the Divisions between the Protestants and Papists, the Arminians and Calvinists, are fairly and fully represented.* [1677-1704] 1st English ed., London: T. Wood for Timothy Childe (Vol I), John Childe (Vol II), John Nicks (Vols III & IV), 1720-23. 4 vols.

Bremer, Francis J. *Congregational Communion: Clerical Friendship in the Anglo-American Puritan Community, 1610-1692.* 1st ed., Boston, MA: Northeastern University Press, 1994.

———, ed. *Puritanism: Transatlantic Perspectives on a Seventeenth-Century Anglo-American Faith.* 1st ed., Boston: Massachusetts Historical Society, 1993.

Breward, Ian, ed. *The Work of William Perkins.* The Courtenay Library of Reformation Classics. Vol. 3. 1st ed., Abingdon, UK: Sutton Courtenay Press, 1970.

Brook, Benjamin. *The Lives of the Puritans: Containing a biographical Account of those Divines who distinguished themselves in the Cause of Religious Liberty, from the*

Reformation under Queen Elizabeth, to the Act of Uniformity, in 1662. 1st ed., London: For James Black, 1813. 3 vols.

Burnet, Gilbert. *Bishop Burnet's History of his own Time*. 1st ed., London: For Thomas Ward, 1724-34. 2 vols.

Bush Jr., Sargent & Carl J. Rasmussen. "Emmanuel College Library's First Inventory," *Transactions of the Cambridge Bibliographical Society* 8 (1985): 514-56.

———. *The Library of Emmanuel College, Cambridge, 1584-1637*. 1st ed., Cambridge: Cambridge University Press, 1986.

Calder, Isabel M. "A Seventeenth-Century Attempt to Purify the Anglican Church," *American Historical Review* 53 (1948): 760-75.

———, ed. *Activities of the Puritan Faction in the Church of England, 1625-33*. 1st ed., London: SPCK for the Church Historical Society, 1957.

Campbell, Helen. *Anne Bradstreet and her Time*. 1st ed., Boston, MA: D. Lothrop Company, 1891.

Capern, Amanda. "'Slipperye Times and dangerous Dayes': James Ussher and the Calvinist Reformation of Britain." Ph.D. Dissertation. University of New South Wales, 1991.

———. "The Caroline Church: James Ussher and the Irish Dimension," *Historical Journal* 39 (1996): 57-85.

Chalker, William H. "Calvin and Some Seventeenth-Century English Calvinists: A Comparison of Their Thought Through an Examination of Their Doctrines of the Knowledge of God, Faith and Assurance." Ph.D. Dissertation. Duke University, 1961.

Chandos, John, ed. *In God's Name: Examples of Preaching in England from the Act of Supremacy to the Act of Uniformity, 1534-1662*. 1st ed., London: Hutchinson & Co., 1971.

Cheney, C. R., ed. *Handbook of Dates for Students of English History*. Royal Historical Society Guides and Handbooks. Vol. 4. [1945] Corrected reprint ed., London: The Royal Historical Society, 1970.

Chidester, Evelyn A. "John Preston: Puritan Divine and Writer of the Early Seventeenth Century." M.A. Dissertation. Texas College of Arts and Industries, 1956.

Clarke, Samuel. *A general Martyrologie, containing a Collection of all the greatest Persecutions which have befallen the Church of Christ, from the Creation, to our present Times; wherein is given an exact Account of the Protestant Sufferings in Queen Maries Reign. Whereunto is added the Lives of thirty-two English Divines, famous in their Generations for Learning and Piety; and most of them Sufferers in the Cause of Christ. Together with the Lives of Gustavus Ericson, King of Sweden; Jasper Coligni, Admiral of France (who was slain in the Massacre of Paris), and Joane Queen of Navarr (who died of Poison a few Dayes before that bloody Massacre). Likewise, of divers other Christians who were eminent for Prudence and Piety. You have also, lively Represented, the divers manners of those cruel, horrid, and inhumane Sufferings, that the People of God have undergone in all Ages and Nations;*

and the Effigies of some of the eminent Divines, in Copper-plates. [1651] 3rd Corrected and enlarged ed., London: For William Birch, 1677.

———. *The Lives of sundry eminent Persons in this later Age. In two Parts. I. of Divines. II. of Nobility and Gentry of both Sexes. By Samuel Clark, sometimes Pastor of Bennet Fink, London. Printed and reviewed by himself just before his Death. To which is added his own Life, and the Lives of the Countess of Suffolk, Sir Nathaniel Barnardiston, Mr. Richard Blackerby, and Mr. Samuel Fairclough, drawn up by other hands.* 1st ed., London: For Thomas Simmons, 1683.

———. *The Marrow of Ecclesiastical Historie, contained in the Lives of the Fathers, and other learned Men, and famous Divines, which have flourished in the Church since Christ's Time to this present Age. Faithfully collected out of several Autors, and orderly disposed, according to the Centuries wherein they lived. Together with the livelie Effigies of most of the Eminentest of them cut in Copper.* 1st ed., London: William Du-gard, 1650.

Clausen, Sara J. "Calvinism in the Anglican Hierarchy, 1603-1643: Four Episcopal Examples." Ph.D. Dissertation. Vanderbilt University, 1989.

Clifford, Alan C. *Atonement and Justification: English Evangelical Theology, 1640-1790: An Evaluation.* 1st ed., Oxford: Clarendon Press, 1990.

Cogswell, Thomas. *The Blessed Revolution: English Politics and the Coming of War, 1621-1624.* 1st ed., Cambridge: Cambridge University Press, 1989.

———. "The People's Love: The Duke of Buckingham and Popularity." In *Politics, Religion and Popularity in Early Stuart Britain: Essays in Honour of Conrad Russell,* edited by Thomas Cogswell, Richard Cust & Peter G. Lake. 1st ed., Cambridge: Cambridge University Press, 2002, pp. 211-34.

Cogswell, Thomas, Richard Cust, & Peter G. Lake, eds. *Politics, Religion and Popularity in Early Stuart Britain: Essays in Honour of Conrad Russell.* 1st ed., Cambridge: Cambridge University Press, 2002.

Cohen, Charles L. *God's Caress: The Psychology of Puritan Religious Experience.* 1st ed., New York: Oxford University Press, 1986.

———. "The Saints Zealous in Love and Labor: The Puritan Psychology of Work," *Harvard Theological Review* 76 (1983): 455-80.

Collinson, Patrick. *The Elizabethan Puritan Movement.* 1st ed., London: Jonathan Cape, 1967.

———. "Puritans." In *The Oxford Encyclopedia of the Reformation,* edited by Hans J. Hillerbrand. 4 vols. 1st ed., Oxford: Oxford University Press, 1996, III:364-70.

———. *The Religion of Protestants: The Church in English Society, 1559-1625.* The Ford Lectures, 1979. 1st ed., Oxford: Clarendon Press, 1982.

———. *Godly People: Essays on English Protestantism and Puritanism.* 1st ed., London: Hambledon Press, 1983.

Collinson, Patrick, Sarah Bendall, & Christopher N. L. Brooke. *A History of Emmanuel College, Cambridge.* 1st ed., Woodbridge, UK: Boydell Press, 1999.

Como, David R. "Puritans, Predestination and the Construction of Orthodoxy in Early Seventeenth-Century England." In *Conformity and Orthodoxy in the En-*

glish Church, c1560-1660, edited by Peter G. Lake & Michael C. Questier. Studies in Modern British Religious History. 1st ed., Woodbridge, UK: Boydell Press, 2000, pp. 64-87.

Cooper, Tim. *Fear and Polemic in Seventeenth-Century England: Richard Baxter and Antinomianism.* 1st ed., Aldershot, UK: Ashgate Publishing Company, 2001.

Cross, Frank L. & Elizabeth A. Livingstone, eds. *The Oxford Dictionary of the Christian Church.* [1974] 3rd Revised ed., Oxford: Oxford University Press, 1997.

Daniel, Curt D. "Hyper-Calvinism and John Gill." Ph.D. Dissertation. University of Edinburgh, 1983.

Davies, Julian E. *The Caroline Captivity of the Church: Charles I and the Remoulding of Anglicanism, 1625-1641.* Oxford Historical Monographs. 1st ed., Oxford: Clarendon Press, 1992.

Dever, Mark E. "Moderation and Deprivation: A Reappraisal of Richard Sibbes," *Journal of Ecclesiastical History* 43 (1992): 396-413.

————. *Richard Sibbes: Puritanism and Calvinism in Late Elizabethan and Early Stuart England.* 1st ed., Macon, GA: Mercer University Press, 2000.

Dewar, Michael W. "Bishop Joseph Hall, 1574-1656: An Ecumenical Calvinist Churchman," *Evangelical Quarterly* 40 (1968): 110-15.

————. "The British Delegation at the Synod of Dort, 1618-1619," *Evangelical Quarterly* 46 (1974): 103-16.

————. "The British Delegation at the Synod of Dort: Assembling and Assembled; Returning and Returned," *Churchman* 106 (1992): 130-46.

————. "The Synod of Dort, the Westminster Assembly, and the French Reformed Church, 1618-43," *Churchman* 104 (1990): 38-42.

Doerksen, Daniel W. *Conforming to the Word: Herbert, Donne, and the English Church before Laud.* 1st ed., Cranbury, NJ: Associated University Presses, 1997.

Donagan, Barbara. "The York House Conference Revisited: Laymen, Calvinism and Arminianism," *Bulletin of (Institute of) Historical Research* 64/155 (1991): 312-31.

Douglas, James D., ed. *The New International Dictionary of the Christian Church.* [1974] Revised ed., Grand Rapids, MI: Zondervan Publishing House, 1978.

Douty, Norman F. *The Death of Christ: A Treatise Which Answers the Question: 'Did Christ Die Only for the Elect?'.* 1st ed., Swengal, PA: Reiner Publications, 1972.

————. *Did Christ Die Only for the Elect? A Treatise on the Extent of Christ's Atonement.* [1978] Reprint ed., Eugene, OR: Wipf & Stock Publishers, 1998.

Duffield, Gervase E., ed. *John Calvin.* Courtenay Studies in Reformation Theology. 1st ed., Abingdon, UK: Sutton Courtenay Press, 1966.

Echard, Lawrence. *The History of England. From the Beginning of the Reign of King Charles the First, to the Restoration of King Charles the Second. Containing the Space of above 35 Years. With a complete Index.* Vol. II, London: For Jacob Tonson, 1718. 3 vols.

Emerson, Everett H. *English Puritanism from John Hooper to John Milton.* 1st ed., Durham, NC: Duke University Press, 1968.

Erlington, Charles R. "The Life of James Ussher, D.D., Archbishop of Armagh." In *The whole Works of the most Rev. James Ussher, D.D., Lord Archbishop of Armagh, and Primate of all Ireland. With the life of the Author, and an Account of his Writings.* 1st ed., Dublin: Hodges and Smith, 1847-64, I:1-324.

Fesko, John V. *Diversity within the Reformed Tradition: Supra- and Infralapsarianism in Calvin, Dort, and Westminster.* 1st ed., Greenville, SC: Reformed Academic Press, 2001.

Fielding, A. John. "Arminianism in the Localities: Peterborough Diocese, 1603-1642." In *The Early Stuart Church, 1603-1642,* edited by Kenneth Fincham. Problems in Focus. 1st ed., London: Macmillan Press, 1993, pp. 93-113, 237, 262-64.

Fincham, Kenneth, ed. *The Early Stuart Church, 1603-1642.* Problems in Focus. 1st ed., London: Macmillan Press, 1993.

Fincham, Kenneth & Peter G. Lake. "The Ecclesiastical Policy of King James I," *Journal of British Studies* 24 (1985): 169-207.

Ford, Alan. *The Protestant Reformation in Ireland, 1590-1641.* [1985] 2nd ed., Dublin: Four Courts Press, 1997.

Fuller, Morris. *The Life, Letters and Writings of John Davenant, D.D. 1572-1641 Lord Bishop of Salisbury.* 1st ed., London: Methuen, 1897.

Fuller, Thomas. *The Church-History of Britain; from the Birth of Jesus Christ, untill the Year M.DC.XLVIII.* 1st ed., London: For John William, 1655.

———. "The History of the University of Cambridge since the Conquest." In *The Church-History of Britain; from the Birth of Jesus Christ, untill the Year M.DC.XLVIII.* 1st ed., London: For John William, 1655, pp. 1-172 (Appended).

———. *The History of the Worthies of England.* 1st ed., London: J. G. W. L. and W. G., 1662.

Gavin, Joseph B. "The York House Conference, 1626: A Watershed in the Arminian-Calvinist-Puritan Debate over Predestination." In *Trinification of the World: A Festschrift in Honor of Frederick E. Crowe in Celebration of his 60th Birthday,* edited by Thomas A. Dunne & Jean-Marc Laporte. Toronto: Regis College Press, 1978, pp. 280-311.

Gisel, Pierre, ed. *Encyclopédie du Protestantisme.* 1st ed., Paris: Éditions du Cerf, 1995.

Godfrey, W. Robert. "John Hales' Good-Night to John Calvin." In *Protestant Scholasticism: Essays in Reassessment,* edited by Carl R. Trueman & R. Scott Clark. 1st ed., Carlisle, UK: Paternoster Press, 1999, pp. 165-80.

———. "Reformed Thought on the Extent of the Atonement to 1618," *Westminster Theological Journal* 37 (1975): 133-71.

———. "Tensions within International Calvinism: The Debate on the Atonement at the Synod of Dort, 1618-1619." Ph.D. Dissertation. Stanford University, 1974.

Gordon, Alexander. "John Preston D.D. (1587-1628)." In *The Dictionary of National Biography: From the Earliest Times to 1900,* edited by Leslie Stephen & Sidney Lee. [1917] Reprint ed., Oxford: Oxford University Press, 1921-22, XVI:308-12.

Granger, James. *A biographical History of England from Egbert the Great to the Revolution: Consisting of Characters disposed in different Classes, and adapted to a methodical Catalogue of Engraved British Heads: Intended as an Essay towards re-*

ducing our Biography to System, and a Help to the Knowledge of Portraits: Interspersed with Variety of Anecdotes, and Memoirs of a great Number of Persons, not to be found in any other Biographical Work: With a Preface, shewing the Utility of a Collection of Engraved Portraits to supply the Defect, and answer the various Purposes, of Medals. 2nd Enlarged ed., London: For T. Davies, J. Robson, G. Robinson, T. Becket, T. Cadell, and T. Evans, 1775. 4 vols.

Greg, W. W. *A Companion to Arber: Being a Calendar of Documents in Edward Arber's Transcript of the Registers of the Company of Stationers of London, 1554-1640 with Text and Calendar of Supplementary Documents.* 1st ed., Oxford: Clarendon Press, 1967.

Hacket, John. *Scrinia Reserata: A Memorial offer'd to the great Deservings of John Williams, D.D. who some time held the Places of Lord Keeper of the Great Seal of England, Lord Bishop of Lincoln, and Lord Archbishop of York. Containing a Series of the most remarkable Occurrences and Transactions of his Life, in Relation both to Church and State.* 1st ed., London: Edward Jones for Samuel Lowndes, 1693.

Hajzyk, Helena. "The Church in Lincolnshire, c.1595-c.1640." Ph.D. Dissertation. University of Cambridge, 1980.

Hall, Basil. "Calvin against the Calvinists." In *John Calvin,* edited by Gervase E. Duffield. Courtenay Studies in Reformation Theology. 1st ed., Abingdon, UK: Sutton Courtenay Press, 1966, pp. 19-37.

Haller, William. *The Rise of Puritanism, or the Way to the New Jerusalem as set forth in Pulpit and Press from Thomas Cartwright to John Lilburne and John Milton, 1570-1643.* [1938] Reprint ed., New York: Harper & Brothers, 1957.

Hargrave, O. T. "The Doctrine of Predestination in the English Reformation." Ph.D. Dissertation. Vanderbilt University, 1966.

Harrison, Brian H. & H. Colin G. Matthew, eds. *The Oxford Dictionary of National Biography: In Association with the British Academy: From the earliest Times to the Year 2000.* Oxford: Oxford University Press, 2004. 60 vols.

Hart, Trevor A., ed. *The Dictionary of Historical Theology.* 1st ed., Grand Rapids, MI: Eerdmans, 2000.

Helm, Paul. "The Logic of Limited Atonement," *Scottish Bulletin of Evangelical Theology* 3 (1985): 47-54.

———. *Calvin and the Calvinists.* [1982] Reprint ed., Edinburgh: Banner of Truth Trust, 1998.

Heron, Alasdair I. C., ed. *The Westminster Confession in the Church Today.* [1982] Reprint ed., Edinburgh: Saint Andrew Press, 1982.

Heylyn, Peter. *Aerius Redivivus: Or, the History of the Presbyterians. Containing the Beginnings, Progress and Success of that active Sect. Their Oppositions to monarchical and episcopal Government. Their Innovations in the Church: and, their Imbroylments of the Kingdoms and Estates of Christendom in the Pursuit of their Designes. From the Year 1536, to the Year 1647.* 1st ed., Oxford: John Crosley for Thomas Baffet, 1670.

———. *Cyprianus Anglicus: Or the History of the Life and Death, of the most reverend and renowned Prelate William by divine Providence, Lord Archbishop of Canter-bury, Primate of all England, and Metropolitan, Chancellor of the Universities of Oxon and Dublin, and one of the Lords of the Privy Council of his late most sacred Majesty King Charles the first, second Monarch of Great Britain. Containing also the ecclesiastical History of the three Kingdoms of England, Scotland, and Ireland from his first Rising till his Death.* 1st ed., London: For A. Seile, 1668.

———. *Examen Historicum: Or, a Discovery and Examination of the Mistakes, Fal-sities, and Defects of some modern Histories. Occasioned by the Partiality and In-advertencies of their severall Authours. In two Books.* 1st ed., London: For Henry Seile and Richard Royston, 1659.

———. *Historia Quinqu-Articularis: Or, a Declaration of the Judgement of the Western Churches, and more particularly of the Church of England, in the five controverted Points, reproched in these last Times by the Name of Arminianism. Collected in the Way of an historicall Narration, out of the publick Acts and Monuments, and most approved of those several Churches.* 1st ed., London: E. C. for Thomas Johnson, 1660.

———. *Respondet Petrus: Or, the Answer of Peter Heylyn D.D. to so much of Dr Ber-nard's Book entituled, The Judgement of the late Primate of Ireland &c. as he is made a Party to the said Lord Primate in the Point of the Sabbath, and by the said Doctor in some others. To which is added an Appendix in Answer to certain Pas-sages in Mr Sandersons History of the Life and Reign of K. Charles, relating to the Lord Primate, and Articles of Ireland, and the Earl of Strafford, in which the Re-spondent is concerned.* 1st ed., London: For R. Royston and R. Marriot, 1658.

Hickman, Henry. *Historia Quinq-Articularis Exarticulata; Or, Animadversions on Doc-tor Heylin's Quinquarticular History. In which, 1. The Aspersions cast on foreign Reformers, are wiped off. 2. The Doctors manifold Contradictions, are manifested. 3. The Doctrine of the Arminians, in the five Points, is proved, to be contrary to the Doctrine of the Reformed Church of England.* 2nd Correct and enlarged ed., Lon-don: For Robert Boulter, 1674.

Hill, Charles P. *Who's Who in Stuart Britain: Being the Fifth Volume in the Who's Who in British History Series.* [1965] Revised and enlarged ed., London: Shepheard-Walwyn, 1988.

Hill, Christopher. *Economic Problems of the Church from Archbishop Whitgift to the Long Parliament.* 1st ed., Oxford: Clarendon Press, 1956.

———. *God's Englishman: Oliver Cromwell and the English Revolution.* 1st ed., Lon-don: Weidenfeld & Nicolson, 1970.

———. *Puritanism and Revolution: Studies in Interpretation of the English Revolution of the Seventeenth Century.* 1st ed., London: Secker & Warburg, 1958.

———. *Society and Puritanism in Pre-Revolutionary England.* 1st ed., London: Secker & Warburg, 1964.

Hillerbrand, Hans J., ed. *The Oxford Encyclopedia of the Reformation.* 1st ed., Oxford: Oxford University Press, 1996. 4 vols.

Hindson, Edward, ed. *Introduction to Puritan Theology: A Reader.* A Canon Press

Book. [Grand Rapids, MI: Baker Book House, 1976] Reprint ed., Grand Rapids, MI: Baker Book House, 1980.

Hirst, Derek. *Authority and Conflict: England 1603-1658*. The New History of England. Vol. 4. 1st ed., London: Edward Arnold, 1986.

Hodge, Archibald A. *Outlines of Theology*. [(1860), 1878] Reprint of revised and enlarged ed., Grand Rapids, MI: Eerdmans, 1949.

Hoekema, Anthony A. *Saved by Grace*. [1989] Reprint ed., Grand Rapids, MI: Eerdmans, 1994.

Horton, Michael S. "Thomas Goodwin and the Puritan Doctrine of Assurance: Continuity and Discontinuity in the Reformed Tradition, 1600-1680." Ph.D. Dissertation. University of Coventry, 1998.

Hoyle, David M. "'Near Popery yet no Popery': Theological Debate in Cambridge 1590-1644." Ph.D. Dissertation. University of Cambridge, 1991.

Hughes, Seán F. ""The Problem of 'Calvinism'": English Theologies of Predestination c.1580-1630." In *Belief and Practice in Reformation England: A Tribute to Patrick Collinson from his Students,* edited by Susan Wabuda & Caroline Litzenberger. St Andrews Studies in Reformation History. Series Eds. Andrew Pettegree, Bruce Gordon & John Guy. 1st ed., Aldershot, UK: Ashgate Publishing Company, 1998, pp. 229-49.

———. "Review of Peter White's 'Predestination, Policy and Polemic: Conflict and Consensus in the English Church from the Reformation to the Civil War'," *Journal of Theological Studies* 45 (1994): 403-9.

Hunt Jr., William A. *The Puritan Moment: The Coming of Revolution in an English County*. Harvard Historical Studies. Vol. 102. 1st ed., Cambridge, MA: Harvard University Press, 1983.

Huntley, Frank L. *Bishop Joseph Hall 1574-1656: A Biographical and Critical Study*. Cambridge: D. S. Brewer Ltd, 1979.

Hylson-Smith, Kenneth. *The Churches in England from Elizabeth I to Elizabeth II*. 1st ed., London: SCM Press, 1996-98. 3 vols.

Ibish, Joan S. "Emmanuel College: the Founding Generation, with a Biographical Register of Members of the College, 1584-1604." Ph.D. Dissertation. Harvard University, 1985.

Karlberg, Mark W. "The Mosaic Covenant and the Concept of Works in Reformed Hermeneutics: A Historical-Critical Analysis with Particular Attention to Early Covenant Eschatology." Th.D. Dissertation. Westminster Theological Seminary, 1980.

Kendall, Robert T. *Calvin and English Calvinism to 1649*. Paternoster Biblical & Theological Monographs. [1979] 2nd ed., Carlisle, UK: Paternoster Press, 1997.

———. "John Cotton: First English Calvinist?" In *The Puritan Experiment in the New World*. 1st ed., London: The Westminster Conference, 1976, pp. 38-50.

———. "The Nature of Saving Faith from William Perkins (d.1602) to the Westminster Assembly (1643-1649)." D.Phil. Dissertation. University of Oxford, 1976.

Kennedy, Kevin D. "Union with Christ as Key to John Calvin's Understanding of the

Extent of the Atonement." Ph.D. Dissertation. Southern Baptist Theological Seminary, 1999.

Kirby, Ethyn W. "The Lay Feoffees: A Study in Militant Puritanism," *Journal of Modern History* 14 (1942): 1-25.

Knox, R. Buick. *James Ussher: Archbishop of Armagh.* 1st ed., Cardiff, UK: University of Wales Press, 1967.

———. "Puritanism and Presbyterianism," *Scottish Journal of Theology* 21 (1968): 213-20.

Lachman, David C. "The Marrow Controversy 1718-1723: An Historical and Theological Analysis." Ph.D. Dissertation. St Andrew's University, 1979.

———. *The Marrow Controversy 1718-1723: An Historical and Theological Analysis.* Edited by Nigel M. de S. Cameron, Donald Macleod, & David F. Wright. Rutherford House Series One: Historical Theology. 1st ed., Edinburgh: Rutherford House Books, 1988.

Lake, Peter G. "Calvinism and the English Church 1570-1635," *Past and Present* 114 (1987): 32-76.

———. "Defining Puritanism — Again?" In *Puritanism: Transatlantic Perspectives on a Seventeenth-Century Anglo-American Faith,* edited by Francis J. Bremer. 1st ed., Boston: Massachusetts Historical Society, 1993, pp. 3-29.

———. *Moderate Puritans and the Elizabethan Church.* 1st ed., Cambridge: Cambridge University Press, 1982.

———. "Predestinarian Propositions," *Journal of Ecclesiastical History* 46 (1995): 110-23.

Lake, Peter G. & Michael C. Questier, eds. *Conformity and Orthodoxy in the English Church, c. 1560-1660.* Studies in Modern British Religious History. Vol. 2. 1st ed., Woodbridge, UK: Boydell Press, 2000.

Larsen, Timothy, David W. Bebbington, & Mark A. Noll, eds. *Biographical Dictionary of Evangelicals.* 1st ed., Leicester, UK: InterVarsity Press, 2003.

Le Bas, Charles Webb. *The Life of Archbishop Laud.* The Theological Library. Vol. 13. 1st ed., London: For J. G. & F. Rivington, 1836.

Lee, Brian North. *British Bookplates: A Pictorial History.* 1st ed., Newton Abbot, UK: David & Charles, 1979.

Lewis, Peter H. "John Preston (1587-1628): Puritan and Court Chaplain." In *Light from John Bunyan and Other Puritans: Being Papers Read at the 1978 Westminster Conference.* 1st ed., London: The Westminster Conference, 1979, pp. 34-52.

Lillback, Peter A. "The Continuing Conundrum: Calvin and the Conditionality of the Covenant," *Calvin Theological Journal* 29 (1994): 42-74.

Lim, Paul Chang-Ha. *In Pursuit of Purity, Unity, and Liberty: Richard Baxter's Puritan Ecclesiology in Its Seventeenth-Century Context.* Studies in the History of Christian Traditions. Vol. 112. 1st ed., Leiden: Brill, 2004.

Lipscomb, George. *The History and Antiquities of the County of Buckingham.* 1st ed., London: J. & W. Robins, 1847. 4 vols.

Logan Jr., Samuel T. "Theological Decline in Christian Institutions and the Value of Van Til's Epistemology," *Westminster Theological Journal* 57 (1995): 145-63.

Longden, Henry I. *Northamptonshire and Rutland Clergy from 1500*. 1st ed., Northampton, UK: Archer & Goodman, 1938-43. 15 vols.

Madan, Falconer. *Oxford Books: A Bibliography of printed Works relating to the University and City of Oxford or printed or published there. With Appendixes, Annals, and Illustrations. Volume 2. Oxford Literature 1450-1640, and 1641-1650*. Vol. II. 1st ed., Oxford: Clarendon Press, 1912. 2 vols.

Malone, Michael T. "Doctrine of Predestination in the Thought of William Perkins and Richard Hooker," *Anglican Theological Review* 52 (1970): 103-17.

Mather, Cotton. *Magnalia Christi Americana: Or, the Ecclesiastical History of New England; from its first Planting, in the Year 1620, unto the Year of our Lord 1698. In seven Books*. [1702, 1820] 3rd ed., Hartford: Silas Andrus and Son, 1853. 2 vols.

Matthews, Arnold G., ed. *The Savoy Declaration of Faith and Order, 1658*. 1st ed., London: Independent Press, 1959.

McCullough, Peter E. *Sermons at Court: Politics and Religion in Elizabethan and Jacobean Preaching*. Edited by Anthony Fletcher, John Guy, & John S. Morrill. Cambridge Studies in Early Modern British History. 1st ed., Cambridge: Cambridge University Press, 1998.

McGee, J. Sears. *The Godly Man in Stuart England: Anglicans, Puritans, and the Two Tables, 1620-1670*. 1st ed., New Haven: Yale University Press, 1976.

McGiffert, Michael. "Grace and Works: The Rise and Division of Covenant Divinity in Elizabethan Puritanism," *Harvard Theological Review* 75 (1982): 463-502.

———. "The Perkinsian Moment of Federal Theology," *Calvin Theological Journal* 29 (1994): 117-48.

McGowan, Andrew T. B. *The Federal Theology of Thomas Boston*. 1st ed., Carlisle, UK: Paternoster Press, 1997.

McGrath, Alister E. *Historical Theology: An Introduction to the History of Christian Thought*. 1st ed., Oxford: Blackwell, 1998.

McKim, Donald K. *Ramism in William Perkins' Theology*. 1st ed., New York: Peter Lang, 1987.

———. "William Perkins and the Christian Life: The Place of the Moral Law and Sanctification in Perkins' Theology," *Evangelical Quarterly* 59 (1987): 125-37.

McKim, Donald K. & David F. Wright, eds. *Encyclopedia of the Reformed Faith*. 1st ed., Edinburgh: Saint Andrew Press, 1992.

Merritt, Julia F. "The Pastoral Tightrope: A Puritan Pedagogue in Jacobean London." In *Politics, Religion and Popularity in Early Stuart Britain: Essays in Honour of Conrad Russell*, edited by Thomas Cogswell, Richard Cust & Peter G. Lake. 1st ed., Cambridge: Cambridge University Press, 2002, pp. 143-61.

Middleton, Erasmus. *Biographia Evangelica: Or, an historical Account of the Lives and Deaths of the most eminent and evangelical Authors or Preachers, both British and Foreign, in the several Denominations of Protestants, from the Beginning of the Reformation, to the present Time: Wherein are collected, from authentic His-*

torians, their most remarkable Actions, Sufferings, and Writings; exhibiting the Unity of their Faith and Experience in their several Ages, Countries, and Professions; and illustrating the Power of Divine Grace in their holy Living and Dying. London: J. W. Pasham [Vols 1 & 2], R. Denham [Vol. 3], W. Justins [Vol. 4] for Alex. Hogg, 1779-86. 4 vols.

Miller, Perry. *The New England Mind: The Seventeenth Century.* [1939] Reprint ed., Cambridge, MA: Harvard University Press, 1954.

————. *The New England Mind: From Colony to Province.* 1st ed., Cambridge, MA: Harvard University Press, 1953.

Milton, Anthony. *Catholic and Reformed: The Roman and Protestant Churches in English Protestant Thought, 1600-1640.* Edited by Anthony Fletcher, John Guy, & John S. Morrill. Cambridge Studies in Early Modern British History. 1st ed., Cambridge: Cambridge University Press, 1995.

————. "The Church of England, Rome and the True Church: The Demise of a Jacobean Consensus." In *The Early Stuart Church, 1603-1642*, edited by Kenneth Fincham. Problems in Focus. 1st ed., London: Macmillan Press, 1993, pp. 187-210.

————. "The Laudians and the Church of Rome c.1625-1640." Ph.D. Dissertation. University of Cambridge, 1989.

————. "Review of Nicholas Tyacke's 'Anti-Calvinists: the Rise of English Arminianism'," *Journal of Ecclesiastical History* 39 (1988): 613-16.

Mitchell, Alexander F. *The Westminster Assembly: Its History and Standards being the Baird Lecture for 1882.* 1st ed., London: James Nisbet & Co., 1883.

Møller, Jens G. "The Beginnings of Puritan Covenant Theology," *Journal of Ecclesiastical History* 14 (1963): 46-67.

Monk, Robert C. *John Wesley: His Puritan Heritage.* Edited by David Bundy & J. Steven O'Malley. Pietist and Wesleyan Studies. Vol. 11. [1966] 2nd ed., Lanham, MD: Scarecrow Press, 1999.

Moore, Jonathan D. "Calvin versus the Calvinists? The Case of John Preston (1587-1628)," *Reformation & Renaissance Review* 6 (2004): 327-48.

————. "'Christ is dead for him': John Preston (1587-1628) and English Hypothetical Universalism." Ph.D. Dissertation. University of Cambridge, 2001.

————. "Preston, John (1587-1628)." In *The Oxford Dictionary of National Biography: In Association with the British Academy: From the earliest Times to the Year 2000*, edited by Brian H. Harrison & H. Colin G. Matthew. Oxford: Oxford University Press, 2004, XLV:260-64.

Morgan, Irvonwy. *Prince Charles's Puritan Chaplain.* 1st ed., London: George Allen & Unwin Ltd, 1957.

————. *Puritan Spirituality: Illustrated from the life and times of the Rev. Dr. John Preston, Master of Emmanuel College, Cambridge; Town Preacher of Cambridge; Preacher at Lincoln's Inn; Chaplain to Prince Charles: Advisor to George Villiers, Duke of Buckingham; Leader of the Jacobean Puritan Movement*, London: Epworth Press, 1973.

Morrill, John S. "The Religious Context of the English Civil War," *Transactions of the Royal Historical Society* 5th Series (1984): 155-78.

Morrissey, Mary E. "Rhetoric, Religion & Politics in the St Paul's Cross Sermons, 1603-1625." Ph.D. Dissertation. University of Cambridge, 1998.

Muller, Richard A. *After Calvin: Studies in the Development of a Theological Tradition.* Oxford Studies in Historical Theology. 1st ed., New York: Oxford University Press, 2003.

————. *Christ and the Decree: Christology and Predestination in Reformed Theology from Calvin to Perkins.* [1986] Revised ed., Grand Rapids, MI: Baker Book House, 1988.

————. "Covenant and Conscience in English Reformed Theology: Three Variations on a Seventeenth-Century Theme," *Westminster Theological Journal* 42 (1980): 308-34.

————. *The Dictionary of Latin and Greek Theological Terms Drawn Principally from Protestant Scholastic Theology.* 1st ed., Grand Rapids, MI: Baker Book House Co., 1985.

————. "Found (No Thanks to Theodore Beza): One 'Decretal' Theology," *Calvin Theological Journal* 32 (1997): 145-53.

————. *God, Creation and Providence in the Thought of Jacob Arminius: Sources and Directions of Scholastic Protestantism in the Era of Early Orthodoxy.* 1st ed., Grand Rapids, MI: Baker Book House Co., 1991.

————. "The Myth of 'Decretal Theology,'" *Calvin Theological Journal* 30 (1995): 159-67.

————. "Perkins' *A golden Chaine:* Predestinarian System or Schematized *Ordo Salutis?*" *Sixteenth Century Journal* 9 (1978): 69-81.

————. *Post-Reformation Reformed Dogmatics: The Rise and Development of Reformed Orthodoxy, ca. 1520 to ca. 1725.* 1st ed., Grand Rapids, MI: Baker Academic, 2003. 4 vols.

————. "Predestination." In *The Oxford Encyclopedia of the Reformation,* edited by Hans J. Hillerbrand. 1st ed., Oxford: Oxford University Press, 1996, III:332-38.

————. "The Problem of Protestant Scholasticism: A Review and Definition." In *Reformation and Scholasticism: An Ecumenical Enterprise,* edited by Willem J. van Asselt & Eef Dekker. Texts and Studies in Reformation and Post-Reformation Thought. Series Ed. Richard A. Muller. 1st ed., Grand Rapids, MI: Baker Academic, 2001, pp. 45-64.

————. "Reformed Confessions and Catechisms." In *The Dictionary of Historical Theology,* edited by Trevor A. Hart. 1st ed., Grand Rapids, MI: Eerdmans, 2000, pp. 466-85.

Munson, Charles R. "William Perkins: Theologian of Transition." Ph.D. Dissertation. Case Western Reserve University, 1971.

Neal, Daniel. *The History of the Puritans; or, Protestant Non-Conformists; from the Reformation in 1517 to the Revolution in 1688: Comprising an account of their Principles; their Attempts for a farther Reformation in the Church; their Sufferings; and the Lives and Characters of their most considerable Divines.* [1732-38] Revised, corrected and enlarged ed., London: For William Baynes and Son, 1822. 5 vols.

Neuser, Wilhelm H., ed. *Calvinus Sacrae Scripturae Professor: Calvin as Confessor of Holy Scripture.* 1st ed., Grand Rapids, MI: Eerdmans, 1994.

Newcourt, Richard. *Repertorium Ecclesiasticum Parochiale Londinense: An ecclesiastical Parochial History of the Diocese of London: Containing an Account of the Bishops of that Sea, form the first Foundation thereof: also, of the Deans, Archdeacons, Dignitaries and Prebendaries, from the Conquest: and lastly, of the several Parish-Churches, as well exempt as not exempt, within the Limits of that Diocese, and of their Patrons and Incumbents: And also the Endowments of several Vicarages: And likewise of the several Religious Houses that were within the same; continued to the Year of our Lord, MDCC. In an alphabetical order.* 1st ed., London: Benjamin Motte for Christopher Bateman, Benjamin Tooke, Richard Parker, Jon. Bowyer and Henry Clements, 1708-10. 2 vols.

Nicole, Roger. "Covenant, Universal Call and Definite Atonement," *Journal of the Evangelical Theological Society* 38 (1995): 403-11.

———. "John Calvin's View of the Extent of the Atonement," *Westminster Theological Journal* 47 (1985): 197-225.

———. "Moyse Amyraut (1596-1664) and the Controversy on Universal Grace, First Phase (1634-1637)." Ph.D. Dissertation. Harvard University, 1966.

Norton, John. *Abel being dead yet speaketh. Or, the Life & Death of that deservedly famous Man of God, Mr John Cotton, late Teacher of the Church of Christ, at Boston in New-England.* 1st ed., London: Thomas Newcomb for Lodowick Lloyd, 1658.

Nuttall, Geoffrey F. "A Transcript of Richard Baxter's Library Catalogue: A bibliographical Note," *Journal of Ecclesiastical History* 2 & 3 (1952): 207-21 & 74-100.

Packer, James I. *A Quest for Godliness: The Puritan Vision of the Christian Life.* 1st ed., Wheaton, IL: Crossway Books, 1990.

———. "The Redemption and Restoration of Man in the Thought of Richard Baxter: A Study in Puritan Theology." D.Phil. Dissertation. University of Oxford, 1954.

———. *The Redemption and Restoration of Man in the Thought of Richard Baxter.* 1st ed., Vancouver, BC: Regent College Publishing, 2003.

Parnham, David. *Sir Henry Vane, Theologian: A Study in Seventeenth-Century Religious and Political Discourse.* 1st ed., Cranbury, NJ: Associated University Presses, 1997.

Parr, Richard. *The Life of the most reverend Father in God, James Usher, late Lord Arch-Bishop of Armagh, Primate and Metropolitan of all Ireland. With a Collection of three hundred Letters, between the said Lord Primate and most of the eminentest Persons for Piety and Learning in his time, both in England and beyond the Seas. Collected and published from original Copies under their own Hands.* 1st ed., London: For Nathanael Ranew, 1686.

Patterson, W. Brown. *King James VI and I and the Reunion of Christendom.* Edited by Anthony Fletcher, John Guy, & John S. Morrill. Cambridge Studies in Early Modern British History. 1st ed., Cambridge: Cambridge University Press, 1997.

Peacey, Jason T. "Henry Parker and Parliamentary Propaganda in the English Civil Wars." Ph.D. Dissertation. University of Cambridge, 1994.

Peterson, Robert A. *Calvin's Doctrine of the Atonement.* 1st ed., Phillipsburg, NJ: Presbyterian and Reformed Publishing Co., 1983.

Pettit, Norman. *The Heart Prepared: Grace and Conversion in Puritan Spiritual Life.* [1966] 2nd ed., Middletown, CT: Wesleyan University Press, 1989.

———. "The Heart Renewed: Assurance of Salvation in Puritan Spiritual Life." In *Transatlantic Encounters: Studies in European-American Relations. Presented to Winfried Herget,* edited by Udo J. Hebel & Karl Ortseifen. 1st ed., Trier, Germany: Wissenshaftlicher Verlag Trier, 1995, pp. 14-28.

Philip, William J. U. "The Marrow and the Dry Bones, Ossified Orthodoxy and the Battle for the Gospel in Eighteenth-Century Scottish Calvinism," *Scottish Bulletin of Evangelical Theology* 15 (1997): 27-37.

Pollard, A. W., G. R. Redgrave, W. A. Jackson, F. S. Ferguson, & Katharine F. Pantzer, eds. *A Short-Title Catalogue of Books Printed in England, Scotland, & Ireland and of English Books Printed Abroad 1475-1640.* 2nd Revised and expanded ed., London: The Bibliographical Society, 1986. 2 vols.

Porter, Harry C. *Reformation and Reaction in Tudor Cambridge.* 1st ed., Cambridge: Cambridge University Press, 1958.

Priebe, Victor L. "The Covenant Theology of William Perkins." Ph.D. Dissertation. Drew University, 1967.

Rainbow, Jonathan H. *The Will of God and the Cross: An Historical and Theological Study of John Calvin's Doctrine of Limited Redemption.* Edited by Dikram Y. Hadidam. Princeton Theological Monograph Series. Vol. 22. 1st ed., Allison Park, PA: Pickwick Publications, 1990.

Rapin de Thoyras. *The History of England.* Translated by N. Tindal. 2nd Annotated ed., London: For James, John and Paul Knapton, 1732-33. 2 vols.

Rehnman, U. Sebastian G. "Theologia Tradita: A Study in the Prolegomenous Discourse of John Owen (1616-1683)." D.Phil. Dissertation. University of Oxford, 1997.

Reid, James. *Memoirs of the Lives and Writings of those eminent Divines, who convened in the famous Assembly at Westminster, in the Seventeenth Century.* 1st ed., Paisley, UK: Stephen and Andrew Young, 1811-15. 2 vols.

Reventlow, Henning Graf. *The Authority of the Bible and the Rise of the Modern World.* Translated by John Bowden. [1980] 1st English ed., London: SCM Press, 1984.

Robinson-Hammerstein, Helga, ed. *European Universities in the Age of Reformation and Counter-Reformation.* 1st ed., Dublin: Four Courts Press, 1998.

Rohls, Jan. *Reformed Confessions: Theology from Zurich to Barmen.* Translated by John Hoffmeyer. Columbia Series in Reformed Theology. [1987] 1st English ed., Louisville, KY: Westminster John Knox Press, 1998.

Rostenberg, Leona. *Literary, Political, Scientific, Religious and Legal Publishing, Printing and Bookselling in England, 1551-1700: Twelve Studies.* Burt Franklin Bibliography and Reference Series No. 56. 1st ed., New York: Burt Franklin, 1965. 2 vols.

————. *The Minority Press & the English Crown: A Study in Repression, 1558-1625*. 1st ed., Nieuwkoop: B. De Graaf, 1971.

Rushworth, John. *Historical Collections*. [1659] Expanded ed., London: J. A. for Robert Boulter; J. D. for John Wright and Richard Chiswell; for Richard Chiswell & Thomas Cockerill, 1680-1701. 7 vols.

Sanderson, William. *A compleat History of the Life and Raigne of King Charles from his Cradle to his Grave collected and written by William Sanderson, Esq*. 1st ed., London: For Humphrey Moseley, Richard Tomlins, and George Sawbridge, 1658.

Schaefer Jr., Paul R. "Protestant 'Scholasticism' at Elizabethan Cambridge: William Perkins and a Reformed Theology of the Heart." In *Protestant Scholasticism: Essays in Reassessment*, edited by Carl R. Trueman & R. Scott Clark. 1st ed., Carlisle, UK: Paternoster Press, 1999, pp. 147-64.

————. "The Spiritual Brotherhood on the Habits of the Heart: Cambridge Protestants and the Doctrine of Sanctification from William Perkins to Thomas Shepard." D.Phil. Dissertation. University of Oxford, 1994.

Schoneveld, Cornelius W. *Intertraffic of the Mind: Studies in Seventeenth-Century Anglo-Dutch Translation with a Checklist of Books Translated from English into Dutch, 1600-1700*. 1st ed., Leiden: E. J. Brill, 1983.

Sharpe, Kevin. "Archbishop Laud," *History Today* 33 (1983): 26-30.

————, ed. *Faction and Parliament: Essays on early Stuart History*. [Oxford: Clarendon Press, 1978] Reprint ed., London: Methuen, 1985.

————. "Parliamentary History, 1603-29: In or Out of Perspective?" In *Faction and Parliament: Essays on Early Stuart History*, edited by Kevin Sharpe. [Oxford: Clarendon Press, 1978] Reprint ed., London: Methuen, 1985, pp. 1-42.

————. *The Personal Rule of Charles I*. 1st ed., New Haven: Yale University Press, 1992.

Shaw, Mark R. "Drama in the Meeting House: The Concept of Conversion in the Theology of William Perkins," *Westminster Theological Journal* 45 (1983): 41-72.

————. "The Marrow of Practical Divinity: A Study in the Theology of William Perkins." Th.D. Dissertation. Westminster Theological Seminary, 1981.

————. "William Perkins and the New Pelagians: Another Look at the Cambridge Predestination Controversy of the 1590's," *Westminster Theological Journal* 58 (1996): 267-301.

Shuckburgh, Evelyn S. *Emmanuel College*. University of Cambridge College Histories. 1st ed., London: F. E. Robinson & Co., 1904.

Smith, Thomas. *Select Memoirs of the Lives, Labours, and Sufferings, of those pious and learned English and Scottish Divines, who greatly distinguished themselves in promoting the Reformation from Popery; in translating the Bible; and in promulgating its salutary Doctrines by their numerous evangelical Writings; and who ultimately crowned the venerable Edifice with the celebrated Westminster Confession of Faith*. [Glasgow: By D. Mackenzie, 1827] 2nd ed., Glasgow: D. Mackenzie, 1828.

Song, Yong Jae Timothy. *Theology and Piety in the Reformed Federal Thought of William Perkins and John Preston*. 1st ed., Lewiston, NY: Edwin Mellen Press, 1998.

Sprunger, Keith L. "Ames, Ramus, and the Method of Puritan Theology," *Harvard Theological Review* 59 (1966): 133-51.

————. *The Learned Doctor William Ames: Dutch Backgrounds of English and American Puritanism.* 1st ed., Urbana, IL: University of Illinois Press, 1972.

————. *Trumpets from the Tower: English Puritan Printing in the Netherlands 1600-1640.* 1st ed., Leiden: E. J. Brill, 1994.

Spurr, John, ed. *English Puritanism, 1603-1689.* Edited by Jeremy Black. Social History in Perspective. 1st ed., London: Macmillan, 1998.

Stearns, Raymond P. "Assessing the New England Mind," *Church History* 10 (1941): 246-62.

Steinmetz, David C. "The Scholastic Calvin." In *Protestant Scholasticism: Essays in Reassessment,* edited by Carl R. Trueman & R. Scott Clark. 1st ed., Carlisle, UK: Paternoster Press, 1999, pp. 16-30.

————. "Vincent of Lérins (d. before 450)." In *The New International Dictionary of the Christian Church,* edited by James D. Douglas. [1974] 2nd ed., Grand Rapids, MI: Zondervan Publishing House, 1978, pp. 1019-20.

Stephen, Leslie & Sidney Lee, eds. *The Dictionary of National Biography: From the Earliest Times to 1900.* [1917] Reprint ed., Oxford: Oxford University Press, 1921-22. 22 vols.

Strehle, Stephen A. "The Extent of the Atonement and the Synod of Dort," *Westminster Theological Journal* 51 (1989): 1-23.

————. "The Extent of the Atonement within the Theological Systems of the Sixteenth and Seventeenth Centuries." Th.D. Dissertation. Dallas Theological Seminary, 1980.

————. "Universal Grace and Amyraldianism," *Westminster Theological Journal* 51 (1989): 345-57.

Strype, John. *The Life and Acts of John Whitgift, D.D. the third and last Lord Archbishop of Canterbury in the Reign of Queen Elizabeth. The Whole digested, compiled, and attested from Records, Registers, original Letters, and other authentic MSS. taken from the choicest Libraries and Collections of the Kingdom. Together with a large Appendix of the said Papers. In four Books.* [1718] New ed., Oxford: Clarendon Press, 1822. 3 vols.

Stubbings, Frank H. *A Brief History of Emmanuel College Library.* 1st ed., Cambridge: Cambridge University Press, 1981.

Thomas, G. Michael. "Calvin and English Calvinism: A Review Article," *Scottish Bulletin of Evangelical Theology* 16 (1998): 111-27.

————. *The Extent of the Atonement: A Dilemma for Reformed Theology from Calvin to the Consensus.* Paternoster Biblical & Theological Monographs. 1st ed., Carlisle, UK: Paternoster Press, 1997.

Tipson, Baird. "The Elusiveness of 'Puritanism,'" *Religious Studies Review* 11 (1985): 245-56.

Todd, Henry John. *Memoirs of the Life and Writings of the Right Rev. Brian Walton, D.D. Lord Bishop of Chester, Editor of the Polyglot Bible. With Notices of his Co-*

adjutors in that illustrious Work; of the Cultivation of oriental Learning, in this Country, preceding and during their Time; and of the Authorised English Version of the Bible, to a projected Revision of which Dr Walton and some of his Assistants in the Polyglot were appointed. To which is added, Dr Walton's own Vindication of the London Polyglot. 1st ed., London: For F. C. & J. Rivington and Longman, Hurst, Rees, Orme & Brown, 1821. 2 vols.

Todd, Margo. "'All One with Tom Thumb': Arminianism, Popery, and the Story of the Reformation in Early Stuart Cambridge," *Church History* 64 (1995): 563-79.

Toon, Peter. *The Emergence of Hyper-Calvinism in English Nonconformity 1689-1765.* 1st ed., London: The Olive Tree, 1967.

Torrance, James B. "The Incarnation and 'Limited Atonement'," *Evangelical Quarterly* 55 (1983): 83-94.

———. "The Concept of Federal Theology: Was Calvin a Federal Theologian?" In *Calvinus Sacrae Scripturae Professor: Calvin as Confessor of Holy Scripture,* edited by Wilhelm H. Neuser. 1st ed., Grand Rapids, MI: Eerdmans, 1994, pp. 15-40.

Torrance, Thomas F. *Scotttish Theology from John Knox to John McLeod Campbell.* 1st ed., Edinburgh: T. & T. Clark, 1996.

Treasure, Geoffrey, ed. *Who's Who in British History: Beginnings to 1901.* 1st ed., London: Fitzroy Dearborn Publishers, 1998. 2 vols.

Trinterud, Leonard J. "The Origins of Puritanism," *Church History* 20 (1951): 37-57.

Troxel, A. Craig. "Amyraut 'at' the Assembly: The Westminster Confession of Faith and the Extent of the Atonement," *Presbyterion* 22 (1996): 43-55.

Trueman, Carl R. *The Claims of Truth: John Owen's Trinitarian Theology.* 1st ed., Carlisle, UK: Paternoster Press, 1998.

———. "John Owen's *Dissertation on Divine Justice:* An Exercise in Christocentric Scholasticism," *Calvin Theological Journal* 33 (1998): 87-103.

———. "Richard Baxter on Christian Unity: A Chapter in the Enlightening of English Reformed Orthodoxy," *Westminster Theological Journal* 61 (1999): 53-71.

———. "William Perkins." In *Biographical Dictionary of Evangelicals,* edited by Timothy Larsen, David W. Bebbington, & Mark A. Noll. 1st ed., Leicester, UK: InterVarsity Press, 2003, pp. 519-20.

Trueman, Carl R. & R. Scott Clark. *Protestant Scholasticism: Essays in Reassessment.* 1st ed., Carlisle, UK: Paternoster Press, 1999.

Tyacke, Nicholas R. N. "Anglican Attitudes: Some Recent Writings on English Religious History, from the Reformation to the Civil War," *Journal of British Studies* 35 (1996): 139-67.

———. *Anti-Calvinists: The Rise of English Arminianism c. 1590-1640.* Oxford Historical Monographs. [1987] 2nd ed., Oxford: Clarendon Press, 1990.

———. "Archbishop Laud." In *The Early Stuart Church, 1603-1642,* edited by Kenneth Fincham. Problems in Focus. 1st ed., London: Macmillan Press, 1993, pp. 51-70, 235-36, 256-58.

———. *Aspects of English Protestantism, c.1530-1700.* Politics, Culture and Society in

Early Modern Britain. 1st ed., Manchester, UK: Manchester University Press, 2001.

――――. "Puritanism, Arminianism & Counter-Revolution." In *The Origins of the English Civil War,* edited by Conrad Russell. 1st ed., London: Macmillan, 1973, pp. 119-43.

Usher, Roland G. *The Reconstruction of the English Church.* 1st ed., London: D. Appleton and Co., 1910. 2 vols.

van Asselt, Willem J. & Eef Dekker, eds. *Reformation and Scholasticism: An Ecumenical Enterprise.* Texts and Studies in Reformation and Post-Reformation Thought. 1st ed., Grand Rapids, MI: Baker Academic, 2001.

Van Stam, Frans P. *The Controversy over the Theology of Saumur, 1635-1650: Disrupting Debates among the Huguenots in Complicated Circumstances.* Edited by Hans Bots. Translated by John Vriend. Studies of the Institute of Pierre Bayle, Nijmegen (Sib). Vol. 19. 1st ed., Amsterdam & Maarssen: APA-Holland University Press, 1988.

Veninga, James F. "Covenant Theology and Ethics in the Thought of John Calvin and John Preston." Ph.D. Dissertation. Rice University, 1974. 2 vols.

Venn, John & J. A. Venn, eds. *The Book of Matriculations and Degrees: A Catalogue of those who have been matriculated or been admitted to any Degree in the University of Cambridge from 1544 to 1659.* 1st ed., Cambridge: Cambridge University Press, 1913.

――――, eds. *Alumni Cantabrigienses: A Biographical List of All Known Students, Graduates and Holders of Office at the University of Cambridge, from the Earliest Times to 1900. Part I from the Earliest Times to 1751.* 1st ed., Cambridge: Cambridge University Press, 1922-27. 4 vols.

von Rohr, John. *The Covenant of Grace in Puritan Thought.* Edited by Charley Hardwick & James O. Duke. American Academy of Religion Studies in Religion. Vol. 45. 1st ed., Atlanta, GA: Scholars Press, 1986.

Wallace Jr., Dewey D. *Puritans and Predestination: Grace in English Protestant Theology, 1525-1695.* Edited by Charles H. Long. Studies in Religion. 1st ed., Chapel Hill, NC: University of North Carolina Press, 1982.

Walsham, Alexandra. "Vox Piscis: Or The Book-Fish: Providence and the Uses of the Reformation Past in Caroline Cambridge," *English Historical Review* 114 (1999): 574-606.

Warfield, Benjamin B. *Studies in Theology.* 1st ed., New York: Oxford University Press, 1932.

――――. *The Westminster Assembly and Its Work.* 1st ed., New York: Oxford University Press, 1931.

Webster, Tom. *Godly Clergy in Early Stuart England: The Caroline Puritan Movement, c1620-1643.* Edited by Anthony Fletcher, John Guy, & John S. Morrill. Cambridge Studies in Early Modern British History. 1st ed., Cambridge: Cambridge University Press, 1997.

White, Peter. *Predestination, Policy and Polemic: Conflict and Consensus in the English*

Church from the Reformation to the Civil War. 1st ed., Cambridge: Cambridge University Press, 1992.

————. "The Rise of Arminianism Reconsidered," *Past and Present* 101 (1983): 34-54.

————. "The *via media* in the early Stuart Church." In *The Early Stuart Church, 1603-1642,* edited by Kenneth Fincham. Problems in Focus. 1st ed., London: Macmillan Press, 1993, pp. 211-30, 243-44, 285-89.

Wilkins, John. *Ecclesiastes: Or, a Discourse concerning the Gift of Preaching, as it falls under the Rules of Art.* 9th Corrected and enlarged ed., London: For W. Churchill and M. Lawrence, 1718.

Williams, Edward. *The Christian Preacher: Or, Discourses on Preaching, by several eminent Divines, English and Foreign, Revised and Abridged: With an Appendix on the Choice of Books.* 5th ed., London: For Thomas Tegg, 1843.

Williams, George H. "Called by Thy Name, Leave Us Not: The Case of Mrs. Joan Drake, a formative Episode in the pastoral Career of Thomas Hooker in England," *Harvard Library Bulletin* 16 (1968): 111-28, 278-303.

Wing, Donald, John J. Morrison, Carolyn W. Nelson & Matthew Seccombe, eds. *Short-Title Catalogue of Books Printed in England, Scotland, Ireland, Wales, and British America and of English Books Printed in Other Countries, 1641-1700.* [For the Index Society by Columbia University Press, 1951] 2nd Revised and enlarged ed., New York: Modern Language Association of America, 1994. 3 vols.

Wood, Anthony A. *Athenæ Oxonienses: An exact History of all the Writers and Bishops who have had their Education in the University of Oxford. To which are added the Fasti, or Annals of the said University.* Edited by Philip Bliss. 3rd ed., London: For F. C, and J. Rivington et al., 1817. 4 vols.

————. *Fasti Oxonienses, Or the Annals of the University of Oxford.* Edited by Philip Bliss. 3rd ed., London: For F. C. and J. Rivington et al., 1815.

Woolsey, Andrew A. "Unity and Continuity in Covenantal Thought: A Study in the Reformed Tradition to the Westminster Assembly." Ph.D. Dissertation. University of Glasgow, 1988. 2 vols.

Index

Abbot, Archbishop, 144-45, 149

Adam, 31-33, 74-75

Allport, Josiah, 187, 205n.171, 209-10

Alured, Thomas, 20n.79

Ames, William, 28, 122

Amos, 74

Amyraldianism, 43-44, 188n.74, 217-20

Amyraut, Moyse, 217-18, 219

Andrewes, Lancelot, 14n.57, 15, 150

Angels, fallen, 74-75, 114-16, 180, 180n.33, 190, 192, 196, 203

Anti-Arminianism, 16, 20, 20n.79, 77, 93, 128, 129-30, 137-38, 161

Anti-Calvinism, 10, 134, 226, 228; and Harsnett, 58-63, 64; and Montagu, 146-47, 166n.124; and York House Conference, 141, 146-47. See also Divine decree (Preston's theology of predestination)

Anti-Papists, 17, 20, 20n.79, 146, 148

Apostles' Creed, 31

Appello Caesarem (Montagu), 146-47, 150

Aristotelianism, 5, 201, 221-22

Arminianism, 31, 43-44; anti-Arminianism, 16, 20, 20n.79, 77, 93, 128, 129-30, 137-38, 161; and English Calvinism, 224-25; and Perkins' rebuttal of universal redemption, 43-44, 51; and salvation of the reprobate, 129-30; and the Thirty-Nine Articles, 143; and universal redemption, 43-44, 51, 158-61, 166-68, 228; and Ussher, 179-80,

179n.32, 183-84; and York House Conference, 150, 151-52, 158-61, 166-68, 227-28

Arminius, Jacobus, 31, 43-44

Augustine, 50-51, 56, 64, 65

Balcanqual, Walter, 213n.206

Ball, Thomas, *Life of Preston,* 3-4n.2, 5, 6n.15, 7n.16, 9n.27, 11nn.41-42, 16, 104; on Preston's anti-papal activities, 20n.79; and Preston's universal redemptionism, 97; York House Conference report, 151, 152-53, 161-62, 163-64n.112, 167

Bancroft, Richard, Bishop of London, 68

Baptism, infant, 54, 125, 125n.58, 135-36, 192n.99, 194-95n.109, 223

"Bare sufficiency," doctrine of, 67

Baro, Peter, 62, 225

Barrett-Baro controversy, 30

Bastingius, Jeremias, 67

Bastwick, John, 22n.87

Baxter, Richard, 19n.74, 163n.111, 173-75, 219; and Perkins, 29n.13, 39n.57, 43; and Preston's concept of the gospel promise, 126; and universal redemptionism, 96-97, 104, 104n.36, 122, 173-75; and Ussher, 173-75, 182, 186, 209

Bedford, Thomas, 187

Berkhof, Louis, 121n.40

Bernard, Nicholas, 175, 186, 186n.68, 210

296